MW00618475

My Dear Amie

Letters Provided by Charles Kelly

My Dear Amie

Letters Home from
Capt. Samuel Camp Kelly

Co. E
30th ALA Regiment
From March 1862 to April 1865

Compiled by Steve Lawler

ISBN: 978-1-6653-0760-4 - Paperback
ISBN: 978-1-6653-0761-1 - Hardcover
eISBN: 978-1-6653-0762-8 - eBook

Library of Congress Control Number: 2023919461

Printed in the United States of America

⊗This paper meets the requirements of ANSI/NISO Z39.48-1992 (Permanence of Paper)

Letter provided by Charles Kelly

1 0 2 0 2 3

Foreword,
by Charles Samuel Kelly

My name is Charles Samuel Kelly. Samuel Camp Kelly was my great, great grandfather. I am proud to carry his name in mine. This letter collection clearly displays the type of man and husband that he was. I hope some of the words he wrote home to Amie, his wife, during the Civil War will inspire you in some way.

Samuel Kelly was my grandfather's grandfather. His son, Richard Bussey Kelly, married my great grandmother, Leonna Bledsoe. I have the honor and privilege of living in the home where Leonna was born in Sylacauga, Alabama. Her father, Francis Marion Bledsoe, purchased this home and farm to make his life and raise his family in the 1850's. It is named Mountain Spring. The home was built in 1843. Leonna was born in the house in 1860. Francis Marion Bledsoe was killed in action during the last week of the War in South Alabama at Spanish Fort.

Leonna Bledsoe grew up in Sylacauga and was raised by her mother. Leonna later married Samuel Kelly's son Richard. They made their home in Calhoun County Alabama, but always split their time between there and Mountain Spring.

I would like to thank Steve Lawler for painstakingly copying and transcribing this collection of letters my family has kept over the years. The transcription is word for word and lack of punctuation and grammatical errors are just as the words appeared on the letters except where pieces of pages were burned, missing, or damaged in some way. Getting to know Samuel C. Kelly through his words will hopefully help you fill in the gaps.

The Lord is writing the story of all our lives. The Bible tells us that in this world we will have struggles. War and the suffering it brings is something no logical man would choose until he is given no choice. Nevertheless, it happened during Samuel Kelly's lifetime. He chose to be the man he was created to be, stepped into hardship on behalf of his country and family all the while staying committed and faithful to his wife. He knew that leading, communicating with, and comforting her were his responsibility. These letters are evidence of the effort he made to serve Amie as her husband. They are a testimony that it is possible to walk towards the urgent and seemingly impossible while not forsaking the important things in life as you go. My hope is that this book of letters encourages you. Thank you for reading Samuel Kelly's words.

1862 SCK Letter Transcribed

MARCH 1862

Camp Curry March 19th 1862

.19 P1

My Dear Amie these lines leaves me well except one of my teeth is Sore, I had the headache last night but it was from not getting coffee for breakfast, the boys used up the coffee I had the night before, I rode on the baggage from Oxford to the camp in the Smoke & ashes, whitch added nothing to my condition, & to add to that it was hot verry hot & we had & we had to walk (they Said 1 ¼ miles) but it was 3 to us, we Slept but verry little the night we Stayed there We got here about 8 oclock we got tents & then to work, we got them all up & fixed off with polls laid on the ground & Straw on them, but we could not get wheat or oats, but we got pine Straw & are pretty well fixed up, John Pike & I went out & filled his tick with confederate feathers & Slept as well as I could Sleep any where (except you know where) I want a tick not a matress & then I can fill & empty as Suits me We have hired a negrow for a cook & washer, When I Say we I mean the four officers, We did not know wheather we would be allowed to mess

1

with the men or not, but it is not common & besides that we wanted wood & pine & fires & water & tents put up & taken down &C&C not because I prefer them as mess mates but I want to be eaven & live at home we give 15 dollars per month

P2

Wednesday evening It rained verry hard this morning & a company from Randolf came in at that time, we had quite a pleasant time to what they had, I was at meeting to night, an old man from Shelby preached, there was Several mourners, I hope we may have a fine day on Sunday as Renfro & Minett are both to preach here, there is already Six companies here, We are in an old field, with plenty of wood and water all around, Thursday morning we eat our first breakfast together this morning, the last of the turkey, but we have lots of victuals yet, We had a Drill this morning, Tom Lewis was our instructor, he is a good officer but I fear he will not be elected Lieut Coln because he is an out Sider, Alexander in the same fix, I expect we will form a Reggiment as Soon as ten companies get here & if we do Shelly will be Coln, The Calhoun Companies prefer Henry, but there is Some Risk to Run & we do not want to let Such a man as Shelly go on uncertainly, Amie I had a Settlement with Alexander & Send you the note I Send this by Sol Dunkin who is on furlow for ten days, he has the ich & tis best for him to go home, I have written all, I believe I know that will Interest you I am well & think I know how to take care of myself under the circumstances I am anxious to make an officer, We have a fine Company of men all well, God bless you S C Kelly

CAMP CURRY TALLADEGA CO MARCH 25ᵀᴴ 1862

.25 P1

My Dear Amie this lines leaves me well & do hope that they may find you all enjoying the Same blessings, I had a Spell of cholic Saturday night whitch turned Sour on me Sunday & I was quite unwell until yesterday morning when I took some canephor & am well as usual, We had Brother John Renfro with us Sunday for dinner & it Rained & Showered So that he did not preach but promised to come again next Sunday ___ Billy McCane was over & So was Minett, We _____ form a Regiment in a few days & Shelly will be Coln, Tom Lewis, John Francis Coln, Wm Richie, Bradford, & Tom Reynolds are the candidates for Lieut Coln, I fear both Lewis & Francis will be beaten, (but both Seem determined to Run) for they will divide the vote in the Calhoun Co, There are already 8 Companies here 2 Calhoun 3 Talladega 1 Jefferson 1 St Clear & 1 Randolf & 3 other Companies at Talladega waiting for tents We have 2 Sick this morning John Price has the mumps & John Rhodes has the measles, John Wilkinson is not well, has caught cold & I fear will end in a Relapse of Measles, Warren Slaton is hopping about yet, he Stuck a knife in his leg, before we left home, there is a free Hospital at Talladega, but the boys do not like to go there, I expect to go out to See bro Renfro, he Said he would come for me Some evening, I have not been to See Ann yet but will after

P2

the Election is over We expect to draw money Soon, in the coarse of another week then I expect to come home, I would like to be at home on the day of our meeting if I can but I may be obliged to come Sooner, I do not want to go until we draw, as there is a goodeal of money oweing me in the Company, I have Sent by Jim Porter for a Sword & I Suppose will cost at least 30 dollars, Amie I got Hamp Graham to buy me Some Hoop Irons (on a note) I Suppose he got them he Said he would pay the note & you can pay the taxes, We have Sent on for the Selma Refit but it has not come yet, you can Send on & get it if you choose, Amie I would like to be with you all, but God knows that I feel it my duty to Serve my Country, I am determine to try to do my whole duty & having done all I pray that I Stand Clothed in the richtiousness of Christ, tell all of them to be good Servants as unto Christ for all must die & after death the Judgement, tell the boys to take care of the Stock & every thing as though I were with you, Good bie God bless you all is my prear

PS Direct to Lieut S. C. Kelly Talladega care of Capt H Mcbees

CAMP CURRY ALA MARCH 29TH 1862

.29 PI

My Dear Amie I am well & have enjoyed myself as well as could be except, we have been two days electing one officer (Lt Coln) who is Bradford, Shelly was unanimously elected by acclimation we have a hard contest for Lt Coln, Major __ 4 days election but have desided on Capt Jack Smith of Jefferson,

Amie I have not got my box yet not your falt, it is at Talladega, I will get it today I gave been wanting to go See Ann but for the election I am going today Major or no Maj, Henry Oden & I believe 3 of unkle Alex Suns in law are here, Dr Patison Lizzys husband is the Captain of a Com, H. O. is frst Lieut, I have become acquainted with them, Capt P went home & in Speaking of the acquaintances he had maid Spoke of me, his wife told him to ask if it was Sam Kelly So we

P2

become more intimately acqed, he was crowded with company & Slept 2 night with me, but we are not together in the election but tis a free thing & will make no difference with Sutch a man, as I take Capt Patison to be, not with Standing H Oden was a candidate All of them are baptist all are as well as I could expect God bless us all, good bie I expect to be home on Fryday week S C Kelly

TALLADEGA 4 ½ OCLOCK MARCH 29TH 1862

.29 PI

(FN letter burned top to bottom on left side
& letter folded to be used as its own envelope)

Amie opened the box & found the letter, I was glad of news that all were well as to pease they aut to be worth 75 cts __ worth from one & ¼ dollars per bushel ___ to wheat hold at 150 cts until you hear from me again flour is worth 10 dollars per hundred ___ Selma as to the horse I do not intend to pay any Sutch price, hold on until I come __e I am on my way to See Ann I will be back

Monday morning, I will be home with in the time Stated, am looking every moment for the cars lots of Soldiers a perfect <u>push</u> I Send this by Joe Hobs_en write good bie

S C Kelly

PS no can _____ a invellope I Send you 2

APRIL 1862

CAMP CURRY APR THE 1ˢᵗ 6 OCLOCK PM

.01 .02 P1

my dear Amie I Rec yours of the 31 today & proceed immediately to answer, I am well at present but was not So yesterday I went to Anns I found all well (Mother & Key was there) & I had a Sunday founder, was Sick enough all of the after part of the night & in the morning could not eat a bite, but I got to the depo & footed it from where I got off to camp about 2 ½ miles, when I got there all were on drill but Soon came in & began to Strike tents for a Regular & thorough move of about ¼ mile I was in the way & wished I had Stayed with Ann all day but, a man came along & Said he would haul a load for a quarter & I Said I had the money So I told the mess that I could not work but I would pay the bill, but I had to Show them how to put up the tents (our own) I did not eat a bite

P2

until after 12 & then it was a piece of lite wheat bread baked & a few Sups of Sassafrasss tea that was all I wanted, I took before eating a few drops of champfer, at Supper the Same, together with a good nights Sleep cured me (not Sorter but well) I have been on drill 5 or 6 hours today, & never felt better I think I Shall be more caucheous here after, Amie you Say it Seems long & So it does but I can meet you before fryday week, I think I can get off on Saturday evening & if So I will meet you (God being willing) At Linseys by 8 PM. I think I had better not let Such a chance Slip, for there is no certainty how long we may Stay here or how Soon we may leave but we have no armes yet, but we may go to the armes, instead of them being brought to us, the most of the Companys are in favor of uniforming (we are not) it will cost at least 20 dollars per man, & besides that all of our men have a good jeans Suit, I believe we are better clad

P3

than any Company here & is well drilled all are well except Slight complaints, as to wheat Well it at 2 dollars per bushel at home, as to mules do not let the fine ones go at no price until you hear from me & as to the Sorry ones you can Spear let them go at the price I put, but only for cash, dry up the credit System entirely, & pay my debts as fast as you can, Mules will be mules before this war ends Say to Lizzy I Sent her letter by Fergerson, Amie I wish you would bring me Some candles & a piece of hand Soap, we have had Some all the time but I had none if I had they were lost in the divide, I have a notion of having my cloth coat altered to a military I have a Set of buttons & I think tis better that than give 15 or 20 dollars for another, I have no use for it the way it is, Amie it is amusing to hear the hum of an army Some are talking Some Singing, laughing fiddeing coughing hollouring crowing & all Such the hum is like bees

P4

Wednesday morning 2 Apr Amie I am well as usual, my bowels are regular we have a plesant morning all up & ready for duty except 2 who are grunty but not Sick, I get along finely with both officers & men I have not got my passion nor Sword yet but am generally known as an officer We put out guard yesterday for the 1st time I expect it will be my time in a few days to be officer of the guard, The Lieut have that to do & the captains are officer of the day, I do not Suppose you to know much about it, but I will tell you more when I See you than I could write in a week, Amie Dear I think that you had better have the colt & old Judy carried to the pasture, Siphax the 2 mules & Lauren, The grass is putting up finely & James promised to yoke Such as would not Stay without, Do not let them Ride Siphax but about ½ the way I

Suppose the colts will follow the old mare & Siphax can be led, 2 of the boys can go & take 2 mules to ride back on, leading Judy & Siphax or if you can fix it better, do so, do not be disappointed if I do not get to Lins but I will if I can, we do no drilling on Sunday, but dress parade in the evening, mearly to hear the order of the next day I must close for it is about 8 when the guard is put out Keep a Sharp watch over the corn wheat Stock & every thing I want to know how every thing moved God bless you all and us all Good bie S. C. Kelly

.09 P1

(FN letter burnt along edge)

My Dear Amie It is pleasure I write to you, on account of our brilliant Success near Corinth, the Report this morning is that our army has captured Grant,s & Bewell,s whole army,s ___ are all doing tolerably well I caught cold & was a little hoarse, the weather is verry dissagreeable, rainy & windy the health of the Company is good, we have 2 or 3 Sick, but Slightly, We mare dissipointed about drawing money, not because there is none, but because, the Sergon,s Report was not fixed up correctly, I think we will get it in a few days, there is a Rush for furlows today & the Coln has Redused the turn to 7 days & tomorrow it will Still be Redused to 6 days & So on until it will run down to the day Coln Shelly is expected, the object is to have all the men in camp when Shelly comes, So we will be Ready

P2

Do not be disappointed my Dear one when I tell you I cannot come before we draw, for it will not do for me to leave before, I am out between 3 or 4 hundred dollars & I am the man to tend to the collecting & the time to collect is when they have the money I Sh__ expect you to Send the flour monday, or as, Soon after as you can get it Ready I will try & Send you Some Sack__ if not in time borrow all you can & Send all at one load if you can, take the RR Agents Rec at the head of the Road to be Shipped to Talladega, Pay the freight if they Require it, the Reason I want it here as quick as possible is, I am afraid they will fly from the bargan, The

Comissary at Montgomery Says he can lay it down at Talladega for 5 ½ dol, I am Sorry I cannot be with you all but Such is the fate of war, May the God of Mrcies be with us all, & guide protec_ & defend us & enable our armies to triumph is the pray of your own dear SCK

Camp Curry Apr 15th 1862

.15 P1

My Dear Amie I Rec yours of the 10th yesterday evening, it was missent & went to Alexandria & came to me dated the 12th, I was glad to get it, I was not astonished to hear you had the blues, but I trusted that you would look to him who is able to comfort & Releeve you through his Spirit & grace, I was disappointed again, on Fryday, I heared that John Hendricks had come home on furlough & Sent me word (by an officer) to come & See him, as he had but a verry few days to Stay, So I accordingly applied for a permit to go up on Saturday evening & Return on monday morning, but was Refused by the Lieut Col (Bradford) So Such is the life of a Soldier, We cannot get furloughs for but 3 days length, So you See that I would get home (by the Stage) at 12 or 1 oclock & have to Start back at 9 or 10 at night, but I live in hope that when Col Shelly comes home we will be better treated, or will oby more cheerfully

P2

John H came out yesterday to See me, but I was the officer of the guard & had but little time with him, he has been Sick, he looks as usual, he thinks he is well he Said all were well at home, he Starts this morning for Montgomery where he is Stationed, I thought there would be more wheat than that but do not know, I was so long Rec Mcginises flour that I thought you would make Some other Shift for Sacks, you ort to Send the flour to S C Kelly Talladega, I expect to be there to Rec it, I Suppose Hudson will fix it wright at the head of the Road, there is a talk of our moving out to Talladega, as we have to guard the Yankey prisinors there, A Special dispatch came last night to our Commandant to prepare to guard General Printess & 150 federal officers & a detail of about

100 men from his Reg has been make, but none from our company, but we will have a chance, the Coln has gone in the county to get guns to guard with , I Rec a Box of

P3

things by the hand of Arheart, It appears that you have plenty at home yet (So mote it be) I did not expect So much bacon, we get beef fresh or Salt every other day, but no bacon & Pickled pork in a abundance, I expect that I have had more provisions than any of the mess, by far, So I think one piece, either Side or ham would have been & abundance, No blame My Dear one, to you but may God bless your generous Soul, I expect to get a letter by hand of Some of the boys, who Stopped in town, & I wait to answer, At tis time the cook Summons me to dinner So I will go & See what he has got, Dinner consisted the balance of the ham (boiled) after all of the frying part gone, corn bread, water, Sugar, butter & Some fried cakes of Wheat dough, with plenty of butter & Sugar on them eat prime, I hought that by this time the boys would have been in but I expect that they intend to Stay to See the prisioners, as the chance to get off is none, I expect to go to Talladega to night or in the morning to See about the flour

P4

3 oclock Talladega 15 John P & Sam Penlan arrived I Rec the letter & was glad to hear that you were all well John brought my Rect for flour it is all Right, I met them ½ way but they came back with me to See the Yanks, as to my coming home I expect to come home when I get money but if I cant do any better I will take a furlough for 3 days, & come you must make out the best you can tell them boys to put the Jack in the Stable & feed & curry & water & attend to him wright Barney is the one to do that, he must not go down, I must close may God bless us all & bless the nation may he give us Strength to overcome our enemies & make them Sue for peace & obtain it upon honorable terms to us as a nation, God bless you, I forgot to tell you I am well & have been Stoubt ever since I Saw you, So mutch that I think I will come again

S. C. Kelly

TALLADEGA APR 16TH 1862

.16

My dear Amie I Rec the flour today that of

Robinsons weighed 225 lbs that at 6 cts 14,10/100 dollars the expenses on it from the head of the road 60 cts, leaving 13.50/100 dollars, I charged nothing for my trouble it all lost

Some but I could not get it out clean, I expect to Send this by Bowman, Enclosed you will find one hundred dollars, he does not know I Sent it, I think I have money enough to answer my purpose without it, If you have any chance pay L Weaver eight dollars & forty four cts, to pay to <u>Ablsolem</u> Mcginnis, the Remain of his flour, As to the Jack notes I did not understand until J Palmer came that there was any dissatisfaction about it, I Simply mean that, if a man breeds his mare to the Jack & that mare has a colt, or is traded that the note is a good one, & if he keeps her & She does not get a fold, that, that note is null & void whether I die or live, And as to Jones wheat a ct it is 5 ¾ bushels wheat at 100 per bushel & 2 years & 8 months int (1 y 46.00/2 y 46/ 8 mon 25=117) 575 int 117X 6.92 ½ cts of that is Fergersons & he ort to collect it, the money I Send you pay Robinson & pay Somebody we owe with the balance, Yes pay J R Graham the note I gave him of 75 dollars just before I left, I do not know when I will get any more, we have not drawed yet, the Yankee, prisoners, 60, officers none under the Rank of Cap came last night, As to the paper I think you had better take an Atlanta paper I am in the biggest hurry you ever Saw I have to go out to camp to night & it is most night 5 ½ oclock

God bless us all Good bie I am well S. C. Kelly

(UNKNOWN DATE)

I am Smartley troubled in the Same bunk with me Jef Bradford lay & he & I were writing, he with a borrowed gold pin & when the dinner bell Rang he was out & I put up my things & waited until I heard him coming & went in to table, he (I Supposed would take care of his own) walked through & left every thing & while at dinner Some one lifted his pen the owner of whitch Says he would not take a 50 dollar bill for, I came back after dinner & went to writing & just as I finnished the other Sheet he came to look for Storys pin & lo & behold it cannot be found, I have no idea that he thinks I misslayed, Strayed or Stold it, but Still I hate for Sutch things to happen about me, I am Still writing with my 5 dollar pin & pencil for _____ I may take this chance May God bless us all good bie my dear one your own Sam

MAY 1862

CAMP CURRY TALLADEGA MAY 2OND 4 ¼ OCLOCK

.02

L Weaver Sir I am in a hurry, the Coln Says we may all go home & vote. You will be So kind as to Send Amie word to Mothers if She is not gone, I will be up tomorrow evening

In haste S C Kelly

CAMP CURRY TALLADEGA ALA MAY 5ᵀᴴ 1862

.05 P1

My Dear Amie I had to travel by my Self for 7 miles before I overtook any one, I trotted all the time until I overtook Brown & White (Nealeys Suns in Law) they were in a buggy & P Nealey along to cary back the mules, I changed with one of them for a Seat in the buggy, we pushed on to town, & passed about 1 AM at the branch this Side we came up with Lt. P. who had gathered up Furloughed & Recruits, to the number of 18 or 20 men in waggons I carried a light for the gang & we knocked along Slowly until break of day, which found us opposite Glovers, I then Saw that we would have to push up, So I lit to walk Severald got out to liten the load & we made in quick & double quick to the depo. We overtook the Stage, got there in time &C

P2

we had 18 neat 5 furloughs 14 of the 28 that came with me Saturday, Amie I Recon I shall have to cut this letter Short, as there is a goodeal to do & if I Sit writing to you I fear it will not be done (Such business is not mine) but I generally See to it, I never eat the Snack you gave me until 9 AM, I then, knocked round a while & lay down at (about) 11 & Slept until 2 PM, got up & eat a Snack, off of Pikes turkey & peach pie, & tapered off on the last of my cakes you brot me & was as well Satissied (or Sassage fried) as if I had been to dinner, I enjoyed the trip last night & after 11 oclock was not Sleepy, I conseder I (or we) made a lucky escape of the Rain, & it would have been better for all of them, had they came in the night, without Rain, it Rained hard just as we came to the camp no one got wet, we Leave in the morning, God bless us all &C S C Kelly

(FN this is written in the margin)
4 oclock PM, & the train comes at 5, it is Raining today S

CAMP NEAR TALLADEGA MAY THE 6TH 1862

.06 .07 Pl

My Dear Amie, I am quite well today, I Stood my trip finely Slept well last night & am in fine Spirits, I Saw Mrs Patson this morning, She looks well, I rec yours of yesterday by the hand of Arheart, I was to busy at the time to read it, but went off to the woods to read & to thank God for his abundant mercies & blessings & especially for the gift of the Savior, (on whome I trust) & Secondly, for Such an help <u>meet</u> as you are, I felt that I did know on whome we believe, We did not Start this morning as we expected but the orders are cooking 5 days Rations today for the trip I expect we will Start, we had 18 recruits yesterday & 11 today we have now 114 men in all, Said, I think we will have a full company in the morning, we know of 4 or 5 more who will come, The band of Music is on the ground & I must go & See them & hear it play, they want to join the Reg but the men will have to pay them (the Government does not pay them) Well I think it a poor Band they have only 6 brass peases & drum, & the expression of the men generally is not to employ them, I am willing to go my part, I tried to have my likeness taken, but he had no cases & is but a poor artist,

I will have it the first chance, I think that in Selma or Montgomery I can do better, Amie you asked me about packing cotton, All I gin for is the toll, if a man furnishes his own, the better, I had rather every body had done So (if they had you would not have had to Send Turk to collect), what not the toll but the rope & baggin, no I do not charge for packing (that is part of the bargan), Tell Barney & all of them that if the Yankees come, not to Run off, but if possible to hide the best mules in the Swamp in the fields, the yanks does not want them but to find out from them all or every thing they know, I am glad to hear from Barney, I believe he would do all in his power for the good of the family, but I think that is a wrong notion for while he was dodgeing around they might come on him & make him go & Show them the way to any where he knew & after he had done all he could (in that way they would take the mule & I do not know what they would do with him) likely turn him loose or take him along to wait on them, No the best plan is (in my judgement) to Stay at home & take the chances, I have no idea that they will kill any one but may, take Such things as they want, God only knows, but I am in hopes that they may never live to get that far in the Country, I believe now is the buying time & now is the day of trouble, Pray for the success of our armies & ask God to give us the victory, that we may once more Return in peace to our homes, acknowledged by the nations of the earth as an independent nation, the will we give unto God the glory, for he has Said, the race is not to the Swift, nor the battle to the Strong but to whome he Showeth mercy, & he has promised to hear his elect that cry to him, Amie if I Should be So unfortunat as to fall a prisoner, I Shall fix up to write, by reading every other line, you will get the Sense of my letter, & by reading

P2

every line, you will See what Sort of a letter the yakees thought I was writing, I do not know whether I can fix it up, but if I cannot do it effectually I will not attempt it, Say nothing about this, but, if you get a letter from me, when a prisioner try it that way, God for bid that I ever should, I will try my hand,

(FN this is where he tries his hand at writing ever other line to be read)
    Amie we had like to have had a Serious difficulty
    but all turned out to be a matter of no importance, We or
    We are at the head of the Road yesterday morning & a pass
Station
    but I Saw that Sort of work would not do & I Squashed it
    one of our men heared one of Francis men, Say Mcbee
    had no Such men, or they knew where to get the right Sort
    of men or Some Sutch expression at Camp Curry 2 weeks ago
    & F S man passed by, & one of our men Said there goes that
Smart an
    one word brought on another until I had to exercise my
authority

(FN the end of test writing between lines)

I pronounce this a failure, but the idea is to write one for yanks & one that is the true meaning of my heart, I have not time to Study it out now, but if I am so unfortunate I think I will

MAY 7TH 4 OCLOCK AM

Well Amie we are about Ready to leave an extra train came up last night & it Stop opsete the camp, we will to go in open cars (I must lay down my pen for I am nearly out of ink & pen bad) we will have every thing aboard & be off in less than 3 hours, we are allowed to take our boxes &C I Suggested to the company, that they leave the Sick mens, clothing at the depo, but Some are doing one thing with them & Some another, the Sick at home are Required to Report (as Soon as able) to May Smith who will be left to take charge of them, My Dear one you Shall hear of me Soon, I have but little to write & less time to write it, And now by the blessings of God I expect to See you again after this war Shall have passed & we as a nation Shall be free & independent, breakfast is now ready & it is not day light, So I must close.

Praise him from whome all blessings flow, Pray for me for the Confederacy for all it is our duty to pray S C Kelly

(This was on a small scrap of paper inside the letter)
(Front)

You will See an advertisement for Blankets & Clothing in the paper by Capt Burr of our Regt You all must do all you can with out disfurnishing yourselves he will be at J V & will pay liberal price, Your new carpet would make Several & you can get a good price at least 10 dollars per blanket, do as you chose about it Sam

(Rear)

PS Since writing the above I have concluded that I would Send 2 hundred dollars that I have no use fore here Sam

MONTGOMERY 11 ½ OCLOCK MAY 8TH 1862

.08 P1

My dear Amie we left Talladega 8 0clock AM yesterday, I was officer of the guard, Coln S Seems to have Some confidence in me (judging by the Repeated calls) I Served all day but not much to do until we got to Selma at 4 ½ PM, then I had to keep the Soldiers off the boat, but to Return to my trip, there was a dense crowd at Talladega, & all the way women Strewed the cars with flours, all Seemed to cheer us on in our cause, even to the negrows, every where were as intent as their mistress, we had Some little confusion, as our baggage train came uncoupled & we left it 4 miles before the word could get through the men to the engineer, (we were in those box cars you Saw there 18 in number all crowded thick as hops) I was cheering the ladies as we passed Coosa Station, hat in hand & the wind blew it out of my hand, at the Same instant a lady threw a pound cake & had like to have hit me on the head, I turned round

P2

& Said boys I have lost my hat where is my bundle & all agreed that I aut to have a name on it & I delivered it over to one of the officers of the Company, I borrowed a hat & in an hour or So I was told that a man who came off of the freight train on to ours at dinner had it, & I Saw him & he gave it to me last night after we left Selma, we got along finly on both until I lay down & thought

Some confusion, on account of the crowd on board there was about 750 or 800 Soldiers of our Reg besides at least 100 pasingers men women & negrows & children &C, we left Selma on board the Southern Republic a verry large & fine boat at 6 ½ P. M. & arrived in this place about 8 oclock this morning, too late for the train, we will leave this evening at 5 P. M. , we were quite tired of being hemed up, Some few Slightly Sick, I heared this morning before I got up, that a man fell overboard last night, I was not inclined to believe it, (but alass it is too true, he was Sleeping near the edge & we met a boat &

P3

at the whistle he (in his Sleep) became frightened & jumped upon his hands & knees & Ran off into the River, he was name Coleman of Patisons Comp & Such is the best information I can gather, Amie I had my likeness taken I Sent it, I think a good one, you can judge better it cost 3 dollars, I must close May God bless us & all of us & the cause that Seperates us is the Sincier prays of your own S May 8, 62

MONTGOMERY 6 PM MAY 9ᵀᴴ 62

.08 .09 P1

*(Written on inside of the envelope that
was used to mail 1ˢᵗ letter very fragile and torn)*

Amie I have concluded to write as I have nothing else to do ,I had this piece of paper, We have had our company on board one hour, We are waiting but I know not when, I am Sitting on the platform, I Saw John Hendricks just as we were going aboard but bide him good bie , as I thought we would Start in five minutes, he Said he was not well, We drew knapsacks canteens cartridge boxes haver Sacks &C but we will get guns at Atlanta , the whole country is alive to the war in this City, they making pikes (I do not know what for they are about 2 inches wide 10 or 12 inches long Sharp on fith edges Sharp point joined on a Staff about 6 ft long, I think I Saw at least 3 or 4 thousand, there is 650 prisoners here of the sutch order black & bad looking generally, they Say they had whipped us at Corinth that they were fiting of the two nations of the _____ I will quit now anon S

4 oclock AM (we left West Point 4 ½)

6 AM May 9th we had a hard time placing packed with men Staff Sitting on every position, we passed through lagrange, one hour after that ___ 18 miles we have better this morning all in fine Spirit the best Corps & the land _____ fine crops _____ had brought us to Newnan through _____ worn out _____ uninterested _____ brooks Sage pretty hillside ____ not ____ except for woods _____ making about ___ mite for 3 minutes

.09 P1

10 ½ oclock AM brings us to a little place called Palmetto 20 miles from Atlanta & 50 from West point, We are getting along finely I have looked for that bad grass all the way but have not Seen any but once, I think there aut to be 4 times as much in the country we have passed today, the land is broken old & poor, We will Stop in Atlanta there we expect to get our guns, & also wait for 3 of our companies who we left last night on acco

P2

unt of cars to carry them, We had too mutch load enough to Stall the engine 2 or 3 times, We are now detained our train was backing out of the way of another, when the wheels of our car came coupled, & the word was fall out, (We were going Slow) & you better know it we fell out I was writing when the train moved (I cannot write when it is moving) I was not fritened but hardly had time it Stopped So Soon, I was 2 cars behind it, If it had come uncoupled when

P3

(FN burnt along edge of letter)

We were Running I do not know what damage cars an train it might have done, The men are working at it now, to get it off of the tracks, we will be off in one hour,

My Dear I know you will be tired of this, I have been well Since I Saw you we are Smokey & black traviling in Smoke & dust, I have a notion to go & wash 11 ½ AM , 25 minutes after 12 Noon at Fairburn, Watering place, J Williams was presented with a nice looking wat_

P4

__ this inscription (on a car __o) Presented by Q V Smith Fairburn Ga, I gave her a card with this inscript Coln Shellys Reg 30 Ala

Signed Lt Kelly

1 ¾ arrived at Atlanta I Suppose we will go on the Same train

KNOXVILLE TENNESSEE MAY 11 ENTH 1862 8 A. M.

.11 P1

Well My Dear one I left off writing at 7 oclock 9th at big Shanty Ga I then lay down Shortly afterwards & when I awoke found ourselves in Dalton, we arrived there at 2 oclock A. M. We thought we were going to Chattanooga but a dispatch from Some where, Stopped us & turned us yesterday morning 9 ½ Oclock, to this place, where we arrived at 8 oclock last night without any accident 110 miles from Dalton

P2

We passed through a number of Small towns yesterday & nearly every where met with the cheers of the people, we thought we could tell the Linconites any where, we Saw none in Georgia, but as Soon as we passed into Tenn we Saw women & men that would not cheer, but Stand & gaise while 9 tenths of the people bade us God Speed, we were presented with flours & at one place the ladies Sent out bucket of butter milk whitch was

(*FN written on bottom of this page upside down*)

The order is fall into Line I am well God bless S C Kelly

P3

taken in with many thanks, Just at this moment I hear the order fall in by Companies, I tore off the leaf I had finished & backed it & expected to Send it by Dr. Mann but could not find him, we fell into line & marched out to where we are now 2 miles North of

Knoxville on what is called the Fair ground, It is an enclosure of about 50 acres, covered with Short clover rather broken than level, we are in a nice grove of large oaks, intersperced with

P4

Short leafed pine in plain view of the far growing, adjacent to a nice Spring of cold water, the whole country from the State line is rather broken Covered over with Clover fields Corn wheat & oats about equally divided, dotted over with white houses villages & barnes &C while the clover fields are covered over with the ritch growth in full bloom, Some of it knee high with lots of horses & mules, cat

P5

tle hogs & Sheep all look fat & fine We have had a hard time (So the boys Say) Since we left Talladega, I have Stood the trip finely if we meet with nothing worse I think we will do well, we drew bread last night but no meat, the bread was loaf & crackers we had one Sholder of bacon but concluded to eat the bread & go to Sleep & have meat for breakfast, So we did & were Satisfied got to bead in the cars about 11 or 12 oclock every man for himself, on boxes floor

P6

or where ever he could I lay on a mess box (in Kart) & by the kindness of Capt P, I was furnished a quilt that with my Mexican I done finely & Slept with out Rocking until nearly Sun up, got up, Washed & was invited by a Capt to take a fish breakfast, which I excepted as a matter of corse I paid 50 cts & think I got value Rec, We Saw Sights yesterday we came through hills dales brooks & vales over rivers & creeks, but the worst Sight I Saw was crossing the

P7

Tennessee River the bridge is I Suppose at least 50 ft above the water, no cover over the track, a long train of cars loaded with the bone & Sinews of the land is a Sight (the bridge is ¼ of a mile long, we were 5 minutes crossing & after we crossed we Ran along the banks, the mountain on one hand high above our heads & the River wide & deep on the other & on we went Rocking from Side to Side, it was enough to make the Stoutest hearts Shrink back

P8

but we were kept by the power of God & were Safely landed at Knoxville in due time, Our Company is all well except for 2 or 3 who have the mumps but all able to walk to this place, that large man that came to mothers that morning last Sunday we left is Sick & left at Atlanta with 1 other, The worst case we have with us is our Lt Wm Landers he is a man not to company but he is Sick, Amie I have given you an outline, I am Sorry I did not write all day

P9

yesterday I lost all the names & distanses of places, but too late I am dirty & my trunk is with the other part of the Reg, I Recon I will get it I am most out of money but think I have enough to do me, I have loaned & Spent for what I kneeded I have no Sword (but Landerses) we have not got armes yet We expected them at Selma & every other place we Stopped at but none yet, in 40 miles of the enemy & nothing to fight with I think

P10

we will get them, but know not when, this Place is under Martial law & I Suppose a good many Soldiers about here, We Saw a Company of Artillery they left here for Some bridge, I See no Sighs of a fight but do not know any thing on that Schore, Write to me on the Reception of this direct to Lt &C care of Coln C M Shelly 30th Ala Reg Knoxville Tenn, Good bie God bless you & us all is my P) S C Kelly

MAY 14TH 1862 4 ½ OCLOCK PM
KNOXVILLE TENN

.14 P1

My Dear A I have not written in 2 or 3 days before yesterday Our other Companies came up & I was fearful that my trunk was lost & got permission to come to town look after it, where I met

Coln Shelly, he Said I was the man verry well Coln (Said I) what will you have, Sir I Shall have a detail of 20 men & put them under you, for to take off the baggage & put on waggons, I tried to beg out but he Said, you are the verry man, So I took it as a complement & knockled under, I was all day & arrived at camp just at dark, I went to the Corn & Reported all done, & Said to him that twice Since we left Selma, have I been on duty all day, well well Sir, did you not know this

P2

a good horse, or Leiut is apt to be imposed upon, I told him I took that as I under stood it, all Rite, Said he, We got all of our things got Set up but had but little to eat, we were either full or gaunt all the time, I think we will do better now, There is lots of provisions in & around this place, but the Sitizins cannot Sell it, to Speculators bacon is worth 25 cts, the whole of East Tennessee is under martial law, I think that the Sitizins are Smartly tinctured with Abollitionsm, but all are mute as mice, I understand that there is, in & around Knoxville 30,00 troops under Gen Cerly Smith, nearly every day Some fellow gets killed by the Sentinels, lots of Sickness, we left all our Sick when we left Talladega except Some verry

P3

Slight cases, when we come to Atlanta we left 2 men, & now we have 16 Reported this morning, all Measles & mumps, We lay out one night without tents We drew our guns yesterday (Rifles) Mine na, or Enfield, I do not know which I will have to leave my trunk, if we go to Cumberland Gap, & am in hope we will not go there, for it is 40 miles from any transportation & I fear we will fair but Slim, & besides that I understand by a courier yesterday, that there is not a Yankee, to be found in that whole country, Every thing Sells with a vengeance here, & Seems to be anything you call for, this is a larger place than I expected & as Rough & broken as the road any where to Knoxville, I must close as the boys who came with me are impatient it is now 5 oclock We are 2 miles

P4

from town, direct to Lt S C Kelly Comp E 30th Ala Reg Knoxville Tenn & on one corner direct the P Master to forward it if we have moved, May God bless you & yours & the cause that now Separates us is the Prayer of your Own S. C. Kelly

PS I forgot to tell you that I was well & have been well, Pray for me, & Request the brethren & Sisters to pray for me, & the cause whitch I deem a Richeous cause, tell all of the boys how I am, & tell them that I yet hope through the mercies of God to get home & See them all in the flesh, after I have helped to drive the enemy from our land & when peace Sweet peace Shall cover us as a garment, So Mote it be

SCK

MAY 16TH 4 OCLOCK P M 1862
FAIR GROUND 2 MILES NORTH OF KNOXVILLE TENNESSEE

.16 P1

My Dear Amie I have nothing else to do, & concluded that I would put in the time, by writing you a few lines to inform you that I am well as I could wish or expect & have been improving ever Since I left home, I was well enough then but you know that I had been Sick prior to that time, I think that I Shall Stand the company now, at first I was not well for 3 or 4 weeks my bowels are regular, & my flesh is hard, Still I am gant, but weigh the verry Same I did when I left home, I do not eat but little (compaired with Some) but am Satisfied with it, I have not got but little money, 15 dollars, is my pile, I have not drew any pay yet & have Spent Several dollars for eatables &C Since I left Talladega, I do not want to do without anything I want & Still understand me, that I have not fooled away money, I am nearly out of every thing except my clothes that I brought from home, I have fully done my part, in furnishing the mess, I have bought me 2 flannel Shirts & one pair drawers, I find Since we have been here that the days are as hot or hotter, & the nights cooler than, in Ala, & when we drill we get wet with Swet & cool off by going in the Shade, & our Shirts feel cool, So I concluded I would try flannel, We Rec orders last night to cook 2 days Rations today & be Ready to march at 4 AM in the morning, to leave all our Sick in the hospital, that we would be allowed only one waggon to the company, that we had to leave all our mess boxes & Surplus clothing, &C, that the officers were not allowed to carry more than 80 lbs, each, So we turned loose this morning

P2

to fix up for the trip, arrangements made & the Sick carrid to the Citty, David Phillips bad with mumps F Payne intermittent feaver, H A Grffin, mumps G. w. Kilpatric Pneumonia, J W Frgrett, Ryley Cooley bowels affection, N. H. Graham feaver, but not bad, but unable to march, orderly B. M. Pike mumps, John Pike Junior Sick Stomach, vomiting J. N. Baker just came up to us this morning Sick with the mumps John Rhoads with a mashed foot, from fall of a barrell of crackers 2 days ago, but nearly well enough to go, Jim Graham nurse, Our Lt Landers is about well, I went this morning & deposited, in the East Tennessee & Georgia R Road Depo every description, knapsacks, haver Sacks, canteens, cartage boxes belts bayonet Scabbards &C&C, I then wrote to May Smith at Talladega notifying him of the Same who will order them forward, the things are all put up in mess boxes, & if the boys come on they must notify the Agent whose name is J Jaques that they are from Co E 30th Ala Vol, & will find the Boxes marked thus id they open the boxes they must not take, but one of each out & not more clothing than 2 Suits & 1 blankett, & be Sure to fasten them up, well, with every thing in them they leave, I do not know where we are going but believe we are going to Kentucky, I Rec last night the information, (through high authority, not publicity) that there was a dispatch from the War Department, that all of the new Regiments of Ala & Georgia were ordered, that the Kentuckians Said, that an army of 30 thousand Confederate troops would come through there State, So mote it be, I will wait till after dress parade, but for fear I do not have the chance

(FN written upside down in margin of this page)

I bid you good bie, but first let me tell you that I have not Rec a word from you Since I left Talladega, but God bless you I know it is not your fault (unless you are Sick) I know that you have written, I Shall write to you as often as practicable, but my dear one, do not be uneasy about me, if you do not get a letter from me every other day, for I do not know what chance will be, Now I Recommend you to look to the living fountain, God bless Good bie SCK

MAY 18TH 1862
NEAR CLINTON TENNESSEE 12 ½ OCLOCK PM

.18 L1 P1

My Dear Amie my last 2 evenings ago, I Said we would move, So at about 4 AM yesterday morning we struck tents & after Some little bustle & confusion we left this place, & came through Knoxville at about 8 AM (we did not know where we were going) & Struck out a North west course, we Stood the trip finely until dinner where we had traviled 8 miles, we Rested about 2 hrs & Resumed our journey through the verry brokenest kind of country, we went up hill & down hills until we arrived in about 3 miles of where we Stayed all night, when we came to a crooked muddy Stream with a good bridge over it, where we Stopped & found a number of

Springs on either Side, the men turned loose & all drank to there Satisfaction, there had a great many failed before we reached there, but Sun was hot & the Road Rough, & I never Saw men fail So fast in my life I do think that there was 200 hundred (out of about 500 that we have) I was Surprised at myself I Stood the trip So well, I carried as large a knap Sack as any one (except Some few fools) & nearly all the time Some ones gun, & in the evening late I carried 2 guns for 2 poor fellows (of our Company) that looked like they would faint, I carried them I Suppose 2 miles, when I discovered that one of them must Rest, when I gave it to him & told him to Rest until the guard came up & tell the officer that he could not go without help, we came to a creek ½ mile

24

before we Reached the camp & I looked round to See about crossing & was told that there was a little log up 3 hundred yds up the creek & was told that there were 200 men wating to cross

L1 P2

So I Said to the men I was not going to hunt a log like a dog, I could wade like a horse, So I Stripped off my boots & Socks Rolled up my pants & waded like a horse, I Suppose 100 hundred waded, We got to wash our feet by it, we got over, what they called bull Run & went on to camp, at 2 old meeting houses, (

So I told the Capt that it was Anty Baptist,) where was a nice branch with Sedars & Rocks, with a Spring, where we Slept on the ground in the open air, I never woke until about 4 A. M. & the first thing I heared that it is raining now, we got up & fixed our Scanty meals, (of cold biscuits & bacon) & got Ready & Started about Sunup, & about that time the Rain began to come in heavy Showers, it Rained on us for 2 or 3 miles, we got here this morning at * AM & all Set up by 12 oclock, lots of them gave out this morning, I am to be on Police this evening, Shelly Complemented me, I hope I am prove worthy of the confidence he has in me, I try to behave myself & do not Say this for every body, I thank God for his abundant mercies towards me & do trust that he will continue them, I think if I do not get Sick that I will make a good Soldier, I am not Capt, but Sometimes I wish I was but every Sweet has its bitter & every bitter has its Sweet, We have with us 65 men & 4 commissioned officers our camp, We (the Reg) are under Brg General Reynolds, I Suppose that there is about 5000 thousand men here, Infantry Cavalry & Artillery, I have no Idea how long we will Stay, nor where we will go, I was disappointed yesterday in not getting a letter, Wm Estice got one dated 14th Said that our baby was Sick, but better, all I heared Since I left Talladega, I Recon you had better direct to Knoxville, So Good bie, God bless you & all that is dear to us

S. C. Kelly

NEAR CLINTON TENN 6 OCLOCK PM 18TH

.18 L2 P1

(FN this letter is burnt at the folds & envelope stuck in places)
(my pen is So bad I cannot write) Since writing the other Sheet, I have been on duty but it rained & I was Relieved, it is Raining _____ Since then we Rec orders to be in Readiness to Start in the morning out on Scout, we are to have but one tent to the company & 6 days Rations cook, to take one Shirt, blanket & Shelly Said that I might carry a gun (then he Said he would not Restrict the officers) We will carry one waggon or to the company I Shall leave my trunk with my clothes except my Jeans coat & pants & one Shirt that I brought from home, one pr Socks together with my old boots Mexican blanket is to heavy I Shall get a blanket from Lt J W Pike (I am pleased with him) we Sleep

L2 P2

together & I call him John & he, me Sam, we are going to leave the negrows, with Lt Landers, who are both Sick (or not well) the men are in fine Spirits, this morning they seemed to be dull, but although ___ they have not Rested more than 6 hours, the Word go tomorrow Revived there drooping Spirits we have the

Staublest Comp of men in the Reg, this morning 3 Comps Started before us & they began to fall back * before we Reached here, I do not believe there was in all them more than one Comp, Ours had but 40 _____ that lagged, Our Co Capt is too St___ is all the object, My dear one I do not want you to be uneasy about me, for I know & trust him on whome we believe, though a Sinner yet Christ is my Shurity & under all circumstances I will do the b_____land of my _____

& land of the brave & the blessings of God (FN this portion written upside down on P1) Rest upon it & all that is near & dear unto us is the prays of your Own S, good bie, & I hope we will meet on earth SCK

MAY 20TH 5 ½ PM
CAMP NEAR JACKSBOROUGH TENN

.20 PI

(Letter folded & used as envelop)

My dear Amie we left Clinton at 8 AM crossing the River
Clinch at 9 to 2 o'clock it is nearly as large as the Coosa & I
suppose that boats run up that high, We entered the town after
crossing, an old deserted looking place on a Rock lodge & Rock
Cort house which looks like it was numbered with the things that
were, I Saw but one business house & that was a commissary Store
it is about as large as Alexandria, but Seems like one good church
house on a hill, (Well Supper is Ready) & J Pike has baked some
good looking bread, I had to bring the water, put the lid on & keep
up the fire &C the bread was good but had no Salt in it, every
fellow cooks his own meal (or eats it raw) I cut a Stick & broiled
over the blaze, a nice piece of ham & ate & am Satisfied, but to
Return to yesterday, We traveled & wated through hills &
hollows, Winding round mountains (or large hills) & encamped 4
½ miles from Clinton, making in all about 5 ½ miles

P2

I had plenty of provisions, that I had cooked at Knoxville 3 days before, I packed it in my haversack, I Started with 10 bisquits & the hock end of a ham, I took one, b, & cut a fresh ham & a good Slice & boiled & eat, I gave to eat, to an old man, & he had like to have cleaned me out, only leaving me 2 biscuits, went to bed under our tent but before I parched me Some corn, We Stretched 3 flies, for the men, It looks like camp meeting, Revile was about 4 oclock A. M. this morning & we got up called the Roll (all well (55) men) Sat down by the fire talked & before we had done a thing had orders to Start, all hands to work & with mutch haste got our things in the waggon & off to the war, with out breakfast lots had none, until 4 ock when they drew 3 crackers ___ all Said we came on through the Same kind of country, described, until about 2 miles back we have Struck a nice vally of about 1 mile wide, we See but little farming going on, See but few men, & believe they are nearly all Linkonites, we Stopped here at 3 oclk PM after traveling 14 miles, I Stand it first Rate, neither Sore nor blistered feet, more anon, Wednesday night 7 oclock, we got up early this morning

P3

& resumed our journey over a Rough Rock Road intercepted on either Side with houses of the ancient Stile & passed Jacksborough an old place of the order of Clinton, we kept on until about 8 AM arrived at what is called big creek gap, the place where <u>Gollicaffer</u> expected to give the enemy a Round, but was betrayed & he then concluded to blockade the Road, (that leads through the mountains along the creek) he had Rocks & timbers Rolled into the Road cut along the Side of the creek (it is not larger than Nances Creek) the fortification is a natural one, two large ledges of Rocks running parrelel about 50 ft between them the height of one 30 ft & the other one 60 ft nearly perpendicular the Road running nearly parrellel across one end the creek between, between those ledges is verry Steep, So one ___ man could Stand above another & a thousand men could Shoot at one without being in oneanothers way, I am well God bless us all good bie (I have a chance to Send it now) SCK

(*FN written between lines upside down*) We expect to go on Soon to Cumberland Gap 25 or 30 miles farther We are 40 miles from Knoxville there are 2 Georgia Reg ___ battery of Artillery cavalry & in all I Suppose 10000 Strong

NEAR JACKSBOROUGH TENN MAY 24TH

.24 .27 .30 .31 Pl

> (*Ink spilled on letter & parts of letter is not legible*)

My dear Amie I have put off writing _____ we were expecting to go to Cumberland Gap this morning, but we Rec orders this _____ go back to this place which is _____ heared that the Yankees were _____ in force across the mountain & the idea was not to be cut off from our provisions which was on the Road from Clinton, which we met this morning about 7 oclock, (but no Yankees) we Started without breakfast, I drew Some crackers, & divided it among the men leaving no 1, Some to crack on in the rain & mud, it Rained all the way, we were Some time getting a camp ground, we were ordered to go to the Right to the top of a hill, which proved to be Steep & at least 300 yds, we got off our tricks & got wood & a fire Started, when we were ordered to fall into line, Some of them thought the line of battle, but fell in & believe that they were as well prepared in feeling to fight as they will ever be, wet cold & hungry, we came down the hill & passed in a nice grove where w Set up & are doing well

MAY 27TH 1862
KENTUCKY & VIRGINIA LINE 11 OCLOCK

P2

my dear Amie I got my letter Spoken of even____ last, I am in command of a Company (Composed of ____ men of Co, A & 7 men of Co. E, our, Co) on Pickett __ are about 3 miles from camp (the way we _____ cannot describe the fortifications, but Say that ____ would take 5 times our numbers to take the gap we are on the extreme right pickett behind what is called Rifle pits, we have but 5 men on post at one time during the day & at night will have half the Co, we have 24 hours provisions with us, My own is 8 biskits & a hock bone (raw) canteen of water, a few dried apples & a piece of tobacco, Our meet is (good) bacon but when fried is verry Salt, I prefer it raw, My Dear A I never had better health in my life, I feel truly thankful for the abundant mercies & blessings, bestowed on me, Oh that God would continue it & give me grace Sufficient for the days, Oh that I could be a better man, & worthy of the confidence Reposed in me, Pray for me, Pray for our cause, pray for our Success & the final overthrow of the Lincon army & for the independence, Peace prosperity & happiness of the Confederate States, Then Shall we Rejoice together & praise him who is able to Redeem us, & bought us with his blood

MAY 30TH 7 A. M.

P3

We had no alarm at our position last night, but heared Several Reports of guns during the nigh, at other pickett posts, there is posts Scattered from here all around this Side of the Gap, 8 or 10 Co on pickett every day, The general came to See us yesterday, he Said upon our vigilence depended the Safety of this army & that if we were attacked we must hold it until we could be Reinforced, at all hazard, There is a Tennessee co close to us, & a N Carolina Reg about a mile off, but a rough way for men to come in a hurry, the timber is all cut down (helter Skelter) for a ¼ of a mile before the pits we are in & Steep enough to make a man blow if nothing in the way, I Slep with Lt Oden last night on one blanket & covered with one, I had a rock for a pillow, with my hat on it, the blue Sky for a covering, I felt that God was my protector, & I am Shure he did for I am well, with all of the powers & faculties which he has given me, I cannot describe the fortifications, even if I were allowed to, I think from the maneuvering that they (the officers) are

P4

expecting a fight, and _____ is that the Linconites are in about 12 miles of here with 15 Regiments, we heared _____ yesterday in that direction, it Seems to be a _____

of mountains one after another any _____look from here, on the Side ___

Ridge Stretched along, appeare _____ the Cumberland (we are on) ____

_____ manning, we are above the ____ of the _____ while every mountain gap ____ high above the clouds wound round the hollows looked like Snow or more like Sands would Spread __ gulf, dotted over with islands ____ in camp 12 N, we arrived here about 10 ½ , I found <u>Pammers</u> Rhodes & Several others, who Returned there was 11 came in Some Sick P Palmer is not Stoubt, I was glad to get a letter but was Surprised to hear that you had not got but one, from me, that one had all, I had time to write every other day until the 17th when we left Knoxville, we came to Clinton Sunday morning (I was on Police) I wrote then & when we came to big Creek Gap one or 2 letters, I do not want you to think I do not write

P5

Bill Johnson is not in our Co (you wrote I could collect his bagg in act) C Evans will get a discharge I wrote it out last Sunday, but it will, have to be Sent to the war department for to be Signed he is Spitting blood & left at Clinton. As to Fergerson Affair Say nothing about it (tell you there is no Redress in military law) The boxes you Sent I have not got, the Stopper of the berry bottle came out & Spilt all over the cake, the box got Smashed on the car & only the letters is Saved, the Sick in the hospital eat the rest & bitters J. P. Said he could not bring it, As to the likeness I do not know but that it was as good as my Sort of men have, an officer aut to look Stern & be prompt & positive, I was not Serious, too mutch to the contrary, as to the brown paper letter, I had nothing else to do but to drop you a few words, I had plenty of paper in my trunk but could not get it out of the baggage car, & as to writing full Sheets this is according to circumstances, at B Shanty I had to write & run

P6

(Written on scrap paper date unknown but with this letter)
(Front)

Direct to Lt. S C Kelly Co. E 30th ALA Cumberland Gap 55+69=115.

(Back)

You need not be Surprised at the backing of this letter, the Scamp must Steel off the Stamps, for they use them for change, & lots of them will not Stick I will try to another way & if it does not go I am not out 5 cts S C Kelly

P6

May 31rst 11 oclock I intended to Send it yesterday but was to late, the Capt came up this morning he is not well but better than when he left, I do not want you to put yourself to the trouble to make me any clothes, I had better buy them, I can get them when I want & as cheap as you can get them, I Bought me another Shirt & a pa pants (woolen) I cut off my old jeans pants (where they were worn or the ankles) & pockets) & made me a par of drawers, I wish I could Send my Shirts & drawers & pants home for I have no use for them here, I have not worn my linen pants or but one day, they are too white & light for this climate, Our picketts caught a Yank this morning he Said he had deserted them & coming to us, but he was crawling when they discovered him the day & night we were out we made no discoverys, Our Co is Reenforced with the Returned Sick, We have 69 men 46 absent & 20 of them at home & you Say to eve one & every body to tell them, that they had better come or Send a Certifficate from a doctor or they will be published & dealt with as deserters, Report to May Smith Talladega or to Capt, I must close, may God bless all of us & the cause of our Country Pray for me I will do the best I can good bie yours affectionately SCK

MAY 28TH 1862
CUMBERLAND GAP KENTUCKY TENN & VIRGINIA

.28 P1

(FN in this letter he explains how the ink got on previous letter)

My Dear Amie I have but ½ hr. to write before courier goes out. I will Say in the first place, I am well (but hoarse) I am in command of the Co. Our Capt. has the mumps fell behind yesterday morning, at a kinsmans, I have 55 men & 22 of whome are sick but 2 are bad all nearly wore out, I Stand it as well as any man in the Reg (I Reckon) mumps is prevalent Sore feet common, Say to Jane Sam P __nds it well, Among the unsound is Bowman (Sore feet), Jack Williams irregular Bowels, R Cooley left (Sick) Journey Do White Do Ben Peace (Sick in camp) Wm Stewart mumps, H Steel, H Wolf just tired & bowels irregular, those are all that are from our end that you would know, we got here about 4 o'clock yesterday eve traveled 42 miles

P2

Since Monday morning 3 days we are on a hill Side (Rough enough) Stretched tents & Slept Steep last night, we are one part in Virginia & the other in Tenn, I have not Seen mutch of the fortifications the road up the mountain is an ess & then an other ess backards & forwards, good road not verry Steep, There is lots of water in Small Hills all around here with plenty of Springs, one Black Sulphur , (Splendid) Our waggons wnt back from the big Creek Gap to Clinton for provisions, I Sent for my trunk for Pike & me, they brought it but left the key, So I have to borrow one (there is but 2 in the Reg that will open it) I can always get it when I can find the man, I wrote you a letter Sunday evening but had no chance to Send it, & no key to put it away, & left it to put in Caps trunk & Some of them turned over the Ink on it, I put it up (not withstanding) in his trunk & this morning Landers is out, with the key, I will write Soon, I want to put on clean clothes & would like you to buy or make me a Shirt & drawers of cotton warp & Wool filling, wove plain, I prefer them died, but would take them white, if you could get black Sheeps wool with white warp, would be ideal my Socks are holding out prime (all whole) yet my old boots were left at Clinton, I got my blanket, we are expecting a fight here the enemy will have to come to us we are all Ready, I have never heared from you yet but do not blame you, God bless us & the cause of our Sepiration   S. C. Kelly

JUNE 1862

(Unknown date but around this time period)

my Dear do not get excited about this & Say nothing about it, But it Seems to me at this times because I am not a Talladegan that they do not Show me that favor as is Shown to those from Talladega, It is a Talladega Concern, May God forgive us all, understand me I have had no falling out with any one, I expect that I am wrong I hope I am in this particular, the Coln has family prayrs every good night, I go up occasionally all have an invitation I will write to you on this matter again, & that is not all I intend to apply my Self to tactics I know that I can learn all I now I have learned, & I can I Read into practice I do not intend to miss many drills, I will close Supper is Ready, & I feel like I have discharged my duty today God bless you & yours good bie my Dear Amie SCK

JUNE 3RD 1862
CUMBERLAND GAP TENN

.03 P1

(Letter has burns around edge)

My Dear Amie I rec yours & Billys last night I was glad verry glad to get it, I was also thankful to learn that you were all getting along So well, I would be glad that the children all would have both measles & mumps for I tell you that childhood is the time, for if they were ever thrown in the army that they would be Sure to have them then the worst place they could have them, But for the measles & mumps ____

__th Ala Reg would have this day 9 hundred men in Stead of

4, I did not know that men could Shun them So long, we have 30 Sick in comp & 45 out or behind 45 Reported for Duty, 3 of them waggoning, , the Capt is not well, we have in all 120 now but I question if we are all together any more our Sick (except the bad cases) are Sent to Lowden, from Knoxville, we had 3 left at K, Rountree & Foster with about 100

P2

others who had no guns were left at K _y or of Gen Smith, The letter was Sent forward by Capt Lee of our Reg, the convalessent are not doing us any good (Scarcely) Some of them did not hold out to get here, R, Cooley (as I Stated in my last) has not come up yet, they travel 40 miles by land & by the time they get here they are almost Sure to be Sick, out of all the S furloughed men there is not one third able for duty, J Palmer is well J Palmer is not I think he had better have a discharge he has not asked it, but I think can get it, Sick men are a nusence to the cause, for it aut to tale one well man to wait on every 3 S men, I had Rather have 40 well men than 70 Some Sick 20 not well but _____ GC, The time Seems long to me but if you can make out without me, I feel like God will take care of me, through this war, nothing would please me better than to be at home (in time of peace) but can I prise anything higher than Liberty No, I will Sacrafize all & even Life itself upon the altar of my country, and just So long as God will give me health & Strength, I expect to battle with the invaders (of the land of the free & home of the brave), or gain our independence

P3

I acknowledge at all times that I am not as good a man as I wish to be but I do not know that I am a worse man than when I entered the Service, I hardly ever get mad & it is the poorest place to pout that you ever read about, brother C. Said he never knew a good man to come out but a worse man, It is a poor place to Show on whose Side we are on, I have not heard but one Sermon Since we left home & that was a Methodist & not mutch in it to feed me, we have no chaplain, I have been on duty or on march every Sabbath (I believe) Since we left Talladega, it will be our (Companys) time on pickett in two more days , we take it by Co Commensing at A, B & C one from each Reg every day the Pickets take in a Spy nearly every day, they (the prisoners) Say that they are deserters from Linconland but they are put in Safe keeping, H Forney is a prisoner in the charge of an old mess (School of Johns) mate at Collage & Suppose is doing well I would like to have more of a variety than we have but except on marches we get a plenty _____ bacon & flour, Soap & candls Salt no Sugar Coffee molasses pickles Rice &C Such things as they cannot get we cannot get, We are poorly fixed in the way of cooking utensils we left nearly all we had we have a Skillett & one pan with 3 tin cups all Said, I wrote to you about my trunk key, I was badly pestered to borrow every time, but J Palmer found one on a Rock out on the hill Side & it fit as good as my own, We cannot buy any thing to eat here at all nearer than 3 or 4 miles & then hens are worth one dollar & everything else in proportion, Butter 50 cts & Scarce at that bread

P4

and meat for breakfast with good cool water & meat & bread for dinner & So on from day to day, but I am thankful that we have that, I got on the way up here 2 canteens full of milk & a little honey, is all I have had Since we left Knoxville, the honey colicked me as usual, I expect that you had better pay Billys master, if you have money, I do not know when we will draw or what I would do with it, I am afraid to Risk it by mail Since you do not get more than half of mine, I Shall number mine written in June this is one, but 2 or 3 Since we came, I want you to cut out the teligraph collum in the Reporter & Send it in your letters to me, if I could get your letters as quick as the last I would not mind it, direct to Cumberland Gap until you hear from me to change, it has been Raning for Several days, we are on a hill Side Rough & Steep mud plenty in the fair grounds, I am Surprised to See that Billy has improved So mutch God bless the child, for I do not know what he is to do in th____ tell him to apply himself for _____ without letters is no man tall esc_____, So far as his natural Strength consi_____s, but to be direct & controlled by an other, I had no idea that there was So little learning in Ala, every body aut to educate there children, if they work night & day to do it, the negrows of our Reg are the best fed & favored than the men, for they cook for officers & if there is any thing left they get it I must close God bless all of us in our Several capassities tell the negrows to be happy in their lot, for God in these times has given them the better place, Affectedly Your Sam C Kelly

P5

(This page is written upside down & between lines of P1)

P.S. I rec your paper & was glad to get it I have Some of my apples yet whitch I crack once & a while, We have Several very Sick m__ Simmons McGill Griffin are worse off there is a hospital 13 miles off but verry Sick men cannot bear the trip, we have these 3 in an old house & a nurse to wait on them but bad at best, I reckon you will call this a full Sheet, It is Raining & nothing else to do, I will close for meat & bread is ready, give my love to all who inquire of me Pray for me for I know that I am not my own keeper, but trust on him, on whome I believe

JUNE 6ᵀᴴ 12 OCLOCK NOON
ON PICKETT ON MAIN ROAD 14 MILES FROM MORRISTOWN TENN

.06 P1

(Letter incomplete)

My verry Dear Amie I don't know that I have anything of interest to write to you, but to let you know that I am disappointed twice by not getting letters from you, there was both times letters out of the neighborhood, & they came through in 5 days, but alass no tidings from my Dear one, far far away, it make me uneasy but I cannot blame you, I think that the paper has given out, or the money is gone or that Some of you are Sick, if the latter do not with hold it from me, if the first, tear it out of that old Ledger, if money Sell a mule or Something less, if you cannot borrow, For Gods Sake do not withhold any thing from me, that

P2

you would tell me if I were there, Get Ves Estice to back them his letters comes through in quick time, My Dear I mean no offence, be it far from me, I would write oftener but I have nothing to write, nothing to write with or nothing to write on but this Black book & it on my knee, Scrunched down on a Rock on the ground, & it will Soon all be gone, I have but one envellope cant buy anything & if I could I Should have to give 5 prices, besides all those things I have no change less than 10 dollars & venture to Say I could not get it change in weeks, but be all that So I will endeavor to write once a week let it cost what it may, & frequently, have to wait Several days to Send it to the office, in our present advanced position

P3

There is an examination of the officers to come off Shortly & I do not know who can Stand a through examination, but I know I cannot, (I may go to the wall) but it Seem like they could not do without me, for I am on duty about every 3rd day, & if on pickett of detached companies I am one of the few, if on battalion drill, I nearly every time have a Company (not my own) to command & in my own Co have all the Running about & finding out the many questions & petitions & do up the dirty work generally, but I do not complain, but try to thank God who givith me the health & Stringth & confidence of the men, with whome my lot is cast, These things you must ponder in your head (& Say nothing) but I know nothing I would not tell you were I in your arms & Sipping the burning kisses, I wont take

P4

Oh that God would interpose in our behalf as a nation & give us the power to drive the invaders from our Soil & that Speedely, & that Peace, (on honorable terms) Sweet peace might over Shaddow us, when words & Rumors of Wars would Sease, when the wearied Soldiers might Return home to their loved one, to meet around the family tables & alters, to Return thanks unto him who Saved them from all the dangers of camp life & for the blessings of peace & for all things, both temporal & Spiritual that we enjoy, I fair Sumptuously every day, I am on Pickett we Send out into the Country & buy chickens milk corn bread butter onion &C, we had enough for Supper & breakfast for 25 cts a piece, but breakfast was late & must go get dinner

JUNE 7TH 1862
CUMBERLAND GAP TENN

.07 P1

(Letter burnt at center edge)

My Dear Amie I have nothing of interest to write you but to let you know that I am well, I consider that above all other blessings of earth (naturally) the best to a Soldier, I prize it higher & do feel thankful to him who is the giver of every good & perfect gift, Oh how Sorry I am for a poor Sick Soldier, who is without God & with out hope in the world, who when he has all the accomidations of a camp life, Suffers for the many verry many let the conveniencies, & kind words of his wife mother & Sister, but in Stead of that the doct__ are careless & rough the nurses curse & Swear to thus & So we have not got but 2 or 3 bad cases in the Co, but about 24 on the Sick list this morning, Steel & Palmer will get a discharge with 3 others in the Co, they will be home Shortly, it is nearly impossible to get the papers fixed up & properly Signed, I think this a healthy

P2

place, I was on Pickett once Since I wrote came in yesterday morning, on the mountain that night it was disagreeably cold, we were not allowed any fire after night, we had no alarm, I was on the Same post as frst time, I carried a Sheet of paper to write you a letter but got to Studding the tactics & had no time to write, You must not expect a letter every 3 days, but I will try to write once a week not that I think or care less for you (God forbid) but because I Shall have more duties & have to apply myself for an examination the course of 4 months, _____ if the officers of our Co were Required to undergo an examination tomorrow that all would be found wanting, & likewise with all of the other Companies with a few exceptions, My last letter I Sent it by Capt Lee a discharged Soldier, I expect to Send this by another one, he is of Francis Company, I do not know what

P3

more to write I wish that I had, Oh J. will tell you that our mess has not got but one of our tents, from Clinton, we all Sleep in it on beds made out of Small poles & chestnut bark, we first drive up 4 forks lay polls from one to another, then lay Smaller ones across, then the bark across them (which is wide enough for a man to lay on one Single piece Slick Side up), we have not got all of our bed clothes yet, P Palmer has joined as bed fellow Since he Ret, we Sleep tolerably well now but not So well as if we had our tick full of leaves, I think in a few days we will get all, that young man Person (the Cadet) has come up & joined our Co, he Sleeps with the Capt & Landers & Truss Sleeps at the foot on the mess Box, So you may know we are crowded

P4

We have been moving our tent today we were Stuck in the Co, we dug out on the hill Side & Set up, I always do my part & wish I could Say that for all, I am just writing this because I have Space, I commenced patching this morning but had to quit & help put up every thing when we got Set up I mean our bed & the tent we (Pike & me)Sent Truss to get dinner & commensed to write the other it Seems to me expected us to put up their bed, but we concluded that we had done our Shear, they are now busy, Dinner is over & you cannot guess what we had, well we had chicken dumplings & Soop, (but had no chicken) it done prime had biskits & water, we have verry good _____ considering we have no Soda, it is worth150 cts per lb Sugar 40 Molasses 2 dollars & none to buy in less 7 miles, I went to a house the other day & got my dinner for 50 cts I Shall go back occasionly, I must close, we have to go 1 ½ miles to drill & the time is nearly come May the God that we worship protect us all is the prayrs S C Kelly

JUNE 8ᵀᴴ 1862
SUNDAY 3 ½ PM

.08 P1

(Written on a scrap of paper)

A I expected to Send this by P Palmer who has had the Capt working for a discharge for a week but the papers is not yet Signed, he will be at home in a Short time 4 others applying & tis as easy to get all as one, We Saw 4 fellows discharged (for desertion yesterday) they Rec it on the naked back 39 lashes with a cow hide & drummed out of camp to the tune of Yankee dood

P2

le, in the presence of 4 or 5 Reg, I was at a burial today the man was from Talladega County died of Pneumonia, Our Sick is improving none but bud Griffin, he has pneumonia, he is better I think will get well, We Rec orders last night to avail ourselves of every opportunity, to Send back all Surplus bag, we expect a forward movement by order of Gen, but I hardly believe we will go, I Saw the order it is not known ____ well SCK

JUNE 12ᵀᴴ 4 OCLOCK P. M
SIX MILES FROM CUMBERLAND GAP SOUTH ON PICKETT

.12 .13 P1

My Dear Amie I Rec yours of the 3ʳᵈ few days ago & was glad to hear you Speak (if on paper) it is a Source of consolation to hear your voice any way, but alass, I must deprive myself of that (only by letter) for the love of my country, We have been in an uproar for the last 4 or 5 days, we knew Something would turn up & night before last Rec orders to cool bread enough for 3 days yesterday, I was on the camp guard & our negrow was Sick, So we had to cook, (or Pike did) & last night we Rec orders to be on line by day light, that every man that could not walk that had not been Sent out would be left on the ground, (the bad Sick) were Sent out to Tazewell 12

P2

Miles, that we had waggons to carry, the convalessent were to walk, there guns having been Sent in waggon, We had 2 that could not walk Sewell Griffin & Phillips (the latter left) about 17 or 18 of the others P Palmer H Steel B Cooly & others Started on to Tazewell & we towards big creek gap, The orders to the Capt to pack all the company books & valuables in one trunk to the company, that he did but all belonged to him except the books that was packed, I packed up my mine & Pikes things in my trunk & expected to leave it at the house of an old Union man, when the order came it was to fall into line immediately with nothing but guns &C & provisions & one blankett to the man and that with out knap Sacks, So I locked it after taking out one Shirt one re drawers 2 pr Socks & uniform & Summer coats all my pills P killer & Champhor but left the last named out in my haste, We left every thing

P3

else & Started 20 minutes to 12 oclock, we traveled to this place formed in line of battle across the road in a Sedar thicket on the hill Side, while in view was fields of corn & wheat fields with the Road in the center, The Coln Said we had come to fight &C while all was Right with Alabamans, The Moon was in eclipse when we Started, looked like new moon & Still increased until it became total & then passed off as it came, it was total for about an hour or more 4 hours in all, we lay down on our arms wet with Swet, & wet feet from adding creeks without anything but 1 blanket apiece, I got to Sleep after issuing cartridges to the men about day light & Slept without interruption until 7 oclock AM, I got up went to a house for water & I got Palmer & I a pone of corn bread 2 quarts butter milk & butter enough to eat it paid a quarter & left when we got back Started out here

P4

5 oclock PM the army is moving & we must go, I am in advance with 7 men ¼ mile, I halt every man passing have learned from cavalry that the Yankees are crossing the Moun in force & not more than 13 miles below here, I guess we will go there to night

13th 7 oclock AM we traveled until about dark last night & camped with out disturbance, I do not know when we will leave, our man Phillips we left in camp was Sent on yesterday, We thought that the Gap would be evacuated, but it is not, I got my Pain killer by S White one of Fracis Co who were on Pickett, he Said my trunk was there but Said nothing about my Mexican Blk, You Spoke of kisses & kind words, God bless you, I have So much to write I do not know what to write, at all events, I know that no man Sacrifised more than I do, & can Say I have had as much pleasure at home as most of men, but all for you & your children, I can live any where until I die, but to let my prosperity be Subject to Lincon, never

(FN this below was written upside down in margin & across P1)

no never, God bless the cause that Separates us & all of us S. C. Kelly

J Palmer is well & J Price I must close I have a chance to Send

JUNE 14TH 1862, 6 P. M.
CLARBORN CTY TENN 12 MILES OF CUMBERLAND GAP

.14 .15 .16 P1

My Dear Amie I Rec yours of the 8th a few hours ago, I am glad to get a letter but I have never Rec a dispatch in one of them, we hardly ever get a paper & when we do it is the Knoxville Reg, I do not consider it Sound or Reliable & if it were both it is So badly printed I cannot make out all, Cut out the most important dispatches out of the Reporter & Send them in with your letters, as there is Room in nearly all of them, We have been expecting to go on every hour Since night before last but we Still Remain we hear lots of grape vine telegraph dispatches, but it is generally believed that the Yanks are 10 miles

P2

down the vally, & that Bartons Briggade, our men, is Still below them 10 miles or more miles, & will bring on the attack while we will advance in the Rear, the Yankees are opposite the gap where they came across & I am of the opinion that they will find out the plan & take back to the whole of the mountain where they crossed, but no telling what a day may bring forth, You Say we had a fight & was uneasy &C, but we have not & when you hear from us again, Arheart Wolf Crenshaw Baxter are Sick & Sent back to Gap more anon,

15th 8 oclock AM at the Same place, Harvey Bridges went back with mumps this morning, We had a good nights Rest last night, got up about Sunrise washed & eat breakfast one cold buisket broiled on the coals I had meat but

P3

did not want it I had plenty of cold water & was Satisfied, I washed my Self & put on clean clothes went to hear old man Cornelius preach, he done as well or better than I expected, he was followed in a Short exhortlaling (by Parson Lane), who afterwards called on the crowd to know how many profesers there were by them kneeling & he Said there was more than half, Then went off with Some of the boys to write for them & Returned at 2 oclock, broiled my bread, eat my meat Raw (lean hock) drank cold Spring water & Set my Self down on a pile of hay to tell my dear one at home, how I have passed the only holy Sabbath Since I left Talladega, that I was not on a march or duty, Oh how I would have liked to have been at home today to have been permitted to have gone with you to hear Brother H preach, It would be no hardship for me to walk, & the

P4

rest of you Ride in the buggy, So as I might See that lovely form & how that Sweet voice that has cheered me & promped me to the performance of every good deed & those Little ones who are the pride of my life, who Say Pa. Pa. & lean to me to decide all those little innocent disputes, (Oh tis gone from me now) & at Liberty to Set down with brother & Sister (in Christ) to hear the good news of good tidings that unto us a Son is given and a child is born, & his name is Jesus because he Shall Save his people, Are we his or are we not if So of all men, I Should be the most thankful for he has kept me by the power of God, through faith, Ready to be

Revealed in the last time, My Dear one I do appreciate home & family as mutch as any one but never do I expect to enjoy it any more until we have gained our independence

P5

I can weep like a child I can mourn like a dove but that will never gain our independence, I must be a man, & fight the invaders So long as they dispute our write to govern ourselves or til it pleases God to take me from the Strife or my health becomes So impaired that I cannot up with the army, I have not heared nothing of the enemy today, more anon

16th am 6 ½ oclock after breakfast of the Same Sort (no varities) I did get an onion yesterday about as large as an egg roasted it for Supper, for which I paid 10 cts this country is nearly eat out but we have lots of government Stores & provisions at Knoxville Morristown & other places, but we are out on a Scout & expecting a fight & carry only Such as we cannot do with out, We)our Reg) have the praise for the best behaved of any that have

P6

Ever passed the Road, The Tennessee Reg are (the Sitizens Say) the meanest to them they take Such things as they want, We always buy, they Say that they can tell well Raised men by the way they do when they come in, We are going to drill this morning, I Suppose they will cook our bread & Send it from the Gap, that's the way they done day before yesterday, It is now 7 Battalion drill, I must go 2 ½ oclock here Still write immediately, I have a chance to Send, God direct you & me &all of us in the way we Should go more anon S C Kelly

JUNE 19TH 4 ½ OCLOCK AM.
CLINCH RIVER 18 MILES TO MORRISTOWN & 8 MILES TO TAZEWELL

.19 .20 .21 .22 P1

My Dear Amie the last time I wrote to you was the 16th, We received orders on the 17th to make up & cook 4 days Rat of bread

& be ready to Stare by Sun Set, we had 2 skillets to the company & 54 men & 4 officers we the latter, waited 2 or 3 o'clock made up dough & cooked on a Rock, we left there between Sundown & dark, we Started in quick time took the mountain immediately, it was cloudy & no moon & I do think that the Roughest feeling Road (for I could not See it) I ever traveled was that night, you have no consception of a bad Road, we reached the River (called Powell's) about 10 o'clock, we had it to wade, Some pulled off briches & drawers Shoes & Socks, I pulled off my socks only, it about twice as large

P2

As Tara pine & a little over knee deep, we waited for the brigade to get over, I lay down on my knapsack under my head & took a Sweet nap but when I awoke I was cold, I went to a fire the boys had built warmed a little fell in & Started towards Tazewell at 1 ½ AM, the moon out & Road better arrived there about Sunrise, 8 miles from the river, had ½ hour to cook Raw bread & eat Raw meat & Started for Morristown 26 miles, we are tired & sleepy but knocked along slowly & arrived at Clinch River about 3 PM, lay down & slept until it was out turn to cross (we crossed in a float) about 5, Stacked arms & Stayed until Sunrise this morning, I do not know how many men is along (but it Seems to me) that there is to many to Retreat, We have Ev

P3

acuated Cumberland Gap & every thing is destroyed the Cannon the large peases & one in particular Long Tom that they had in Mexico & our Side took it from the Yankees at Mannasses was Spiked & Run of the bluff ¼ of a mile high & all the balls canister & grape followed, the powder magazine blown up, (one man got his face burnt off him as the Irish man would Say) the tents & clothing & cooking vessels provisions & every thing was destroyed except a few, my Trunk was busted open & myne Pikes, & Landers things put in, Pikes, & put on a waggon, but one Lt told me it was thrown off, So I do not know whether or when I will ever get it, I think we have passed 200 waggons

P4

today, We have not got but 2 men that cannot walk & I believe they are all with us & before us, H Bridges is bad with the mumps, but can walk on, & not being confined to line may make the trip, now about 7 miles to Mtown, RR there, We crossed the Holston River in flats & think that there was 100 in crossing at one time, about 9 PM a grand Sight it looked all the world & the Rest of man kind was assembling there & that I Saw was only one Brigade & before we got all across Bartons Brigade came,

20th We camped about 1 mile from the River & 4 from Mtown, drew Rations had but 1 Skillett & 2 lids, with 3 pans to make up in, we Ran them all in double quick all night, Some got Some & Some got none, I offered 20 cts for 4 biskits but did not get them, I had 3 biskits &a piece of ham, that I brought from

P5

Cumb valley, I fryed 2 of them eat one with a piece of ham cooked in the Same & at the Same time with 4 or 5 other mens Rations at the Same time, all in a Skillet that will bake 7 bisk at one time, So you See that I have 1 bisket for dinner & one for Supper & none for the other 2 days, but I will make out I can get if it is in the Co & besides that I can do on less than any one you ever Saw, I believe that is the great Secret to health to a Soldier, I can & have done 3 biskits & a little Raw meat 2 days & was Satisfied & had 6 or 7 good ones & meat in my Sack if I was at home, I would (or did) eat more in one day than I do in two, I do believe that I have fallen off, but to the contrary my britches is tight enough to Stay up without gallases, I have not fattened much but my flesh is hard, I am not Stiff nor Sore nor feet blistered, have helped along the weak, & thanked God that

P6

he has been merciful unto me I take it as I find it, Rough or Smooth clean or nasty, can make out on what any body can, I have actually eat bread that my dogs would not but do not be Sorry for me, but pray for me, that God will Still give me health, Yes health above wealth above promotion above every thing in this life, but that good & perfect gift of God the forgiveness of Sins, Well my Dear I have not told you these things to make you Sorry but to Show you that we are determined in this war, & that I am willing to undergo any hardship or privation for the cause, time Rolls on Rapidly as ever I Saw it in my life, it is not half the time I know the day of the week or month, we are here Still 9 AM I do not know what we are waiting for there is Some manovering of the

P7

waggons, every one has their own opinion about them, I think that they aim to Send them the gravell train to Knoxville, they were brot over here to be guarded last night, I think that tis move will give to the enemy the whole of, E, Tennessee, I See no other endorsements in this Country for me, the people are (with a verry few exception) the poorest most ignorant & worst looking I ever Saw, dirt eaters, but they have to eat Something & verry few have any thing else, the first wheat I Saw cut was the 18th Some fields is fine, nearly all So Steep that they have to be cut with <u>Reep</u> hooks the crop is not near Ripe yet, the corn is from is from 2 blades to knee high except one field about waist high the Rows runs Round the hill , too Steep to even walk up (a mayjority) & where ever they can get a Spoon full of it is a place for honey, I got a bate, dearest it will make corn or Wheat or clover, night before last I eat it with out

P8

water or bread & it did not hurt me, I eat lots more than I ever eat at once, I will try it again the 1st chance , even at 25 cts a pound, 1 ½ oclock PM We were ordered in to line, as we thought to go on to Morristown but we left faced Recrossed the River at 2 ½ & Struck out for (I do not know where) but I Suppose to meet the enemy who it id likely have followed us, more anon,

21 7 ½ oclock AM, We left in the direction of Tazewell traveled on til night where we camped on the top of Clinch mountain, we lay all round about here, I could not find a place level enough to lay down & I with Several others went into a garden & lay among the plants, We are in hearing of the Yankee Cannons, on the

root we are going, I do not know who they are firing at, 12 oclock they were firing at our advanced guard, I must close God bless good bie S C Kelly

P9

22 4 ½ P. M. I cut the Subject Short yesterday & expected to Send it off immediately but it (as many other things) turned out a failure, I have wrote all day for to Send but there is no Regular mail now, We left the top of the mountain about 10 AM, & came to this place 1 mile from top, in a nice burch & oak grove where we can Sit in the Shade of one there all day, on a Ridge full of Roots & Rocks, we have been expecting to move every moment & last night at 10 oclk we had to draw & (cook) 2 days Rations, to carry the flour in barrels up a Steep hill it dark & all the men had been a Sleep, we after So long a time Succeded in getting it & the bacon to the camp nearly ¼ of a mile, we had but one oven as usual. I & Pike maid up dough & he went down into the Tennessee Reg & cooked it in frying pans, While I picked and

P10

cleaned & old hen that I gave 75 cts for put to boil in a Tennessans camp (kittle I had borrowed) we got bread done & camp kittle all Sitting up Steep with about 2 lbs bacon & about Six lbs of flour made in to dumplings to Season it, by about 2 AM, We lay down & left the boys cooking to tend to it, we had good oak Railes to make fires of, We Slept until day light when Some one told me that Tennessan had come for his kettle, I looked down to See what I Should put it in, all the pans was in use & I Saw nothing to hold it but the empty flour barrel, no, no, don't, don't cried ½ doz, well let me have a pan Said I, all in use Sir will I will pour it on the ground, for I promised the man to let him have it when called for night or day, done or Raw, & picked up the kettle & Some one thought to empty the flour out of the pan

P11

back into the barrel, & I emptied it into it leaving 5 or Six dumplings Sticking to the bottom but no matter & double quicked off, just in time to get it into their waggon, but as I Started I Said to the Co pitch in fore thing eat it up, for I expected we would be off in less than 5 minutes & when I got back it was all gone (except the Soop or Sop, or truck0)except one little piece of bacon & a dumpling about an inch Square, but Pike had Saved me the neck, but in the fight it lossed all the Skin, So mutch for the first chicken I ever tried to cook myself, but it was all Right for me for I had the colic, the first time Since I left Talladega, I eat a piece of bread & a cup of coffee boiled in a cup mashed in a bag (we bought 3 lds at the Gap) I took a dose of P killers & got well directly, I kept minsing last night & drank lots of branch water (the Spring being muddy

P12

now) My Dear you know now that I have nothing to write I must quit & See the Race after the Squirrels, 2 men are up 2 trees after 2 & at least 100 men on the ground more Anon, Well it is now 7 PM I have eat Supper consisted of cold bread & Raw ham & an onion Roasted, I feel well enough after my colic this morning, I carry my Bible in my coat pocket, it is verry heavy but I could not bear to let it go, I do not Read it as mutch as I want, I Read it every day, I must close there is So mutch of this I hardly know what I have written, we will evacuate this valley, but we are Scattered about to get off the Sick & army Stores & then we will get up & head, I guess we Chattanooga, I must close 60 of us here Scattered plum home, May the God of battles be with us all & give us Such victores as may cause a Speedy peace Good bie My Dear

24TH JUNE 1862
GRANGER CITY TENN 13 MILES FROM MORRISTOWN (IE)
THE SAME PLACE OF MY LAST LETTER SENT BY MAIL 4 ½
OCLOCK AM

.24 P1

My Dear Amie we have been Running about So mutch that I have not got your letters Since I left Powells Valley, the last was dated the 8 June, I have nothing of interest to write you but we are on pickett & heared that Lt Carpenter was going home, (he has Resigned Sick) & I thought that I would let you know that I was yet Spared & ask you to help me thank God for his abundant mercies towards me in giving me health & Streangth & in passing through this war So far with as little trouble as any one & also that I am Respted by both officers & men, & if I have an enemy I do not know it, of all men I aut to

P2

Ema Pease Send this immediately to Mrs A E Kelly respt S C Kelly

Be the most thankful We (my Sqd of 25 in all) had a fine time yesterday, we Sent out 4 miles & bought 5 chickens 3 or 4 lbs butter 2 canteens of milk 1 of molasses all but the chickens we are Saving for breakfast, we made dumplings & had 2 ovens full (Splended) all of which we eat with forks of Sticks & had enough, if had had more Some one would have been floundered, We Started Several out by light this morning for 1 buckettt of honey & canteens of milk promised yesterday, all of what we got yesterday cost only 200 not a dime apiece, I & Palmer went in the morning to the Spring & at the house got 2 pones of corn bread for 25 cts that woman is cooking bread for us, we swapped flour for meal & pay her for baking, there are 5 of our Reg there & one Tennessean (Sold) we were in the house & he was Skulking around

P3

among the children 2 little girls one 9 & the other 6 years old, the older came in & the other about 60 yds Started to the house, when he tore her down & She Screamed, but we though She had hurt her Self, but She Shreaked out again when the mother Sprang out & cried out Come out here boys, we bolted & he took to the mountain, we followed him 3 hundred yds & he turned down the hollow & made good his escape, I had on 2 canteens full of water but there was but one man before me & I should have Shot at him but for him, be the man before me had no pistol, if I could have Shot him it would have give me more good than to have killed ½ doz Yanks, the woman Said that She was glad when, P & I came for he had been there longer than them, She wished I Shall Report to his Coln immediately when I get to camp & all Say that

P4

hey know him, he is of an Irish Company Raised about Nashville, It is Raining a little this morning the first time Since we have been with out tents & we left them at the Gap, the 11th, I believe that we do as well without as with them, we do not want to Stay more than 2 days at one place, we wear out all the leaves & it becomes dusty, I had my 2 Shirt washed yesterday one a flannel over S & linen bosom Starched, I mixed, I have a nit Shirt & I use my thin coat as an over coat, I have 2 par of your drawers, I wear one par a week & then Sun & whip them & make them nearly clean, this is the frst time I have had a chance to wash, from the Gap, I paid 20 cts for both, We have lots of tellegraph about the armistice, the Rasing the blockade of England, France & Spain & the combined forces of the world, but I for got to tell it, is all Grape vine, I must close May the God who has ____ Still protect us is the Prayr of ___ own Sam C Kelly

(FN this below was written upside down & in margin of this page)

I Send this with Palmers because we are Scarce of envelops & Scarce of every thing else in that line

JUNE 27TH 8 AM

.27 P1

Well My Dear one I was relieved of officer of day at 6 PM & returned to camp found it all quiet, Seen A and the Co had Rec letters, it gave me consolation for Some in the neighbor hood to get letters, I know that nothing Strange has taken place at my house or they would have mentioned it, Capt J Francis is going home to gather up the men who are Scattered about at home of the Regt, I learned that Maj Smith is Sick, he has never been with us Since we left the letter I Sent by Carpenter never Started in 2 days after I gave it to him, Lt Landers has tendered his Resignation he complaines of not being well

(This is written in ink across P1 Mrs A. E. Kelly at home)

P2

we were in a hard Rain day before yesterday, & it has Rained all the morning & it bids for to rain all day, in Showers we Rap our blankets around us & Stand round trees & do the best we can, I have kept dry only my out Side clothing, we do not know what is on foot whether peace or war, but we know we have trained here for Some cause, it is coming a hard R & I must close I am well, do pray for me, I feel like you do, May God bless & Serve us is my Prayr,

direct to Morristown Tennessee

Good Bie God B my Deares Amie your ____ S C Kelly

JUNE .29 .30 JULY .01 .02
GRANGER CTY TENN 13 MILES FROM MORRISTOWN
SUNDAY MORNING 9 OCLOCK AM

.29 P1

I was Rejoiced last night when Hobs came in & brought me a letter from you, I was thankful that you were all as well as you were, I Rec this morning by mail yours of the 21st was Sorry I Said any thing in my last about it, I hope you may be Spared from all diseases as our enemis, I do Sympathise with those who are afflicted at home & more especially with the poor Soldier in the army, I expect that you had better feed away the peas & Sell the corn, you Say you cant think of any thing to write, I have nothing to write as to wanting to See me that is out of the question, So long as I stay well & I had Rather be well & be without Seeing you than get Sick & take the chances of getting well or home, Sick men

P2

fair So badly, Our Dr is the laziest & most indolent man you ever Saw he gets more Cursing than all the Rest of the Regs, I think P Palmer Paid me, or else he Said that he forgot to pay me, tell him I drew up & got Signed his discharge & Coln S Sent it on, God bless the children tell Billy not to forget his book, for a man of learning is a perfect man & without he is only a tool for the learned men (naturally Speaking) knowledge before wealth, for he can get the money if he is Shrud. Tell the negrows that they are well off (if they do not know it) they have plenty to eat & wear good houses to keep them dry & only to work & have there victuals cooked all by day light while the poor Soldier who is defending them have to cook night & day march night & day & carry from 16 to 30 lbs and with out Clothing, Sleep in the woods as lousy as hogs, have no gospel preacher

P3

(*FN this page of letter very faded & hard to read*)
unto them, while hundreds daily diddling in there sins & when God _____

_____

_____ amon

30th 10 oclock AM well my Dear A. I have been busy since I left off yesterday & have made out

P4

2 muster & payrolls, & one monthly Report & have 2 more to make. I Recon no poor fellow never had less to do with accounting to what was Required, but I Said before I left home that I would do the best I could under the circumstanced, & So I do yet & if I were a president today I would do the Same, I try to exercise Reason, & what little judgment I Have, I have all of that Sort of work to do in our Co, it Rained yesterday twice, I had my blanket stretched on Some Rails & Some out to lay on I do __ me, I must close we are now to muster for pay, I think we will have lots of money but the Rule is to know what to do with it, more after words, Review over all in & want to cook, Some one has Set the oven on the fire & now it was interesting to See the boys with biskits & meat in hand & of all the frying, this is my peace & that is my biscquit, &C all frying at least 10 at a time

JULY 1862

JULY 1ST

P5

July 1st 7 ½ AM breakfast over (which was) a piece of ashcake (wheat dough) & a piece of boiled beef, You have no Idea how good bread Such is, the ashes does not stick mutch as to corn, the Rest of the Co are on pickett except one from each mess

The negrow (Truss) has come up, he is glad to get with us, he has been verry Sick & faired but Slim, he is baking ashcakes for the Rest, I was left to make out those Rolls, I had a piece of plank about a foot wide & ½ long, & the paper was ½ as long as your table (& to Small at that) it was brown paper & a damp day, So do not know whether they are correct, all of the Co books & nearly every thing else left behind, As to Some not liking Coln. S. I can Say that I do not like every thing he does, but neverthrless I would not exchange him for any man I know, in the Service or out of it, Some men grumble because they have to come to the war, & grumble after they come, & would

P6

(Lower corner torn off letter)

grumble if it were other wise, Shelly is good to his men, but he has to obey, his superiors, just as I have to obey him, If we had any way of cooking we would draw more than we could eat, Some wast it, Some eat as mutch in one day as I will in two, in a word I cannot eat a days Rations in one day, I heardly ever eat ½ I carry, Some always hungry & out always begging (mad & grumbling & not infrequently Sick) neither Coln. S. nor myself got a whole Shot in our coat but Capt Samuells did (at big creek Gap) while on pickett, by a bushwhacker who

ran home & Ss gun snapped & that is all of it, Tell J Hobbs wife that he got here safe & is well, to write to him, Direct to Morristown, that She kneed not Send him any clothing, there is so mutch uncertainty, You Say you put off writing, I Rec some of yours but I Supposed you wrote al least once a week I want you to number all you write in July &C I will do the Same, I can get your letters sooner than ____ _____ because of the abundance of _____ at Montgomery _____

them to distributing

P7

Well My Dear one, I do hope that God has answered the prayres of his people, in giving us a Signal victory at Richmond, Coln Shelly has just come from head Qrters & Says that Gen Stevenson has Rec an official dispatch from Richmond of the Signal victory & complete Rout of the enemy, it Rums thus that we captured 1 May General 9 brigade Gens a number of Colonials & 39 thousand prisoners, that they have thrown down there armes & dispersed in the ___mps & are being taken prisoners, Throwing up there hands & begging for mercy, That it amounts to a perfect overthrow of the grand army, Thank God for the victory if it is not So large as Stated, It is a great blessing, & we Should thank God who givith us the victory, I believe it will have its influence even upon this part of the army

P8

Say to Graham I will take 25 cts per lbs for cotton, I would like to know what spurred him up, he was whipped the last time I Saw him, I have never been whipped God is just & hope & believe that he would not let an unjust & irreligious Nation overrun us, Who mearly ask the privilege to be free & independent, & who have fought & will fight (in the fear & under the protection of him who givith us victory) until we are subjugated & then they will not get but little cotton I want Turk to thrash all the wheat he can, as long as it will pay, then I want them to make brick, no more danger of them than of the corn & every thing else, of the Yankees, in fact less, But one thing must not be neglected the gin damn, he had better get Some one to advise with him, Some one acquainted with water power I want it done up So as it will never break I Reckon you

P9

do miss me at home, from what you Say, I miss you & home & all the enjoyment of home & family, the blackberry tramps & garden towers & happy wife & children, I Still live in hope that I will yet live in enjoyment of that Peace, that I have prayed for, I live through one war & now believe I Shall live through this without firing again, I thank God that I have Sutch a praying wife, Still pray for me I am a poor Sinner & unless kept by the power of God, I would be lost, as to my getting a furlough it is out of the question

, Where is Fanny & Key, you Speak of getting another & I reckon you had better get Miss R She is a nice girl from what I hear, John R (her brother) is a good Soldier, Sell the cow (my judgment all the time) beef is worth 10 cts here & was worth that in Talladega

P10

but if you meet a chance take 25 or 30 dollars for her, Tell Virgil to take good care of his pants that I have but one Par & my Shoes nearly wore out I have but one white Shirt 1 nit 1 flannell, 2 coats 3 par Socks 2 Drawers, I have nearly Ruined my uniform coat, my old hat is getting worse of ware, have never cut my beared Since I left Nor do not expect to untill get home, I change my clothes, often & am not loosing, I have taken & given away all of my P killer, except one dose, Some times I have a light touch of colic, then I use it, I have never taken but few of the S. Pills, & them you Sent me more, I do not know what Sort they are ask Dr Bowden & write me, If you get wool make me Shirts & drawers of

P11

(Corner torn off this page)

Of the kind I wrote you lest the war closes & I come home lousey, I think that it is a poor chance, to Send go ahead & make 40 yds more of cloth & I hope we will yet live independent, Poor peoples Sons in the war may aut to Send back their money & those at home aut to write to them in that way, Some among us will Spend all they earn, as to the color of clothes Shirts & drawers any color Brown or yellow or one thread of black or brown & one white, no matter what, or white if you cant do better, The kind cotton warp & wool felling wove plain, Since I left my trunk I have had to carry my bible in my pocket, I have Read it as mutch again as, then May god bless us all & Save us as a nation & Spear _____enes of home to _____

JULY 2OND 7 OCLOCK

02 P12

I thought that I would close but I find the other Side written on & I neglected to Send yesterday, I think we will move about 1 mile, because this place is Scarce of wood & it is getting So filthy, the weather is wet, not mutch Rain but cloudy & occasional Rain, we have not heared any war news write to me about the Jack the hogs the mules, how many goats &C, I expect that they had they had better get Some boards, this Summer to Recover the house & kitchen, You cannot get nailes, but you could have them patched, Do the best you can &May God bless you & yours is the Sincere prays of your own SCK, give my Respts to the Brother & Sister S

PS men & S Penland are well

JULY 5TH

(The next 2 letters are Amie's
June 16th with Sam's reusing Amies letter by writing between the lines
upside down & in the margins)

JUNE 16TH AMIES LETTER

P1

At home June 16th 1862 My dearest S As I can send this by Hobbs will write we are all up but not very well Billy he has been sick he had a chill last saturday but is up at present he has been sick for a week but is up, fanny did not have the measles her and Torie & Toby great no have them. My children are through with them. There is a great deal of sickness, and no medacine. Miss J Bavrd is very bad & Johnny graham, P Westbrook lost his wife last Saturday, I do not know what was the matter she was not sick so ____, Mrs John Graham is very unwell & fear she will have a hard time of it yet. I do not any news I have been at home so close for the last five days. Roberson and Hall have gone after a thrasher, J Davis will have one too _____

___ and Turk will start their men 1 week we will be done ploughing by that time. They have laid by the house piece if it raines soon it will make good corn. I have agreed to let old Albert Alexander have _____ corn in the morning at _____ J Bensons wife is to have, 4 or m5 at I thought at 75 cts. I do not think we can spare much. Did J Palmer pay you 75 cts for John Bates, if so you can write to me I find an order from him to you among your papers he wants to know it is paid, I do not collect much but pay some as I go, I gave Dr. 10$ the other day to buy me a bit of quinine if he could get it at J. he said I had better give it than to do with out if we had much sickness which I agreed in fear. The children are in a great fuss talking about you they all want to see you so bad. I do wish you could take a peep at home once and a while.

P2

Sam sends howdy and said he wants to see you mighty bad, does wish you could come home. We are getting along very well considering you are so far from us but what did you mean by saying in your last if I could do without you, you would stay till the vandals were whiped. I thought I was compelled to do without you no matter how much I disliked it. I do not know but what I would say come home if I thought it would do any good but I try to bear it as well as I can. I saw Mrs Benson this evening she said all was well. John Easley is sick but was thought to be better. I went to Grahams to set up but so many came in. I borrowed Mrs Halls mule and came home to write to you. G Hobs I did not know his tale that he would start tomorrow. Lovl Alen another writes back that he does not like Shelly he has no feelings for his men and thinks they never are he does not get always get enough to eat either but do not say any thing about it only watch, some are always ready to grumble and find fault and there is none perfect. I heard that you or Col Shelly one had a hole shot through your coat but do not believe it for no one can tell how it could. John Stewarts second daughter ran away last week and married a wounded soldier by the name of Formby she was about 15 years old. My time is to short I cannot think what I want to write only I want to see you and could tell you many things. My last paper had no news. I will send any of importance if you are sick do come home immediately. Ms Bowman is very uneasy about Bowman also C Evans folks he has not yet. Read your bible and live at the mercy seat trust god and do your duty and all will be well. May the god that ralys the heart of man direct and keep as is my prayer write of ___. I got 2 letters in June Good bi Amie

JULY 3ᴿᴰ 1862 4 ½ PM

.03 P1

(Letter written over top of another also part stuck to envelope & torn)

Camp near Clinch Mountain Well my Dear one I Rec your favor of the 28ᵗʰ yesterday noon and was glad to hear from you I know that you Love me _____

_____

_____

P2

about Sunrise we heared heavy cannonading in the direction of C gap ____ _____ we Supposed it was the 4ᵗʰ July celebration, all quiet now, the wind blew last night cold & it was clear, the Sitizens Say that is the coldest Spring & Summer that they ever Recollect ___ that there crops are back wards, I Saw one Pi___ about as high (the best of it) as high as my head, Tenn is the last place to live in in time of __e, I think we have found the place (if even) where e ____ children looks out the top of the chemnes _____ the cows come home, they have no waggons _____ I do not See any, the worst old ploughs, hau__ ___ thin as a Saucer & about the Size, they gather c____ the hill Sides & throw it acr__ 40 or 50 & So__ places 100 Rows in

(Rest of letter missing)

JULY 5TH 7 OCLOCK
.05 Pl HIS

*(SCK letter of July 5th written between
lines & in margins of Amie's letter of June 16th)*

My dear one I have Some paper in my B Roll but your letters
are accumulating on me So mutch that I though I would try &
Send them home, I have them all I believe & paper is So Scarce &
high & I have no way to keep it & besides you are a good Reader,
Do not miss understand me about the letters accumulating, I wish
I could get one every 3 days, but to know that you are all well &
in fear of God once a week is better than 4/5 of the men in the army
do, There is a men in our Co who have not Rec a letter from there
wives in a month, I would not know what to think , the longest I
have ever waited was from about the 13th to the 28th June but did
not blame you, I though Something was the matter, I went
yesterday to a house to get molasses, light bread baked Palmer
with me, we carried 10 lds flour & Sat down to wait about 10es
AM, we Spoke for dinner whitch came off in due time, we had
bacon & beanes, fried ham, Rice grits, corn bread, &C & topped
off on green apple pies honey & Sweet milk, for which we paid 50
cts each, then we were in good plight to Rest, Sat down & talked
with the old man (who we found Southern) until about 4 oclock
PM, when we were told our bread was done, we got 2 pones, one
of common, & one of a large Size, paid the old woman %0 cts for
her trouble &left for camp, we weighed it & found that we had 16
lbs of the verry best kind of bread, which is ours & Pikes
allowance for 3 days, The other Soldiers went there to get that
yeast to put in there bread, but She told them that they were not
the man She made it for, & the next one that would come, would
try to persuade her that the man She promised had been there, &
She would not bake for him, & She had better bake for them, No
She Said the man I promised is not yet come & after a while when
I came She Said to her daughter & old man that is the man, I
believe the Reason She wated So long was, because when (I paid
her the day before for the C bread,) She gave me one dollar for ½

dollar that I told her & gave it back to her, I could have kept it & cheated her out of 50 cts just as easy as put it in my pocket & She never knew it, but I never thought of taking advantage of her ignorance, It done them So mutch good when I handed it back, that it was worth 50 cts to cts to me, I have tried to be honorable If I a Soldier & have to Shift about, honesty is the best policy, My Dear you know that I have nothing to write by Such as is in this letter, but I would tell it to you (& more too) if I were with you, Pike & I have with drawn from our old mess, & given up the negrow, we have been thinking of it a long time, he has not earned his victuals Since we left Talladega to us, he has been unwell for a month or more & if

P2

he had not lost a day, when have nothing to cook but flour & bacon & nothing to cook it in, no Soap to wash & nothing to wash in, & feed a negrow on the best (or Such as we get which is the best hams) at 33 cts & I do not know for flour & what it comes to as much to divide with him, fellow carry for his and tote & our dues besides (that pay 4 dollars per month & run to the Doct for him), I know it will not pay, I can boil meat or eat it Raw, I can do with it or do without, (as long as most of them) In every Respect the Capt does not tote far, & is a great Spunge, but we bare it in our hearts, & it is better to give than to Rec, We all parted with out a word there is Some grumbling in the company, about the money in his hands, belonging to the Co that Ryan gave them, they Say he is might Stingy, of it & Some Say he is using it himself, His end of the Co complain more than ours, All Say he is partial, I expect Sam Penland has given me fits in his letters home, but I only done to him what was my Duty & have nothing to take back, not neither in the Service or out of

it, he was detailed as Corpor all of the guard next morning 8 AM, the time passed & that night at roll call no Sam, next morning Same thing, he Stayed down there about the waggons, because Johnson the Act 2n master Requested him, I Said to Capt that

was his duty to inquire into it, well I will, & it went on So until the whole Co complained about it, & the Capt would not & I Reported him to the Agt, & then the Capt had or Said he had, had him detailed for that purpose, S told Johnson I do not care what & then come & told me that Johnson Said he Ranked me & that he could detail a man out of my Co, I Sent him word that he was a liar (or both) that he was nothing but a private at 11 dollars a month, act as assistant 2n Master in the name of Capt J C Francis, I have not heared no more of it & S has Ret to qrts, in Stead of riding all over the Country as <u>lucky</u> boy Private Johnson, Cleaver fellows will met, I write this to let you know that I know my duty & Rights & if need be will fight to maintain them, I have never had a difficulty & do hope I may not, I will yield if I think I am wrong, but Right never, I can get my washing g done for 25 cts a week, I got my Shoe mended, my pants will Soon kneed patching, my watch is good as good as any in camp, I Sleep with it on, & Some times my Shoes, I change my clothes every week, if I cant get them washed, I Sun & whip them, May the God in whose care we are, Direct us & Save us from the Sinners death & our country from the hands of our enemies, & that the name of this Confederacy Soon be written, (& acknowledged) among the names of nations of the world & Peace be Restored on honorable termes is the pray of your own Loved one S C

S is verry Shigh, J P told me he was mad P told him that I did not ask him and at odds & Best to do it up, They hat one other as bad as any two in the Co, Say nothing, but Listen you will hear it among the Whitesides

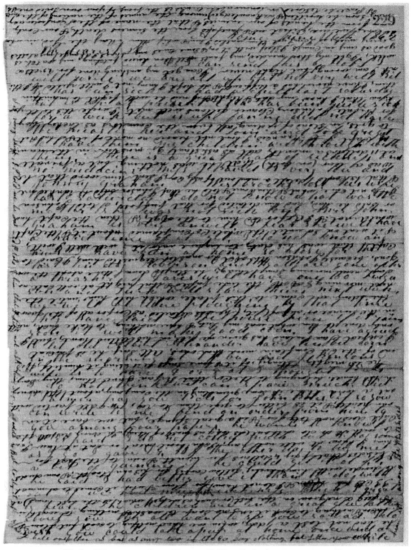

(July 5th example of how difficult it is to transcribe these letters which are written between lines & in margins)

JULY 6ᵀᴴ 1862

.06

*(Sams letter of July 6, 1862 written diagonally
over top of a portion of Amie's letter unknown date)*

P1 HERS

The weather is cool and cloudy for the season Billy is making hats out of wheat straw that looks very well he is nearly done on 1 for him and 1 for Dickey they do first rate We are having beans peas potatoes & beets now how I do wish I could send you some

P2 HERS

my chickens are small my turkeys nearly all dead I think I shall eat the turkeys. Mrs Whiteside sent me some green apples that smell & taste very well how you would __

___ them I often think of you. May god bless you and keep you in the way you would go. I do pity you Amie

6ᵀᴴ JULY 5 OCLOCK AM

.06 HIS

My dear Amie we are ordered off we will have to Start in one hour, I understand that we will be off for Bentons Brigade who down about Rutledge 15 miles South East of here down the MT at the Same place that we have crossed twice before, Several Sick Price Wolf Watts Ducket Phillips Garrett Hollingsworth

6 Oclock AM we have Struck tent one is all we will be off Soon all packed & Ready the tent S__ned off they are falling in good bie God bless the world

S. C. Kelly

GRAINGER CITY, RICHLAND VALLEY 4 MILES SOUTH OF BEANS STATION 1 PM. 6TH JULY

06 .07 .08 P1

My Dear Amie I mailed a letter at Beans Station. I wrote a slip in it, we crossed the Mt early but the Steep Side was to go down which we tripped of rapidly, we arrived at the Station about 9 where we took the Right hand on the way to Rutledge, to join Benton's Brig, who have not one suit, no knapsack no nothing, they call them the foot Calvary because they travel so well, this is a nice valley & in the white Settlements, I am waiting for dinner at a nice house where the Regt are lying around the spring, well Dinner over & I tell you I got my money back, I Do not envy any one, I had Rather

P2

crack a crust at home than to have the best dinner in E Tenn, but I must make the most of my absence, Well I had squirrel (I got the head) irish potatoes, beans, corn & wheat bread, coffee (with Sugar), B Berry Pie with B. B. Jam, Syrup Sweet milk &C&C all for 25 cts, lots of officers & men eat, the man has plenty of negroes & has been all the time Southern, It Reminds me of home visitors in carriages, & on horseback came Ladies & their husbands & children all E Tenn are at home, the married men, but alass Alabamans are in the field, & I thank God that they are not like E Tennesseans, more anon, It is now nearly 4 o'clock & we have got 6 miles to go, I got my Knapsack hauled, through the kindness of Qr. M. Johnson, I wrote of in

P3

My last, God bless you Good bie 7th 4 P. M. I have spent a lazy & idle day for which I am ashamed of, I aut to have Read my bible, but have neglected to do any thing to profit as I know of, I do not Recollect when I ever done so little good, We came about 4 miles last night & camped at a nice spring an old man (Passed) & woman this morning, I got a good breakfast for 25 cts we left there

& came to this place where is a poor place to camp except the water, which is any Sort you want Red Black & White Collaborate, Freestone & limestone & on a nice creek to wash in, I do not think we will stay here long,

4 Oclock AM 8th it is cool this morning the mail will Start out

P4

immediately, I have nothing of int To do, Wolf is with us, he is not Stoubt but can follow by having his gun &C hauled, J Palmer is not well (Secret) he wants to go home & is putting on, the whole Co are talking about it, I must tell him of it (as a friend) I will Try to do better today, I must not be idle, I must Read or write every da, may God help me to live worthy of the vocation where in I am called, Bowman is just Bowman yet, he is verry profane but obliging, Arheart is well & I believe has got out of the notion of the conscript doing him good, J Thackerson makes a good Soldier, May Peace be Restored & we Return home Soon it my prayr, God grant So mote it be, May God bless you & yours & answer your prayers, God bless us all Good Bie S.C.K.

P5

9 oclock A. M. I found out that my letter would not Start until 5 P.M. I did not know what would turn up during the day, & I thought that I would get a letter but put it up, that our moving was the cause of my not, It is 12 & no mail, I must wait but feel like I cannot be disappointed, Palmer got E's, she partly wrote at your house I thought that, that was to answer me a few days, So I took it, If you can find out when Capt J Francis is coming back, & Send me a good par Shoes, Stewarts of good lather with he bottoms ½ inch wider & on the Same last of the others & a pare of pants, Do So if not I can get them here, I forgot to tell you about Ingram Morgan that colt is bound until the debt is paid tell Robinson to tell him that I will have the mare &

P6

colt both levied on & Sold if he does not pay, I will not gene at 5 month old but 40 dollars, 12 ½ Well My Dear J Francis has

Returned he brought letters for lots of our Co but none for me I have to take the Company of 47 Privates & 5 non commissioned officers & go on pickett, to Start at 1 PM I must close, there letters tells of Several who were killed in the fight at Rmod I must close my love to all good Bie your own, S C. Kelly

(FN SCK letter of July 10ᵗʰ & 11ᵗʰ written between lines of Amie's letter May 24ᵗʰ this letter was torn & burnt had to be repaired)

MAY 24ᵀᴴ

P1 HERS

My dearest S. I wrote to you by the Palmer boys which I hope you have received before now. We are all but I think is taken the measles. She does not complain much. Virgil is complaining _____ nothing serious _____ his foot but it will _____ well soon as it has been opened and run some he nearly sicks me out of the bid of a night. There is several cases of sickness in the neighborhood. Tuger is very low with the plur and B Bridges is sick. Turks daughter is very bad off. She had a baby night before last and had the ___ before Turk says it will run them both close to live, but that is because P told T do not know. We had the hardest rain day before yesterday I ever saw both lighting strikes hail and another rain yesterday. The ground is miry. The boys have planted out our patch with potatoes. I think must have a patch some where else. I want to beat you at raising potatoes if I can. They are near over the corn the second line and the wheat is turning and will be ready to cut in a few days. The gin house price will make 200 bu so Turk thinks. Some of the oats will not make any thing on accord of the rust the patch towards Sadig a _____ the others look _____ last night and spent the night _____

robed a bee gum this morning that was very _____ I thought of you and wished you had some. She gave me a bowl full to fetch home so we will have honey for several meals. I was so sorry to hear of so many sick in camps. May God watch over them and you for good is my prayer, and keep you from temptation as well as from evil. Virgil talks a great deal

P2

about you and nearly always says you will die and they will bring you home to bury you. I told him I did not know that they would do that much as mush as would like to have you buried here where I could rest by your side if I should out live you but that is a gloomy theme so I will ___ it pray in God to shield you and_____

_____ back safely. _____
My cabbage do not do well Barma says _____ the rust like is on the wheat. I know they die nightly. I have had them replanted 2 or 3 times to no purpose. Dr Hughes has come home to Stay he tried to get a furlough and he could not so he got mad and resigned and came any how he let Jim get off at his wifes house and then told he had run away and gone to the Yankees and Jim came that evening. I do not think he shows much love of country.

_____ at ft. Pillow but got as far as Corinth and turned back without hearing from him. People here are asking 5 cts and 100$ for wool in the dirt burrs and all cant you get me some in Tenn for less than that. I do not think I will buy any at that price will make cotton answer my purpose if I can. I have been busy weaving all the week on all the negro boys pants they will do them first rate for winter if I could _____ wool for there coats _____ My dear one _____
must not do like Hughes but defe_____ country to the last if need be and God will protect you. You know I miss your cheerful voice on occasions but I hope it will not be long till we should meet again on better times for which let us all pray. I am out of paper I have sent to Rome but it has not come yet. It yet has the appearance of rain. There was a considerable hail at Teagues this week and cut the corn and wheat all to pieces nearly. God bless you good bye your own Amie

SCK LETTERS OF JULY 10TH & 11TH 1862
CAMP NEAR RUTLEDGE GRAHAM CO TENN JULY 10TH 1862
5 ½ OCLOCK PM

P1

My Dearest Amie My letters here have not Rec one Since the 2 ond dated the 28th this morning there was Several Prather, Alexander, Slaton & others got I expected one, I think I write one every 3 or 4 days, I have ___ing to write but have an opportunity of Sending it by Lt _____ of our company who has Resigned, If they get Rid of me it _____ not be in that way, I will Stand the examination & it _____

I will have _____ to the Ranks, I do not believe it was _____ goes by favors, John Francis Luit two of them ____ board (but the truth is he did not want them himself) a Capt has a great influence who acts as Lt, or who goes to the ball, Lt Vinsant of Johns Co is better than two thirds of the officers in the Regt, but he was not from JV nor Talladega, Ours is the back woods, wool hat co, not a man in it from those cities, John Francis Returned day before yesterday, he never knew anything about home or any body, he promised to See you, I believe in fact he gave me but little Satisfaction about any thing, he is dead (nearly) with the big head & Seems like feels himself above me, as far as a brigadier, above a 4th corporal, I may be desired but if there is any mutch excelance to him I have never Seen it, In a word I think if I had gone home, that I could have brought more letters than he did, I believe from what he Said that he Slipped off to keep from bringing, keep these things in your heart, I get along finely with officer& men, I have not had any chance _____ Since we left the _____ Capt keeps them hot (Secret) I th____ he has Smelt a mice, he has applied himself closely, but between us is no officer & the men under him do (nearly) as they please & besides that he is a man of no decision (in confidence) I have to do all the business (he comes to me as I Should go to him) keep these Sayins in your heart, the Staff officers (or Some of them) hat him, he is a clever man, but as full of conceit as he can hold, I heared the agutant curse him the other day, because the men

P2

Officers did as they pleased they Say tome frequently that our Co aut to do thus & So I tell them I am not the Capt & on two occasions they have told me they wished I were, I do not desire it but I would like to have a good Captain, Well I was going out on Pickett when I wrote last, I had a time of it on the public Road & at least 100 passes _____ all carry passes whites & blacks _____ yet Some _____ but all talk & no Sider, I have but about 10 dollars & that will not last me long I Swapped off my last linen bosom Shirt to Lt Vinsant for a linsey Shirt, I have now 2 of them (all I have) 2 Par drawers & one old par pants, one thin blanket, both my coats, all I want if my Pants were patched & Cavalry cannot carry mutch we moved again today about ½ mile, Our mess Settles today we owes 29 dollars & 28 cts each all Said negrows hire & all, I have Spent that mutch on more out Side lots of which I have let go in _____ & forgot, but I have furnished 23 dollars in cash So you See I only owe 6 dollars on that Score, I had 2 teeth pulled today they got to hurting me, I have a notion of having 2 pulled, the ones just behind the eye teeth but I thought I would consult you, they trouble me (not ache) but I have to pick them before I get through eating, I have always had that to do but my hands were not So greasy to get my knife out, I will close & if time will write more in the morning, God bless you & yours your own SC

6 oclock AM 11th It is raining a little this morning Coln Shelly & Brad _____

_____ by the men, I Saw both this morning _____ a Sleep' Palmer is Sick (mumps) Benson Ret yesterday, 7 or 8 more but none bad, I wish I had Something to write this is a general writing, May the god of all the earth guide us all, I heared that L Weaver was dead Dick believes it, he is well, he is well, may God be with us all & bring about a peace is my prayr, I have Sent this now & had a notion to tear it up but it is all, I love you most dearly & love to get letters from home but do not get my Share, Oh that I could write Something good bie SCK

CAMP NEAR RUTLEDGE GRAINGER COUNTY TENN JULY 13TH 1862 2 0CLOCK PM

.13 Pl

(This letter has holes in it)

My Dear Amie I rec yours of the 8th last night I was glad to get it & Sorry to hear of the death of Sutch a man as L W, I was also glad that you found all well at home, I was also glad to hear that I had been blessed above many in a crop of wheat I also in oats, for I expected that they would not pay for cutting, you must take particular care of the old oats (if any on hand) write me word about them thrash out the others & keep them Separate take care of what corn you have, mind & do not let the cotton seed go, they will (if the war ends) be worth 1 dollar per bushel, are you going to make any peas or pumpkins, if you are not you had better (at odd times) have them thrashed out S__ned and put in one end of the garden, the hulls far away, if ____ will be any cotton to gin, have the dam fixed, you had better let it alone, & may be I will be home before you make another crop, I want brick made, they will Sell, is Billy gone back to School, or is the School quit, he must go, how dus Syphax come on, is old Martha able to pull you, have you weaned the colt, if not, put it in a Stable and feed & water it a week, then mussle it & carry it off to the pasture at Mothers, & have the mare brought back, try her to Alexanders little horse if that horse is not there try the John Bently horse or any other to Raise a colt except Penters, I will not give the price, is the bacon holding out, will you have any to Sell, is the old Sows got pigs, is the Shoats got to be hogs or are they Shoats yet, poor or fat, is the goats more trouble than profit, or will they pay, if you kill any you had better get Sim Weaver to tell you how to tan the hides, Tell me how Turk & T gets along thrashing how mutch they have thrashed & what they are doing with the toll also about the Jack,

&C&C I was glad to get your Telegraph the 1rst one was delayed Some where 5 days, the last letter I was expecting, it was as late as any thing we had, do so again write at least once a week & for fear I do not get them wedge in one every now & then for good count, I believe you when you Say you wish I could come home, So I expect the whole family is of the Same desire but I am a Soldier fighting for the Rights of my Country, uncompromizing until we have gained them or do as thousands have done, lay my life on alter

P2

of my country, pray for me that God will Still give me health & Strength to battle on until that one great thing is accomplished, Then Shall peace come, Then Shall the Soldier Return to his Loved ones at home I would fain come home (but not to Stay while my Country calls for help), if it were for only one day, but cannot, there is but 2 ways to get off & I doubt, but one for me, the one is to get Sick (as brother Smith was) & get a discharge, or Resign, It Seems to me that it would be better for Dick Weaver to get Substitute than Dave, he has a family & is but a private, I Sympathize with those who have lost Relatives in the great victory, they helped to win at Rmon I do pitty the woman at home more than the Soldiers I am glad that Key has considered to come to See you, is Fanny Dead or married I have not heared , You kneed not Send me paper for I have no chance to take care of it, if you can put up with Sutch I can write on yours as I have done Several times, I expect that yours will be opened if you do not quit Stuffing them So full, I Still love to get them Still, I fear I Recon the corn Shrank & wasted, I am glad to hear you have money, plenty it is more than II can Say, I have __ dollars & do not know when we will draw, QR Master Johnson is going ____ _me to make his bond he could have made it here, but he would not got home then if you See him get him to bring me a pr Shoes I can make out for clothes a while longer, Mexican B gone to Yankeedom, I told you of all in a letter before, I Some times fear I write the Same thing over & over, but do not mean any harm, I forget It is So, Some are lousy, I am not, have never Seen one, on me, I change every week, It is not So, I am not Maj, (but would like to be) I do not know how that could Run the vine, Maj Smith is with us & is worthy, I was not deceived & Johnson more So, J Palmer is not well (he is after a discharge or furlough or anything to get home, So Say 2 thirds of the company) I hate to tell him, but must he looks bad he does not eat mutch, S P does not believe in his Sickness, we are getting on well enough in the woods, that letter I Sent by Landers I want you to burn (FN the rest of letter written upside down in margin) My Pin Staff is a Stick with the pin tied to it & the ink Soaks in it & you See the Size all over this Sheet, I am officer of the Guard today, I make me a fishing hook out of a kneedle & Cought a mess of Sardines day before yesterday (Fryday) the next day the men cleaned out the branch went in & felt under Rocks &C & cought them all, they looked like those I use to catch at home, I had 23 cought in an hour or So, I ____ us all, hence forth & forever amen you own Sam

JULY 17ᵀᴴ 8 AM ONE MILE S OF RUTLEDGE

.17 .18 .19 P1

Dear Amie we are on the march. We struck camp this morning fell into line, took a vote for 3ʳᵈ Lt I M Person (the cadet) was unanimously elected. we then took line of march & for now stopped just where the road runs into the main road & do not know which road we will take, We left the sick in camp 13 No Among them Bowman (Slight) Penland (fever) Wilkerson (Weak) Wolf (Slight) White (not mutch) if any thing, we have 56 rank & file, John Thomas (Wingos Soninlaw) fell down (as he Says) & shot off his middle finger on his right hand, night before last on pickett, We had Several men come in this week, One of them Said he Saw you in Jv but did not Speak to you

P2

I expected to a letter this morning but did not get a letter, I Supposed you wrote Sunday, Arheart was appointed Orderly, until B Pike comes up, I Shall close fore the present with my best prays on you & yours

18th 6 Oclock AM We left the Last place mentioned at 11 ½ oc AM it Rained &

went towards Knoxville in the direction of Blanes X Roads. it continued to Rain incessantly (as did on the 4th July last year) all day & increased in the evening we traveled about 7 miles & took up at 3 ½ PM, wet to the Skin, we turned in at the yard gate passed the Spring & creek (both muddy) & deployed on a hillside covered with trees & high weeds, I stopped at the house, out of the rain, where I stayed all night, got a poor

P3

Supper Slept on the floor & under wet blankets, payed him 50 cts & this morning & Returned to camp, it is the first house I have Slept in Since I left home & should not have done that but I was broke down in my back the day before, I could not get up Strait without pulling up by Something, I was lots better yesterday than I was, but was Smartly worried last night, I felt like I am better Still, If I have 2 or 3 days to Rest I should get well, I was taken as usual with out any cause as I know, it was the frst time I ever Reported, not able for duty, I was persuaded to stay at camp with the Sick, but could not bear the idea for you to hear that I was left, I got my Carpet Sack halled & am glad that I came, but I walk easly, You must not be uneasy about me for if I get So I cannot

P4

go I think that I can get a furlough & come home (I am not at all Sick & am healthy) but I hope, I may not get the chance on Sutch terms not because I do not want to come home, but I do not want to be Sick enough to get a furlough,

I do not know where we are going, there is a large force (Several Reg) Infantry, Artillery & Calvary, We have many cooking, but less to cook lots of the men are out of meat, & we draw tomorrow evening, I have enough to do me plentifully 3 days, I hardly ever eat ½ I carry, Some of them will eat that much in 1 ½ or 2 days, then they beg & do without. These are the reason that Some write that they do not get enough

P5

J Palmer has got well, I told him that over ½ the Co. was talking about him (& it nettled him) he went to the doctor (as he Sais) medicine that cured him in a night, & the next day was Rep for duty, I feared to tell him but am now glad I did, It is now two PM & we hear we may stay Several days, No news & am not in any fights to write, I See a patch of cotton at nearly every house it is Small but has Some blooms, they all Raise there own Syrup out of Sugar cane, it turns my teeth black, I intend to Send ½ of that Spool of thread back to you, it is in my way & besides that I will not use it up in years, I use Some of my buttons Sometimes, I borrowed a Par of pants & got mine washed & patched, my thin coat is about done

P6

Linseys Wash is making money, they all charge 10 cts a garment, but the last one of them Say they had Rather make cotton than Stay here, Truss I believe is the triflingest one in the Regt, he is out of money (he Says) he does not wash good I got another to do mine, I am put up at a house & intend to Stay until I get better (if I can) I hope I will be well in the morning, The man of the house told me that he was So crowded that he could not take me in, I Shall go back to the Co,

19th 10 Oclock AM I am Still but ½ , I went out on Battalion drill commander of the Co this morning, I took 2 of my Dr Cowden pills yesterday they worked me well & although I slept on the ground in the open, I feel like I Shall get well Right away, May God grant it So (more anon)

P7

9 Oclock PM I now have a chance to Send off my letter I do it greatly disappointed the male came in & no letter for me, Why do you not write Jim Gratiam wrote that you were all well, but does not Suffize, I have not Rec one Since the 8 or (it was written), Sunday morning 7 oclock I am better, well we have had a bad night, I lay down & Slept well until about 12 when I was awoke by the Rain in my face, I Rained verry hard, we huddled as best

we could under blankets Stretched & by tree for about 1 hour when it Seased, the ground being wet I went to the fence placed 2 Railes Side by Side lay down doubled my blanket, to keep off the dew, went to Sleep & dreamed I was at home with

P8

my Right hand tied up, I Slept dry, You have no Ide how we can Shift, I found out yesterday by going to See the Coln that the mail would go out today at 12 oclock So I concluded to wait, I went from there to a blackberry patch about a 1 mile where there were thousands, I thought of the days of old Langshire but alass you _____

We are to move today about 1 mile, Our mail does not come by Morristown now, that is the way I account for my not getting, but J. P. got one dated 3 days ago, I wait in hope, May the Father of our Lord Jesus Christ be with us all & guide us in the way we Should go is the prayr of your own dear one far far away, May Peace be Restored & I Return to my loved ones S C Kelly

P9

(Written in margins of the letter must be a PS)

If you make me any Shirts you must have them fine & of the Same Size & length as my others with 2 pockets in the breast, I prefer a jeans coat to a cloth, gray Jeans but I Suppose you could not get it cut Right if I were not there, but you had better have the Shirts 2 & 1 of drawers, & have me a par of Shoes made & Ready to Send by the frst chance, tell bull S. to make them ½ inch wider & on the Same last & good leather, one of these were planky, Wide bottom & good job

SCK

I got the old women of the house to patch my coat for which I gave her ½ the Spool

JULY 11,1862 AMIE'S LETTER WITH SAM'S JULY 21 22 WRITTEN BETWEEN LINES ALSO LETTER BURNED SOME &

TORN & REPAIRED DATES ARE QUESTIONABLE

.21 .22

.17 AMIE'S

At home July 11 1862 My dearest S. I again seat myself to drop you a line and the war news. glorious news, from Richmond God grant it may prove the last great battle we will have to fight. We are all up Dan is complaining some. We thrashed our wheat yesterday and made 105 bu. The bottom field made and the boys made 6 ¼ bu they are not done the oats yet the blue oats are good but the graying oats only made 4 or 5 bus. Miss J Baird died yesterday and we are going to the burying this morning. Son Fergerson came home last night he is on his way to Chatanooga, has been sick a long tome but is well at this time. I shall go from the burying to J Grahams and see his babe it is very low and then to Robersons and stay all night. Dickey has a very bad cold and cough. I fear he will be sick. Tom has not _____ the measles yet and no sign _____ I spent the most of Sunday at Grahams _____ all well. Bro Smith will be at Liberty Sunday and preach. Step over and hear him you say you are good at walking and that would make some body else glad. He wants to buy land in the neighbor hood he says. He cannot get to Texas, he does not preach much, his back is still weak. I cannot fill this shut you can. Write on the vacant side and send it back. I would not write now but for the telegraph news in the Reporter. It has been nearly 2 months since you left the last time and it looks like 2 years or more. how I wish you could come home and stay, but be a good soldier fight hard and we will conquer some day. may god protect you and save you from harm and timtation and bring you home safely is my daily prayer. I do want to see you so bad has Hobs got to camp G_____

SAM'S LETTER .21 .22

GRAINGER CO 4 MILES NORTH RUTLEDGE TENN

P1

Dear Amie we _____ 7 miles South of Rutledge 8 PM last night

_____ time, we had a plesant time though verry warm __ arrived at opposite the old camp about 12 oclock, We Stacked arms & unrolled blankets & spread & lay down in an old eat out clover ,F, Slept without rocking until 3 when we were aroused, took up line of march & Stopped at this place, an old Ritch man by the name of McMichael, who furnished breakfast to many, I did not, I had a piece of lite bread before & eat that, we are this morning nearly out of every thing to eat, than we ever have been, there is not one pound of meat in the co & not one biscut to the man (cold water bread at that, leather hoe cakes if you please) Some of the messes have a little flour, & many cooking it, I had 3 of the Same Sort bisk gave 2 away & eat with a little Sour B Milk, part of the 3rd our Rations are at Bs Station about 7 miles from here, we will go there or else we will have them hauled here & draw today, 12 Noon, I Rec yours of the 17th by the hand of Pike who arrived yesterday morn our _____ I was delighted, he Says that S Penland was out of his head _____ not mutch Sick, Griffin is at Kville, I fear that I Shall _____ the things brought by Steel I am _____ out them a while, I wish you to make those Shirts but do _____ them but if I had them I Should Sell these I have as they are to large & Short,

22ond 9 oclock AM we found our Selves Ready to march by Sun Set (last night) we Returned to our old camp at the Sulphur Springs, arrived here at 9 ½ PM, making a Round of about 28 miles Since thursday morning, Staying at one place 3 nights & 3 days, apparently to no purpose, We found our Sick doing tolerabley well S. P. is verry weak & when he doses talkes in his Sleep, I consider him out of danger, all the

Rest up, I Rec your favor of the 13th by Griffin, he is at Knoxv, he mailed it, I was glad to get it, my letter comes in Showers (though not your fault) We had 4 men come in with Pike, I am well in my back, I know the cause, I got So, I had my hair cut & beard trimed & went in the creek, Come out in a hurry & went on drill, I took cold that night & the next day my teeth Seemed to be all Sore, & that evening after drill (when I was hot) Sat down to rest

& when I got up __ could Searesly Straten, I was Sorry I had my beard trimed, Some of it was 5 or 6 inches long, I had about ½ the length cut off, I had my hair cut close, & now eve_____ Saying how gray you are getting In So mutch that I have concluded

P2

I will have no more use for Sissors during my Say in the war, As to peace I know nothing of it nor do I believe the tenth part , I do not blame Fergerson for backing out, I would be glad that brother S. could buy land there J. Palmer talked like his place Suit him, I think that brother S. is mistaken about the victory at Richmond, we gained a glorious victory, I expect an all out fight there, I care not what Penland or any one else Says if it is not the truth, I know Pike to be a gentleman & a Soldier, I intend to do my Duty regardless of any ones friendship, without favor or affection, I do not dislike my Capt, but Some of his ways does not Suit me. I think him a clever man in his way, I know request it of you again never let this fault finding letter live or be Seen except Some one Sees it burning, I hope you will forgive me for troubling you with Sutch a mess, I hope God has, I was asshamed of it, & will try in future to do better, I try to reconcile my mind to disapointment, this World is full of trouble, but we must _____ the measure of our prays God bless the children, _____ we are well (& all) & that their lots may be cast _____ pleases, I hope Martha R will be advantage to _____ that you may be as a mother to her, John is not well _____ he is off driving a wagon, he is a good Soldier, key might Stay with you at least one 3rd of the time, I hope She may hear from home, now they have captured that Scoundrel Critendon, Oh I forgot to Say we drew Rations in time yesterday to cook & eat, Pikes Wife Sent him the nicest coat of jeans black & White wool mixed, I want you to make me one if you have to give 1 ½ dollars per pound for wool his coat could be Sold for 30 dollars & will wear out 2 cloth ones that would cost 60 dollars each, May S. has Sutch a one, there is no clothing to buy here, we are considered in the field not in quarters, I had but 5 dollars but borrowed from May S. 10 d, If we were on the RR I Should Request you to Spend Some of your money in coming to See me as I couldnot come home, but No use talking at the length of these letters, I tell you nearly all & I Some times have a Pencil & Some times pen on my knee & on any thing, now writing ____ one , you knew not for I trust, I know in whome I depend upon _____ the war to a Speedy _____ wrote this with home made ink, Close Save us in heaven when we are done with time is the Prayr of you &C   SCK

JULY 23RD 7 AM

.23 Pl

I eat some Alabama cake yesterday that Pikes wife sent him , it was a Rarity, Griffin came up yesterday, he brought my paper &C I sold it for at 10 cts per sheet & 3 involepes at 10 cts, I had no place to carry it & the men wanted for present use, all is quiet this morning, it is cloudy I cannot think of any thing to write, our sick is increasing all that come in are on the S list, we had even 20 this morning, out of 79 in all, I was officer of the police yesterday, I am good at that & had a Company one day of 100 privates & 10 non commissioned officers, had 1 Spade 1 old axe (duller than any you ever had at the S house) with which I used to make crobars of Rails & Shrubs of bushes my Co. were armed with pikes of the above named & brush brooms, 36 of the P & 50 of the latter the ballance to use there hands, to carry off rubbish with the Pikes they dug holes & raked the offensive Substance in it dug dirt with the Same & covered up

P2

I would close I cannot write the paper is damp I think the Capt. is the worst home S Sick man in the Co. I am well & hope that these lines may find you all well I forgot to tell you J Price has come from the Hosptl at Bs Station, he said that they are Raising Regulars, that they get a bounty of 100 dollars & a furlough until Peace is made, that he saw 2 men getting furloughs, that he heared that there had been 2 full Co raised from there to Morristown, among the Soldiers S Penland is better this morning I wish that

Peace may come upon us Suddenly, oh that God would Rule & Super____, to that end that the Southern Confederacy may Stand among the nations of the eart free & independent, acknowledged to be able to Sustain her Right, May She become a God fearing & God Serving nation & now My Dear Amie I bid you good bie, praying that God will direct us Sustain us, keep us, give us health Strength, wisdom, knowledge & understanding, to fill the vocations where in we are called, to live to the honor of his name, that he may give us grace Sufficient to the day, Yours S C Kelly

(This slip of paper was in this letter)

Direct, Lt. S. C. Kelly Co. E, 30th Ala Reg Vol Knoxville Tenn

(UNKNOWN DATE J. B. PALMER TO AMIE)

Mrs Kelly Lieutenant Kelly is so buisey so buisy making out a descriptive list he hasent time to write any more we are ordered to cook 3 days rashings and be ready to march in the morning at 6 oclock we haven't any I dea where we are going

Yours respectively J. B. Palmer

You will find inclosed A fiew lines please send Emey Palmer and will oblig

JULY 17TH AMIES LETTER WITH HIS LETTER OF JULY 26TH WRITTEN BETWEEN LINES

JULY 17TH AMIE P1

.26

At home July 17th 62 My dearest S. Your of 10th & 11th by Lt. Landers come to hand yesterday & I assure you I was glad to hear from you. I wrote the 7int giving the particulars of Singers death and the boys names that fell at Richmond that we knew, A B Graham was not dead the last news. Graham was to start to here last night. T Ledbetter was wounded. James Weaver is supposed to be killed or taken prisoner his body could not be found same of Capt. Mclellan. Dave Mc is wounded Frank Ware killed James Hubbard killed Lou Alexander and M Abernatty killed and a great many others I cannot now call to mind. I never saw as much distress in my life everywhere I go someone is in mourning ones that fell at Richmond. Oh this cruel war when will it end and let the dear ones return home to cheer the lonely there. God grant to send us peace on honorable terms and that speedily. All the soldiers write that peace will soon be made for my part I wish how soon but do not see any thing to justify the conclusion for England and France are both uncertain and Lincoln has called for 300,000 more troops. Bro Smith was here day before yesterday he was trying to buy Furgason out gut F backed out, he looks bad and limps a little he said we did not near whip the Yanks at Richmond they are reinforcing for another fight. We heard that your Reg was ordered to Richmond but I did not believe it. I know S P had a falling out with you for some cause he wrote home that J Pike was the best office and a long ways the cleverest you had but you know Sam and it is not worth while to mind him he will get mad and pout round awhile and so does his mamma before him but clear your skills before your maker and

P2

never fear but what you will come out right. I am sorry you disliked your captain but it has turned as feared. He thinks he knows it all. I stoped in JV to see J Frances thinking I could send you paper and envelops and a letter but he was gone and had been for a day or so and I did not see him. I was disappointed as well as you but we must expect disappointment in this sinful world. Kay is here I do not know how long she will stay. She is a precious child. We are all up but Dickey is unwell he has strong symptoms of flu and I fear will have a bad time of it yet. We are through with the measles. now if we can escape the flu we will come out pretty well after all. Miss Martha Roads is still here she is nearly naked and a slow hand to work but I will try to bear with her till you come back. H Steel will start back next monday night. I do not know whether to send your jeans pants and some shoes or send you the money and let you buy for your self. I could send the money easier than the things unless you are on the railroad. I wish it was so I could come and see you or you me. I do want to see you bad I can scarcly bear it but what can not be cured must be endured and I will have to wait as bad as I have too. The boys are done ploughin the corn looks better than any corn in the neighbor hood. We had roasting ears day before yesterday that we got out of the garden. We have a big piece peach pie every day and how I do wish my dearest had some. I never sit down to eat but what I think of you and wish you were here to help us enjoy what we have. We had strange visitors yesterday. Bill Stewarts 2 daughters spent the day they made them selves as agreeable as they could, no doubt of that, we had chicken pie for dinner and Mary Tarpinder said she wished

P3

John has some of it she said she would willingly do without if he could have some. The ambulances and waggons of Vandorn's army passed this way going to Chatnooga. They had some of the pettiest mules I ever saw there was not many men with them. They had went by Atlanta. They looked stout & rough. The Yanks may run when they get after them. There is no news now all quiet at R and I am afraid that ment big fight will be in Tennesee and you will be in it. I have not got any wool yet and will have to pay 175 cts in the shirt when I do which is rather you do. I sent you some paper and envelops this morning by Griffin and will sent this by Pike tonight and will write again by H S next monday if I can. You say you have a notion of having 2 teeth pulled but thought you would consult me. I would dislike to have them pulled unless they ached. Could you not have them pluged and save them. I will want a new set when the war is over if I should live that long and I would dislike for you to be without but you can do as you please about that. I fear Dicky will have a severe time of it he is rite sick now. Maybe he will be better by morning. Singer did not have a will he was insensible from Wednesday till saturday morning when he died. his family are in a great deal of trouble about it he did not talk any about dying either. The goats are doing finly if you call having young ones doing well they are so fast we cannot have any to kill the old Billy look very bad. he is so poor . Dicky is sitting on the step and I sitting in the door. he says tell dady he is sick and come home and see me. Dan went to mill yesterday and broke down. he had to go back this morning and bring it home he got his grinding at Ackins old mill. I am afraid it is not good. Dan said he saw a bu of wheat ground that only made 15 lb to the bus. I

P4

did not weigh our but it made more than that. We have all turned hoop makers or remodling old hoops and they do well as new. we take them up so they are not near so large. I reccan that pleases the men. The bugs are eating up my cabbage. I fear they will not do any good this summer. We had a light shower today but not enough to do any good. it is thundering still in the rain corner. We had a good rain last week but it is so hot it does not do much good. The corn is twisted as bad as ever. I sold P Palmer 10 bus corn and after he got it in the waggon he told me I would have to wait till you sent his money and I could not help myself Mrs Benson also got 2 and Mrs Boles is to get saturday 8 or 10 bus. I am in hopes graham will make a support. I have about got the baggin and rope making by taking 2 bus of onions in part pay. I wish I could send them to you. has Bill Stewart and John Palmer paid for there rope and Baffin if not how much. My new clock will not run it has been stoped 2 weeks. I think I shall send it back to our bro

Graham. There is bad tales out on him about drinking too much but am in hopes it is false. do not say any thing about it. Key sends her love she say she misses you so much talking to the children and playing with them and lots of other things. I like the plan of you writing back on my letters particularly when written in ink but when written with a pencil it is hard to make out some times. I think you improve in writing very much go on improving and you will make your mark one day. may God help you so live that you will not be ashamed in coming days. I want you to be a meek follower of the savior and a useful one too to your fellow men. I would not do all the work and not study any. I would let the cpt do his part. May God be direct you and keep you from harm Amie

I will send your pants and shoes by H Steel you had better meet him at the Railroad if you canto get them.

CAMPED NEAR RUTLEDGE JULY 26TH1862

.26 Pl

(His written between lines of Amies from July 17)

My Dear Amie I rec yours of the 21rst last night by Steel I am glad & Sorry I hope that Dicky may be better by the time you Rec this, I am well, I fear you will be uneasy about me, I am well in my back, I will try to be more careful, it must have been my own imprudence I miss took, I am writing on this sheet the same way you wrote, I have nothing of interest to write, Steel brought my Shoes, I am very well pleased, they are to large, I fear they will wear out my Socks, they are good at the heel as any were else, my Shoes fit so well that that they do not wear, I have one pair of blue mixed ones that I have not worn but little, my pants is worn out & kneed the 2ond patch, I can make out for a while, I can make out with out my Shirts until you can make them,, you want to know about the colours, white <u>warp</u> or black & white & black filling of ___ ____, I can get Some jeans of Henrys he is discharged, he will stop & see you, he Says that they made it for his brothers & him & I got the promise of him to let me have his part, You go & see it at the Boyds old place & if it will do get it if you have to give 3 dollars per yard, if it is nice gray jeans, if it is a little dark tis all the better, I want you to have it cut double breasted, with a Strait collar, Cannon can cut it by the old patterns of my brown coat of last year, he must make it longer with 2 rows of buttons on the breast & ___ & be hung a little longer, as to the pants I do not want no stripe on them, as to buttons any good button will do, whether brass or not, I believe I had rather have them covered with the same than brass on any thing else, do not buy the jeans if it is not nice, I am verry proud & do not want to be inferior to any one, I am kneeding a hat worse than any thing else, I think you can make my clothes and Send them by Some one who will be coming, You may tell it that all the furloughed men are expected to Return or Send in another note from a doctor immediately or they will be published as deserters, (it the order) will be published in the JV Republican, J S Palmer accused me of writing Some thing Scandalous home about him, I denie it & besides that I marked what I

P2

Said (Secret) & I know you have more Sense than to tell anything I Say in confidence, to Sutch a Set, just Say to me whether or not you told Emma or any one else that I Said any thing disrespectful or not, I believe & So does John that Sam Penland wrote it, the expresion was this that She thought that instead of them being at outs& writing every thing against one another home that they aut to be friends or the best friends to one another in the Co, So you can See that the Saddle does not fit me & I do not cort the friendship of any man, I was always independent enough, but if possible more now, J Palmer acknowledged to me that he did wanted to go home & So do I & I may have Said to you that he did but you did not tell it, I know not in a way to make _____ So the company talked about him & I told him as a friend (to our Selves) & I believe it helped him, be careful what you Say for they are all envious of me may God give me grace Sufficient for the day may he guard us in the way we should go, We had 5 men come in from home yesterday & to day we have 79 in all 17 Sick 5 discharged yesterday, the old company got Some blankes & after I wrote out one entirely he took the job in hand, I was glad of it but it is a light job to fill a blank form, I have been drilling the Co ever Since we come back here except one he always has Some excuse, I am glad of it I love to drill on Battalion Drill. I think that but few of the Capt besides me, I know the Coln does not scold me as mutch as he does Some of them, I Sometimes am corrected on the field, but I am willing to learn & I have never been insulted by the Coln, the men all Respect me as an officer both in our Co & in the Regt, I know that I have Some influence with Colns & Maj,

I never dictate but Sometimes Suggest & he Says, to me (Strictly confidential) that when he wants certain things done he knows who to call on, I call myself the police of force, I do hope that I am not vain, I try to be humbled, but must I not tell you I will tell you all I hope if I can but See you I do not talk it to others but my dear wife I would tell you my whole heart if I could, Sam Pendland looks better this morning, many of the Rest any mutch Sick, Tode Wolf & Lum Evans applyed for a discharge but could not get it, I think the Capt is anxious to come home he is not popular with the Staff, they do not talk to me only confidential concerning him, he Said the other night that if the Co would Say So he would Resign & go home, no body Said I do not care one Straw, but would hate to be in his Shoes

P3

You may have Railes Split & fence in that pasture, I do not know when they will get them, I Suppose they can get Some over in the big pond next to Davis's fields & then I reckin the balance in the bottom, I do not want them to go cutting down all the timber & Splitting but little but to Recollect them if it will not Split in the Summer it will in the winter, I want them to make brick this Summer & fall there is no Cotton co pick, I would like to know how mutch wheat they thrashed & whether they are done & what they have done with it, J Palmer & Bill Stewart did not pay me for the Rope & the baggin of that Bag, So P Says I do not Recollect, tell Robinson to tell Anderson Morgan that I will have that mule lened upon if he does not pay me, I will give him the worth of it but will not give near 40 dollars, You might have the dam Raised & gin out that Cotton in the house it will help the new ground if it is dry weather, I wish you would put me in a pen or two in your next these I hope do fit me this is the 2 or 3ʳᵈ one I have tried, I jobbed it against a rock to break it but I tried it again & it Scratched it I have a Staff, I wish I had Some thing to interest you, I want you to Send me the telegraph news you can put them in the foldes, You know the that the way you fold them they are thicker on the edges than in the middle, take an iron & press them down as to my bottle it is, I never expect to heared it, I think Fanny Miller might com e & See you & Stay with you but you are out of the range of her acquaintances, I hope your Sister come on Since her Sad loss, Horses is high here, De G bought just Sutch a waggon as that gray of J Graham & gave 250 dollars & 35 for a Saddle the Same man Sold 3 mules the Same day at 150 each nothing fine one a 2 year old, You kneed not trouble yourself to give H G back his note I gave him 5 dollars on the one the mare lost last year they were not born in ____ weather have you forgotten the interest countes & a dozen other things, I understand from your last letter that you gave him 1$ for making my Shoes you must begin to look about for leather to make their winter Shoes, I expect that if you have a chance you had better Send my pants I do not know where I can

P4

get any we are in the woods 17 miles from any where & not mutch there, Morristown about Sutch a place as Cross Plaines only a Road passes there, If you would writ with the very pail ink, & I with the deep (we could manage the thing So as the yanks would get but few letters), I carry my Jackets full all the time, I Set down & tore up to or 7 the other day, I cannot carry but little paper, I was s Sorry you Sent that, A peach pie would be a luxury especially at my dears table but no use talking, I have a notion going out tomorrow & See what Sort of a dinner I can get, God bless the children Dicky I do hope that he may be Sparred you & all the rest On that, I could See you all if but for one day, but I am a Soldier of my country fighting for the rights of my family & Country, My dear one I have never grumbled at your not writing, but I think you mistaken about the length of letters, if yours are the longest I certainly write the most & be that as it may I have nothing to write except to tell you all of my ups & downs & Sayings, I tell you So mutch that I am almost ashamed of my Self I thought that I wrote more than any man in the Regt nearly, Coln Bradford Says I am the beatingest man to be always writing to my wife he ever Saw, My Dear one had you Rather have me home

Sick or well in the army, I had Rather be well in the army, Oh that God will give me health Strength, Wisdom knowledge & understanding to fulfill the vocation where in I am called to the dread of the invaders & may peace burst forth upon us in all its brilliance is the prays of your own dear & then will I Return to the wife of my youth & the children of my Strength to enjoy that Rest whitch has cost so many precious tears So many hardships preservations & So many precious lambs & lives, I Reckon your letters have all come, I get one every week Send them if they are opened you do not loose mutch, I Borrowed 10 dollars of Major S the other day, You kneed not Send any yet, I could draw if I wanted to, I try to guard against my temper but the co do as they please, only when I command & then I have to be pretty crabbie, but generally work off well, In camp is a poor place to act the Christian but I do as well as I can constantly I try to Read Some in my Bible every day but not enough, May god forgive us all of our Sins & Short comings, & give us grace Sufficient for the day is the prays of one who loves you dearly God bless us Good Bie S C Kelly

JULY 8ᵀᴴ
(Her letter gives names of killed & wounded at Richmond)
(SCK's letter of 27ᵗʰ July between
lines of Amie's July 8ᵗʰ edges of letter burned)

P1

At home July 8ᵗʰ 1862 My dearest S. With a bleeding heart I seat myself to write to you from Sinyys, he died at 6 oclock saturday morning and was burred Sunday he was sick 3 weeks he was insensible from wednesday morning and speechless nearly, He first had pneumonia and then the fleem, and last the brain fever. I got there friday 1 oclock and he never spoke or seemed to know _____ thing he suffered a great deal and died _____ hard. He did not have a will they are _____ troubled about it. David is there he will get a substitute if he can, all advise him to do it there was a great many at the burrying and every one nearly in distress about some dear one killed at Richmond. James Weaver is killed, Frank Wear, James Hubbard, M Abernathys son Alexander, Dr Burton, Arch Graham, Tyler Ledbetter, Clim Smiths son others that I cannot now recall. Capt Whatley, J Farmer, Jake green, 2 Woods, Humphries and a host of others wounded. I just know I never saw such times. May God make bear his arm in our deliverance and that speedily is my prayer. I found all well at home but Tom he has the measles, but not much sick, he is the last. Miss J Baird was burried last _____ also J Grahams baby and Andy Brown. I do not know what is passing in the neighbor hood. Dan was sick last week. Barna is with the thrasher Key is here also. Miss Martha Roads the girl I spoke of getting to live with me she seems like a good girl but not know much and cannot read or write. J Slope in town yesterday to see capt Frances but he had left. I intended to send our paper and

P2

by him. I will send by D Pike next week if I can. I hear of a great many letters are broke open by the Soldiers I reccon they were after money. Bro James has sold our corn there was only 60 ¼ bus, and he paid me yesterday at 1$ a bu, and I paid Stifers 32.27 2 notes he held against you, and yet have seventy odd dollars. You say I must sell a mule if I am out of money, I had rather buy than sell. I have plenty of money so far and keep getting _____ the along. What has become of your Mini_____

blanket have you lost it with your clothes _____ _ould be sorry for you to lose it. I heard belou____ that some of the Reg. were lousy is it the case, do try to keep them off you. I would hate it so bad for you to get lousey. I heard this morning that you was elected Maj. Is that so. I do not believe it. I had rather you was a good soldier than Maj. There is not so much danger. We are festering for a fight at chattanoga. Oh may the God of battle shield your fate ____ how could I bear to hear you had fallen and no one near to close your eyes or wipe the death damp from your brow. May God save us all and keep us in the way we should go. We are needing rain the weather is dry and hot and but like it was for our sins that these things come upon us, may he forgive us, and cause our face to shine once more. Truly _____ are trying times and who will be able ____ . I will leave half this sheet for your to write back on. I send it with Mother. Write to her and tell her how to direct letters and where to. You do not know how much I want to see you, but for this cruel war you would be home but be a good soldier and may be it will not be long till we can set at home together, write of ten my dear one, good bye A

Near Rutledge Tenn July 27ᵀᴴ 1862

PI HIS

My dear Amie I at a house of a nice family waiting for dinner, I want to get out of the noise & bussle of camp once and a while, I can rest & it Seems more like passing the Sabath day in the way I Should, that in camp I Stayed until after inspection which came off at 8 AM then come here 2 miles & after Resting now Sit _____ to write you a few lines to inform you _____ I have nothing of interest to write you but you li ____ read long letters & the one I wrote yesterday I could not Send until this evening So I concluded to gorge you own out on a great long Rigamarole about nothing at all, This is the first time I have been out of pickett unless on duty, the first pass I ever carried this is a nice valley narrow & thickly Settled, the most of the people are good livers & a good cal of intelegance a good many negrows, Rutledge is a little old one horse town about as large as Alexandria & I believe the county Seat of Granger County, I am a little uneasy about being So far from the Regt we are expecting to move Some way Soon, I heared that the 52ᵒⁿᵈ Ga ordered to be Ready, 4 companies of the 31ˢᵗ Ala left yesterday, Martial Alexander has Resigned, I was told by a man in the co that he had has never drilled the co one time yet he has fallen off lots, 3 other capt in the Regt resigned a few days ago, Our Regt is improving in numbers we have the largest E Tenn, Our is double as large now as

Donleys they have had tents cooking utensils &C and have been generally Stationed while we have done with out & run all over E Tenn, Tents is all a humbug, I would not have one in the Summer time I had Rather take the Rain than be bothered with one & besides that they are unhealthy because they will not Stand up unless they are fastened close to the ground & then the flies is So bad, We have not been bothering with flies Since we left the Gap & I know there was two thousand to the tent, It is about 12 now & I must examine their books to See if they are not Baptist

P2

Yes here is Southern Psatnist by 1 grave &C with the name (I Suppose) of the gentleman of the house who is absent in it Mr I said, M Lowe Rutledge Al So trials and Sufferings for Religious Liberty & the old family Bible that lay on the Stand, Dinner over which was a good fried Dinner with plenty of pies S Cakes apple butter Serves home made ____ up &C I found as I went out an old Tennessee Baptist _____ & read a Sermon of Pendeltons in fact ____ nearly all in it, Settled my bill with the old lady, chatted a while with her & two nice daughters took leave of them & about 3 oclock PM proceeded to camp & to my Surprise found all gone but the Sick & convalessent, they left with in 15 minutes after I Started, I am at camp & the Regt is at the top of the mountain about 2 miles off, there was a fight over about Tayswell this morning last about 2 weeks J Palmer was on the mountain on pickett

I will close I Shall close that bless you & me & all of us, I Shall go on in the morning if they do not come back to night, they left all but blankets we cook & Send to them

S C Kelly

ON TOP OF CLINCH MOUNTAIN 3 MILES WEST OF RUTLEDGE 7 ½ OCLOCK AM JULY 28TH 62

.28 P1

My dear Amie I Sent my last written at camp, but I understand that it did not go, I tried to get Some one to come with me to the Regt but I found no one out of about 200 Sick & convelssent & about Sun Set Judge Tunley of JV came & Said he wished Some one go with him So we Set out up the Steepest Roughest Road possible I had my haversack with 3 bisquits & Some other trinkets he was on a good horse, he proposed to Ride & tie but I told him I was fleet & he had been to Richmond to See his Son & had Stayed with them 3 or 4 weeks his ankles & feet were Swelled I clipped along & out traveled his horse, So mutch that he had to Rest him, We got to the Regt about dark the Judge is the frst one to See us, he Says that Graham did not find Ab, his Son was all through the fight & not hurt, we are waiting here for orders I Reckon I believe we will go back to camp, we cannot haul up the mountain they cook & pack it on horsed to us

P2

There is lots of Skulkers in every Co we have 80 men & when you Say, that all the weekly men drop out nearly half will Skulk 38 of ours, but the battle was in hearing, we aut to have about 60 men with us instead of 42 I was determined to follow, but Thanks be to God who giveth me health I do not want to be uneasy about me, I think I am well

Aug 1rst 8 ½ I will beat Tunley home the Co is Started good bie SCK

AUGUST 1862

KNOXVILLE AUGUST 1RST 1862 8 ½ OCLOCK AM

.01 P1

(This letter is burned in places)

My Dear Amie I am on my way home, Do not be uneasy I am well, but I have to go by Selma I am on the mission of gathering up the furlough men of the Regt if the car does not Run Sunday I cannot get to blue Mountain before monday night, Now Suppose you get in the carrage & come down to your Sisters Sunday & then I can come home with you when I come, I Send this by Mr. Worlie one of Sargts there is 6 others with me all from other Companies We left the Regt night before last at 9 Oclock PM come 6 miles

Slept till day (under a Shelter) & came on to McMillen Station, got on at 8 AM came to Knoxville by 9 & could have gone on through but for getting transportation, So we had to lay over until now If Dickey is too Sick you cannot come I hope he is not May God continue his blessings upon us is the prayr of your own Sam

PS I expect to Start imme__tley or in ½ hour at furthest S. C. Kelly

Near Dalton 5 ½ Oclock AM go Strait on I ___l be on as Soon as possible ___ willing good bie SCK

P2

(PS written on old letter from Amie)

PS My Dear Amie I expect to go up home monday evening after Pike comes in the morning if you could Send Billy down with them Sunday with old Martha & the buggy I could come back Some time monday night or tuesday morning he could Stay at his aunts until about 4 or 5 oclock monday evening & then come down I can come up on the freight train which is about 1 hour Sooner than the passenger whitch is due our ½ past 6, I am uneasy about you all if it does not Suit, I can pay my weight on the Stage, If he come I will See him & if not I Shall take Stage, is it better to Send & Save the 4 dollars or not, I feel the use of the mare buggy & boy will be worth more than 4 you decide

I am as ever your own Sam

(This written over Amie's letter)

You know the paper but I am at the Station waiting for the train to move S

P3

(Back of PS Amie's letter)

and setting up J R Graham had a congestive chill yesterday and came very near dying but is better this morning The two Fannies are still with me the are precious girls I do not know how I could have managed if it had not been for there help, I feel like the Lord has provided for me and given me strength in the hour of trial May he sustain us both in every privation. I sold Jo Forney 100 bu wheat at 5.00 per bu. He paid me 300.00 I will let him have more if I have it to spare he is buying for the government. The __ ___ was all dried up yesterday they claimed Mr ___ on the toll and Fergason refused to pay it and the assessor

SEPTEMBER 1862

WEST POINT SEPT THE 5TH 9 AM

05 P1

(First time he mentions his slave Dan being with him)

My Dear Amie fear you will be uneasy about me but I have been as well as I could wish We have got along Slowly ___ Shure we left Selma on the night of the 2ond, but got on a Slow boat & were until thursday morning 9 oclk getting to Montgomery to late for the morning train, We got on the 4 oclk & arrived this place 10 Oclk last night where we will have to wait until 2 this evening, all well I have 87 men besides myself & Dan, he Seems to enjoy the trip is

P2

verry handy & will be of great Service to me if we both keep well Our provision are about out & if they were not would Spoil, I had to draw bacon & crackers for the co in Montg bacon & crackers had the bacon boiled, I Saw a man from the Regt, who left monday he Says the Yanks proposed to Surrender on Saturday (condition only) but not accepted, they Shelled us all day Sunday no damage done, we did not fire a gun, he thinks they will Surrender Soon, my dear A I do not want you to be uneasy about me, but pray (on continue) to for me, may god bless you all & all the Sam

SEPT 07

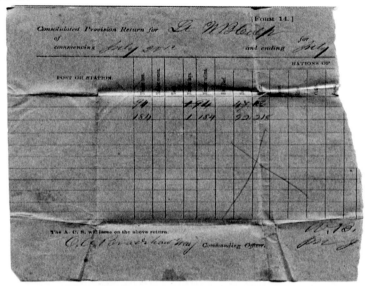

(Envelope was made from a Provision Repost dated July 20th ending July. Has # of men 184, # of days 1, # of rations 184 & flour 213)

FAIR GROUNDS KNOXVILLE SEPT 7TH 62

.07 P1

D Amie I am here but expect to leave today on the 11 oclock train for Morristown we may not get off but I hope we will, I fear I shall not be able to get these boxes & my trunk any farther, For dan is a hard Road to travel I meet with dissipointments on ever Side the officers about haughtly & dodge about & do not fix me up Soon enough, I saw Henderson he has had jaundice he wants to leave here I fear if I leave my (forgot a word) I shall loose it I would send it back but that is a risk it is worth ten dollars

P2

to lug as I have done with those boxes If I did not have Dan I should have left them long ago, G Raburn helped as long as our provisions lasted I will do the best I can, Mr Millener is discharged & is waiting to carry this we are all well, give your Self no uneasiness God bless you, I hope that I Shall come home Soon when this cruel war is over I am in the way good bie S. C. Kelly

SEPT 12TH 1862

.12 .13 .14

*(The envelope is made from flowery
wallpaper probably taken from a house along the way)*

SEPT 12TH 1862 CAMP NEAR CUMBERLAND GAP

.12 P1

My Dear Amie we arrived here day before yesterday after a goodeal of trouble with the boxes I got it all through but if I had not met with our Doctor (a new one) I would have been compelled to have left them I got along well with the men & have no doubt that I made many warm friends though strangers before, they all Obeyed & Respected me & I done for them the best I could I found the Company getting along as well as usual, I am Capt with the least dissatisfaction all I hope will work well, I have been very busy Since I come back I have drawn 4 hundred & fifty dollars my wages up to 30 Aug I am dated Captain since 2 Sept

P2

I only had 7 dollars when I got here I let Warlick have one hundred to buy me a Sword in Atlanta he has not come up yet. I bought a pistol for 35dollars & have paid Maj Smith & others 5 dollars I have about four hundred dollars I Shall Send you 3 hundred, You had better take up the Swan note & the balance use as you think best pay it out, I am going to Send this by a discharged soldier a Dutchman by the name of Adler, Say nothing about it till after you pay it out I have not let anyone but Pike know I have drawn, there is here too many wanting to borrow, Send me the dispatch in your letters I must close by Saying I am verry anxious to hear from you God bless you S. C. Kelly

(this written in margins)

I Send you 5 fifties & 3 twenties 250X60X<u>310</u>

write to James to rent out the land he must	250
advertise & do the best he can with it Say to	071
J Palmer he aut to have drawn his money on his	795

discharge ___ he has another paper Send it me & I ____ get it if I can So busy SCK

.13 .14 P1

Dinner is about over they Swap bread for meat, & lean & borrow, & not unfrequently quarrell, but they generally laugh, the one in fault, out of countenance, & by Sutch exposition as, fight it out, you are no kin, put up your knives, keep on Shirts &C&C

14th 12 oclock well mr Johnson will not Start today & I have a chance to Send by Mr Pretchdl who lives in Talladega nothing has turned up Since yesterday, we were drilled this morning in the Skirmish drill, they are talking of Raising out of the Regt a company of Sharp Shooters & picking the men, I was ask if I wanted a position in it, I am Some what opposed to it unless I go with it because, it picks out the Stablest, bravest, best men in the companys, I do not believe I will take Stock, I have heard

P2

that our Capt will be Rejected he is very mutch confused I do believe he has got to the point where he wants to go home I do not know what he will do I believe that I am popular with the men not only of our co but with the other companies I intend to try my hand the frst try opportunity Some of our men Say that I am as ill as a Cat, So I am when things goes wrong, but when write all know that I am Friendly & family this you must not Show, I Read Some in my bible every day but (ashamed to Say it) not as mutch as I aut, I try to live a christian life but hard work, May God bless us in the capasities he has called us to fulfill, Protect Sustain & keep us from harm, & Super rule all things to bring about a Speedy & honorable Peace is the P of your own Loved one Sam Your always

.17 HIS BETWEEN LINES OF HERS .09

.09 HERS P1

My Dearest S. I been thinking for several days of writing but had so little to write my paper stopped and I was so at home I had no news, and then I was not very well for several days. But I was glad to get your letters 1 from West Point and the other from Knoxville. Barna has been sick for 2 days with this bowel complaint. I am in hopes he will be well soon. Sam took a fool and ran away to get yesterday morning and has just come back because Mr. Turk asked him why he did not bring the buck to the house as he told him and said he would whip him and went on and Sam commenced replying no please masser when T told him if he said another word he would give him 50 and went on to work and Sam took to the woods. I think Sam was in fault. Mr. T says Sam has been trying himself since you left he thinks he is mad because you did not take him in place of Dan. The rest are all well. I do think Barna could manage next year he will do himself but the boys will not mind him

Sam will not mend he is so small, but I am in hopes he will do better when he gets older. They have taken up several yankees about here one near High Wilsons and 3 between here and the river and Bairds. Anderson

P2

And 2 of Fosters negros for stealing Anderson to sell and give them 200 lashes apiece what is the world coming too May God make bare his arm and work for our salvation we have gained another great victory at Manassa plains also Kirby Smith in Kentucky and taken a great many a prisoner. I am busy making the children new clothes out of old ones, for the meeting hour. I do wish you could be here and go with us may God spare your life to come to us again it hurt me worse for you to have this time than it ever did before but my trust is in God that he will keep you still. Mary Bryant was very sick at mothers when I left she miscarried I recon but was only 2 months along Fannie came home with me she is a precious child I do love her so much and she is so smart she can get more out of Martha than I can if I could only keep her I would be satisfied. I am afraid Barna is going to have a bad spell he says he does not feel any better. I have sent for the Atlanta inteligencer it is cheaper than the reporter but have not got but 1 yet and that was several days old. I am anxous to hear from you when you get to the Regmint. Will Weaver payed yesterday going back to the camp also J Green and I Crook. Write often and may God preserve you from harm and danger. I send half sheet for you it is ruled so close good by Amie

17 HIS BETWEEN LINES OF HERS

P1

Camp of internment Near Cumberland Gap Sept. 17th 1862.

Dear Amie It was with a great deal of pleasure I Read your letter you have no Ida how uneasy I was getting about hearing from you, You must not think for 3 or 4 days of writing to me, but write every week Shure whether I get them or not, I Shall be uneasy about the letter with the money in it until I hear from you, I am well & enjoy myself as well as I can, I have had lots to do Since I Ret but do not know but what I do best when busy, I found the Company matters & papers in a Scattered condition If I had you to help me I could get along So well, Seemingly I was glad to hear of your Short Spell of Sickness, Thanks be to God that it was nothing worse I think I understand those Short Spells, I am in hopes that Barney is well before this time & that you may all get along well, Sam ort to have 100 lashes & if he dont behave himself I Shall Sell him certain if he was on the Alabama River he would Soon learn how to behave himself, I think Dan will do finely, he trades on apples & washes, he made 5 or 6 dollars one day & two or three another, he has me 2 Pikes and Palmer to cook & wash for, we are messing with Lt Person who has a negrow to cook for him he Person has Rendered himself verry unpopular in the Company, He is awful lazy, & the worst glutton I ever Saw of his age, He will be up to old Natty Parks if he lives, the boys give me 3 dollars per month for board, their own Rations furnished, Dick Weaver

P2

is Speaking of Sending Wash home & if he does he wants a transfer to my Company & mess with me, I think Francis will not like to give him up, I have a notion of withdrawing from Person, J Francis has bee as thick as a thief with me Since I come back but I know, he wants promotion Coln Braford will Reign &C he has cousined around me to find out if I would not go with him &C Maj Smith into a battalion of Sharp Shooters, S the Lt Coln, F the Major & I the Senior Capt. but I tell you I had Rather have a Talladega cousern than Sutch a consern as they can make, I know that our company has been the tail end all the time, but it is not the fault of the Talladega officers, No I had Rather be under Shelly than Coln anybody, I do not Seek promotion, I am one notch hier than I wanted to be, but under the circumstances I am Capt undoubtedly & I will try to be Respected according to my merit, John F is ambitious for promotion & I fear cannot wait he is haughty & abrupt only at Sutch times, I think that I will get along with officers & men both in the company & out of it, Capt Dr Patison is the Senior Capt & if Coln B Resigns will be Major, unless he will do as F wants him (Ie) let him pass him, & if he P does not then F intends to quit the (consern) Regt and form a Battalion of S

Shooters (Say nothing about this matter) I have not been with the Co but little, have been fixing up Descriptive lists & discharges, we ar Still in line of battle & cook quarter mill

P3

We had Rather be Pickett than here are on Pickett every 5 days can See the Yankee Picketts about 1 mile off, the boys nearly all have body (guards) lice on them I went to the river today to wash, I looked good but found none, we have wore out the leaves, they have had but little chance to wash, we have Roll call every two hours & drill in the manuel of arms, & inspection every day but upon the whole we are doing nothing & tired of that & the yanks are in full possession of the gap and I think will hold it we are not going to attack them there & they are not going to come out, Dan Sends howdy to all we are well enough to eat his cooking there is some grumbling about Rations, J Palmer has the toothache & Says he will have it pulled, W Slaton is Sick with chills Some more complaining none mutch Sick the 31st has gone to Babtist Gat Some 12 miles from her, We are awaiting orders we have 2 days Ration of bread cooked, Jim Graham has not got his discharge yet & Coln Harley Says that he will not Sign it for that was what cought him there, Jack Williams & Lum Evans both transferred to an artillery Co, & I believe both Sick of it

May God of his infinite mercy have mercy upon us upon our cause & our army & enable us to triumph over our enemies, until they Shall Sue for Peace on terms honorable to us as a nation is the prayer of one who loves country, life Wife & liberty, Home and Children but Sacrafize all for all S C Kelly

SEPT. 18, 1862
CAMP OF INTERNMENT NEAR CUMBERLAND GAP

.18 & .19 P1

(Daniel SCK's slave letter written by friend)

Dear friends having an opportunity of a friend to write you this morning. I gladly embrace the moment. I know you are anxious to hear from me and how I like camp life. I arrived here on the 10th just one night before Master Samuel did. I met with several gentlemen with whome I was aquainted. I was very glad to see them, and they equally appeared so with me. I entered on my duty the next day, which I presume you are all aware, is cooking and waiting on Master, Which I take great delight in. I also met with some of my own culler, who is performing the same kind for officers. Our task is quiet light which affords so much time to work for ourselves. I am washing for good many of Masters Corn. The soldiers are all kind to me, and pay me fair prices, for my labor, enabling me to make fair wages. I am well pleased with camp life, and I feel more like at this time a white man is my friend, this morning than ever I did before. The hard labor which the soldier goes through, and the exposier they have to bear, goes to prove to me that the white man is my friend in the south. I am sure I will never complain of hard times any more, and if it is Gods will for me to return home which I hope

P2

it is. I will be a better servant than I have ever been. I hope you will not give mistress any room to complain to master of ill treatments to her. I am fully convinced that it is your duty be kind to her, and to try to preserve, and make all you can for her and her children to live on. I have no fears but you will all be humble and kind to her, and the children. Not only to her but to all of the families of men who are in the army. This I believe is your duty, and not only yours, but the duty of all slaves. You should be quiet and make no disturbance to harm the peace of any family, who has given up their families so willingly in the defense of there injured country. If only you could be here for a few days and witness the manner soldiers has to live and the anxieties they have for their families welfare, that they have left behind their, you could not forever shearing tears for them. After the labor is over and a good portion of it is preformed of night thus is a sign to them. To see them, To see them in bunch spreading there blankets on the makers earth nothing but the woods to screen them from the dew or cold rain is far worse treatment than these servants have to under go.

P3

I can a sure last nigh was a great one with me. I was a woke about moon rise, with the noise of the enemies, suppose they were burning up their magazines. We discovered a tremendous light instantly from the fires burning up what they could not carry off withum. I suppose it was an hour until day when they commence firing off their cannon. I have no idea the number they fired off but it was many a one. The roaring excelled any thing I ever heard. News has come in since I commenced writing that they have left, and that our calvary has been in the Gap. I suppose our force will take full possession of it to day. If we were there I might write you much news that would be interesting to you. I want you to be sure you give my love to all my collered friends. Tell the young ladies I would like to see them. Please get Mistress to write for you and send me letters. I will write you as often as I can reasanably can. Your affectionate friend and relative.

Daniel

P.S. This leaves me well, also Master Samuel. I hope this will find you all well.

DAN'S LETTER
SEPT 19TH

.19 P3

(Slave letter written for Daniel by friend)

This morning we are in the gap. My conjecture was correct. The enemy left yesterday morning, and we entered the gap. A great many things are left unharmed, while it look as if they have destroyed many thousand dollars worth of various kinds of property. Oh the work they have done, in preparing to fight us here is immense. They have thrown up brest works of all kinds. The cannon pits they prepared is the finest work I ever saw and shows plainly it was master workmen that superintended the whole affair. But with all this they left it with fighting. Law me it would do your eyes good just to take a view of it. The mountain is high, and the timber all cut off for miles around. A great many tents are left standing but cut and riddled into doll rags. Guns, ammunition, cannons, axes, pick axes, spades and every thing else you can think of was left too tedious to mention. Our forces are currently traveling here from several miles around and has filled up a lazy flat in front of the gap. O; I never saw so many men in my life. The wagons and men have been coming in all night. This is a general letter to you all. I must close yours truly.

Daniel

(To his friends & relatives at home)

.18 .19 & .20

.18

18th 5 oclock AM to early to See how to write the Yanks have been blowing up every thing Since 3 oclock the brightest fires & the most Rumbling Reports Support that they are leaving we have orders to pack up & be ready to march at a moments warning it is Raining a little would be glad of a good Rain not Rained any Since July on the boys all in high hopes in mutch haste I remember this the day of thanks giving May all be engaged God bless us & you all S

Cumberland Gap Sept. 19th 1862.

.19 P1

My Dear Amie The Yankees evacuated the Gap yesterday. We arrived here about 10 o'clock. They destroyed everything, burnt up the stores, ammunition, tables & riddled their tents which was left standing. Scattered hats, caps, shirts, pants &C&C all cut to pieces. I feel like I am fully repaid for all I lost at the gap precisely 3 months ago they have buried their cannon, burnt their small arms & ammunition. All of the boys got something pens, ink, paper, books, camp stools, candlesticks, tin plates everything. I got nothing because I did not know how long we would stay nore when we would go & besides I had command of the Company & had not the chance, I have as much as I want to carry, I sold my old jeans pants for 5 dollar & my old coat for ten & Dan Swapped for it & got 5 dollars to boot I also sold to Perkins my old hat for 5 dollars. I have no use for 2 calico Shirts I sent Dan down to the Johnsons where I left my trunk to & carry my boots to put in it & told him to sell the shirts for 2 dollars a piece

P2

I do not know whether he sold them or not as we left before he got back & when he Ret to old camp had to cook our Rations & bring forward to the gap which brought night I saw him last night (we were on pickett) we got our suppers, but I do not know how come out trading, the Sun is now about an hour high & he has not brought our breakfast yet, We expected to be called in this morning to pursue the enemy but Suppose we are waiting on Rations, The troops were coming in all night long & wagons running both ways We are all relieved by the Yanks evacuation they have done more work than we had before we left, I Suppose 50 thousand dollars would not more than pay for there labor they are evidently afraid of us judging by fortifications more anon God bless the cause

12 noon we are still on P we expected to be Rel but have not I heared that the balance of our Brigade had started on our Regiment cooking

P3

(Part of envelope stuck to letter)

expect to start _____

heart _____ to _____ have Read it all & do not like it mutch you can Read it & Read it to the negrows Sutch portions as you like nothing verry objectionable in it (except the tone)

The Yanks were well fixed up in the way of camp life for instance they have their telegraph (wires) lines in full operation as far as they go it extended at least 1 ½ miles this Side of the Gap if they had been successful at Tazewell they would have had it there in 24 hours after the fight, Morgan Kept them in the Gap 2 weeks longer than they intended to Stay (by using there telegraph & a factious name) by telegraphing them that he would soon have them plenty of provisions &C&C when they

P4

found out the trick they soon Skedaddled & they went to I do not know where. We heard Some firing this morning Supposed to be a fight. Our folks are putting a telegraph line from Morristown to this place when we get it we can have the old Yankee one Repaired & then we can get it up to Camps. The whole Country is laid waste where the Yanks goes nothing left. Crops eat up, fences burnt, gardens trodded down & rails burnt. Tazewell is a waste. I will close with the benedictions, the best I can wish SCK

20th 5 ½ AM My Dear Amie Still here but Still expecting to Start we have our Rations cooked & apparently Ready. I have my trunk & all I brought along, Dan is Sick was very Sick last evening, I think with cold, the 2 nights here has been cold & verry windy, I gave him Some of my Strong pills & think he will be better as Soon as he begins to Stir, I have one hundred & 90 dollars I thought of Sending it to you but I had better keep it for fear it has to be left god bless & save us all good bie Sam

Sept. 25, 1862 10 A
76 miles North of the (Gap) 18 miles of London

.25 P1

My dear wife A I am well but Dan is not nor has not been Since we left the Gap he has cold I carried his provisions yesterday & with much ado he kept up We are marching day & night & Sometimes short of provisions but we have never Suffered I said yesterday that I could walk with any man in the Regt my feet are blistered with my shoes & I put on my boots & I am doing verry well now It is a poor mountainous country water Scarce and

P2

dry dust deep &C apples Scarce but was plenty we get a part of what is going my men have been unruly but I will Straighten them out I am anxious to hear from home, but we have no mail Old Gen. Barton drunk Col. Shelly & others have reported him & I hope he will be cashered we are doing well now plenty to eat. expecting to start immediately to Richmond and Lexington Ky we are wasting the whole county I am in hopes that Dan will get well Dr. B is paying good attention to him Report says that no Yanks this side of the Ohio River

God bless good bie in mutch S C Kelly

OCTOBER 1862

OCTOBER 4TH 2 ½ PM

.04 .05 P1

My Dear Amie in hast I write to you, I have a chance to send this by Phillips who has a Substitute who came with Wingo I am well & have been all the trip Dan is well I hope will stay so we are near Frankfort Kentucky ordered to march keep this note S C Kelly in love God bless us

P2

About 100 yards from camp in line while the Army is moving I do not know where we are going nor how we will fair. Ky K is alive in our cause 30 thousand have Rallied to our standard the women cheer us on Cannon were heard towards Shelbyville 30 miles off Ky is too good a country for us to ever give up we have had a hard march for 200 miles or more.

P3

My Dear one I Send these notes to you because I do not kneed the money this one is on this man that brings it he Says if he has money enough he will pay & perhaps Stay all night I think him a gentleman & he can tell you many things I cannot write

P4

I Said I made the other note in a mule trade So I did I bought him for my Pack mule Rode him 5 miles & a Sick Lt ofter me for him & I concluded that my feet were Rested So I thought 90 dollars was not made every day Say nothing about what I write about it as I have never told but 2 men what I gave, I hope that God in his infinite mercys will protect Sustain & keep us in the way we Should go Pray for me continually SCK

P5

(Versailes) is one of the best secession towns in the State, Dan is a good fellow, Jack is Rascally & Love is in a peck of trouble about him & is mad at me at Shelly at the cSS at the world, & Sick (home Sick) & Sick in the hospital, more of the mind than body, (Dunking for a discharge at Frankford), Say nothing about this the Doctor Says he never will Sign his discharge, that is hes mad & Sick, I believe that Dan will Stick if Jack & Wash & others will let him alone I have lost Since we left the gap 3 men) Journey fell off a bluff one night & nearly killed himself but no bones broken he will get well Adkins at Same place with fever & L Alexander, W Slaton Sick & has to be hanled Pearson Do we have, 8 or 10 complaining have in all 74 men & the 2nd largest Co in the Regt (Frances largest) I have them in order pretty good disciple but had to be Rough with them 8 oclk well my Dear I have just Ret from breakfast at an old widow & Son who is a widower all kindness have an invitation to dinner this is a great place I wish I could See you today, & tell all

P6

The note Refered to I made it in one day in a mule trade it is on a Lt & Maj S all good but I have as mutch money as I want to carry & I might loose it, if I get the money on it I will Rect them, I have 75 or 80 dollars with me our money is good here (in places) but when we can buy it is about ½ as high as in our County & double the price of gold & Silver, Lots of bacon & flour here I must close for I am in a figgett I have good bie SCK

5th 5 ½ oclock we left Frankford about dark after we crossed the River the bridges were fine & the greatest excitement prevailed, we are forming a junction with Buckner, Bragg & Smith we marched all night or nearly So we come 16 miles & are now this Sabbath morning at a butiful place

OCT 5TH 1862 12 OCLOCK NOON VERSAILES, KENTUCKY

O5.P1

My Dear Amie I had closed up my letter twice but we are still on our own awaiting orders & expecting to move every hour we arrived here about 3 oclock this morning all right with me except a Sore throat I lay in the Rain the other night without my blanket we were drawn up in line that morning expected a fight & the old negro that had the mule (Refered to) did not come up, but Stayed with the waggons, It is Rumored the yankees are in possession of the City of F, it is also said they have taken 15 of our waggons, among them is A Brown, Reves Shaw & others belonging to our Co I may write the Same things in the different letters but I forget what I have not Said I understand that Buckner Brag & Smith are all here (I have seen the 2 latter) together with their Brigadiers Barton, Stevenson, Reynolds, Reims, Ledbetter, Churchhill & others it is the largest Army we have ever been in I have a notion of going to my Dinner

CUMBERLAND GAP OCT. 23RD 4 OCLOCK P.M.

.23 & .24 .25 Pl

LETTER 1

My Dearest Amie I rec two letters today of you 1 the 6th the other the 10th believe me I was verry glad to get them & was truly thankful you were all so well & more especially that I was yet in the land & among the living after one of most fatiguing marches that any set of men ever went through dust, but little water, half the time on ½ Rations ¼ rations without marching night & day& I have had no blankett for the last 12 days until last night, we passed an old horse but a sick boy on him with our blankets & provisions he got lost off & we never came upon him until we found him sick at Cumberland find horse stolen & he laying there, I was afraid of lice & done without until Dan found

P2

me one 4 days ago & Sold it to Palmer & then we lay on the ground & covered up with it, I have not got any lice on me but it gave me the chills I Reckon I have kept up but have been quite Sick 2 or 3 times I feel thankful that it is well with me as what it is, Several Sick nearly all fell out I started with 77 men & one night had but 12 men up the Road has been Strowed with Sick all the time we let them go ahead last night I have but 38 men I have lost none dead or taken prisoner (I believe) except Jonney who was sent to Richmond, I am better than I was I have walked 18 miles today & crossed the mountain, eat a little fresh beef & ½ bisquit, will get 2 bisquits apiece today, Daniel is the best boy in Regiment is Shifty & Smart, got well in about 4 days he has been worth 50 dollars to me this boy I must close Do not be anxious I Sent 390 dollars just before we left the gap God bless S C Kelly

24ᵀᴴ 6 OCLOCK AM

P1

LETTER 2

Well my dear I thought I could Send it off last night but could not We had a good nights Rest Cooked & eat & have 2 days Rations on hand all appears to be cheerful this morning Dan had an old lame horse given to him, on which we pack our blankets &C Our trip into Ky Seems At a glance to be a failure, but not So, we have 3,000 waggons loaded with provisions, 5,000 mules, 2,000 horse & beef cattle, no drilling. We have made a with draw & the Reason we suffered is because we had to keep everything ahead & fight the enemy behind who annoyed our Rear all the time until about 70 miles back, We were in battle array twice but the enemy would not strike, We expected it every moment. we must to have had a hundred thousand, or in a word more men than I ever saw, they were coming in from 10 AM until after dark two ways, we Stayed in line until next morning & they did not give us fight when we turned Southward for Cumberland Gap. we were in hearing of several fights but were never engaged. it is reported that Bragg, Buckner, Breckenridge & Smith held a council & all Said fight but Bragg, I do not know whether that was so or not but we were disappointed in not getting a fight after So much hard work to get up to them, It was also Reported that we were ordered out of Ky by the War Department I know we have been in a hurry some times & then again we would stop (as we thought) for 10 minutes or Stay 10 hours very irregular

P2

5 PM well my Dear we are at Clinch River crossing after a trip of 17 miles, Sometimes fast as we could walk & then very Slow owing to the Road waggons before & behind this is only Cirbys Command Bragg is on our Right B Ridge & Buckner I know not where, This is a good country but desert now where this Army has passed, fields desolate, fences burnt, gardens trodden under foot & Stock killed &C&C Some families eat out & Ruined, we did not destroy much when we went out, but alass all of Ky as a majority is against us except the women God bless them that are for us Love Alexander has got up with us, Jack Ran away at Salvasa 12 or 15 miles S of Frankfort H Steel was Sent forward with the Sick he and J Hayes (the Latter heared of a days travel back) behind, it is nearly dark & we are not yet across it is cold but no killing frost until 4 or 5 days back. I left 5 Sick in Tazewell H Bigger & Little Pike, Argo D Boozer S Reeves, J Benson Slaton E. Stice have been Sick early all the time but up, Bowman & Arheart both broke down together with many others

I had last (this the 25th 6 oclock AM) 65 men & 5 Sick, Well my Dear the 310 dollars Sent home by Adler about the 15th Sept you have not Said anything about I have not Rec but the 2 letters Spoken off, You may have mentioned it before, I dreamed you got it & was Satisfied I wanted you to pay Swan & Montgomery as to the cotton, you can exercise your own judgment, but this is a bad time to weigh cotton, tis so dry, get JRG to weigh if he is not interested, I have about $85 that will answer my purpose, I have no chance to Spend this or it would have been, I trust in God that he will yet Save me as he has done & you & yours & the confederacy may yet be freed from her enemies SCK

(Written in margin very small)

PS because papers Scarce bad Scarce generaly

CLINCH RIVER 21 MILES EAST OF C GAP E TENN. PM OCTOBER 25TH

(Written on front of envelope)

THE POLITENESS OF W. WADSWORTH
(Written on back of envelope)

Dear Sir I am Sorry to trouble you but in one who has traveled twice across Kentucky & my ____ _____ has not heard a word from since 20th Sept & besides that by this method She will get in 8 or 10 days Sooner than the ordinary course of Sending it to the Distributing office at Montgomery, You will confer a great favor on me if you will forward it immediately. Yours Respt

S. C. Kelly Capt. of Co. (E) 30th Regt. Ala. Vols.

PS paper scarce SCK

(This letter has no date probably November 1862 but has names of men)

P1

I Suppose that there is 6 thousand ____tual men at this place & think the place as near like Seragordo Mexico as ever I Saw, but we have the position that the Mexicans had there, the Rations are Scarce bacon & butter is worth 50 cts chicken mostly, Our mess is getting through with the money fast, we have to pay 25 cts for bacon 6 for flour, all we get some Sugar & molasses no nothing & Some times the commissary does not want to let it go, I borrowed Some but do not expect to pay it back, I do wish I did have had Some thing to interest you, I would give a dollar for a letter, I take out the last one I got & Read it occasionally, Capt Said Send his Respects to you, The valley from the gap varies from ½ to 2 miles wide, it is nearly one continual lane, Some fine houses wheat & clover fine, but little corn planted, Rocks is a natural production fine Stone fences, fine Stock, I will close, I wish by the help of God over come our enemies

P2

A list of the men that are with us those marked with an ess off Site their names Sargt J. D. Hollingsworth, Corp S. M. Penland Corp J. W. Williams (S) N Argo (S) 3 Boozers, B Baxter J Benson 2 Browns, Andy & (Ben S) Bowman (S) Harvey Bridges, Sam Bowling (S) Parson, B. A. Cornelius, 2 Cannons (S) Ducket, Wm. C. Estice, Fannen, A. C. Griffin (S fever) 2 Griffith, Mendy

Henderson, Jackson (S) Hugh Kidd, McDill, McCollum, James Peace, Ben Peace (S) R Prater, 2 Reaves 3 Sewells (S) Simpson (S) W Slaton Wm Stewart (S) H Steel (S) Shaw (S) Shell (S) John Thackerson S C Taylor H Wolf (S) James Young S Young (S) these others have came to us Since we left Knoxville Landers, Thomas, J Massey, McDille, I think that the men will get better in a few days Rest we have been put through, Coln Shelly Says that we have Stood the march well but looks verry mutch like all would fail, I must close I have not dressed yet the mail will go out this day, I did not know I would have time to writ this but pushed it I have Repeated but for the Reason given S C Kelly

OCT 27 1862 5 PM CAMP NEAR RUTLEDGE TENN

.27 .28 Pl

(Wrights about how bad conditions are)

My Dear Amie we are in a Rather confused State we came over here night before last the wind blew cold & during the night an occasional spitting of snow or sleet got up in the morning after a bad nights Rest on a hillside on Rock & brush by one of the worst Smokiest fire into an old fashoned Regularly built, Snow it Snowed all day & the hollows were covered about 12 inches deep or at least 6 inches on the level ground you may imagine Something about it when I Say the wind continued to Shift all day on every Side of our poor fires made without one splinter of lightwood & with one dull axe to the Company, I stood it as well as I could. I sat on a rock covered up my head went to sleep & like to have broke my neck, the snow on my blanket on my back got to be about 1 inch deep, In the evening we built a shanty, hauled a load of straw, cut wood & built a fire, Slept under wet blankets comfortably, Dan was very sick both nights, I gave him medicine last night & he is better today, I am afraid he has Pneumonia the Doct Says he can cure him in a few days, today has been pleasant & the snow is nearly all melted off, we expected to

start off this morning at 7 o'clock & we fool like turn in & burnt up our Shanty to make a fire, So now wee are now drawing 2 days

Rations to be cooked tonight, we expect to go South either to Savannah, Chattanooga or Corinth uncertain, J P will tell you all he knows & that aint much about what we are going to do, I had no time to write when he started, more anon, Dan has supper about ready & I am hungry &hearty, God bless you all Sam

28th 10 oclock AM well my, D, Just as Supper was Ready (which was stewed beef & cold biscuits) Capt Dr Pattison come around I insisted on him eating with us telling him I was disappointed in getting Sugar & coffee, he Refused saying he had got a good supper & invited me Round to drink with him, I accepted (as a matter of course not having had a drink since the woods was burnt) went Round drank & talked with the mess who consisted of Capt, Lt Oden, Lt Hescock & Lt Wallace all of whoom are intelligent & gentlemanly officers & Sat until 10 o'clock took leave & Returned to my qrters (about 50 yards off) found the whole mess in a

P2

perfect glee cooking up 2 days Rations, the men drew sugar & coffee at the Rates of 3 pounds to the 100 men of coffee & 5 pounds of sugar (one days ration) just enough to make them one good mess, they had drank it & no Sleep nor Slumber to there eyes we layed down about 11 oclk we got up Right about ½ hour by sun (no roll call) I eat breakfast had coffee made in cup of the old grounds & parched flour (which looked like ground coffee) try that I Say it is the best Substitute yet easily prepared, I think wheat ground & used without boiling or Sifting will be the trick, I heard a few days ago that Barley is the best Substitute know, it would be better to grind it first Save trouble, breakfast over, I procured a camp kettle for the Company to scald the lice in, I am superintending it myself, I let each one get his water & boil his garments & take them to the branch to wrench or dabble as he pleases no need talking about lice, I have seen on a mans coat collar in less than 2 inches 5 of the old big ones & ___ as many as the filling crossed the warf, I knew that there was lice but I had no ida to what extent. I tell them that they will kill colts & hogs &

they will torment & they will Suck the verry life blood out of them, those that are So verry lowsey all look pale, I have Dan off scalding ours also (he is not well but great deal better, fever blisters all around his mouth) I am clean except I got some last night which I did for I felt one on my neck, I Strip every day or So & Search, have never caught but 3 off me & they were fresh emergent but it is nearly impossible when you See them crawling on men like hogs on a hill Side Rooting for acorns, Some favor writing, lots washing, no Small number with Shirts of cracking, no Soap, clothes ragged, Shoes nearly worn out, Several men in this Regiment bare footed, hats tattered & torn, beards long & loose as wild asses main, no gospel preached unto us, Oh that God in his infinant mercy would have mercy on us as a nation God only knows when it will end, Into his hands Lord I commit our destinies with all that we have & are Praying this to forgive us our Sins & bring us to a Speedy peace with the nations of the earth & the name of CSA may be written with the names of the nations & God our God Shall have all praise for our Redemption,

I need some socks & if you have them a good pare of coarse jeans pants mine is to thin, I do not know as I need anything else, Dan aut to have a good coat but I can buy if do not have it Ready, nothing would give me more pleasure than to be with you, but alass this cruel enemy, Save me a Suit at home less I come home Some time lousey as a hog, I have no ida when I can get the chance but will come if only for 5 days, I am So Sorry for you, Oh that God will Restore you & your health, Tell Barney to go ahead & be part to business for on him I Shall have to depend & be contented with his lot for if he was to have to have to work 20 hours in 24 & fair as he does would be better than the Soldiers life, I have hard trials & ups & downs Standing between officers & men (have become hardened) have Set my face as a flint & intend to Stand hard Ships as a good Soldier trusting in God my Savior who has kept me Safe thus far & I believe will bear me Safely through the Storms of war home to that humble (though wounded) cottage where lives my dear ones, All be industrious be honest go to hear the gospel preached, prepare in life for death & in time for that awful eternity where the worn duth not & the fire is not quenched,

Sell the cotton if you think best, get James to live with you if you can tell him to Rent out the old place & do the business of the estate & I will make it all Right

S C Kelly

CAMP NEAR RUTLEDGE EAST TENNESSEE OCT 27/ 62

.27 P1

(From Daniel SCK's slave)

Dear mother I take the present opportunity of dropping you a few lines to let you know how I am getting own this leaves me very unwell I have been very sick getting better now Just completed a long and tiresome march of some four or five hundred miles we have been nearly all over kentucky I saw a heap of things that was very pleasant and interesting and some that was not so pleasant one passing through harisburg kentucky I saw a sight that I shall never forget there was a battle fought there the day before and I never saw the life of dead and wounded men in my life but thanks be to god I have got back into tennessee again times are hard heare and I tell you what it is camp is not the thing it is cracke up to be when it comes to paying too dollars a Dozen for bread and small biscuits at that it snowed here all day yesterday the snow was some four or five inches deep heare this morning and we had to stand out and take it all Dear mother if never live to see you any more I want you to give my watch to Sister

P2

Dicy I was offered 40 dollars for it in cash a few days ago but would not take it for I had promised it to Dicy before I left home as soon as we draw some money I will send you some some 18.19 dollars and want you to save my boots for me and not let the boys wear them out for maybe I will get to come home again give my love and best respect to all of my friends especially to the young girls if we go down south which is the general belief of the people

I intend to come by home to fulfill your promise I want you to send ma a letter once and a while for I would like to hear from you all tell Sam and toby and Dicy and fanny and tom and Eller and Miss Elizabeth and nirgle and Dicky all howdy for me me and Moss Sam gets along together mity well he could not have taken better care of me if I had been some relation of his and I have told you all the news I will bring my letter to a close by saying farewell
    Dear mother for this time
    Daniel kelly

NOVEMBER 1862

CAMP NEAR LENOIR E TENN NOV 4ᵀᴴ 1862

.04 P1

My Dear Amie I just bt me some paper (which cost 8 ¼ cts. Per sheet) & conceded I would write you, to let you know I am not well but better I have been sick 3 days, I went home with J Hendricks at Knoxville & got foundered on fried batter & baked apples & Sugar., it cholicked me (yes just now moved & turned over my ink all over my paper, hand & on my coat & pants which are very much abused) for 2 days without an operations for 2 days Since then the worst kind of disentery I have not taken anything & think that I will get well by being prudent, I bought me a horse, bridle & saddle in Knoxville which I rode here 26 miles just in time, he cost me my pistol (which I had got verry tired of & 35 dollars 70 dollars out, he is a good young horse but like many others both Soldiers & horses had a hard time in Ky, I have almost concluded that if we take the cars here, to Send Daniel home by land with him, he is to good a horse to loose & too much money to give for 2 days Ride, he would be worth in Ala in the spring in good fise 150 dollars, he is a traveler

P2

It is only about 200 miles he could Ride it in 7 days, but if we go by the gravell he is not for sale, I think the Signes are good for us to go to Murphyreysborough or Nashville, thousands of troops are passing dayly on the train South, I Suppose from Va, There are 5 or Six Brigades within 3 miles of here, lots of our Regt sick none of my Co bad, that are with us I have 67 men Pike & I 69 all said besides 6 waggoners out of 110 men, H Steal lost in Ky, Boozer & Journey also, Oh My Dear I am So anxious to get a letter of you, the 10th Oct is the latest date, want to know whether you Rec 310 dollars in the letter Sent by Adler if not you write to him (he did not know that the money was in it) & inquire if he did not bring a letter for you & where he mailed it or what he did with it, at the Same time write to Mr John Collins (brother of Jessee) about Adler & say to him that I sent 310 dollars in it & if Adler had ever got home &C, Direct both letter to Cropwell, Lt Clair Co ala I also want to know whether you Rec a letter brought by M P Phillips from Versailes Ky with 2 notes one on Moore & Smith for 85 dollars & the other on Phillips for $10

P3

I Reckon if the $310 is lost that you had better Sell Cotton to pay the Maughney note or 10 bags at 20 cts which will at least make one thousand dollars as fast as you get money pay the debts in a word, I think by Selling 10 bags cotton & what Stock you can Spear next Spring & what money I can Send you can pay every debt that we owe, if those indebteded do not pay but little, One thing certain all I owe has to be paid war or peace live or die, while I Shall loose hundreds there is due me in the Co at this time owe me at least 200 dollar & my wages are 260 dollars due, We have been fixing out Muster Rolls & pay for 2 or 3 days we or the men will draw 4 months wages, I intend to try to get some that is owing to me We owe Montgomery near 200 Swan near 200 Graham 200 or more Cary Estes 350 Dr Cowden 87 ½ but Some credits Maughney 800 by this time all Said 1800 dollars more than I thought, I may have forgotten hop I have in my favor, I Shall try to Send you all the money I can Spear to pay on those debts & you collect every dollar you can on my act, I have 25 or 30 dollars enough to answer on my own purpose, My Dear I think you aut to Sell the wheat at least 75 bushels 150 I believe you had you aut to let he

P4

people have it for Seed you had better have the locks changed, I am confident that Some were Stold last Spring, ½ bushell & ½ peck per acre will be enough to soe per acre, & I want 25 acres in the Todd field sowed as I directed Barney 16 bushels will be enough, I hate to Say a word about you using flower, but ____ off 75 to Sell 16 to Soe & it leaves 59 for use Since that leaves over a bushell per week or 4 lbs per day as mutch as 5 men draw here, while you have corn bread bacon beef chickens Kidds vegetables &C&C all the family numbers 13 I believe, while we have beef we have no bacon nor pork unless Saved over, Do not take this wrong My Dear one for God bless you, I believe you do the best you can, but the poor of this world what will become of them, I only want to impress upon you a Since of Strict economy & the certinty , that our debts must be paid, you Said in one of your letters that James was up there making up a School he can get it & I am willing for him moving up to the old Rhodes house & take Shingles & cover it & St it any where he pleases, teach his School & attend to my business just as he would his own (with your consent) & I will pay him for his trouble, I think he owes me that Service under the present circumstances, May the God of battle still watch over us & may we be more humble & more dependant looking to him for help in every time of kneed S C Kelly

Tell J P if he is not gone that we are here now do not know how long for (26 miles South of Kon on the E T & Ga Road) my Respects to all who inquire after me Direct to Knoxv SCK

.04

(Sam talks about Daniel his slave)

12 Noon Daniel is well & is a good boy my intrest & welfare is his, he Sticks close as a brother, Says he had rather live in Ala as a slave than be a free negro in Tenn or Ky, Says he had all chances to leave me but preferred to go with me, He said that he had

mother them a hundred dollars that we were ready to start home, he gets along with the men verry well buys, Sell borrows & lends, is cleanly in his person & cooking, I must close do not be disappointed if Dan does not come for I do not know how I could Spear him will Yours truly affectionately & Fraternally S C Kelly

Lenores Station Tenn Nov 9ᵀᴴ 1862 9 oclock AM

.09 P1

Mt Dear one I am only tolerably well I have not been well but able to be about I think that I will be well I have taken medisin, my leven did not act but have been improving 4 days Dan has been very Sick I fear he will not stand camp life he is affected in the same way in fact & 2 thirds of this Regt is in the same fix Coln Shelly has been quite Sick he has Ret to camp, the weather is cold we sleep cold have but few tents, a negro is so bad in the way Sick I am a good notion to send Dan home, I do not want to but I fear he will not do me any good this winter, J Pike has got cross I am afraid that he is tired of cooking for me but I have not eat but little & they have drawn

P2

& eat my rations & Dan's, I Sent him off to Dr. B's tent where he has a Sick negro where he can be attended to, Tell J Palmer to hire Halls Bill & bring him with him & I will send, D, home, I do not intend to do without one if I can help it my duties are many to many too cut wood & tote & cook We have not brawn money yet but will, We (or General Barton) has been contending for the 50 dollar clothing & by both which he says we should have if so those who have not drawn will get about 140 dollars, I think one man from a co will be Sent home with the money of those who want to Send, I am in a hurry this old man is waiting he can tell you his Story I can not get a Blankett for myself I would like to have socks an over coat & a blankett but I do not expect you can get the 2 latter, I will kneed a pair of pants Dan the Same. I bought him a coat, we will draw today. My Dear I am opposed to Selling cotton for less than 20

P3

cts & not more than 10 bags at that, & I know that with that mutch & what I can Send you & what you can collect that we aut to pay all out debts except Cary Estes, & I had Rather have it in cotton than money to keep, as to Turk & the Boys &C I told him they might help gather Jim Ts for my taking out, D, & every thing else (he will do Right about it) (my paper is damp) I am in a hurry & cannot compose my mind as to Salt we get plenty & I do not know what you will do, but I believe you will do the verry best you can, I Rec your of the 28th 4 days ago, Tho one verry Sick in my com, good many complaining, Several bunking for a discharge (among them L Alex, Arht, Cornelius &C) Say nothing of that, John Rhodes is with us & will Still driving, Must close God bless good bie May God Still protect us & Save us is my Prays Yours most affectionately S C Kelly

November 20 & 23, 1862

(His between hers of Sept. 19th hers)

P1 HERS

AT HOME SEPT. 19TH 62

It has been so long since I heard from you. I cannot stand it much longer. What has happened to you. I have not heard a word since you left Knoxville. Do write to me I have trouble enough with out that. The Negroes are trying themselves in this country. Fosters stealing soap and meat or anything they can lay hands on and gets Bairds Anderson to sell or bring back here for Patience to sell or that is there tale. I do not think Patience is in it but they tell it and Crops Jack was taken up and things found in his possession that came out of Grahams store. He accuse Bill Whiteside they took Bill up and found a key that will unlock our crib and Youngs grocery which he said Dan gave him before he left he said they had been in Young grocery 2 or 3 times with it but Young took off the lock. He also says they been in Grahams store he had box of white gloves he says he had taken meat wheat and 10 or 12 bushels corn from the old man his master at different times and that he helped Dan to measure 3 bushels of wheat here the Saturday night before he left and Dan took it to Gar Sims on old kit. He says he never knew Barna in any manner but the key just fits the crib that has corn in it. I have the key. I was in hopes he told this tale on Dan & Powell because they were not here to speak for themselves for they tried to bring in Halls Negroes but I supposed they cleared themselves. Sam has been doing better since he came in and Turk whipped him he has cooled down completely. I do not think Barna could manage him he is big. Davis Stewart & Powell came home night before last. Davis was wounded in the arm at Manassases he is improving he will stay 3 or 4 weeks. Jeb Harris was killed and Littljohn and Capt Lee, I am taking an Atlanta paper but do not like it.

P2

The meeting commenced last saturday at Liberty and closed yesterday, I joined by letter none by experience, Bro Martin took sick and left and bro Canfield remained he is a pretty fair preacher, but we are so cold nothing but the power of God can thaw sutch cold profesor, & that he would shine in our hearts by his love and cause us to wake up to our duty, yesterday was thanksgiving we met as a church and I assure you the soldiers were not forgotten may God answer our prayers and send us peace, Montgomery thinks peace will be made soon sometime this fall, & that it may for I do not see how I am to do with out you much longer, I am afraid it is a case with me any how, and if it is how can I get along without you for 9 long wearisome months who will comfort me and cheer me up no one can do it as you would, but what can not be cured must be endured, May God sustain me.

2 of our hogs have died and I fear others will and the we will not have enough for our meat, unless we buy and that would be hard. Fannie Miller has had the toothache very bad for several days. We were on the eve of starting to Bowdon to have it pulled but it passed before we got off so we gave it out for today. Toby had 1 pulled this week. it is raining some. the boys will get done

the fodder today if it does not rain too much. They pulled for Roberson 1 ½ days this week . we yet owe him 1 day whitch they will pay next week. High Wilson died this week. I do not hear of but little sickness truly god has blessed us in that respect. Mccain gave me nice little Billy Goat. But it was small and our goats whipped it and I recon killed it we cannot find it no where. The sisters of Liberty church are going to make bro Martin a suit of jeans and give to him. I was so sorry for him at our meeting, he came rite dirty and says he has made up his mind to wear cotton, better thinking what was in the hearts of his sisters, may god prosperity undertaking for his name sake.

P3

Fannie is still here but I am afraid she will not stay much longer if I could keep her on Reg, I would be so glad , she suit me so much better than Martha does. I am very busy picking my wool to send to the factory. I shall send it next week. I sent the waggon to the shop this week. It will be done the first of next week. The man that is fixing it joined the army will leave soon for the seat of war. I do wish you could see the children they look so healthy and stout and talk so much about their Pa. A soldier stopped here for dinner, not long since and gave the children 10 cts. a piece. They were so proud they did not know how to behave. My garden has come out a great deal. I am in hopes I will have plenty of cabbage for the winter after all my fears to the contrary we have a stand of tunipes at last. But the weeds grew this wet weather as fast as any thing else. I had 4 bu of dried peaches and I bought 1 of apples from Mothers Maria. I wish you had some of them occasionally at least. The church made up bro Canfield 7$ yesterday I gave him 1 as my. and 50 cts minutes. I will send you one if I can when they come. but may be you will be at home by that time. A waggon load of Soldiers have just passed and saw fannie standing in the pasture and 2 or 3 said loud enough to be heard there is a pretty girl there is a pretty girl and how I did enjoy the joke. It pleased me better than there laughing at the waggon tongue when you were here. Aunt Pollys Hillman was with the waggon he is going to Virginia with Newton Porter, It has rained so much the boys had to quit pulling fodder. And I will send Barna to Loves Alexanders to get me a billy goat, If he can. Marshall Alexander died last week of black jaundice he was at home when he died. how does Dan stand camp. Pink Palmer went to Taladega and would not receive him and Barker the shoemaker. They took Tom Cox and several others, that I do not recollect now.

P4

I stay at home so close. I do not believe I can fill my last page. Jane and Em were well yesterday. they are complaining of not getting letters, others what is the matter are you pregnant or sick or do they not allow you to write, I do think some of you might write, if not all. I am not mad but I fear you are sick, and the Lord only knows how I could bear to hear sutch news as that without coming to you, but I may come if you get sick may I not do say yes for that would be some satisfaction. I want to send this tonight so I will close, may the God of armies protect you and bring you back in peace and safely and may he put his spirit in you as a captain, and cause you to first favor in the eyes your men. God bless you . Tell Dan to remember if he has die and if I never see him again. I want to meet him in a better world. Good bye,

A E Kelly

PS Patience says to tell Dan howdy for her.

November 20th 8 am
On top of Waldens Ridge about 85 miles S West of Knoxville in the direction of Murfreeysbourough (Murfreesdboro)

.20 .23 his between hers
P1 his

My Dearest Amie We left Camp Benton (or this place 25 miles S Knoxville) last Friday morning. We came on to Kinston on Saturday night in good time where we stayed until Monday 12 o'clock when we took up line of march & came 11 miles. Slept all night left early the next morning. Being in the advance traveled 17 miles & stopped in good time but yesterday we were the rear & my Co. was the Rear Guard. We got along tolerably well till 12 when we struck the mountains & it commenced raining & the waggons stalled & it continued to rain until night. I made the horse pay me. Dan had a time & was after night coming in 8 oclock all muddy had fallen down several times but when he came he had bought me some butter & potatoes. It rained until my boots ran full of water. I was only wet from my thighs down having on oilcloth over my shoulders. It was about

8 o'clock when we got to camp (Rear Guard). No axe to cut wood had to gather old (toby tuck as Virgule says). Thought it cleared off & after a so long a time got to sleep. About 12 o'clock got orders to start now. We drew Brandy & I thought it would be good medicin. I took a drink all kept sober this morning we set out at 9 oclock. Sunday morning 8 AM we are waiting orders every thing packed upready. We are at Jasper.

23rd November we have been traveling increasingly in the daytime. Since we left the Mt. I haven't had time to write in daytime & no light at night. No pine in this country & no suffice to start it with. Doing finely on this march I ride & command the Co. about half the time then Dan takes him & strikes out & comes up to camp with corn & always something else to eat he has bought. He sells apples & enough to keep us in butter, chicken, pork, potatoes &C&C makes some money besides. I have done better since I have been by myself. I have my own fire & cooking & J & Dan eat together more than half the time, for I cannot wait to eat one at a time. I have just 40 men with me & it is the 3rd largest Company. J Pike & several others sick were sent back last Monday among those were Roundtree, R Cooley, W Garrett & Johnston. None of them much sick but Pike. He had the fever& had had for several days. I tried to get him a furlough but could not. I fixed

P2

he was present & got up his papers & drew his money. I had drawn up to the same dates Aug. I suppose they will be sent around on the train (RR). We are going through to guard the waggon train (our Brigade). All the other Brigades went on the cars. This is called a post of honor just sutch as we always get (a post of drudgery & hardship). The road is good, nothing muddy nor dusty. The nights are cold & the days pleasant & everything would work well if the men had clothes, blankets & shoes. Half the Company kneed some of these things. Several are bare footed & I am very sorry. Palmer deployed I expect him to come to us at camp Barton & he should aut to have come. I fear we will Suffer before he gets them to us. we are under very strict orders & we have Some troubles with the men. they are not allowed to leave the ranks on no pretence without a guard with them to bring them into line again. we have a rear guard of 4 men to the Company & the Capt. or Commandant of the Company & required to march behind them to see they all do there duty & if not to put such double dutys on them as the merit of the crime deserves. Such as carry 2 guns on their knapsack & such likes all eating of walnuts & persimmons are strictly forbidden there are thousands of them close to the road Side, I have brought all my 40 men in every night since last Sunday night unless a man gets sick & is excused & hauled by the surgeon. I have but one to sick to walk but all seem tired, we march 11X18X20 miles a day & have to cook our rations at night, we are generally late drawing flour & beef by the time we get it cooked & to bed it is 12 o'clock, then up by 5 or 51/2 o'clock at fartherest. Only 3 skillets & 1 kettle to the Company. I have enough cooked every morning to do breakfast & supper (hardly ever eating dinner). I get up at 3 or 4 oclock AM. We are all getting very dirty have had no time to wash since Friday week & particularly lowsy, you kneed not doubt it any longer, I & Dan are lowsey but not lost if could get chance to wash & scald we can clean them out, Col. Shelly is not well & hates to sick as bad I do. I must close for I am sitting on my sheep skin writing on my knees. I received this on monday or Tuesday night with one dated 11th Nov. I suppose this sheet followed me through Ky , it told me things you supposed I knew (& tales I do not believe) all right I do not get the letters, if So I would ask you the same things So often. I am glad to get them from you My Dear though 2 months old, No time for love letters now though I love you none the less. God bless us all & do us good, Yours SC Kelly

PS It is now 10 oclock & expect we will stay all day but uncertain as wind, I will close it up & Send Dan back to town to mail it S C Kelly Capt Co (E) 30th Regt Ala Bartons Brigade Tenn

NOVEMBER 24TH 11 O'CLOCK AM
LOOKOUT MOUNTAIN

.24 .25 Pl

Camp 30th ALA, Lookout Mountain 8 or 10 miles South of Chattanooga

My dearest Amie I commenced this yesterday but had a monthly report to make out & besides I was sick with swimming in my head & sick stomach. I also have a very bad cough, feel better this morning & hope that I will be well again soon. I have not taken my medicin yet, the Doctor said I had better not until I know better what was them matter with me, that it was a derangement of the stomach but I was fearful that it was a spell of Pneumonia. Saturday morning almost day light we received orders to get ready to move immediately & it pouring rain & the wind blowing cold, we gathered up & started about sun rise, up the Lookout Mountain, we expected that the Yankees would shell us as we come up but it was so cloudy & smoky that they could not see us, we came on the top about whitch was about 3 miles & then faced South on the top about 2 miles further, where we stayed all night, arriving there about 11 AM next day which was Sunday. We moved to this place which is about one mile back, reken on account of wood & water. The seased Saturday about twelve but everything was wet & we had to send back to camp for rations & some of the men had eat all they had & one day ahead so it was very scarce last night. We had orders to be ready to move at a minutes warning & to cook up 3 days rations, which took nearly all night. After 11 o'clock last night they were killing horses, there was a shelling yesterday evening on the Right, the

19th were in it & this morning there is a ½ dozen Report about it, had the Regiment went off last night I did not intend to go with them, for I was reported sick but I hated the idea of staying behind, a thing I have never done when the Regiment moves I have always led my Company but we have not gone out yet & every thing is quiet so far as I know, it rained last night & this morning but has seaced now but so foggy that you cannot see more than one hundred yards on the Mountain, beats any place for heavy fogs, that I have ever seen.

The health of the Regiment is good, considering we only have but few tent or flies. My Company (the largest in the Regiment & perhaps the Brigade) has but 2 tents & 2 flies, one tent is mine & the Lieutenant, our cooks, John Allen & Babe Pike & Sgt. Palmer stay with us, the men, that have neither stretch blankets & if there is a plank or board in ½ mile they appropriate it to there use. Not so horrible as seems to one, who is in a good house & good fire but time will tell when the Army goes, this mountain abounds in tiny hens & in one week every tree that will do at all for wood within ¼ miles will be cut. Oh it is a sight to be on the mountain & see the enormous & able camp fires & then to think of

P2

the amount of provisions for one day, for the Army that is now around Chattanooga, a pound of meat or flour to the man & 2/4 of beef, of meat not less than 100,000 lbs. Of beef it will take 150,000 lbs. if they were to average 500 lbs. apiece, think of it, one bushel corn weighs 55 lbs., then it will take nearly 200,000 bushels of corn per day. Who then be surprised that rations are scarce occasionally. I am not here to Chickamauga Station is 12 or 15 miles & to add to that all the teams that haul the provisions has to be fed & a 1,000 more that are hauling ammunitions. It is to much for me to see how one man can do it & I hope that it may be so managed that the Yankees will be compelled to get off of our soil & sue for peace according to our terms.

Chickamauga Station Nov 25th 12 ocock M My Dear I write I am with a sick a squad. The Battle has raged since 12 yesterday, our forces are down from Lookout yesterday & this morning they took position on Missionary Ridge. Our Brigade were not mutch in the fight yesterday they were guarding gaps, or rather Picketts. M Sewell of my Company was killed, The Company was under Pike, Arnheart on Pickett, I have not heard of A. I am on the sick list, but better, likely the Company are in it today, good bie God bless & save us all. Your own Sam

TENN NOVEMBER 27TH 1862

.27 Pl

My Dearest Amie your kind letter & valuable things came Safe to hand last night. I was so glad to hear from you & I expected that you would send me a par pants & socks but did not expect the blanket nor coat I kneeded a blanket & bought me a coverlet nicest sort for 7.0 dollars. I also bought (or swapped) for a par of socks gave a dollar to boot & also gave for a pare of boots for Dan 25 dollars his old shoes were worn out entirely, my boots are hard by soiled. So you may see that we are very well fised up I gave the coat you sent me to Dan we are getting fised up to house keeping verry well. I had for dinner ham best kind bacon sweet & Irish potatoes biskits & corn bread. There plenty of bacon sometimes beef from the Commissary I settled with the Comsry today for the month Sept my bill was 7.50 dollars. Oct I do not expect will be so mutch for we were in Ky & half the time half Rations. I settled Pikes & Persons Bill all in the some myself all the same. Since the 1st Nov I have been to myself & have not bought of Comsy but little had had more bought in the County & in fact have lived better & done better than ever I have since I have been in camps. I had rather do as I am doing & not make a cent for Dans hire than to have as myself & get 20 dollars per month he makes enough to fed us and the horse easly, he paid half for his boots, Bale Pike was elected Lt today. I am afraid he will be rejected he is a poor chance but nearly as good as is in the Co. Bill Camp was 5 Sargt or Commissary of the Co. he will do I have 41 men with me only one sick (Gaylon) You speak of the sickness in the cattle I think it is Smut in the field, when I am there I have it every bit pulled & stamped to peases & my cattle never die with it, It may be some thing else, but I doubt it. The negroes will not pull it when I am there unless I watch them.

P2

I have turned over the last drop of ink I had. I think you had better buy nails & fix James a house. I would not build it to close better move the house when we kneed it, but you and him for that. Well I have borrowed some ink but I look for someone to knock it over as J Pike Cooly Thackerson Garrott & 8 others in all have just come to camp. All say that they are only tolerable well Pike looks poorly Lt. Landers came with Capt McBee to join the Co. together with 3 others. As to Tom Estice taking the old plank he never did it when I was there nor would he have taken it had I been there but let it go & if any of them claim the old house tell James to move it out of there & if for nothing else make firewood of it. Do not let Halls man nor Duke, nor no one else have it if you give up the house old Toms, one of them will claim the patch also as to my comming home & directing that is out of the question. I have never doubted not for one minute your loving me no never, but my dear believe me, I will come home every chance I get on honorable & fair turn is as to love & love letters this is no time for that, these are the days that tries mens soul, I do not envy J Palmer his happings he has ruined himself in the Company & has betrayed the trust reposed in him, No my dear one is I do not get to stay at home until I get it on the terms that he & Jim Graham has. I will be here when the war is over he P stood the chance to be Lt. But he but he did not come & the men kneeded the things . I have ordered him to camps immediately & if he does not come I shall have to Report him (it my painful duty what they pay me for) I have to be faithful & true I screen no man I am pd. 130 dollars per month & as a good soldier I set my face as a flint & endure hardships I can say in truth that I believe I am a good Captain & will eventually be as well beliked as any Capt in the Regt. By my own men especially . I am as strict & tight as Dicks hat band &

come as nite seeing every thing as well as ever I have frequent applications to get transferd to my Co. as to the size of the house, suit yourselves. I am verry sorry you get so low down, would to God that I could be with you or could cheer you up may God give us grace sufficient for our day. I know J P does wrong, you say you cannot git wool, lots of solders with cotton clothes on & scarcely any shoes & the branch frooze over all day but does not seem very cold. I think if you have not sowed wheat yet you had better have it scratched in the days are short & the dampness will rise enough to sprout it & I had rather have it scratched in dust than rolled in mud. I am sorry you have to give so mutch for salt & cant get it at that, but maybe that those law's and works will do something better. God save us all . I am sorry you are so hard run about meat, I do not think you kneed be afraid of of beef. Dick is with us he says he writes every chance so do I & now I tell you, You kneed not expect me to write so often as I used to, but will every chance & my Dear one do not go crazy about me, for if I die it would do no good, but I yet believe that I shall yet live to see the S Confederacy Shine fourth in all its glory & we meet in peace around the old fire place with our children & servants to praise God who is the author & furnisher of our. My Dear one still pray for peace & especially for one who has chare of 112 men (of all sorts) who feels incompetent of the task, tell the church to pray for me, that I may hold fast to the profession I have maid & not fall a victim to temptation & to satin give them all my love, tell them not to be discouraged in this the hour of our countrys trial but trust in God who will give us victory & peace the darkest hour is just before the breaking of the day & then Oh then burst forth the morning sun (So mode it be SCK)

P3 WRITTEN BETWEEN LINES OF P2

PS I have not answered all the points in your letter but it is night & you & I must do the best you can & it will be all right with me S C Kelly

December 1862

Camp near Manchester Tenn Dec 3rd 1862

.03 P1

My Dear Amie I have been thinking for several days that I would write you but the weather has been cold & I was very badly crowded in tent & Capt McBee was here & I in the time got a permit for 24 hours to go out to Mr Millers. I ran over my time one day but all went off well. I found them all well except Sims he is not well but able to be up he has been a prisoner but is now exchanged & his Regt. Disbanded & Reorganized. He has not rejoined the Army I insisted on him to come & see us & join my Company for I thought that I could give him a Luminance (as I am confident that I have not a man that will stand the examination) he says that he cannot stand the infantry service, but promised to come & see me Old J L was just as ust to be, I found his wife a pritty woman, nice & cleaver was well treated by the whole family, Kitty is as large as Dice & is a nice girl Newt & Ben are little towheads between the size of virgle & Billy I thought of going on the train but it was 12 miles back to Tullahoma & only 28 by the Road, So I did not know what train,

P2

So I concluded to ride my soar back horse, I left Manchester at about 10 Oclock AM & arrived there about ½ past 4 PM after kicking over the roughest kind of Road I spent the time verry pleasantly but it was so short the people are in a Strain in this country. Miller is speaking of going to Ala. He says if he stays & our Army falls back that the Yanks will take all he has & likely abuse & insult his family steal all his negroes or set them free among them to walk about & claim to be lords of the land, where as on the other hand if he goes to Ala his negroes with wives from home will run away & he looses them but he thinks that he had better save something than nothing, they cannot carry off his land & if they do Confiscate it when we will have gained our independence that will return all the property found, he is of the opinion that he can ship enough meat & bread to do them one year by hiring out all but the little ones he will have to leave all his furniture, but better live in a cabbin without any than have nothing at all in his old age he says he is too old to plough he askes me my opinion & at first I told him to stay

P3

& after we had talked it over & he gave his views I am of the opinion that he

had best move he had written to Gladden & G told him that he had a plenty of land & houses &, but Miller does not want to plant a crop but hire out you might ask what will he do with his corn &C Sell it to the Army at a high price the Government has pressed all the surplus took in the whole county only leaving enough for home use, Miller says he thinks he would like our country, Albert is in the service . My Dear I wish I had some good news to write you we have a powerful Army about Murphreysborough & a big fight expected, we are about 30 miles South, in order to head them if they were to attempt to flank us, we are on a line of battle (on the extreme left) 14 miles long Regt after Regt & Brigade after Brigade, Stevensons whole Division, held as a Reserve. We may stay here all winter, or we may move any hour they are skirmishing nearly every day, but we can find out but little, we have but 3 tents to the Co, but expect more as soon as the coms can come to Manchester (this is an arm) but the Yanks burnt the bridges & they are

Repairing.

P4

I sowed two blankets together & made me one. I & the Pikes are entitled to one to one of the three but if we take it, we have either to take in men or let them stay out in the rain, & I must shelter Dan, or a white man for one will take up as mutch room as the other so it is a hard case either way, for Dan to be pushed out that will not do & for him to stay in a tent & a white man out that is not fair, So I gave up the tents & furnished my own & cook &

eat & sleep to our selves, I fair mutch better to ourselves but I have to sleep with Dan, I do mot like that mutch but I had rather sleep with him than with a lousey white man, I can keep clean of lice by doing this way, but it looks shelfish, I have a card on my tent, don't lay in my tent the men are getting boards today to build a shelter, Dan is gone to town I have a notion to make Rails & build me a house, I can do it there is lots of good timber here & plenty of water, it has cleared off but yesterday & last night, no use talking, but Blanket tent did not last.

4th 1 ½ Oclock PM Mn D A fully intended to send this yesterday but the thing is verry irregular yet & the p mail was gone before I knew it nor do I know when this will get off, Dear one do not be disappointed if you do not get letters for I tell you there is so many thousands of letters in the mail is that

P5

They (I believe) destroy them, I think some times that I aut to get more letters but when I hear men say that they have not Rec a letter in 2 or 3 months I think I aut to be thankful of sutch, I do not blame you nor do I want you to blame me, for I know that I have an interest in you and your prayers, the last letter I Rec McBee brought me dated 18 & 19th Nov this is the 4th 15 days & may be 5 more, but I still look on, I know you write & I know some of them will come, the more we write the more we will Rec in proportion, So you must not get out of heart but hop on, hope ever, pray or pray ever trusting in God who has sustained us this far through dangers seen & unseen to us & who is able (in his own time) to bring these troubles to an end &us together as a family, to praise him, from whom all be leaving flow, I was verry mutch disappointed when I Retd from Millers & McBee gone, I intended to send several mens money home by him I have it in my hand & do not want to keep it, if I were to loose it , they would want me to pay it out of my effects at home & that would hurt, I have 5 or 6 hundred & could have drawn 3 or 4 hundred of my own wages & sent it all, but alass he could not wait, Miller proposed to loan me any amount had

P6

I wanted but I told him all about it, he said that I was not like the most officers, I said that I could not spend it, unless I was Stationed & buy every thing I buy every thing I kneed, but do not want to waste it, I want to & must pay my debts whether anyone pays me or not, Dan makes enough to keep us in anything we can get to eat (at the highest kind of prices) besides flour bacon & beef, which we get at the Commissary, & have something near 100 dollars of my own money yet, every thing is high green apples sell at 7 & 8 dollars per bushel & the speculation (Dan & 2 or three others in my Co) buy at that & sell at 50 cts per dozen, plate pies (the size of our tin oblate) Sell at 50 cts as fast as Dan can hand them out & make the change, Dried fruit at 25 cts per qt, I have Dan cooking some of those you sent me he is going to make pies, & after what we want he will sell the rest, I had mutch rather have peaches, I have not been out of fruit in a month every thing else in proportion, but I say My Dear I have never had any fruit as nice as that you sent me, it is it is pealed & the cores left out, Sam Penlands wife sent him some & some butter & he is not with us, so I have kept it more than a week & have no Idea that he will come soon, So I have a motion to confiscate the whole bag, I found some papers in a little sack, whitch

P7

had I known were there I would have had out smoking, I have quit smoking except When I am bound in my bowels, or have the toothache, which I have had ever since last night, It did not hurt me but had a many a time & I concluded that I would have the nerve killed, it has quit hurting & I hope the bad times is over, I am sorry I had that one pulled at home, & if I were to get where I can I will have another put in, the place, the gum is sore yet, & it so mutch in the way eating, J Pike had got well enough for duty & Bale Pike is acting today as Officer of the Guard, I was Officer of the Day yesterday, our Regt has undergoing a considerable change, May Smith to Lt Coln, Capt Dr Mw, C Patterson to Major (he is a clever man but no Officer) (more than I can say for Lt Coln

Smith) he is a verry poor Officer, Capt Francis was verry mutch disappointed, H Oden is Capt & 2 others junior to me, we have changed places in the Regt according to Rank, but not change our latter, I am 2 on the left wing, Anderson left, I am glad to get out of the center, I am anxious to know whether James had come & whether he has build a house or rented, he aut to be in the Army one day & see what men can do we can make with out either saw, wedge, or foot, split them with an axe, but we had some braces made today & will carry them with us, 300 hundred 4 foot boards will cover a good big house & I have a plenty of the verry best timber in the bottom while oak on the side,

P8

we are getting better fixed we_furnished one axe (in my Co) & 2 draw 2 more, so you see we have 3 axes if I had 6 & 2 iron wedges & 3 spades & 2 mattocks we could build Shantys every where we stopped a week, I do not want to encourage stealing but the Army <u>hords</u> every thing else & I thought that it was no harm to take an axe & if I had the chance I would finds 2 more & when we moved we would carry them with as guns, for if we put them in the waggons they steal them, I am trying a new send 5th all well & sleeting

God bless good bie

Yours affectionately S C Kelly

DEC 6TH 1862 5 OCLOCK AM
CAMP NEAR MANCHESTER TENN

.06 P1

My Dear one I just started a letter day before yesterday, I believe but I under stood that we would leave here in the morning (I do not know where for) & Johnson was going home so I concluded that I would write to let you know that I & Dan are well & hope we may stay as well as we have been since we left Lenors Station, nothing worse than toothache has aided us, Yesterday was a bad day on the soldiers it snowed until noon with the winds high & after that the smoke, the smoke, but we have no fire to black us, if we had I do not know how black we would get, for my word for it I cannot keep clean, not even my hands I have been up 2 hours built a good fire warmed water washed clean as I could (but it froze to my beard) washed feet changed clothes from head to foot except vest & coat, got on my new pants & am well pleased, I made Dan follow suit, he blowed & shivered mightly, but I make him change every time I do, & no excuses, he is now getting breakfast, bisquets & sausage, which an old acquaintances of my Father gave him, & after breakfast

P2

he is going to the country to wash, preparatory to the anticipated move, my hands so cold that I can hardly write, I am sitting in my tent writing on a box, with a good fire at my back & candle stuck in front of me by running tallow on the base & sticking it to it, it is about out & I must get another, I said at Mr Millers that I had been trying to buy candles but could not, So Mr M would give me six when I insisted on not taking but two, I must close now for Dan has summonsds me to breakfast, it is not day yet,Day light left over when we get up this morning the moon was in eclips nearly total, I must quit again & have the Roll Called, So my time goes, always busy, I have to write nearly all day making descriptive list of all the men in the Co,, Well now my Dear I have sorty gotten through my morning duties & will say that I confiscated S Penlands butter to help out my breakfast, he had some dried fruit also, I think I shall sell it, I have just Rec & Red your letter, it came by hand May Allen of Talladega, I was glad to get it, being the frst since the 18 & 19th Nov I was glad to hear that all were well, I could not read it without tears filling my eyes so full that I bearely could see to read I do thank God for sutch a wife, for one who depends on him

P3

the creator & finisher of our faith oh that we could trust wholely upon him oh for the blessedness that once I knew oh that I could serve him more & better, Oh for a moment to praise my God, a heart from sin set force Prey on hope an, prey for me for I acknowledge that I am to often forgetful of my Strong tower of my Back of my heding places who is the Christ the Son of the living God, I think you are Right about the preacher if it is the money & that only let him go where he can get it we always pay & pay enough without paying a part of the bad Subscription, Either of the others will Preach for 100 dollars & maybe that Bro S is not the man as to those men at home, that is what some of them were working for, they went to Atlanta & Small Pox was there & they got furloughed home, they will be like the old man was, when the old woman killed the bear as to Palmer I guess I have stured him up by now, I have got all you sent, as I wrote before I do not Kneed anything now, in your line, I am glad that James is going to build, mutch the least trouble in the course of one year, I think I will send you some money but I do not know whether Johnson is going yet, he is going to get

P4

shoes blankets & all for the Regt I am verry Sorry you are so hard run if you kneed any money borrow it I can pay it soon, the Smoke is so bad, I have moved 8 or 9 times & now I have settled the fire & put it out the sun shine pleasant but the snow melts slowly I know that there is no credit on Pendersons notes & I owe him for brick & work , consequently the kneed of a Settlement, I know a woman or either me is a poor hand to collect sutch debts, do not make any more of the same sort

H Foster Says he paid his R & Baggin debt, but I think after all credits with the 2 dollars he pd Turk he owes us 540 dollars he I guess is at home, I had Rather

B Bridges had gone any where than to my Co, I already too many like him (Shinkers) Old Billy Thackerson wrote to me to join (as a Subst) my Co, I wrote him I did not want him, that one of those long names was enough in a Co, Since I wrote the above J T told me that old Billy was in Hospital at Lagrange Ga with Rheumatism guessed Right, I am glad you have not the power to make peace fear you are to anxious, it is for you & your wrights & our children, that I am fighting, but for me I could live my time out in a free negrow Republic, but the wives Sisters mothers & daughters of Soldiers, make them endure hardships & psirvations, God will give us peace in his own appointed time, I hope you have your Room covered & when you are in your cabin & it Raining or Snowing, do not think that the Soldiers cannot stand it, not so all dangers are not deaths,& although I am under a blanket tent, I Sleep warm eat hearty, laugh at trifles & by the buy the time flies Swiftly Round,

P5

Now my Dear one do not tease me about coming home you know that I love you dearly & you may know from henceforth & forever that I love you too well to disgrace myself you & our children by coming home on a flimsey excuse, I thank God that he has Supported me thus far & has given me health & Strength to undergo what a many a man has fallen under I will come every fair chance but I do despise a Shinker so bad, that I think I shall be pretty mean crazy before I Shink, as to Capt McBee he is not fit to be a corporal, as to my men minding it those with me are the Sort to do there duty & they do mind it & talk hard of every one Palmer could not be elected corporal in the Co all say he is a pulk & C you must learn to enjoy yourself & make home, home without me, for I tell you again I have no idea when I ever will be at home, but I yet think that I will live this war through & see you & yours at home, after we are a nation Do not get out of heart but cheer up, cher up, brighter & better days coming, & I hope soon, I know I do not write as often as I use to, but not because I love you less but my duties are more & my facilities less & I am not near marched down I donot know how mutch men can endure I may get killed in battle but I have never had any forebodings in that way I think that we will get tents soon & we will have more waggons to transport what we have, the government is doing all it

P6

Can to Supply, it is poor in sutch things, cut off from the worlds trade, but it has done10 times as mutch as the world thought it could do, That blustery night, will do I Recollect it I got up at 12 oclock when the tent was so crowded that we or larger portion had to stand up, I never Slept any more until about 10 oclock next night, I can get up any time, or set up to any reasonable time & not feel the Slightest inconvenience I am glad that you feel like your lot was in pleasant places, So you have kneed, but every sweet has its bitter, & every bitter its sweet, but Stand fast in the hope, & having done all, Stand clothed upon the _____ of Christ, I am Satisfied that you are in _____ & would make living with ½ a chance, They were fighting out beyond Murfhreysbrough (as you heard) Thursday week they Run our cavalry in, but the infantry fell upon them & run them back 7 miles killing about 40, so Capt says I would take a paper & not be dependant I Suppose, Sutliff (an old aquantance of ours) has brought out Bryan he was as poor as Duke when we left Tenn< Lots of Tennesseeans will be poring into Alas I must close for I am So cold that I cannot write I Doubt your tiring me down, talking I am a talker & can sleep or let it alone, eat or let it alone talk or not write or not, under all circumstances do the best I know God bless good bie S C Kelly

DEC 10TH 62
CAMP 30TH ALA BARTONS BRIG NEAR READYVILLE TENN

.10 Pl

(Missing some pages)

Dear Amie I have nothing of interest to write but that I & Dan are well & have been all the trip, I wrote to you by (as I thought Johnson) but found out that he was going by montgomery & Selma, & M Runnally was going direct home so I sent the letter by him, that letter was written a day or probably 2 days before I sent it I expected P to go but he did not get off & the day before I sent it (Saturday) it Snowed all day & that morning I sent it (Sunday), I had no time, but would have had nothing to have added except that we were well & that it was verry cold & we were going to move immediately & I sent some money home by Johnson that belonged to Soldiers in my Co who were not up with us, the money I aut to have sent by McBee I sent you

Two hundred dollars, one of which you must pay to Harvey Briddes & take the Rest the other ten I paid for him, for the mule he bt in Kentucky Your money may be left at Jacksonville with Judge Wood that is where he will leave the balance, I had that money on hand & did not want to keep it, So I thought best to send to you & when they came up I could draw from qr Master on my wages & pay them back I have 105 dollars yet but I owe J Palmer 83 or 5 out of that There is now about 400 dollars Due me for Services Rendered as Capt which I can get (or borrow) at any time I have bought lots of little trickes & conveniences Since I have had my horse mutch as I could not carry with out him, I lost 30 or 40 dollars

P2

In Rec & Paying out the money to the company I rec 7707 dollars & in making change (Supposed) gave them sometimes 2 bills stuck together, It was all new & packed up straight & stuck together as close as wafers, My Dear do not sell the cotton at any price, for I think that we can get money enough to pay our debts as fast as they want them Pd & If you had the money for the cotton it would (I think) at 20 cts leave you a Surplus of from 6 to 9 hundred dollars & my wages coming in (or a portion) every 3 months besides what is owing to me (Some of whitch) will be paid this winter, will keep you in money while there is an influx of money & a deprecation of the it, every one is lite I am. Want to pay their debts while money is plenty at the same time, I know that it takes lots of money to buy every thing you are oblige to have If you Kneed any money borrow it for a short time, cant you get David Weaver to get you some Salt, I saw a letter from him, he said that the Salt Co that he & Gladden & Draper were in would make their Salt clear by that I suppose they will have some to Sell, You & James for that, between you You must do for the interest of the family as though I were dead, for I am so far off & know so little about what is going on there & little communication is so uncertain & I have my hands & head full of other business & So I say act for yourself & at all times I am ready to Render you any assistance I can in the way of advice, but you are not bound to take it, it is (in your judgement) you act otherwise all wright with me

P3

12 oclock noon Well Dear one I have written all the paper that I thought I could have news to fell, but as you are So fond of long letters & they verry often, I will Scribble on more & tell you now it will not be worth the paper besides the trouble writing mailing & paying postage, yet nevertheless I have at this time nothing else to do, & nothing would give me more Satisfaction than to talk with you, if but fore one hour, & as I am deprived of that Satisfaction (voluntarily) I will give you first a description of out last march &C&C We left Manchester 8 ½ oclock am on Sunday morning, ground frose & covered with Snow verry cold but the Sun Shining the Snow did not melt but verry little all day except in the Road & fair places to the Sun, the Road Slick as ice & Several men crippled themselves by falling, at 10 or 12 oclock the Road got Sloppy & about 2 or 3 commensed freezing again, we Struck camp about 4 in a piece of wood land where the Snow had not melted at all it was 5 or 6 inches deep, we cut wood built fires Raked away the Snow eat hearty Slept well, got up early & Resumed our journey to this place whitch is 24 miles from Manchester N. W. & 12 miles from Murphreysborough, the 2ond day was warmer & yesterday Still warmer & today quite pleasant, the Snow is about all gone I do not know how long we will Stay here, nor where we will go, We heared that Morgan had a fight & took 1,500 hundred

P4

Well the 1ˢᵗ days march, Dan Rode about 3 miles in the morning & then I Rode to camps except a mile or So that I let Andy Brown Ride who was Sick then Dan took him & went foriging (as we call it) he got into qrs about dark with corn enough to feed (Snukes) night & morning four hens a bushel of Sweet potatoes & a qrt of Molasses, the potatoes Sold like hot cakes at the Rate of 3 dollars per bush, but the hens no go, for there was no Salt, no lard not been in 3 or 4 days drawn all out & none to get (nor have we drawn any yet) So he had about enough to Salt one (whitch he got for that purpose) he cleaned all of them cut them up in his bole put the Salt upon them went to bed about 10 oclock, got up in the morning at 3 & commensed cooking & by good day light had all done & breakfast eat, the most fried chicken I have Seen in the army he had fried it in bacon greese & I tell you it was good, but the peases So large not well done, I got as many livers & gizzards knecks &heads & feet as I wanted, he commensed Selling it out by the qrs worth & Soon Sold out all we would Spear at the Rates of one dollar per chicken we had enough to do for dinner next day & that night he bought 6 whitch he Sold for 50 cts apiece quick (they were Small Size to fry) last night he got butter & Molasses , and a Sholder of fresh pork he also day before yesterday gave one dollar for a pt of Salt whitch Salted every thing & the Sholder of meat, gave 12 ½ cts for it, he generally Sells off enough to pay for purchase & make what we

P5

and what the horse eats & Some times a few dimes besides, I have to feed my own horse, the Regulations does not Say that I Shall not have one, but it does not feed horses belonging to officers of the line (from Maj down) he is a Splendid Riding horse but poor & his back has been verry Sore but nearly well now & he is mending up fast as I ever Saw, I get him 30 years of corn per day Sometimes in Shuck & no fodder) whitch cost 25 to 50 cts I thought of Sending him home, but not until I am not allowed to keep him, I would not have walked the other days for 5 dollars per day, besides other advantages Dan has gone foraging now I give him a pass & he can pass the picketts any where or time he does not like to go ahead he is afraid of being captured, he has got to Ritch to wash, he hires our washing, he has a bad chance to wash, So few vessels, I hope I may always get along as well as I am doing now but I doubt it, if we go toward Murphreysborough there is So many Soldiers there, I was in hopes we would go close to Millers, it is about 20 miles, a little too far to go often, I think if we

Stay here long that I will go out there if I can get off but times is pretty Squally now, we keep out a heavy pickett all the time about 1 & a ½ Companies from each Regt, there is Round & about here 5 or 6 Brigades (Stevensons Division) (& of Smiths Corpse) & at Murphreysborough Braggs & Shelvyville Brickenridges, I Suppose that Gen JE Johnson has come to take the Command of the whole, I am hungry & Dan has not come back & I broke the christal out of my watch night before last

P6

So you See my codition &under Sutch circumstances I Shall verry Soon be compelled to close this long letter all about nothing at all, I expect to have to go on pickett this evening Lt Pike is out now with 14 of our Co I have with me 47 men & the 2 Pikes & myself make 50 out of that no 5 are Reported unable for duty 2 of whitch fell down & hurt themselves, (one bad) I think they will be well in a few days, the others not mutch Sick (Riley Cooly one) I left 4 at Manchester barefooted, there was 95 out of the Regt in the Same fix my Co are as well provided for clothes as any, I believe better, I have a good Co & pretty well broke & One of the largest in the Regt, I will quit, more after a while, Well no dinner yet, I put my watch in my pocket christal out & in rotting about I broke it, I went in to the 40 Ga Regt where I understood was a workman but he like many others had gone home, not deserted as you might Suppose, not mutch of that, I had my tooth plugged yesterday I think it will do well, Still it is Soar & now my Dear Amie I believe I have told you all I know unless I could see you, I Saw you last night in a dream you were as familiar & noble as ever I Saw you in your characteristic noble wommanly bearing &C I am in hopes that by Some hook or crook or Something else that I will get to come home Soon, I do not know how but honorably for whitch I keep my Senses I do not intend to come home any other way, I have dreamed about you two night in Succession, do not be disappointed if I Should not come I may not come in 12 months the Lord in whome I trust only knows, We may Stay here 1 day or we may Stay longer who knows, Direct your letters to, Capt S. C.

Kelly Co (E) 30th Ala Regt Bartons Brig Manchester Tenn, I am Waiting on my trunk because of this _____ _____ being dirty, May God direct us in the way we Should go & our Rulers in the management of our National affairs & bring peace out confusion SCK

DEC 12TH 1862
CAMP SHELLY 30TH REGT ALA VOLS BENTONS BRIG READYVILLE TENN

P1

My Dear Amie I have written you 2 days ago a long letter, put it in the bag & this morning it had not gone, we have no mail communications here I do not know why, I am expecting a letter from you when we get a mail, I still wait I know you write but the many thousands of letters fill every thing to overflowing, I think I am quite lucky about getting letters I still expect to get while you can write & there is mailes to carry them , we are in the same place yet except we had to move about one hundred yds to square out the camp & arrange the companies fires& I am yet well so is Dan he is a big eater& I am afraid he eates to mutch sometimes, I have nothing to write except that we are getting along verry well, John Hendrix was to see me yesterday he is well & is qr master of his Battalion it is equal in Rank of Capt & gets 10 dollars per month more, He says that he had Rather be Lt or Capt, he has more writing to do & more Responsibility, but he has a horse to Ride & he brought his negrow back with him he passed our house, but Said it was in the night late & could not stop without loosing a day, he is camped about 4 miles of here, on the <u>Lavern</u> Road, I do not know what else to say, Yes we hear cannonading nearly every day, Yesterday we heard about 20 guns, we have not heard any today, the enemy is at Lavern & beyond, which is 12 miles north or NE of Murphreysborough, The boys guess that we are going to leave in a few days

P2

Because we have got ever thing cleaned up & got to drilling

Coln Shelly drilled yesterday, he is laid up today, he had a conjestive chill 4 night ago , I fear he will fail if so we are gone up Spout as the saying is, there was one man died on guard post this morning in our Regt he ate a hearty breakfast & went on post (Camp guard} & when the Relief guard came Round they saw him fall & he died in a few moments, Supposed had conjestion, My informant was an aquaintance of his & I suppose it correct, the man is dead for there was a detail to dig the grave, we are fiscing up for rain or snow the men some of them are making Sedar boards, we have burnt Sedar nearly all together, Since we been here, it makes a hot fire, but we got an order this morning not to cut any more Sedar, There is lots go good wood close here now but if we stay here a few days longer it will get scarce, Some of the men are building chimneys to their tents I have not done any thing of the kind, I & the 2 Pikes have taken one of the tents & 2 other men join in with us & we all warm & cook by the same fire, We are getting pretty well clean of lice I have not had any in some time, but the men have so little chance to wash that it almost amounts to an impossibility to get rid of them, I searched diligently today & had I found one I should have killed him Shure, We drew Salt yesterday I do not see why we did not get along (better) swell as when we get salt, the way they do they put the beef on to cook & then throw in the Salt, the Sop is as Salt as brine &

P3

    meat fresh & not infrequently Raw, So the thirst for water is insaliable & the Disentary (or indigestion) Sure to follow While without Salt they do not drink so much water & dry there beef & thin fry it in the bacon greecc &does fine, I am Satisfied that people at home use more salt than is actually necessary for health, I know whin I was at home that the vitals were saltyer than I liked besides the whole Army more or less is afficted with

    scurvy & fresh beef is the idea for that, I believe I have written all that I can Recall of now for I have written this is the 3rd letter since this day week, Oh that I could see you & be permitted to stay with you if but for one year or one month or even for one week I could tell you all about many things that I can not write or I forget or in my judgment not worthy writing better days coming & I hope soon May God enable us peace prosperity & plenty & that he will enable us to win the prize of our independence & that Speedely So Mote it be

Dec 13th 9 oclock am My Dear I have not had a chance yet to get off my letters & this morning drew mine from the mail I now have a chance to Send it by (unckle) bob as we call him, who belongs to Capt Burr of St Clair Co, he will pass by our place on the Stage going home or furlough as he calls it, I have nothing to add except that I would like very well to carry them myself, We are Required to stay in camps & have Roll Call every ½ hour today Coln Shelby is to unwell to drill today, I fear we will have to do without his services a while at least

P4

Lt Coln Smith is at home & May Patteson is behind with the Barefooted crowd at Manchester So the command of the Regt, if Shelby fails will desolve on Capt Francis

(I fear it will make the Big head Strike in on him & kill him, if not it will most) he is actually the best chance after Shelby in the Regt, I have been expecting it to rain since last night it is warm & cloudy with, wind high, Smoke quite disagreeable

4 Oclock PM 13th well Amie (D) we have just Ret off of what is turmed a Brigade drill, Gen Benton was on the field with his aides we preformed about the same evolutions that we do on Reggimental drill but the order proceeds from the General through or by his aids who carry it to each Coln on horse back to each Coln an aid or order bearer, We have more time to Rest than when on Reggemental parade, It is something new to us, We have been in Sutch a Skedaddling position since we have been in the Army, that this is the first Brigade drill, The General sent word to the Coln & he was able today to announce to his men that President Davis would visit our camps tomorrow, I hope it may be so I would like to see the old veteran Soldier & Christian, I must

wash & brush up & put on my best for the Rea & more because it is Sunday & I am officer of the day tomorrow, I had Dan build him a Shanty out of a blanket for himself, I had us live sleep with a horse, he twists & turns & throws his arms about so bad, Still he is clean & clean of lice, I make him wash & keep clean, Dan is a good boy but I fear he will not be any account if he should live to get through the war, he will get in sutch a lazy idling habit, he is pert & is well beliked in the Co, I shall have me a bedstead put up in the tent ore ½ of it & sleep to myself, we have 7 or8 blankets & covers between us & when we stop a day or so draw straw, I wish that I had my bed tick it would be quite the trick, but I guess I will make out without it, Reckon Shurly Palmer will leave before you get this if he started the 10 I shall look for him in 4 or 5 more days but the__ __h ills he has may him yet another month that is all the hope I have now of a letter soon, it is not rained yet but still warm & cloudy it will come soon, May God who is Ritch in means have mercy on us & keep us & guide us & bring us all home in peace is my prayer Good bie Yours SC Kelly

DEC 14TH 5 OCLOCK AM SAME PLACE

.14 Pl

My Dearest Amie I had just commenced my breakfast when a Sargt handed me 3 letters one from you whitch I now proceed to insure was not brought by Palmer but by Some other means I took a chill I gasped & is at home today, I am in hopes you Rec mine by Nunnaly before this time, it will Show where I am & c I try to be thankful, that we were all well at the time of your writing, It was verry cold but you will see that we made out better than one in a house would expect I am Sorry verry Sorry that James cannot live with you I do not know where you will get a man that will do, they are so verry scarce I have no one in view, Suppose you & Barney try it, without you know that you get a man that will do, no man with more than one family will not do, Still trust in the Lord & all will be Right as to Jim, G,I have no power over him no more than any other officer, he was transferred from our Co &

Regt to the 31ˢᵗ Regt & then they assigned him to the hospital, be careful of his money & him, the Devil will have his Due, in the day of accounts H Steel is already ordered back by me & you can tell it in the neighborhood , that I Said I had ordered him to Report at Knoxville where he could be exchanged, & that I said that if they die not mind some of them would be Shot for laying out as some of them were doing as to Bowman every body knows that I am not Smart, but at the same time know that he is a fool he had better Ret immediately I do not hate the fool, if I do it is because he is a fool

P2

God knows my heart I do not hate him, but he hates me because I compelled him to do his duty he wants to do as he done when he went home, as he pleased, & that will not do a Soldier, he must have no will of his own, but to do the will of his Superiors, I think that & get along as well with my Co as any Capt in the Regt & I know that 9 months ago that I was unpopular not care one cent for that I intend to do my Duty & make all the Rest do likewise I ask no odds, I grant no favors not more to one than another I think the Some times that you urge me to mutch about coming home I want to come, but not bad enough to do so as Some others have, bear it &the time will come when I will come home, Into the hands of the living God have I Committed myself & you and all we have & are, it is guard morning & I must go I do not know what to say about Billy except he had better go to School you must determine that, I am glad you can get cands, I believe I would get 2 pair how many bags of cotton have you to put up will there be any cotton to gin & Co I look for Arheart & Some others & Some others I do not look for at all until they are compelled to come, It is the General opinion that there will be a big fight here for the Yanks are fortified & will not come out to attack & we will not attack them in turn, If you can get

Salt & I hope you can I think best you kill the Steer, you can

Sell it if you do not kneed it you have never said whether you Sold any wheat or had any to Sell, will you kneed all the corn &

fodder, will you have meat enough, I must close God bless us all & Send us peace on honorable terms is the prayer of one who loves you Dearly good bie SCK

DECEMBER 14TH 1862

.14

> *(Transfer was written on back of letter dated Feb. 3rd 1862)*
> I hereby consent to the transfer of private W____ Mc Dill of Company ____teth Regt
> Ala Vols to my _____ _____ Regt, I have in my company two brothers of said ____ ____Dill

Camp Beulah, near Mobile Ala	Bush __orces
December 14th 1862	Captain Co. L 18th Regt

Ala Vols.
Approved
R G Jnze
St Col Crndy 18 Ala Regt

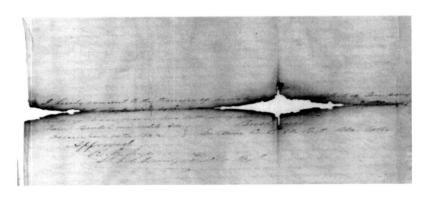

DECEMBER16TH 1862
CAMP SHELLY 30TH ALA NEAR READYVILLY TENN

.16 Pl

My Dear Amie I started you a verry long letter or Rather 3 letters day before yesterday, but I have a chance to send you another So I write, we are all well except 4 in the Co who are

Reported Sick none of them bad J Palmer Ret day before yesterday evening, he tells a different tale to what Capt McBee as he terms himself told, we all took it for granted that he was not mutch sick & I wrote him (Palmer) a pretty sharp Letter, Still McBee said that P told him to excuse the matter with me, I find out of P, that McBee did send him (P) word after he got home, not to start back before 25th Dec, it seems to me, that McB wanted (P) to get in a scrape, for he knew that I was disappointed in Ps not coming back, So I was & it all grew out of what McBee said, We could hear all the time that Bought ((Franciss man) was sick, but no one believed from what McBee said that P was sick enough to stay & C If that will give Satisfaction well if not I have no apology to make, I have nothing of interest to write J P told us all about the Bogus money _____ Surprised at some folks, Some I am sorry for ____ Some I am not surprised nor not sorry God send how _____ that they may get their just deserts, tell virgil that I got his present (the Little p of corney yarn) he sent me, God bless the children, where there is little, but little en____led, & the widow gave as mutch as any

P2

Our Co is out today on Camp guard & pickett 14 So it will leave but a small co here I expect that you had better get Ivy, from what Palmer says I do wish that will do well in getting some one but I cannot tell who will do or not, I thought Turk was the verry man, but we see that we were deceived he will not do only for himself, I think that he aut to have made the Shoes, to make up some of his lost time, Let it go, The Devil will get his dues if you never Frank Rountree Sends 35 dollars to his Father min this letter you will send him word & let hi9m come & get it, I will close Dan Sends some Yanke Shinplasters got at the Gap, May God bless all whome we should pray for write often if I get them well if not not mutch lost

Your Own

Sam

CAMP NEAR READYVILLE DEC 19ᵀᴴ 1862 AM

.19 P1

My Dear Amie I do not have time or next day to write I now embrace this opportunity, We are going to Start to Mississippi tomorrow we will march from here to Murphreysborough & then take the cars, I am afraid that we will have a time of it, I want to go by Mr Millers but I fear I shall not have the chance, I am mighty troubled about what to do with Dan & the horse but I have concluded to send him home, he will bring his clothes & blankets & I expect that you had better stay keep him at home until I send you word, for I know in Reason that he will not do me mutch good in Mississippi, I am a little doubtful about Sam getting home but I will Risk him, he may fool me you must write to me _____ _____ after you get this do not let ____ ____ Stage _____ without you have a letter on it, Dearest Capt SC Kelly 30ᵗʰ Ala Tracys Brigade Selma Ala, We are put into an Ala Brigade the 20 Ala 31ˢᵗ 33ʳᵈ 46ᵗʰ & 30 all under General Tracy an Alabaman the Georg-

P2

ians in a Ga Brigade under Barton and another Brig the Tennesseians together & every State troops together, I am glad of it I think they will do better, We expect a fight but we have been hunting one a long time, I hope that (if this war is to be decided by fighting) we may get at it soon & that God will give us a victory on every field until our enemies are obliged to Sue for peace & ask pentanes for all the depredations committed since this crewel war has been going on, I think that Dan wants to go home, but I think that he also wants to come back to us again, but I do not apprehend he will be any trouble to you, I do not believe a word about the tailes told on him about his stealing he is trustly at camps & has been of great service to the Co all the men Respect him except two or three, who envy him because he has more liberties than they, John Pike loves to curse him every chance he gets when I am not present, he does not want him to cook for him at 3 dollars per month but would like to be in a mess so far

P3

As a fire is concerned , so as he can make him take up all the filth of mornings get wood carry all the water & c all these things keep in your heart, I & Palmer mess together & have our fire separate I think when Dan leaves us that I shall take a man from the Ranks to cook for me & excuse him from all other duties

4 Oclock 21rst my Dear we are at Murphreboroug & have orders to be Ready to start in one hour, We are going to Jackson Miss if you write Direct to Mobile I am well, there is lots of Soldiers about here I saw lots of our old acquaintances, Jes Ingram among them I cannot get to come by home do not be disappointed, all in the same <u>fisce</u> it would not do for all to goby & consequently none are aloud to come, I will close & leave the Rest for Dan to tell, may God bless you & all

Good bie yours affectionately SC Kelly

22nd 12 oclock noon well my dear we are on the cars about 130 miles of Murphreboroug

P4

We got up this morning at 3 am & went abord at __ it was my Co & 1 other, we were left off the 1st train & got on the 2nd with the 2nd Regt Coln <u>Bricks</u>, we got along finely until within ___ ___ miles of <u>Christiaocis</u> we exit the car my ____ ____ ____ broke into (_____ ____ one _____ we had to unload ___ ____ any where we could we _____ ____ ____ ____ the Regt ___ ____ ____ ____ we wasted total ___ ____ I was disappointed in that we ____ _____ _____ gave it out, then I Repacked to send Dan but found out that we would not start yesterday& I got on my horse & went out to Mr M & left the horse & c for him to Sell or do the best he could with him, they are all well Sims is to start today to join Co A that is at home, he also belongs to the Army, he came home last week bare footed & nearly naked, he is as mutch Kelly as Sim, I did not want to give up Dan & I thought that M could Sell him better than you

DEC 21 5 OCLOCK AM

.21

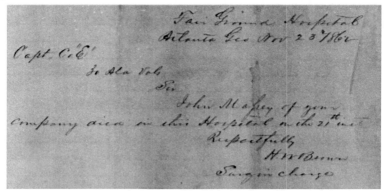

Death of John Mafrey Nov 23 1862

(On back of death notice his letter)

My D I have concluded to send my horse by may wells who lives on B Play I do not see how I can do with out Dan is here & the poorss of Soldiers he cannot get on the cars & he is glade of the chance to get him I will send one good blanket to save his back & my spurs, together with good bridle & Saddle you can fatten him up he is a good horse but badly abused

I must close God bless good bie

Yours & C   SC Kelly

PS Wells is ok with us, he was first in the notion & then out, he agreed twice to take him & as often by & I think he will be sorry yet before he gets Round on open box car, he said it would cost so mutch & I did not intend to pay his expenses

DEC 24TH 1862 11 OCLOCK AM

.24 P1

Amie Dear we arrived at 12 oclock last night, tired after being crowded on box cars, we Shifted cars got the better of it & left at break of day, we arrived at Ringold 8 oclock am this morning, we are now stopped at Dalton for a few minutes, we will pass Kingston where Wells, who I spoke of is going home, I now pause to let you know that I am well Dan also, I have several complaining in the Co, mode several sick, I have 57 men with me, all want to come by home, the balance of the Regt except the Co are gone on, I do not know when we will overtake them, but I am afraid to come by home, I could be there at 10 Oclock tonight but alass I must my Country & obey my seniors as I am obeyed nothing would do me more good, but & but & if & if, We passed lots of Government hogs in fields ____ _____ ____ _____ up evy

.24 P2

morning & hauled off to the soap & oil factory, we passed one of those Factories & the Stench was awful & hundreds of dead hogs laying around, of all the detailes I ever heard of, I think that the worst would be for me, There is lots of Small Pox here, but they say that vaxination is a shure preventative. I got my watch fixed, I am trying to write as the cars runs, I saw Old Billy Thackerson in Ringold with the Rhumatism, his arm in a sling & stick in the other hand, looks just as well as usual, I have not Rec a line from you since Palmer came, am anxious to hear, my letter I expect are at Murfreesboro but no use to me now, I hope all will work Right some day, I must close by wishing you all the blessings that God bestowes on his children, Yours Fraternally S C Kelly

Calhoun Ga 9 oclock PM all Right so far nothing worth relating within a 15 or 16 miles Kingston

ALABAMA RIVER DEC 27TH 1862 9 OCLOCK AM
ON TOP OF WALDENS RIDGE ABOUT 85 MILES S WEST OF KNOXVILLE IN THE DIRECTION OF MURFREEYSBOUROUGH (MURFREESDBORO (ON TOP OF WALDENS RIDGE ABOUT 85 MILES S WEST OF KNOXVILLE IN THE DIRECTION OF MURFREEYSBOUROUGH (MURFREESDBORO) ON BOARD THE STEAM BOAT ROBT WILSON)

.27 P1

My Dearest Amie I Suppose that you got my letter of the 20th to 24th inclusive, It left me at Kngston, We came into West Point without changing cars, arrived at that place at 4 oclock PM Christmas Day, all day we were met on Roadside by the ladies, old men, boys & negroes, amid the cheer & white hankerchiefs of them & the loud wild yells of the soldiers, Rendered more so by (the Ring of evils to our land) & whiskey, bought at the Rate of 16 dollar per gallon, I bt none I drank none, we were as the same train as the 23rd Ala, who had there share, Our Co none got drunk, but if I had laid the example, it would have been as bad as any, that night we lay over at WP & until 11 oclock yesterday, Alkahol Reigned, he had his subjects cursing swearing & even fighting in spite of military Rule, knives Pistols bricks belts & sticks

P2

all wild to carry out their findish purposes, one man lay (or fell) down on the tracks & the train Ran over him killed & mangled deplorably (So says Rumors & if it is not the case, I think & wonder that even one was killed) This was the _____ _____ of troops, Then I got Supper early & went to bed on top of the car, out of the silt & way of the drunk men who kept _____ _____ all night & rested well got up early had a nice Breakfast of Sausage fried corn bread & loaf B & C the liquor gave out & the troops, before us had poured out all that could be found in the place, we changed cars & Set out for Montgomery Ala at 11 oclock am & arrived there at the same hour PM Dark & Raining we were moist crowded than ever, I lay on top (this bad writing is caused by the shake of the boat, Some times worse than other) I put my sheep skin on top when it began to rain, I kept dry but we

P3

had a time last night in the Rain, changing from the cars to the boat We had to draw 2 days Rations & get them aboard had to leave our Sick in Hospital had to take care of all the ordinance stores of the Regt & only two Co I being the Senior officer, We lost Rily to the 25th together with 6 others all came up but Coly, We left 5 or 6 Sick at Montgomery Lt Bale Pike among them & worst of all he had like to died with <u>Desentary</u> _____

One oclock PM Dinner over & we are in about 2 hours Run of Selma, has Rained all day we have made a good exchange from cars to boat, part of our Regt went by rail to Mobile, we will take the Rail R at Selma & go to Meridian & from there to Jackson Miss, We are on a good boat good fair I pay 2 dollars extra of my transportation, had a burth, breakfast & dinner, fair good for these days, Two other boats behind us loaded with troops, I wish that I could

P4

interest you in a letter but I have nothing that I now think of Oh yes I know that you will be interested to know that I am well, I do feel like that I aut not to be so ungrateful to God the fighter of all enemies, Oh that I could praise him more & serve him better, Why Oh why am I spaired in disease & even death while many who are as good by nature & praise fall by the way Side, Surely I will be a better man hence forth, Oh that I could be a better Officer & even more efficient Service to my country, I cul my incompetence even to be Capt, Oh pray for me that I may serve my Co ____ in what so ever ____ that God in his providence may place me, but I tell you in truth that I do not seek promotion (nor do I now see any chance for it) but to be an efficient Capt, I had Rather today, be the Capt, as ever a Coln, knowing my ability, I am Capt & will do the best I can

1863 SCK Letters
Transcribed

January 1863

Four miles South of Vicksburg on Rail R January 5th 1863, 8 oclock (am) .05.06

.05 L1 P1

My Dear one I left off writing Just before we got to Selma we landed there just before dark, in the mud & as quick as possible got all on cars, we left for <u>Monoppoli</u> 10 oclk PM in full tilt & arrived at 4 oclk am 29th Dec unloaded, built fires, eat breakfast washed & by good day light were Ready to move but from Some cause we turned & it was talked about that the Sitizens were going to give us dinner& about 9 am we were turned loose to a long table Spread with vegetables of all kind (nearly) Some bacon & lots of beef we directly empyed all the dishes & they were Refilled & some of them the third time, breakfast over we sholdered arms & off to the wars again we gave the ladies three hearty cheers & went on a bord a Steamboat or the

Tom Bigby, R, we proceeded up that R 4 miles where we landed & took a horse car that Ran down to the water went quarter of a mile & got on a regular old box cars bound for Meredian (Miss) here we came up with Coln Shelly, Sick (or not well) & as ill & Snappish as an old car, there I got of him your letters sent by Johnson who I saw in Selma & told me that Shelby had them

P2

I was glad to get them, well we left the R & arrived at Meredian 9 PM, unloaded packed & Repacked our baggage at ½ past 2 oclock AM left for Jackson where we arrived at 7 am, Stopped there got lots of Sugar, I am tired around ran up & down on the cars until about 10 oclock & we let out for Vicksburg where we arrived at dark, unloaded went down to a Govment Bakers drew & eat boiled beef & homeny bread, went back to Depo put all our baggage in a house & left for line of battle 4 miles (where 5 companies of our Regt were) Coln S with us it dark & pouring down rain & had been since dark, I took out one blanket & left the rest with Dan with the commissary Sargt at Depo , we had a hard time that night , the hills steep & slick & of all the falling down I ever saw, we traveled on until 12 or 1 oclock & were completely lost, Stopped in an old field, toted Railes 3 hundred Yds built fires in the mud & Sat there & nodded (& it continued to rain) until 4 AM, where we took the back track went about one mile took the Right hand & went one mile & turned into the hills at day light because the yankes were Shellin constantly every one that passed, we Stopped until we could find out the way & while there tired as we were had to pull artillery up the hill, 25 men can pull more than

P3

8 horses, we pulled up until we got the batery up the hill whitch took till 8 or 9 oclock & left for our position whitch was to deploy as Sharp Shooters along the old road just above the one we were in, in the morning but Still farther down, all the morning heave Skirmishing were kept up from before day until after night we were not allowed to have any fire & it was pretty cold we were that night put out on pickett & after about 10 oclock were Relieved by a Ga co & we ordered to join our own Regt & deploy as Skirmishers in an open field close to the Byo where it was thought

the enemy were going to build a bridge, that was a memorable night it was so cold I was afraid some one would freeze, I fear many are frostbit in there feet, we left next morning past before day light & got off in a hollow where the cane were so thick that a man could scarcely get along & so steep that he could not lay down unless propped against some thing, we did poor resting that day, but at 12 a flag of truce from the enemy came in & after a while the Yankee detail came to bury there dead, whitch had lay there since the fight on monday it was in plain view of the hill we were on & about ½ mile we heard the fighting as we came from Jackson & they were badly whipped with a loss as they admit of at least 1,00 killed & wounded, our loss in that fight would not exceed 20 killed & wounded, they undertook to storm one of our Batterys & had to cross the byo at a narrow dry place & our men in ditches & the cannon on the hights mad it to them a field of blood, it was in a corn field & there dead lay thick, I Sat on the hill & Saw the blue coats carrying off

4P

the more unfortunate & I did not count them but believe I Saw them move at least 200 on a Spot of from 10 to 20 acres just along this Byo for 8 miles was the line of battle, woods on the yankee side & an open field on ours varing from 4 to 8 hundred yds & just outside the field the Road & back of the R the hills & hollows & cain breaks where our men were kept secreted, & the Sharp Shooters on both sides were popping away every chance they got, there woods were that they were in, were dressed in long mass, So mutch that they could be within 40 yds of the bank & gus could not see them, they said that Vicksburg would be theirs by the 1 rst of Jan but alass for them on that day they Skedaddled & has not been heard of since, When their flag came over both sides seased & both came in sight & got to hollowrin & lots <u>bantering</u> & lots of men on both sides met at the byo & talked & bosted & joked for at least an hour that night, our 2 co had to go on that old field & deploy as Skirmishers half of the men up & watching at a time that was the cold night, & during the night we heard their waggons going off & never have heard again Since they fired there Salutes in honor of as they would say there brave dead one Brigade followed them to there gun boats next day taking several prisoners & Some prisoners the next morning after we heard them going off, we moved just above the Road in the old Road & dug a ditch & lay there one night the Raniyest kind, next day went to camps in the hills Stayed there 24 hours, Come over here last night at dark, had no supper & no breakfast until 10 oclock

JAN 5TH 5 OCLOCK

.05.06 L2 P1

My Dear I have just learned Coln S is going home, I take all I said about him for I believe that he was sick, & if well a gentleman & an officer, but to say the least of it he hurt my feelings worse the time refered to, than he ever had done, but I know by experience that an officer sick can be nearly teased out of his life, there fore I freely forgive & take back all I said against him, I have said & say it now that when he is well & at himself that I would not exchange him for any man to be Coln over me, every thing is quiet here we have a butiful place to camp, the frst we have struck in Miss, we heard that had gained a victory over Rosencrantz in Tenn & had taken 5 thousand prisoners, also there is a Repot that the enemy have Mobile, I hope not, II must close by saying that I am well & hope that God has had mercy on you & yours that he will still guide us, Safely through these troubles & that we may meet soon after we have gained our peace Yours affectionately SCK

.06 L2 P2

January 6th Well my dear we are all well, Some are lightly complaining, I was so glad to get you letters, Still I was sorry to Read in it that you were on a stir, my dear one do not take things to heart but take it easy do not fret, I take things easier than I use to, I want us to trust in God who has kept us thus far, I think that I will send you some money soon there is now 4 months Due me, I expect that Turk will do as well as any you can get, You can swap off the old buggy if you choose, I suppose the 3 or 4 bags of cotton you speak of, is toll cotton, that will make us 21 or 2 in all , if the Ropes are busting off the bales you had better have them repacked in iron ties, have all them put under shelter & leave & the air can pass through under them, I do not know about tending cotton, I think the less cotton the sooner the war will end, I believe if every bag of cotton in the Confederacy was burned up that the combined nations of the earth would force a piece but so long as we Raise cotton, So long it is smuggled

.06 L2 P3

Oh my Dear one do not be low down, Oh that God will give us grace sufficient to the days be cheerful, trust in the Rechdeaness of Christ, prey for me who is exposed to all manner of temptations, Be sire & do not sell out your corn to close, You will have to let it go by the bagful until harvest, Say to Robison that I have been over a good portion of the Confederacy & that my place is not for sail, tell him that Tarripin valley is one of the first places in my estimation & that my place is the verry first,, it is the heaven of Rest for me on earth, the place where my loved ones are, If you can get any thing out of the old mule Dukes, has do so, You can get Graham to attend to it, if you can send billy to school, do so, give him an education virgil is to young unless the school was verry handy, We do not fair as well in some Respects as we did in Tenn, we get beef in place of bacon ^ corn meal instead of flour, but Sugar & Molasses in abundance, Sugar is only worth 12 ½ cts per pound & Mol 18 per gal, bacon 90 cts

.06 L2 P4

This is a poor place to forage, there is so many Soldiers, 2ondlythe people are generally Ritch & thinly settled & have had Soldiers here so long they are tired out, Dan is gone to wash today, All is quiet, I haven not heared but one bom today, I was vaxinated the 2ond time last Wednesday I think it will take, I vax dan 3 days ago 2ond time for him, I must close as the Coln is going to start God bless us

Good bie my Dear SCK

Jan 10th 1863
Camp 30th ala Near Vicksburg

P1

My Dear Amie I Read yours of the 31st Dec last night just in time to read before dark, we have no fire & this sorry wood is verry good to Smoke, but poor for light, I think that I wrote you a letter from the 19th talked inclusive in which I gave you an account of my horse & C that one I sent by Tom Wells. He left us at Kington Ga I left the horse at M Millers for him to do the best he could with, I fear that they are in the hands of the Yanks as it is Reported that Bragg has fallen back to Bridgeport, I was so Sorry for you, I could not come by, but it was positively against the orders & if I had come (although I could have staid there 48 hours & then got to Selma in time) my whole co would have so attested as a gang of birds let out of a net, & I would have now been under arrest, & as I stuck all the rest but Cooly, all the best my men stuck up as well as any & lots better than most of theres, No man could want to come worse not to

P2

disgrace himself, but I was Capt of Co E & the Respectibility of the co Depends on the Captain, I had official notice that S M Penland was sent from Hospt to Rejoin the Co with out delay that contradicts his furlough tale, is lasly coming back, I thought that he was left accidently (but may be on purpose) I have fixed up Bensons papers & Sent them to Judge Woods, & wrote to Fergerson about it, I suppose I can fix that matter of H Bridges, You must find out from him how mutch he drew &to what time, & if he drew any commutation money do that Sure, I got myself into it by drawing for those men & expecting them up in a few days & they drawing in Hospital, You see Judge Wood the first chance & 2 know whether he has Rec a letter from me & if E Y Reaves family has got the money I Ret by Johnson for them, he did like Bridges, J Wood will pay you over the money if he has not already Pd it out, It has learned me one thing never to draw for any one who is not present, I can savs my _____

P3

I was vaxinated 10 days ago & have a nice sore at this time, I has never hurt me except when I hurt it by laying on it, Dans I think will take this time no cases of

S Pox in camps but not more than half of the vaxinated had any effect, I account for it in this way that the men are so poor & so worked by this bowel affection that it will not effect, Some have been tried 3 times, I can send you one months wages, if I had a chance whitch would help pay Graham, I have not drawn it because I have

45 or 50 dollars & that is as mutch as I want here, where there is nothing to buy, I thought that you would collect Right Smart on the notes this winter, I lost the note Bowman spoke of, if you have not got it why not send Billy back to Lucendas to School he aut to go but better Stay at home than go to a poor teacher, Tell Dickey that the Yankees always run just before we get ready to fight them, I was in hopes that they would get done ginning soon & then let the water go until I get home, for I know you cannot get any body to fix it up ___ would not engage to gin annother lb after what is in the house

P4

I am Satisfied that you will have to do for yourself every one for himself & the Devil after all, James has not got time nor more of the Rest, all after the Dollars if they are Confederate & as some say worthless at that, Still my Dear one do not let these things disturb you do the best you can trusting in him whose eyes never Slumbers nor Sleeps & who hears the cries of the widows & orphans as to the buggy I would send it to E Robberds & get him to fix & have it fixed, & pay him his charge & let R keep his as it is so mutch better in his estimation than any bodys else and as to the Room covered I hope that you can make out until the war is over & I then I will or have done a better Shelter than that hut ever afforded 9if the Lord of haste spares life & health, I know that you are nearly without a house, I am quite Still I feel thankful that we are as well as we are, these things are but a picture of what we might be, be contented be

cheerful ___ mynful always abounding in the procseses of the Lord
& you will be happy God is our fri___ & Father & Christ is our_____
_____ than a brother, he Sticketh close

P5

(Writing above margin)

4 ½ ocock PM I thought I was done but I must say something
about that nice little motto, It looks like you do miss me, I just sit
before the fire until breakfast & now you have all the Room I feel
like I would like to be there but not mutch ____ when I was there
my mind was not upon home but with the army I know you love
me dearly but your love is fully appreciated by me, I am doing as
well as I could expect under the circumstances & do Sincerely
hope that the war will soon end if so I shall Ret as soon as possible
never dreaming of leaving you again to go to another war, May
God of his infinite mercy have mercy upon us as a Nation & bring
about that peace on honorable turmes that we so mutch stand in
kneed of & then will we sing to his praises SCK

Jan 14ᵀᴴ 1863

Camp 30ᵀᴴ ala Near V

.14 .15 Pl

My Dearest Amie I am well & hope that these lines may find
you enjoying these good blessings Yes it is a blessing to be well
Dan has written a letter (or got some of the boys to write it) I do
not know what he has written, You can Read it & will have to read
it to the one it is addressed to, I have nothing else to intrest you
that is the height of my _____ (_____) All is quiet in camps it is
wet weather, though we are doing finely, now we get 5 new tents
a few days ago, & Dan found an old one where the Tennesseans
left, those with mine make 7 in all, the best part of the Regt, had
all our tents trunks & cooking utensils we got our trunks 2 ovens
& one tent all the Rest gone we were & are now every man in
public property of wet nights we can all crowd in the tents just 60
in all Some 8 or nine Reported Sick none Seriously ill, we drew
beef & corn meal Sugar & Molasses (I must Drill)

P2

Well my Dear Drill is over & it was a poor one, I acknowledge to you that I am getting verry tired of the Service, I do wish the war may close, Still I know that I aut to be more thankful than I am for Shurely goodness & mercy has followed me thus far while officer after officer soldier after soldier has Sickened & Some died I am yet Spaired, blessed with health & Strength to do the part assigned me in the great war of independence Oh that

God for the Sake of Christ would continue those blessings & mercies upon me & bring me at last (where peace is Spread over us as a garment) home to my (long left) Dear ones at home to enjoy his blessings, to praise him who has Redeemed us & Saved us as a people & as a family

3 ½ Oclock PM 15th I am well it rained all night & has been Snowing all day (at times) God bless you & all of us Yours affectionately

Husband S M Kelly

JAN 16TH 1863
CAMPS 30TH ALA NEAR VICKSBURG MISS

.16 P1

(*Letter to A M Stewart about cheating men out of money*)

Dear Sir my object for writing to you is to inquire about a letter Arheart wrote home to you, for J Stewart, J Palmer told me that Bill Stewart told him that Arheart had written that I had cheated the boys (a good many of them) out of from six to eighteen dollars, Arheart denies the charge, I also deny the charge, Now I ask you as an honest man to send me that letter or the part that partanning to that matter, if no sutch matter , Say so emphatically, there is a lie out & if I am acused of having _____ dishonestly, I shall have the matter investigated, & the guilty party shall suffer if any guilty party there be, & if Arheart did write that is unjust un___ifiable, malicious & Slanderous, & I have a Recorse, If he did not write it then Palmer or Bill Stewart had willfully, maliciously & discustedly lies, Mr Stewart I have the pay Roll one of three (we make on every payment Dr M

P2

C Johnson has another & the other sent to the War Department, all of these are alike & each one show that each Soldier is due so many dollars & cts to the Government & that leaves him so many dollars & cts whitch last amount Pd in & over to each one proof positive in Black & White & all others Ready to admit that I have talked with Lt as not my place to draw for them but Johnson could not get __ paid ___ any other way than by the commanders of companies drawing & paying out to their camps, we were ordered officer & I worked nearly all night to get each one paid & I Rec & Recupted for 1700 & lost in the project between 40 & 60 dollars, I hope no one believes it if So I cannot help it, I never expected to be popular after I got to be Capt, if I were it would be an exception to the general Rule, but that has not detered me from my duty, I have but one way & that is to do my whole duty as far as able Sink or Swim, I have the Results with my Judge where as I have paid more than expected, the company seems to be pretty well satisfied, I have no apology for what I have done as officer

 Capt S C Kelly

JAN 18ᵀᴴ1863
CAMP 30ᵀᴴ ALA NEAR VICKSBURG MISS

.18 P1

My Dear Amie I just now learned that I could Send a letter by hand whitch I brief in & haste to write you a short letter to let you know that I am not so well as I have been I have been Suffering intensely with the toothache for 24 hours, in fact when the weather is cold it hurt me, I have considered to have it pulled out. It is one the opposite side of the one I had pulled when I was at home & on the lower jaw, It is an eyetooth the weather has been verry cold & is now, it Snowed 3 or four days ago & in places is yet snow to be seen although the Sun Shined yesterday & today, it is too cold to write with pen & ink, unless I had more time & more news to write, we are on a kind of Second bottom, no fire & but little to burn but green beach, poor fire Smokey hurts the health of the troops is only trouble, I have none in the

P2

hospital here (Brigade Hospt) Several of Frances men have Some thing like the chicken pox, Some of them Right Sick, there is Some talk of us going to Texas (all Supposition) I wrote to Milus Stuart about that letter, Arheart denies it, & Says that it is J Palmers lies, that he will not tell the truth & C the he , P has told lies here since he came, &C, &C, One of them on Bill S, has told lies P has Bill to lay his upon, You get all the information you can about it, Palmer, Says also that Jim Peace told him that after he (P) left that Arheart & Love Alexander were giving me a verry bad name (or to use Peaces words) that they were giving Kelly hell, this J Peace denied & Says that he never heard of it, that Palmer made it &C Love Said that I was the cause of him loosing his negrow,(all I deny) I wanted him to take the negrow with him to the hospital, he said, he said no, he must cook for the mess & must make something, So I said no more & had no controle of Jack at all, he never ask me take any

PS I have not Rec a letter Since Bowman came, I think it time I must close or get more paper You can find out all you want to know about the matter in question from Turk, Mrs Whitesides & Mrs Robinson (I guess) May God bless all that is our duty to perform Love to you SC Kelly

JAN 22ND 1863
QUARENTEEN CAMPS OF 30TH ALA NEAR VICKSBURG MISS

.22 .23 FRONT

My Dearest Amie I have been thinking for several days that I certainly would get a letter from you, but none yet, the last I rec was the 5th of Jan from your precious hand, but I have not neglected writing & I believe that you have not neglected writing & I believe that you have written, I have been looking for Sam Penland, but he has not yet came, Quarenteen Camps, means that we are cut off from the Rest of the army, as is Said to get Rid of Small Pox Frances company is off ½ mile farther & his Sick 16 or 18 are off ¼ mile farther at a negrow quarter One other Co, Capt Andersons, has one case, it is also off, the 8

Remaining co are all together & no cases of Small Pox or varialloyd, I Saw Dick Weaver, today, he is well, he says that all the cases are getting better, I do not antisepate mutch danger, Still I may have it, I have been vaxinated & it took well, So did Dans, & nearly all the company have been vaxinated, Francis company came by Mobile & were there all day, that may have been the Reason that they were first attached, the weather was cold last week that also favored the disease, It is pleasant now & I hope that it will Remain so, We are better located than before we moved so far as wood & water, the Regt is in a verry demoralized Situation, 18 out of Companies in one night the S Pox the excuse, none of mine I think they will Stick, I am sorry that I commensed to write on the Old Coarse paper Move amen good bie

My Dearest in haste & write all getting on well I have a chance to send it this moment God bless good bie Yours affectionately & fraternally SC Kelly

.23 back

23RD 9 OCLOCK AM
CAMP QUARANTEEN NEAR VICKSBURG MISS JAN 23RD 4 OCLOCK PM 1863

.23 Pl

My Dearest Amie I again attempt to write to you not that I have any thing interesting to write, but that at this time I have nothing else to do, Still it is _____sk for me, my pen, you see how it splatters it __ my five dollar pen, but like its owner is tired (or rather worn out) in the service, if I were with you I could tell it you, faster than I can write with my pen, but this is the best I can do now, I feel thankful that I have the priveledge to write to you & more so to tell you that I am well, I have not had my tooth pulled out yet, I do hate to loose it, Still it is hurting me a little at this time, (changed Pens) I wrote you a letter yesterday it started this morning(changed back) I do not know whitch will reach you first I did not get to fill my paper nor do I know whether I can parade matter enough to fill this, (that is worth writing) It is now

Raining & every prospect for a wet night we have lots of Rain in this county there was some heavy firing up the River yesterday & today, the Report is that there is

P2

a considerable force of Yanks landing, the balance of our Brigade is gone back from _____ to the Rifle pits, Ready to meet the ___ndals, More amen, 11 Oclock Am 24 all is quiet this morning no news from the gun boats, no firing, one of Fraces men died yesterday he has not been well for a long time & took the S Pox & died of a complicated disease his name was Rutledge, he was vaxinated but did not take, all who have vaxinated & it took, it goes light & they are all getting well, 1 case out of the 20 have died, am of the opinion that it will not go harder with the Regt than the measles did The fact is, the <u>veroloyd</u> in a well man where he has been vaxinated is not as hard as measles, I am not at all alarmed Still I may have it, my Scab come off yesterday, I Shall send it to you, you can use it if kneed be, or keep it, it will do my time here after, for years to come, I have another that is nearly Ready to come off the excitement of vaxination is Raging, Some

P3

have been tried as many as 6 times, I despised to be confined, but while we in Quarantine, we will not be in battle but of the two I would choose the battle, My Dear do not give yourself up to uncrtiness but pray for us, & trust him who has kept us this far & has promised his blessings to those who follow his peacefull, I am in hopes that Something will turn up in a short time that will bring us home in peace God only knows, in wh__ hands is the destination of men &nation _____ know that I want to come home, but ca_____ say that I am home Sick, (whitch is bad _____ for a Soldier) I dream of home & of you & I _____ that you are all well, Oh it is a plesure _____ dream about home especially when they are of the Right sort, whitch is nearly always the case, I Saw you Reading a letter from me whitch I had brought you, you were in your ever day dress, not dirty, but not so well fixed up as usual, on account of the work on hand, Still you were hearty Read & well, I fear from the dream that Dickey is not well

P4

I am expecting a letter, & I wait to read its continue , My Dearest one I expect that you will both laugh & cry over this letter, but you must look over my imperfections, I can tell you all my heart & I know that it is properly appreciated, Where are those days of solitude & happiness, for eleven long years (though short to us) they to have gone like my youth & the 12th though attended with Seperation from one another hardships, & privations, it is too __ Saddest of the dozen is gone, & I yet _____ growing (as I fall prematurely _____ but all these things Shall never _____ from my duty, I trust in God & _____ believe that these gray hares Shall _____ come in peace to the grave, It is the call of my country, for you my wife & those helpless little ones, my Mother & Sister & that inaleonable Rite of a brave people to continue to be free, that we get home & all that is near & dear to us, pray to God that he may continue to give us brave hearts & strong armies, that we may verry soon overcome our enemies, & Return home to enjoy that rest that has cost so mutch Sacrifice

Your own Sam

In Camp 4 Mile Bridge Vicksburg Miss Han 29th 11 Oclock AM

.29 .30 P1

My Dear one I have concluded to write you a letter, to let you know that I am well & the Co is in as good health as ever it has been, there is now 71 in all & only 2 or 3 Reported not able for duty I think that they are well pleased with the position I am not I had Rather be with the Regt, they are at the 12 mile bridge across Big Black, I told you that in my last letter you may not get but one, & if you get both, it will not be the frst time that I have written the same thing twice I do not know whitch you will get I also want to send with this one I wrote the 23 & 4 & also a copy of a letter I sent to Milus Stewart whitch you must keep Some one may want to know what I said I will close now & write the balance tomorrow, as it will not get off until then,

8 Oclock AM 30th My Dear Palmer is going to town today, I have no ink, so I will close with pencil we are all well, this is a poor place to get my_____ _____ _____ ___ _____ _____ _____ we got a little flour at 33 cts per ___ & scarce at that, how are you off for

sugar & molasses, we get Sugar at 12 ½ & molasses at 90 cts, the difficulty is the transportation, the Government has all the cars prifsed & they are bringing in Soldiers & carring out Sugar & molasses, I am in __ mighty heavy ___ ____ ____ looking for Coln Shelly _____ _____ ____ ____ ___ _____ ___ _____ ____ ____

friends & Receive to yourself a double portion of both, May God bless us all & ____ ___ SC Kelly

FEBRUARY 1863

(Fragment)

are Stationed 4 miles from here to guard the RR Bridge (my Co) Frances & Andersons on the other Side, the balance of the Regt are at the 12 mile Bridge, we are doing finely nothing to do but to post Sentinals, in fact we have to guard the 2 & 4 mile bridges we have divided the Com I Sent 12 men to the 2 (m) & have the balance at the 4 (M) the health of the Co is as good as it has been Sam Penland came up Monday I was glad to hear from you Still I am Sorry to hear of the Sickness of the family, I expected something bad __ ___ I dreamed of it, I ____ ____ ____ with ___ ____ done ginning after ___ ____ where did all the cotton come from, you say you have 6 or 8 bags yet to gin (19th) I should not gin another tick but what was already in the house I had a letter written but could not send it & come to town this morning & conctuded that I would drop you this, to let you know where I was & how I fair I do not like the business I had Rather be with the Regt, another of the S P cases died it is not Spreading, you will hear from me again Soon, I think I have a chance to send this off immediately   Your Own S

CAMP 4 MILE BRIDGE OF VICKSBURG FEB 5TH 1863

.05 .06 P1

My Dearest I Snatch this opportunity to let you know that we are well, Dan has not been well for Several days but is well now, I had several pills I gave him 2 doses, & he is all right now I have a chance to send this to Yall today so I shall not write but little now, I think that J_____ will get a Discharge & then I will write again & will send you some money, the Co has drawn, Noah paid me but would not pay JP for wheat & corn got last Feb, I Rec a letter of Milus Stuart, it Denied for Arheart So the lie is between Bill & J Palmer Relative to my cheating the boys out of money, I have I have wrote to you about it but the letters are so ancient that may be the first you know of it, I also sent by mail a copy of the letter to you, that I wrote to Stewart, I have not drawn any money yet

P2

but can when I have a chance to Send it, We are getting on very well Bridge guarding none in the Co bad Sick no Small Pox, Francis has lost 4 men another Calvin Turner today with it (no one you know)

Dick W was well the last I heard of them, Francis Co is nearly all Sick only 12 or 15 for Duty, it will go through the whole Co, I went to Vicksburg yesterday to get the money changed, One of the Coldest Snoy & Ranyest days of the winter, I walked 10 miles & got to camp at sun down & it pouring down, So mutch that the fires were all Rained out, I went to bed, & Slept as well as could be expected, &thank God I feel well this morning as ever, All is quiet about Vicksburg, a Yankee Gun Boat passed down the River 2 mornings ago, She fired one that at the S Boat Vicksburg, our guns opened on her She kept cutting, no damage done on either Side, I got a Slip from JR Graham 24 Said that Sam was verry Sick, better the day he left, M S & date 27 Say you were all well I have not Rec one from you since S Penland came, I am anxious about it, God help us all Your own SC Kelly

6th 7 oclock Am find out how mutch money, Bridges has drawn & write to me all well this mor, God bless good bie I must close or miss the chance

11 ½ Oclock February 8th 1863 Camp 4 miles bridge of Vicksburg on Southern R Road

.08 .09 .10 P1

My Dearest Amie I have just Rec & read your letter whitch gave ma a greateal of Satisfaction, I am thankful that you are all yet Spared, Still I was afraid to hear from you, I had almost given out the Idea of looking for a letter as I had not rec one in so long a time I could get letters from Bowden WG & Milus Stewart & all around, Still no letter from my Dear one of whom I had Rather had a line than a Cart load of letters of disabilities accompanied by a certificate from a Dr, the first intimation of Sams Sickness was a slip Coln Shelly brought me from Graham, dated 24th, I had heard in your letter of the (I forget the date) that Barny & Toby were sick I Rec of Bowden 27th that S, would likely make or die, but in a PS that he was better, I am glad that the Yanks have not got Millers negrows, nor My horse, he did not look like mutch horse but cost me 75 dollars you can keep him or Sell him, if he has improved mutch he is a good of his looks, I am glad that you are sending Billy to School but I do not know where to, Here is your expression, I Started Billy to school yesterday, but it Rained all day So I did not Send him today he is going as a day Scholar & if we get a School here I will send him & Virgil too, from the letter he is going to School Somewhere in the neighborhood, close enough to come home at night, whether to Miss A or Some one else, I know not My Dear I write this not to

P2

Hurt, but to let you know that the letters are uncertain & if you have explained in a former letter I have not got it In a word I may explain to mutch you do not in some instances enjoy, I know I

Read it (or dreamed) that you would not send to Miss Julia, A, My Dear for give me for at this moment I am Suffering from toothache, I have not had a chance to have it pulled, as all the dentist are in & have been in Quaranteen Since I have concluded to give it up, It seems like it is ¼ of an inch longer than any tooth in my mouth Tell the boys Billy Virgil & Dicky that Pa is an old man with head & beard nearly white, that they may, Rip & Run now, but when I come home that they will have to be Still only when they aut to Run, but that I think I could wallow all three of them now, May God bless the children & keep them from the eavle, Oh my Dear wife do not spare the little fellows because their Pa is not, nor threaten them with me, but correct, where correction is necessary in that that mild and Christian like manner that becometh a mother & one too who professes to be born of the Spirit of the living & true God, train up our children in the way they Should go, Calling on the name of the Lord in Seplication & prayrs, with Songs and thanksgivings for his abundant mercies bestowed on us, who he has kept by the power of his grace thus far & that he will can long bring us together, to enjoy Peace

P3

and now my dear to J. P. I think from all the lights before me, that Arhart will prove him to be a liar Right, Mr & Mrs W. says he L, A. Spoke in the highest terms of me, J. P. Said that L A, Said it was my fault that his negrow was lost, (That I denied) If I was the cause of L.s negrow being lost would L. P. speak of me to Mr & Mrs W. this I Saw a letter yesterday from Mrs. G to her Son N. she denies ever saying un J. P. presence that she did not want N. to get Arheart to write his letters & I believe I wrote to you, what Peace denied before me, that was about Arh & L A giving me the devil after J. P. left I Rec a letter from Milis S, in answer to the copy I sent you, he denies every word of it yes here is his own language as to mr Arheart, stating that you cheated the boys out of money is untrue he (A) did not ever intimate the like, What Bill S. told L. P. I cannot tell, Somebody Capt has told a lie & I hope you will succed in finding out the Right one, So I will & Sorry am I to say it I believe it is J. P. Milus S. Said that he had Sent the letter to Arheart, by mail but he had not Rec it yesterday, When it comes I Shall call the opponents up face to face & will Read both letters & let the Company deside who has told the falsehood or more than one, Arheart & Palmer are at daggers points A would not pay him, Noah paid me 22.50 is the worth of 15 bushels corn at 1.50, You mistook 28.50 what you see,

P4

Noah also paid J. P. after he got that letter from his Ma

There is plenty of Sugar & Molasses her but the R Road is so pressed that there is no chance to send any home that JRG found out, Bill Stewart had a whetemore & if that is the one he owes me for the Season that was year before last, the colt will be a year old this spring or summer, I know nothing about what was done last year, the best I Recollect about it is that he traded off the mare, & I Said that She was not in fold, Has Tom Esliee ever paid you any, I think you have 2 or 3 notes on him, half of the largest is Fergersons , Still he Fergerson may have it, It is a joint note I gave Lon Ferderson a note for 10 dollars also Sherdan one for 25 or more for cotton bt at Sail, those notes I wish you to pay soon, I did think that I could send you some money but I fear I cannot draw it, I think that <u>Jouurney</u> will get a discharge if so that will be the chance, I Still want you to see Bridges & find out how many dollars & cts he drew with the 50 you paid him, as to the other that is Reaves that Wood got that all come out Right, if he hadnot drawn there he would have been entitled here he got that from Wood, he (Reaves) is now with the Co As to Steel & Coolly that they will have to be Reported as Deserters, I have wated long I am bound to Report them on my next monthly Report on the frst of march, tell Bowden that I wrote his to

P5

Yes Coln Shelly has Ret have not seen him but once, he is not well yet but better he is at the Big Blad_ where the 4 companies are, they were expecting an attack, by the Gunboat that went down by the city, It was thought that she would go up & destroy the RR Bridge but she has not ventured up, Rumor says she is laying down the River about one or 2 miles, Others say she is gone to Netches , We are having quite an easy time here, nothing to do but guard 2 bridges, they are 2 miles apart, I sent Sargt Camp & 12 men down there they stay all the time this one here we keep 12 men at the end of it all the time but Relive every 24 hours, the Company are verry well satisfied with the position, there is 72 of us the largest co in the Regt, I suppose, Andersons co is on the other side or end of the bridge, It is across a little muddy Stream about ½ as large as Nancees Cr__, The Bridge is 150 or 200 yds long & is at the hig__ place 50 ft high, It is what is called a trus__ Bridge, the country is so hilly & no rock that all those hollows where water Runs are trussled , this is the Oldest & worst RR I ever saw, Scarcely ever a day & night passes but what a train Runs off, or some accident happens between here & Jackson a distance of 40 miles, Francis co Still 1 ½ miles from there & his & Andersons Sick further Anderson lost one man of S. P. today Francis, Noah Jenings

P6

F has now lost 6 men Calvin Turner (old preacher Bens Son) is 2 Rutledge 3 Moore 4 Calvert 5 & Page 6 Anderson, Ginn, W whoever it is you quote, is mistaken (I do not know who you mean I wish that you had written the name) It is the Small Pox but Said to be verry mild, every 6th man that has had it has died & I fear that more will die yet I saw Dick yesterday he is Closer than I wish to be We have not been with them in 3 weeks & more, Still Some of us may take it, they come through Mobile & were turned loose & frolicked about 24 hours I conseder it verry dangerous now but did not at first I hate to take less than I said for the mules where will you turn them to grass, was the old field Rented for me this year, id so

Send them off there or get the price, that horse is lazy without _____ur, write to me about him & old <u>Merth</u> & Sy____, If Bryan doesn't have to go to the war Sell him Big Bone, for one thousand dollars, I will not take less,

Feb 9th 10 Oclock Francis has lost another man Willingham &
more will die I Suppose I Rec a letter from Ann She semed to be
glad that I had written to her She told me of her afflictions in the
family, I will answer her soon JL His at Kingston Tenn, he is the
quartermaster of the Regt, they have joined a Georgia

P7

Battalion, whitch makes 10th Confederate Regt

My Dear I hardly know what to write I write so many letters I
forget what I have written or what I have not I have wrote 4 or 5
letter since yesterday morning, I Sometimes Rec as many as 3 or 4
letters a day, from absentees and there friends the most of them
are to answer I am generally busy, I have worn out my pen at it,
John Rhoads has got to the Regt, he came through with the train
he was up at the Depo today, I did not see him, they say he is well
& fat as a bear Ann Requested me to write to John, I think I Shall
we can buy plenty of paper pens & Ink in the city, good paper is
worth from 2 to 3 dollars per q__ I cannot draw any money, I had
the papers all ready, but did not want to draw until I saw whether
Journey would get off, & it is to late,

F or Johnson Rec an order to _____ all the funds & Stores on
hand, so he is aff____ to let me have any, although there is over
four month due me, I paid my commissary bill for Jan 17.65 cts be
sides we foraged lots, It will cost me, to keep Dan at least 30
dollars per month he is so wastefull & hearty, butter at 1 dollar
per pound & pork at 35 cts, looks like he eats it, as th__ it was
given to us, I am confident that it takes as mutch to do him one
day as it does me 2 days

P8

& especially any thing else but beef I eat the most beef & JP is
but verry little behind him, he P is nearly always complaining&
says that he does not eat but little & lays it on Dan, I know I nearly
always leave him at the table, & after he gets through Dan licks
up the balance little or mutch, I have to teach him economy, Yes
sir I am just as saving as P, I can become in a few words more I
will tell you that I do not get along as well as I did before P, came

to board with me, he is the most unpopular man in the co & I let him stay with me because, there is not another man in co that would do him Justice, We had like to have fallen out the other day but he Succomed, he is abroupt & insulting & Still he is good to me, but is an incessant talker, you may keep this in your ____, but hise things are tabu , Some heavy fighting today at a distance, towards the Yankee I know you will be glad twice when you get through this more tomorrow as it will not go out till 10 oclock tomorrow

10th 7 Oclock am well Dan is grunting I Suffered with toothache all day yesterday & last night am going to have it pulled today God bless you in all your ways, Oh that he continues his mercies upon us Yours aff SCK

IN CAMP (FEB 13TH 1863) NEAR VICKSBURG 3 OCLOCK PM

.13 PI

My Dearest Amie I rec yours of the 5th yesterday, it came about as soon as any, I have ever got one, I think that it is a good plan to pay the money instead of putting a Stamp on, a Stamp is too easily taken off, or at all events they comes more letters without than with stamps, I was so glad to get it but was so Sorry that you are not well, I feared it, Still you never but once intimated to me that you were not Right (tis your old disease I guess, the whts) I am so sorry for you, Oh it is bad enough to be Seperated from you, without knowing you are sick Oh that God, our God, in whom we trust would have mercy on us as a family, as a nation & bring about Speedy peaces as the poor tired Soldiers could Return to there loved ones at home, who are in many instances the grater sufferers We have just come off pickett today, from Warnertown, whitch is 9 miles down the River, we started about sun rise on the morning of the 11th & arrived there about 10 oclock AM most of the men without any thing to eat, I had Snack & carried plenty to do me (we Lt Persons & I) (Palmer not able to go) they eat their breakfast after they got there (Some few having nothing) & that was all that they had until the next evening about an hour by Sun,

& when the Rations came it was corn bread brought by men from camp, left there for that purpose, there was joy in camp & they eat & were Satisfied, on cold corn bread & some few had molasses & perhaps a bit of bacon breakfast this morning ditto, all quiet all the time we were gone, Rations Still Scarce, & Do not know the cause, no prospects of a fight

P2

The line by Pike, I hope you understand it now, but for fear you have not Received my letter, I will Say that I had no time to write, & was Sorry I Sent it, but thought you could write on it, & P would tell you all about it, In a word I had carried

S Penland, down there to Stand his trial, was going to tell you, that he (S) would try to make it appear here & at home that I was to blame, they made him forfeit 2 months wages, & 90 days hard labor, I hope you have got the money 720 dollars I sent by old Parson Williams, & have applied it in the way you spoke of, as to old Burnes, note, is it not given one day after date, if not wait till it is due, My Recollection is that it is a cash note, I fear he does not want to pay, or has not got it to pay, Sell no more on a credit, the weather is good & has been Since march, came in except the 8th 9th & 10th verry Rainy & high winds, My Dear one do not work so hard, when you work, may be that is the cause of your not being well, by all means have those old tooth Toots pulled out, I an Satisfied that bad teeth are inquereous to health, the Doctor can give you a li9ttle Cloriform & it will not hurt you bad, if I am not there, that is out of the question, I see no chance for me to get home, unless General Tracy has all the officers examined & they turn me out for incompatency, If they have to be examined (whitch will not Surprise me) I Shall go before the board, & if incompetent, I go to the wall, I am not going to Resign, & they will have to office the company by men outside of it, then I am coming home & Stand the <u>consequences</u> & never intend to be a private in the Regt, things change & men change, Coln S is up for duty again, he looks pale, I Rec a letter from Mother & Mary B, Mother told me about James also one from J Hendricks, I have one written to Mother now, I

P3 WRITTEN BETWEEN LINES OF P2

Have not heard from James, he had some money & did not know what to do with it, I told him if he could do nothing else let you have as mutch as 500 dollars, do not put yourself to any unnecessary trouble about my clothes, I can make out a while yet I have a set of buttons in my trunk, that I got in Montgomery as I came from home, Oh my own Dear one, I had rather you had your tooth fixed than the nice large Bcloak, I have not been to vixbg in 4 weeks only on duty & if Sutch things are here they are hier than any where else, I hope you will consent to do without it wont you any how until next winter, & may be I will be at home, You Say you wish I would see the boys, God bless the children, Oh that God in his providence would permit me to be at home as I was want to be, I do hope when I hear from you again you may all be well it is nearly night & I want to send this out tomorrow, whitch goes soon so I must close Gods blessing rest upon me & hope on you good bie, Your own SAM

14TH 5 OCLOCK AM My D I am Still well this morning Palmer is better he had the chills was not mutch Sick, I think him well, I like our preacher well, he is a young man a Baptist & a good preacher, he is educated, I went to see him last night, he has served as private all time in the 20th Ala Regt, his name is Underwood, I must close the sun is not up yet & Breakfast Ready, & lots to do today good bie S

In Detached Camp at 4 mile Bridge From Vicksburg on Southern R Road Feb 14th 2 ½ Oclock PM

.14 .15 L1 P1

My Dear Amie I Rec yours of the 7th late yesterday evening I was so thankful to Read its contence Surely the Lord has been merciful & kind unto us, in housands of ways, where of we ort to be thankful Still I feel like that I do verry little in Return for all his blessings unto me Oh that we could be more dependant more humble & more thankful than what we are, My D I wrote that note in a hurry & did not discover that I had not dated it the 6th of this inst, this letter of yours came in one week, I hope before now you have Rec one or two that will give you more in detailed than the note I have been writing to you about every 4th day, I Started my last the morning of the 10th, I write so many that I forget what I have or havenot written I Rec Sometimes 3 or 4 per day the most of them have to be answered, I Rec & answered one, of Ann, One of James whitch I have answered today, I wrote one to mother all this week besides other letters of a business charater, I have every man in this Company depends on the Capt for every thing

L1 P2

that they cannot do themselves, Still Some of them hate me I judge I think they are better Satisfied than they ever have been with me but thanks be to God I can say with a clean conscience it is without a cause & they have no Recorse, Tell Billy that I Sympathize with him, I know Something about the jaw ache or pneuralza, I my last I told you that I was going to the city to have my tooth pulled, So I did & if possible it hurt me worse for the next 24 hours than before I am now well, it has hurt me at short intervals

since, I hope it is all over now, I had not chewed on that side hardly a bit in 4 months & every week or 10 days it got sore & long, I had it plugged but to no effect I was wandering up & down the streets of the city hunting a Dentist, or doctor to pull out my tooth when I saw to my great Surprise an old gray headed, gray bearded man that I Recognized in the person of old Brother Buck, he as a mater of corse did not know me, but I followed him Round the corner & walked to him & told him who I was & where I Saw him, Oh yes Said he it was your kind wife, that Said I was so mutch like her father, he asked me of you &C, & sent his love & best wishes to you, he Said that he was there to see his lad of 17 years who belonged in the 46th

L1 P3

Ala, he looked at my tooth & Said that he could pull it if he had the tools, that he had pulled thousands, but

Says he, my dear Sir I would not have that tooth pulled, In a few moments the vehicle came that was to carry him & he bade me a hearty good bie & I Resumed my Search for Some one to pull it out I finally went to the Post Surgeon but he Said that I would have to go to the Hospital, So I after all had to go there not a dentist nor Dr in the place to be found I was Sorry that night that I found the Hospital, So great was my Suffering, but all is over now & it has quit hurting My Dear I try to interest you, but Sometimes I am ashamed of Sutch stuff, do you enjoy Sutch letters, I have no news of general character except what I can give in a few words & that likely I have written to you ½ doz times, You Speak of Snow we have Rain in place of , Some little Snow once or twice You ask if it was ever so cold when I was at home I guess so, but 2 is warmer than one, Oh I did not expect Snooks (the horse) to look well, but he is the best of his looks I ever saw, like many a poor Soldier has worn out himself in the Service of his Country& today there are thousands of Soldiers look just like

Ll P4

him as nearly so as a man can look like a horse I thank God that I am in better condition The Reason I Said that I would not gin cotton, was because the dam is in Sutch bad fix & looks like that they will be all winter ginning the crop, last year by this time I had ginned about 150 bags (I believe) If brother Smith comes I hope I Shall see him, but a bad chance to get any grocerys on the RR, as to our going to Mobile or any where else I think it doubtful until we get entirely clean of S Pox, No more deaths Since I wrote you Tuesday, I can get this paper for 2 ½ dollars a qn I could send you some if a chance presents itself. Journey got a transfer to Hospital duties, he will go to Rome if they give him a chance, Tooth apiece lost, I wish that you would get Porter to fix you up a new Sit, while I am absent & then if I were to get killed or die, then it wouldnot be Said that she is a Sitting out &C as to w \ Woods do not trouble him about that matter all worked out right, HY Bridges what he drew & what you paid him just makes the amount up to the 31 Aug, he is now entitled to 69 dollars, whitch you can pay him or I can if he comes up (I drew for him the last time Just to Straten the books) if yo0u have it if not he can come on to the Co & I can pay him

L2 P1

Feb 15ᵗʰ 9 Oclock AM My D I think that it thundered & Rained as hard last night as I ever heard it, Our old tent is just about as crowed & leaks as bad in proportion as your old house, I am glad that you have Something good to eat, more than I can say, we have flour beef coarse meal, & Sifted it in an old tin pan with nail holes jobbed in the bottom We get plenty of Sutch as it is & all but the beef & meal is good, I am in hopes that I will be at home time enough to Sleep on that carpet, yet before it is worn out, I am glad that you Sent for the Baptist I also am so glad that H & G had an interview & each one no doubt had to acknowledge, their faults, & I hope that it is finally Settled, Where is Graves & what is he doing, I think that Perry Anderson is all Right, My Coat is Smartly abused, I have to make a pillow of it, I think that it will hold out until you can make me another in the last of March or Apr at farthest, My pants holds out verry well, my boots , if I could have about 25 cts worth of work done on them, would last all Summer Dan will

L2 P2

Soon kneed pants, his boots will be gone long before mine, John Rhoads is waggoning down at the Regt, I Saw him, he is well, For fear that you do not know our condition I will here again Say that 7 Companies of the Regt are between here & Jackson guarding the bridges across Big Black R that Francis co are between here & there about 1 ½ miles from here in Quarantine Camp (or ort to be) the well men ½ mile from the S.P. cases who are in a negrow quarter, Andersons Co are on the other end of this B the 4 mile B & my Co on this Side except, Sargt Camp & 12 or 13 who are at the 2 mile B, the Brigade, Tracys Ala Brig are about 4 miles from here, below the city close to the River, all Seems to be quiet another Yankee Gunboat passed down by the City night before last, She floated down nearly opposite the Citty (it being dark & foggy) before She was discovered, when we opened fire on her She Raised Steam & let out, I expect without being touched, & I think without Ret fire, The men of the Co Seem very well Satisfied with our position none bad Sick, except Noah Graham, I Sent him to hospital day before yesterday

L2 P3

he had a kind of Choleramorbus & weakened verry fast I have not heard fro him Since, Bowman has got up, Arheart Rec the letter from Milus S. that, I wrote for, I have not seen it, but heard truthful men say that there was nothing disrespectful in it, of me, J. P. is tried in that & can be in ½ dozen other tales, So Says the Company, All about his bad Sickness at home, & after he Started & got as far as Rome & having to go back on account of chills, there is men in the Co who came with McBee, Say every word not so, & they Say that nearly all he told about McBee is false, I am Sorry Really Sorry that he will do so, he seems to think well of me, & I have always Respected him, &C&C I hate it, but today I think more of him than I do some, My Dear I write this exclusively for your own eye & yearn, I am not injured nor Slandered, & this is the last line I expect to write about it, I Rec a letter from James, he Says that he has collected Some money belonging to the estate, & asked what to do with it, I Said if I can Rec it in peas, for him to pay it over to you, If not in that way & none

L2 P4

Of the Rest, do not want it in part, for him to pay you as mutch as 5 hundred dollar I had Rather not get it unless in the way of peas, The government owes me nearly 6 hundred, but I do not know when I can get it, I have about 1 hundred with me, enough to answer my purpose, I hope, I think that you can Sell & collect enough to, answer your purpose, but If you get any from him pay Asap if it is not paid (I have forgotten) pay Swans note first & then commence on JRG, & Stick to him as long as you owe him a dollar, I am in hopes that we will wind out of debt in a few more months, the Lord Showing us money and now my Dear one I know that you will not complain of the Shortness of this letter, if you do not complain of the length & Simplicity I will be Satisfied, I do not know when I can send it but as soon as I can, Oh that God our God may Still guide us in the way we Should go that he will uphold us by his Spirits power that he will protect us , & defend from all our enemies, that he may keep us as in the hollow of his hand, & Rule all things so as to bring about peace, & let the weary get home is of your own S

FEB 16TH 1863 10 OCLOCK AM IN BED

.17 P1

My Dear it is still raining & I have not got up out yet but had to get up to write some papers & I concluded that I would send you a few lines to let you know that we are all are well this morning, It is the wettest time I ever saw nearly, Arheart brought up the grand letter (he belongs to Camp Squad) yesterday the letter Said that as to Lt P. I believe that they are all satisfied, but at this time there is a great deal of dissatisfaction on the part of Capt Kelly, he is <u>tyrannical</u> as the boys Say, but I Suppose at this time there is not a Co who are pleased with there officers &C I acknowledge all that was in the letter to be So, for we were at that time, all worn out & tired, & as ill as a set of cats, P. Says that B Stewart told him & I expect he did Say Something about it but if that is the letter

(& I have no doubt of it) It was magnified from a mole hill to a mountain, this is all I expect to write about it & I write it Specially for you I Saw Capt Francis yesterday he says that his men are all doing well

P2

no more deaths since I wrote before, One of his men who went to town yesterday says that another boat passed up the River but did not seem to know mutch about it, I have not had a paper since Friday, I give 25 cts for 2 papers every day I go there & one dollar for my dinner I would not mind that but always have to wait until the 2nd table, or Risk being Run over, So great is the Rush they Remind me of hogs Round a slop trough but the naked table without a cloth & the greedy Rascals ____up the glasses & the waters have not time to more than give you something to eat, I get Mutton or beef, potatoes cabbage turnips &C in a word the best hotel I have struck in all my travels lately, no bacon nor flour doings nor chicken fixings, I have not cracked a chicken bone Since I have been in Miss, but Sugar & Molasses lots, I must close, the BR got out of order some where yesterday, no train until after night, I hope you will get this Right soon God bless you & all of yours, me & all of mine & all for whome we should prey Yours affectionate Husband S

Im Detached Camp at 4 mile bridge on Southern RR Feb 29th 1863

.20 .21 L1 P1

My Dear Amie I wrote you a letter dated 7th I answered commensing on the 14th the (day after I Rec it) I finished & mailed it on the 16th, I have been looking for a letter but have not Rec one oweing I suppose to the derangement of the R.R. it has not been regular for nearly a week quite irregular it is of the tracks at this time at the lower bridge & the other night one of the trussels gave way & the engine plunged headlong into the abyss & killed one man dead & Scalded 2 or 3 others badly & one man missing, suppose to be under the engine, The incessant raines that fell for three days & nights Rendered the Road impassable, at any other times but war times, they have got the engine up & will in a few days have every thing moving ahead, there is lots of hands on the Road always busy, the Yankeys has been throwing Shells into the city 2 days (all quiet today) with but little effect the first day they killed a dray man & his horse, yesterday they killed a woman & hurt a child or two, & Struck off a mans arm with

L1 P2

a piece of a Shell, the River is yet rising it is nearly all over the whole bottom on the other side, it is Said that the battery that they threw those Shells from was consealed on the opposite side & nearly opposite to the City, Our Side did not Return the fire I expect that we are well prepared for their Reception, & Still they have several hundred negrows always at work on the fortifications, To my surprise today Bill came into my Qrs. Some one asked him what he wanted he Said that he came to See mas Sam Kelly, I am the man I Replied, (but for my life I could not Recall his name) your name, Bill sir Oh yes, Simmys Bill yes sir, he looks a little broke but I knew him but could not locate him, he Said that he had been here at Vicksburg one month, working on the Rifle pits & planting Cannon, that he had been Sick for a week, but had got better, I asked how he found out that we were here, he Said that he met George Loyd on the street, & G knew him & told him, he had been to see Dick, who he says is well, & thought that wash was there

L1 P3

with D. Loyd told him, but L did not know that he had sent him home, Loyd is in the 31st Regt, in our Brigade Charles also, E Zells & others I have seen them frequently I do wish that I could get a letter every week I think that you do write that often, do you, if not my Dear you must, I write oftener than that, but at this time I could write a volume if I had the matter, I have the time Bill Said that he had not heard never heard a word from any of us since he left Ala, that he lives about 80 miles South of here, his masters name was Buchhannan, that he had a good home & master, that he had never Rec a lick since he had been in the State, that his young master was in the army & he was going home next week & then coming back to wait on him promised to come back to see us, Dan knew him on Sight, Bill Said that he never would have known either of us, he was well clothed, but said that he

(while Sick) could not eat the beef & had spent all the money he had, I gave him one dollar & Dan gave him Some I did not ask him how mutch I was glad to see him & glad that he seems satisfied he had spent so mutch time with D. he did not Stay long

L1 P4

I have not been to the City this week it has been so wet until yesterday morning the weather is dry now Sun Shine & windy all well some dry off Noah G has Ret from Hospital, I wrote you in my last that I was in the City for that purpose, he had a bad spell of Choleramorbus, but soon recovered, he as I say foundered, Sam Penland is under arrest, for drawing to mutch money, he had drawn up to 31st Oct & I asked him when he drew to he said 31st Aug & I so marked it on the pay Roll & drew for him accordingly, Last week Johnson Rec notice from Knoxville Hospt that he had drawn to 31st Oct & he Johnson notified the Coln & he ordered me to arrest him he S thought (it Seems) as I had not Rec notice of his last drawing, that the uncertancty of the mails, that he could draw again, he says now that he forgot, Coln S is up today & will order a Corts martial, he will be apt to loose as many months wages as he thought to gain, if not more than will be light punishment if he had given me given me his Descriptive list it showed that is what he should have done, but instead he consealed it until the fuss broke out, & then produced it just in time for it to be evidence against him, Say nothing about this, except some one asks you every body will know it, but I do not want you to tell it first, Journeys papers has not Ret yet, I will close may the blessings of god Rest Remain & Abide with us, & with the Confederacy is my prayers Your Own Husband SCK

.21 BETWEEN LINES OF .20

L2 P1

21st 7 oclock all well this morning I thought of going to town today but have deferred, there was heavy cannonading last night about 11 oclock at the City, it was thick & fast lasting 30 minutes, We have not heard the Results, I hope that they took a Yankee gun Boat, My dear I forgot to say to you in my former letters, not to give the Right of way to the Rail R Co they are as able to buy I Shall charge one thousand dollars, for it. In tax paying I think that I am allowed the exemption of two thousand dollars worth, one for the Mexican war & one for this, You can see about that, Ask Barney if Dr Teague will Sell his wife for cotton. I have concluded that if he will that I will give him two thousand dollars in

Confederate money or in cotton at market price. I will close as it must go soon or not today S

In Detached Camp at 4 mile Brigh on SRR Feb 22nd 2 Oclock PM

.22 P1

My Dear Amie I sent by mail a letter yesterday but now have a chance to send one by Noah Borugh or Francis Co who is discharged on account of <u>piles</u>, he will start in the morning. Our boys are sending money home by him I do not like the arrangement mutch & besides that I have only about 140dollars, I expect to draw soon, but I do not know how I am to get it to you, I will draw 5 months if I draw at all 5X130X650 dollars I suppose I will owe the odds, that is, 90 dollars, I owe Bridges 25 (or you one) I owe Johnson 24 dollars, my Comissary fill for this month & some other debts, I could if I had a chance (that I could Risk after a few days) Send you 6 hundred dollars, whitch you can use either in paying debts or other wise as in your judgement seems best, My Dear I have no Item of news to write except that at 12 oclock noon today there was a heavy cannonading below town whitch lasted from 5 to 7 minutes it was thick & fast, I hope that our folks took in a Yankee gun boat (out of the wet as the boys say) we have not heard from there, All is quiet now, the cars has not got to making regular trips yet, but will, I hope in a few days

P2

Well my Dear Dan made a Rise yesterday of a piece of fresh pork & 9 pounds of Flour from Comy & bt in the country a pound of lard & a dozen eggs at one dollar each, So as this morning as Sunday (I believe) we are fairing Sumptuously, I Slept Right Smack till breakfast, then washed & eat Set my traps for snow birds took my seat by the fire place on my little box got the History of the first year of the war, after tying a string to the trigger to throw the trap, provided they were slow & Read & catched birds till 11 Oclock, I had 10 that I saved & several got away I think that I shall have a nice fry yet, I Said fire place, Yes I have a Shelter made of boards by the Side of a bank, & the fire place dug into the bank, It does

Scandalous well, it Rained all day yesterday & I sat there & Read every paper I could get my hands on & did not get wet, Our tent is too small for to put a chimney to, or to full one the 2 Pikes, Palmer & my self, all stay in it Pike of one side & Palmer & I on the other, Our trunks on the back end, or rather at the head of the beads, I have me a

P3

writing desk over my trunk, the trunk the seat made out of one plank about 3 ft long & 13m inches wide, fixed up on 3 little forks, When I go to bed I turn the trunk, along under my desk & when I want to write I turn it the other way, Beds Yes we have confederate Soldiers beds, made after this Stile (I Said nothing about bed Steads Recolect but, beds) we took some 5 ft boards & lay down on the ground flat for the chord, then we set one up on the edge, at each side & at the foot, (the trunk at the head in place of) then it looks just like the Runing geer of a hens nest (only larger) then we get all the clean dry leaves & throw in, then an arm full or two of small cain leaves & all then put down one or two blankets according to the weather & cover with the same number mor or less, Oweing to the same circumstances pull off coat & boots, for heading & that is the best Soldiers bed that I have met with in the war, We have a passage of between the beds of about 9 inches, the tent is small & old, & the beds necessarily are narrow se we lay down & Spoon & when one turns over the other is almost compelled to turn too

P4

Dan has him a bed in the old tent he found, after the same order, he & his mess, with us constitute the Staff, as the boys say, it consts of the 2 Wilkinsons, Warren Slaton, G Raburn, & Journey, We are all enjoying ourselves finely, We have a cat that some of the boys got some where, & the other day some one shot an Owl & broke his wing, I suggested the idea of a fight, so the cat was brought & held up by the tail & the Owl by the wing & to the fun all the company came, the Owl was conquerer , I gave the boy 25 cts for the Owl, & had Dan to cook him, it was a boiled Owl. For we had not an eye of greese to cook it any other way, I have done worse than eat Owls, I have given you a few of the incidences of Camp life, I hope you may be interested, I write Sutch Stuff in the absence of Something more interesting & you love a full sheet so well, My Dear one I do hope & pray that the Lord will Bring about in some way, that is honorable to the Confederacy a permanent peace, Oh that he will jet continiew is blessings upon us as a family & as a nation, Pray for me, that he will give me wisdom & knowledge & understanding health that I may serve

P5

(Written in margins)

my Country in what so ever capacity duty calls that I may have a praying hart & contente spirit Always giving thanks unto God for all his blessings

Good bie your own S

PS We have not had a mail this week anxiously waiting for the RR Repair The firing I spoke of was the Yanks Salute mall I know or hear I drop in my pen

PS I Send you this sheet I can buy this sort at 2 ½ dollar a quire, 2 sheets does not make a very fin large letter good bie My Dear Amie

FEB 28 & MARCH 1 & 2

IN DETACHED CAMP AT 4 MILE B ON SRR FEB 28TH 1863

.28 P1

My Dearest Amie I cannot write to you with out Regretting my Misfortune in not getting a letter from you, I have not Rec a letter since the 7th Feb I had not time when Lt P went or I should have written more, the Corts Martial I commensed to tell you about passed off by putting S in the guard house, he is there yet, I do not know what the sentence is, the balance of the Regt went from the Big black B to the bridge the day after I was there we expected to go, & yet expect to, Soon, I have been busy all day making out muster rolls, we expect to be paid off, but Coln Shelly was here at our Qrs today to muster us, he says the probability is that we will have to wait other 2 months all the boys are in hopes that he will not get any body else to take our place as Bridge guard, they have to be guarded my Dear I am verry tired now & think that a little Recreation is good, So as Peter Said I go a fishing I will tell you what luck I have when I Ret good bie God bless you more amen

MARCH 1863

MARCH 1ST 4 OCLOCK PM IN THE BRIGADE ONE MILE FROM VICKSBURG

.01 P2

My Dear A I Said I would tell you more when I came from fishing, I was catching minnows (4) when a Co of men came to take my place at the bridge, It was about

4 PM & we gathered up & left about Sunset, we had 5 miles to go & arrived at 8 in the night, the wind blew & the moon shined bright, So we had a plesant trip, waggons enough to take all our things, We stopped to rest & one of the men had a fiddle & struck up a tune, a darky of the neighborhood came up & we had him dancing by the light of the moon, we had our fun & being Rested we struck out for camp, All able to travel but Slaton Duckett & McCullas, Slaton is pretty bad off I shall send him to the Hospital (Disentary) Several others complaining, we do not like the prospects here, nothing to buy & the beef is too poor to eat so we will have to live on Rice Sugar molasses Salt & corn bread, but it

.01 P3

may be for the best, I am convinced that Soldiers as a general thing eat to mutch, I am standing it well on poor beef, God grant that I may always have as good health as I have since I have been here, I weighed, the other day, without Over coat 167 ½ lbs 2 ½ more than I ever weighed in my life, I am not greedy but can eat a little of a most anything, I believe it would kill me to eat as mutch as some men eat, but every one to his notion,

My Dear I have got to believe that there will not be a fight at this place Our folks took two of there gun boats a few nights since & blew one of keep them from Retaking it, I have not Rec a letter since the 13ᵗʰ written the 7ᵗʰ I thought I was doing finely then, I hope & pray for you if I cannot hear, I know that you have written & I guess that they will be in after a while, I wish I had something that would interest you It will be morning

.01 .02 P4

before I send it out & I have been to busy all day to wash & put on clean clothes, digging off & leveling my tent & fixing up my bed, we lay out doors last night, without fire & Supper good bie more in the morning,

2ⁿᵈ 6 oclock AM My Dearest I am thankful that I am well, the weather good, I wrote to you that I thought Dick W had S.P. I am glad to say he has not, Francis Co is still in Quarantine he lost another man (Powers) had another new case last week, (Cooks Son) I have forgot what I have written in this I expect that I have written the same thing twice in some instances my D. I want you to send ma a box of eatables by Pike (Small) & of sutch things as will keep longer a bottle of B berry wine, I will soon have some calomel, strong pills & some Quinine a small quantity to have. Some clothing my coat is warring slick & looks old my Pants have worn to the frasole , Coat & pants I shall kneed, my boots are Ripped & I cannot get them mended If you make me coat & pants it will be Summer soon after let them be a little Darker than these & fully as fine, thes fine clothes will out last the coarse Pants you sent, I believe you may have S to make me as good a pair of calf shoes as he can on the same last, Lt Pike cant bring them maybe some one will come home for them

P5

(Written in margin)

I must close this sheet is all I have & it is borrowed I have carried it since Pike left in my pocket My pen is bad & consequently bad writing You may think this morning paper but it is the necessity of the time good paper is worth 3 dollars per 20, I hope I shall get a letter today

P6

(Written in margin)

S Penland is still under guard I cannot find any one that knows the sentence the Regt being out on Pickett 8 or 10 miles down at Warrington, they started yesterday morning will be in tomorrow, May the God & father of our Lord be with us all, watch over us for good, keep us from harm is the Prayer of Yours own Sam good bie

In Camp with the Brigade One mile from Vicksburg March 3rd

.03 P1

My Dearest Amie I wrote you ma letter 2 days ago, but now have a chance to send one by hand, by Old Parson Williams of our County I have not Rec a letter yet, but still have to wait on, I would be so glad to get one & in it learn that you were all well & doing well, I told you are, I am scarce of paper & besides I want to send you some money I must count before I can tell how mutch, Yes while I think of it, you must send me, that note, I sent you by Phillips, Signed by Moore & J. R. Smith, they are both here now & I think that I can collect it, by giving a Recpt in lieu of the note, Send by Pike without fail, I drew yesterday up to last Feb 6 hundred & fifty dollars I had about 130 on hand but paid some debts I owed 45 or 50 dollars Comissary bill included, I owe the company 10 dollars, 7.34, Well I will send you 650 dollars & if I get that of Lt Moore I will send you 80 dollars more, Lt Moore is going on pickett will be back time enough for me to get it if I can get it without the note, that will leave me one hundred I have sent Dan to town today to have my boots mended this mud Rots the stitches & they are bursting all to pieces, the leather is good yet not a break in it they are done unless I get them mended & I doubt that, Dans are also worn considerably, I think that he can make out about clothes yet a while he can wear mine after I quit them for Summer he bought him a pair of shoes of Journeys, his papers have not yet come, I suppose that you can use the money I send you, pay Swan Montgomery & Graham, Yuse your owe

Judgement whitch one frst I think we owe L Weavers Estate on a note I want to

P2

pay all my debts as fast as I can Lt Person has come back to the Company he is well & looks well he is desirus to mess with me although he has his negrow with him, he is a verry poor cook but a good hand to do what he is told Dan cools & old Henry waits on him, Person brought a fine supply, had pork sausage & butter, besides cakes & a bottle of wripe BB he said that he Stopped at his unkles in Miss where he got it, he was quite liberal I think that he will do well now, well the mail has come in & no letters for the Co except one from Lt J W Pike dated the 17th Feb Bale broke it open, no news of a grand character except that the health of the neighborhood is good, I hope from that, that none of you are bad sick. Still cannot account, for my not getting a letter, I do not want you to with hold any thing from me, on account of Sickness or misfortune to any one of you, If you yourself are sick, get some one to write to me, & let me know the worst, Oh that I may be prepared to meet the trials & difficulties of this life, with a Christian fortitude, Still My D I cannot believe that you have neglected writing unless you are sick, Mrs Pike wrote that she got her letters Regular once a week do you get mine, I write oftener than once a week I shall close for the present God bless us good bie

3 Oclock PM. I have seen Lt M & he will pay me so I will send 730 dollars that will pay some debts, I expected that James has paid you some on the estate in some way, I wrote to you both about it owe Cary & Stice 5 & 25 or more dollars if you can find out where he is, pay as long as you can without Redusing your funds too low, keep plenty for your own purpose, Oh that God will continue his blessings upon us, Oh that we maybe thankful for the mercies he has bestowed upon us & keep us as the apple of his eye, is some firing this evening mostly on our side, PS I gave Mr Williams 10 dollars to carry the rest to you 720 dollars, SCK God bless you all & all for whome I should pray good bie SC Kelly

NEAR VICKSBURG MARCH 4TH 1863

.04

My Dear Amie I forgot to tell you one thing about the interest on those hundred dollar bills, you will observe that they drew 2 cts int each day & they were issued on the 18th & 22ond Oct last, The 18th of this month there will be about 3 dollars on each one, So 3 fives is 15 dollars, When you pay them out you count the int Sure that will pay the old man, & more, understand I paid him 10 dollars out of the 730 I sent, whitch leaves 720 dollars, In a letter sent by mail written the 1st I wrote to you to send me a box of eatables by Pike, Something that will keep longest also a bottle of wine B Berry or my sort of bitters Rather have bitters, also some calomel, Quinine Strong pills & seems like I have forgotten something else, I shall kneed some clothes as soon as you can make them, for fear you will not get my last I will tell you again I want my coat & pants as fine jeans as this was a little darker than these, I only need them, as to the shoes tell Bill Stewart to make them on the same last (9ns) of good calf (or if you have a good goat skin) Send these things by Pike if you can get them ready, do not starain yourself too mutch I must close My love to you good bie your own SC Kelly

IN CAMP NEAR VICKSBURG MISS MARCH 4TH 1863

.07 P1

My dearest Amie L.A. & H. Steel came in yesterday & brought me a letter, dated 24&5th Feb. I was so glad to get it, I am sorry that Patient is sick, but hope she will be well long <u>eve</u> this letter reaches you, I have got a new pen, & am writing on paper that cost 3 dollars per Quire so I must underline it, I hope to write this hand in making out nearly all my papers that you can read it as fast, as I can print, I will say to you that I am well & Dan is too, I have the largest Company in the Regt. All up some complaining but all able to be up, H Wolf is worn off, he has paines in his legs, & cannot sleep at night, W. Station I sent to Hospital, have not heard from him lately, I have 79 men & 2 officers & myself make 82 present, we have lots of duties to do here the details come thick as hail, yesterday I had

26 men on duty, but heavyer in consequence of a diserter being shot, 2 men to dig grave & 2 to be on the guard that escorted the Prisoner to the place of execution, the balance were on guard Brigade & Camp or Fatigue duties or police &C&C, I being the officer of the day (Reggemental) The Prisoner belonged to the frst La Regt of Artillery, Charge was disertion (& rumors says that he & 2 others that was shot yesterday in two other divisions of the army in & around Vicksburg spiked 2 cannons) they were shot I saw one of them, Reath & Sink under the discharge of 12 guns 6 of whitch were loaded & all took effect in his body, he being tied & blindfolded to a post, Shroud on, he died in a few minutes & was laid in his coffin on whitch he rode to the place or accompanied by the preacher, the General asked him if he had any thing to say, he said he had not, the preacher bade him good bie & in a few moments all was over in the presence of thousands of Soldiers formed in a square of three sides, one Regt after another, each Brigade on a square, with artillery men in front, these Prisoners were taken on bord the Indianolal before Vicksburg a short time ago, thus ended the lives of 3 base scoundrells , all of them were Dutch Irish or out landish, We are scarce run for provisions we have not drawn beef but once in a week & it was not fit to eat, I drew some bacon & flour myself but the men do not, but it is at an enormous price, I understood that the General was going to send off the Sugar & swap it for bacon, that I think will do, for we can do without the Sugar, when we get plenty of molasses, I fear getting Supplys worse than the Yankees, We are planting batteries right in the city, in every cross street, tearing down houses out of the way, I have not been to the city in 3 weeks today, had no business, had we been in Quarantine I thought it a hardship, I am doing as well as I could except, but I do want to come home so bad, but I try to pass the time off the best I can, Remembering at all times I am a Baptist, tis true I do not live up to my profession as well as I would like to, you must pray for me & I will try to live to addorn the profession I have made with a well ordered life & godly & bious conversation, S. Penland case was read out on dress parade in

presence of the whole Regt, the sentence was the forfuture of 2 months wages & 20 days of hard labor, he has not entered on his labor yet, I made a talk to Coln Shelly in behalf of H Steel & the Coln Said to put him to duty, who would be a Capt of a Co of men that had no influence, Coln S is sick, I fear he will not do any more good soon, but Still I hope better things, he is either down or up, My Dear I do not blame you for my not getting letters, I know, that you would & could write unless sick, I think the stock hogs on hand, if well attended to will make you meat another year, nearly as many as you had last year & then some of them died, after they were good big ones, If I rscolect, The goats I believe you had better put the goats in one of the fields & there let them stay, if sutch a thing can be done, & what have you done with your sheep, I think they too might go in one of those large fields & stay, there is lots of picking around those ponds, or will be soon, & I do not believe that 4 or 6 head would hurt the crop, bad

P2

Put the goats in the bottom field & let them eat briars in the swamp, Still be governed by you & Mr Turks judgment, your knowing all the circumstances You Pittty us this cold winter in tents, we have done Remarkably well, I pitty you in a cold Cabbin that leaks just about as bad as our old tent, but I hope you better days when I can build you a tabernacle to shelter us & be at home to relieve you of the oversight of all out doors business, May God in his mercies fast this war to a speedy close, & I may he still uphold me, & the cause for whitch I am this day separated from you, Pay Tom Estice in a settlement 5 dollars for damages done his cow, All about it is he has been a long time making out his act, I proposed to pay at first but he hesitated & I thought it was all over as we had a settlement long since (if I recalled Right) If Fergerson collects that note on Tom, You had better when you & F settles pay him the note, I gave Lon Stoneact 10 dollars I think, all right about Bill Stewarts act, that was my recollection, whitch one of the Nabors paid you & what was it for, was it Slaid N. pd for the mule or some thing for some thing else, I suppose that the Burnes you speak of, sending T.

to see is the one that bought the mule & he is the man that is speaking of buying the Jack, do not sell him on a credit to anyone, I think under all the circumstances that you aut to get 1200 dollars for him. I would not take it if I were there, but that alters the case, If any one will pay you 1000 or upwards, may be you had better let him go, but what will you do with the money, In this case as in all others, I mearly give my opinion & will be satisfied with your decision & and acting for you aut to be better than I do, I here & you there, Is it the mule colt, or is it __phax that has the scratches, have they ever plough my new horse any, can you sell any of them, & at what price, keep them until you can get 150 dollars, for the ___ sorryest ones & then sell, unless some other circumstance forbid, I have no idea you will even get the worth of horse, I do want Syphax altered, I want Barny to work him a little, just enough to break him, let him B ride him a little but he must not be handled about like they did the young mules, I wish I was there to go with you to the smoke house & see the contents & help you eat those old sausages, send me some of them by Pike, Risk it, at all hazzards, I think the chance for furloughs, is played out, but I am among the first to go home on business, as nearly all officers have been since I have, I shall catch the chance, the first hope, Oh yes you can bear it & then you will appreciate , whether I am advantaged or not, you may think that your task is hard, but I thank God tat you are as well off in every respect as you are, Still I do dully sympathize with you & really wish that I were there to help you to bear the burdens of the family, As to J,P. I know how to manage that case, it is all quietted down & he is ganing in situation of the Company, he is at head <u>Ders</u>, Arheart has injured himself in the Company by telling too mutch, he knows no bounds, I advised P to say nothing & let it slide, So he has, I reckon that he P could get in a mess, Still I told P last night that I could not bord him at 3 $ per month & he says he cannot give more, when I took him in he drew plenty of Rations & (could get bacon from 19 to 2h cts flour from 5 to 10 cts &C now his Rations is no meat or some we cannot eat, while we have some all the time I buy at the Comissaries at 33 1/3 for flour & from 50 to 80 for bacon, so he cannot afford to give & I afford to take it, P. I think is improved, he treats me well & I must acknowledge that I respect him, althought he will talk too mutch some times, You say you fear to hear from Dan, he is well, but is verry imprudent, but I attend to that, I really believe he thinks lots of me, & is ready any day to quit the army when I do, but not till then unless he gets sick, he does not make mutch money now washing, we do not draw any soap

P3

You may know that by the look of this paper, Still I change my clothes regularly,

& have them scalded, So as to kill the vermin, I am clean of the, I wrote to you that I sent Dan to town to have my boots mended , he paid 4 dollars the 2 pair, worth in common times about 50 cts, I think that my Boots are gone up (as to saying is), my shoes are pretty good yet, but I thought if you had time you had better have me a pair made just so by the coat & pants, my old hat will last forever or to long for me, it is like I am old & ugly, I thought that I would get me another, all the officers have thrown them away but 2 or 3 in the Regt, It is no joke I am grey headed & my beard is turning fast, it seems to me that all the black hear is shedding out, but I feel like a boy & cannot realize that I am old, it hurts me to think that I am old, for people to say that I look like I was 40 & 45 yrs old, that I could pass the conscripts &c&c, but all is vanity of vanities, Old age is hororable & gray hears ornimental in this war time, I am gld you are sending Billy to school, tell him I say he must learn fast & learn every thing he can, for it is the education that makes the man, tell him that I feel the lack of a thorough education, that the man without it, is the hewer of wood & drawer of water for him that has, I ment just what I said about Dick Weaver, I thought you understood that his Company has Small Pox & he was closser than I wanted him to be, I saw him about 10 days ago & told him I believe he had it, but I learned that he had not, they are still in the old camp no new cases lately, No my Dear, not I think hard of you for writing nor for not, Rec your letters, but I mearly ask you to write the name unless you are sure

I will understand it, & I assure you nothing gives me more pleasure than to Rec & Read one of you long letters, I sometimes think that I write too mutch stuff, in my letters, but it is to you my Dear & if you are satisfied I am more than compensated, although I have a bad chance to write, I fully appreciate your advice, but think I can manage the case of Palmer, I am sorry you told Robinsons wife any thing about it (they to talk to mutch) I expect that R is making every effort to get Ritch, So mote it be, I am glad that I am considered worthy to keep Company with the big man of the Regt, I would not occupy the position I am in if I were not, Still I defy contradiction that I do not associate as mutch with my Co as any other Capt in the Regt & I tell you, although I have my faults & my enemies, I believe I am mutch Respected by my men as any officer kneed be, also in the Regt both by officers & men, Still I know that I am not as good an officer as some others, but as an honorable truthful gentleman in this situation, I can tell this to you & you can do as you choose with it, You say you had rather I was a private under a good Capt, than be so troubled, I would be troubled were I a private, I had rather be a frst Lt under a good Capt, but that is the rub I am not mutch troubled, I dispatch business in a hurry sometimes & can come as mean saying what I think aut to be said as ever, Mother could, My Lt Persons (the Cadett) has come in a week or 10 days ago, he is a right sharp boy, he complimented me the other day by saying that he believed that I was the best Capt in the Regt, all that may sooth, but I tell you I feel my incompetencey, but I do the best I can without fear favor or affection, It is no small job to govern a hundred men & make all day their duty, there is so mutch hipachryphy in the world, May God have mercy upon me, & give me understanding I do hope that Dr <u>Carden</u> will not have to go in the army, I cannot see how you all the whole county could do without him, My Dear you express yourself pesterd about Palmer, give yourself no uneasiness about that, Tell the precious children that I am as they are want to see them, but that they must be good children & mind what you tell them & then I will love them still the more

P4

My Dear I laugh at the ida of your feeling old, I want you to have your teeth fixed with a new set, & then if you should ever be so unfortunate (or fortunate) as to be a widow you might marry a man too old to be conscripted, I want you to have them fixed for my sake, if it is covenant & every thing else considered. I fear my Dear you work to hard to feel Stoubt like you use to, but you weigh enough, but I one time in my life can beat you, I weigh 176, If I were at home I think that I could appreciate home, & I believe that I would stay there & be an humble farmer all the days of my life, I am glad that you are better pleased with Martha R, I hope that she may yet be of advantage to you & you to her, John Rhodes has Ret to the company from the waggon yard, he is well & makes a good soldier, I was in hopes my Dear that you would get so you would not dread storms & winds so mutch, true there will be no storms in heaven, if we are ever so fortunate to get there, trust in God & thow shalt be saved, You ask me if I see any prospect of peace, I cant say that I do, Yet every day is one nearer to the end of troubles, & I think that the Confederacy is in a better condition than ever before, Still the race is not to the swift nor battle to the strong, but to whome God showeth mercy, May he show us mercy, Our Chaplin has come at last, J have not heard him yet, he is to preach tomorrow thin I will judge of it whether it is gospel or Stuff, Dan went to the city this evening he got me a paper, nothing in it but stuff, My Dear I expect to send this by Kirby a man that lives about Oxford who came to join the company but was Rejected by the Surgeon, will I think that I will have paper enough once I believe that I have written nearly all I know whether it intrest you or not, I sent you 720 dollars by old man Williams the old Preacher, this may get home before it, I gave him ten dollars to carry it to you, Now My Dear I have drawn this mutch 75 dollars at Knoxville 450 at Camp Investment (525) as Lt, 130$up to 30th Oct at Vicksburg & 650& up to 2ond March 780$ as Capt making in all (1305$) thirteen hundred and five of that amount I sent you 310$X200X720X1230 twelve hundred and thirty dollars but one hundred dollars I sent to H Bridges whitch leaves 1130 dollars, pretty good well done for a little old Capt, but I gave you great credit for what you have furnished which saved me money, I have not stinted myself, It is so dark I shall quit for tonight &

Dan says Supper is ready good night God bless you

8th soon in the morning, I broke the chain in my watch & have no time, My Dear this is Sunday , I hope I will not be so busy as last Sunday, it looks like it will rain today, it Rained a perfect storm night before last, & our bed clothes were all wet last night, but it was warm & I do not know that I feel any the worse of it, My Dear I was thinking last night that maybe I had better buy me a coat as it may hurry you to mutch, in fact I am certain that you will not have time to make one & send by Pike, or I could do without for some time yet, do not put yourself to any extra trouble about it, I would like you would send me one of those confederate candles, it is a long wick dipped in beas wax & Rapped on a corn cob, Send me a piece of soap. It is as scarce as greese & it is scarce as hens teeth, I believe that this letter contains nearly all I know to tell you, I must close, I have a notion to send my over coat, I have not said anything to R about it, if he takes it it will be to Lensey Weavers, Oh that God in his providence will still watch over us for good & bring Peace out of confusion when the nations may all be at Peace & god our God shall have all the praise good bie SCK

MARCH 17TH 1863
IN CAMP 30TH REGT 5 OCLOCK AM

.17 Pl

My Dear Amie I Rec a letter of you the 15th that was dated just one month before in whitch you asked me several questions that would have been attended to before, had I Rec it in time, but I suppose you have desided before now, I thought stronge that I could not hear from Sims Miller, has he not been to see you is Fanny & Key going back with him, I cannot send you any Sugar & Molasses, every one going has so mutch to carry, You must make out on as little possible, we are fairing better than when I wrote last, we got plenty Bacon & meal, I have well continue, I did not Recollect that I owed any RR Stock, except 125 dollar or the Iron book as it is called, If they call on you for it pay it, I do not want to give the Rite of way, but if you have given it, all Right for your actions are valid, I am glad you did not pay

H Steel, If I never get to other he will never get that, tell Martha R that John has been with us a month, he is well, I hurried, I want to send it by E. Hiatt, Journeys papers have come back at last, he is assigned to duties in the Yazoo City Hospital, S Penland is put to duties today, the health of the Co is good, Some slight complaints, W . Staton in Hosp yet, was bad off, a few days ago, we are drilling lots now& the whole Regt Rust, verry busy generally, I am well as usual, Dan is washing, he does fine, You will see that Requisition on the other side, paper is scarce & I though I would not have time to file

P2

My Dear Amie I hope I will get a letter today, I am so sorry for you, May God bless you & Save you from harm, & give you health & strength is my prays, Oh that he in his providence would bring about termination of this war, in honor to us a nation, have mercy on us, on our enemies, & Save us from, Sins as a nation, Coln S. says that Gen S. Read a dispatch of a naval victory at Port Hudson, that we sunk 2 gun B burnt one, crippled 2 so as they had to be toad off & Cut off 2 above the batterys, that we are sure to get, all is quiet here good bie again your own Sam

IN CAMP 30TH ALA MARCH 20TH 5 OCLOCK PM .20 .21

.20 L1 P1

My Dear amie I Rec yours the 8th, the 17th, I did not Reply because I had that morning sent one by Elisha Hyatt, who started home that morning, he carried some Sugar an for whitch I believe he said he gave 40 cts per lb. Every thing is verry high, boots are selling for 60 dollars a pair & every thing else is that proportion, I also sent one by mail on the 13th, I also sent one by <u>Bangle</u> dated the 23rd or 4th, It appears that you had not got that one, but may be (but I think not) that 21st Feb was the one, here after I intend to keep a record of the letters I send, So as I may know whether you Rec, &C I am anxious to get a Receipt of the one JB Williams, with the money in it, hardly time yet, I am glad Pike gave you sutch encouragement about me, but we had an easy time then, to now, we drill about 6 hours a day & stand guard & pickett &C, but I contend that it is

.20 L1 P2

an advantage, Rather Our Rations are good now & if any are a disadvantage for, Since we have had plenty there is more sickness in two days than was in a week before, In my co out of 80 men yesterday I sent 12 to the Hospital, & had excused from duty 8 or 9 more among the later was Bowman, Sal Durkin & others you would not know among the former were John Price, John Wilkinson & John W Thackerson, I hope we will be healther now, for yesterday we moved out of that nasty hole, we thought that we were going to Sniders Bluff, (about 15 miles up the River) but were stopped 4 miles above the City, just in front of those Rifle pits we occupied when we first came to this place, we are on the field that we were deployed as Skirmishers, those long to be Remembered night, when we were drenched with rain & not allowed a spark of fire to warm, In a word it is the same field foot frost bit in, we are well pleased with our position it is a new Camp no soldier having

.20 L1 P3

I was trewly thankful (to hear that you were all well once again), Oh that you can still stay healty, my Dearest I fear you are not well, do not hurt yourself at work, Swan I fear is a poor Soldier & I think lacks all of being a gentleman, make him a tender of the money before witnesses, & mark the date, if he does not take it, I will say no more on that subject (it is unpleasant) If the Government <u>arestes</u> the cotton let it go, & the corn, they will leave you enough to make out on, & give up the balance, for the Soldier must be fed or the thing will be soon plaid out, I am delighted to see what faith you have, Oh that he would come increase our faith, the Lord will provide, It appears that mules are in demand, You kneed not doubt but what you will sell (Mun) at 150 dollars, You talk like you want to keep the horse, but if you can spear him let him slip, I think he ort to bring 200 or 250 if he was here & fat, I could

.20 .21 L1 P4

Sell him for 3 or 400 maybe 5 hundred dollars, I know a horse that was bought in Tenn, when poor for 125 dollars that the owner asked 150 dollars &I would not be surprised if he did not get it, he is no better horse than mine, <u>br</u> a nice figure use my our own judgment, as enough, I know he will yet improve (more in the morning)

21st 6 oclock AM, we went on pickett last night, after dark & left there at day break, all were quiet, we were on the bend of the broad Miss, just 2 miles above the City, Some firing up towards

Sniders Bluff this morning, In a dispatch, it said that Maj Pelham was killed in a Skirmish, I suppose it John P foe he was chief of Artillery with the Rank of Maj, the mail is done gone out, & I may be will get one letter from you today, So I will close by saying that we are well (Dan & I) no cause to complain, When you write (direct) Capt S.C. Kelly Vicksburg Miss 30th Regt Ala that is enough words & letters in each word, written plane & marked paid but no stamp Your own Sam more amen

PS I have carried this paper ready folded in my jacket, I left my trunk the day we came over, it come that night I was glad you sent that letter from your neace, I had never heard of them, I am sorry for them God bless us all

21ST 5 OCLOCK PM

.21 L2 P1

My Dear one I Rec a letter sure enough this evening dated 14thjust one week ago, I was so glad to get it &

read its contence especially that part that Said we are all well, all the objection I find to it is it was to short, I think my D you might write more, I can Read any thing you write, & I give you long in return (generally) you think you have no news you could tell me if I were with you a volume , tell me about the children, the negrows, the horses, the Jack, & especially old Martha, & Syphax &C&C all that is interesting to me, I think you are mistaken, for in your of the 8th March you say yours of the 21at Feb came to hand yesterday &C, and the one I Rec today, dated the 14th says the same thing, yours of the 21 come to hand yesterday, &C I think you mistaken but had Rather it had said yours of the 2ond or 3rd or 4th March come by the hand of Old Parson Williams, money all Right, I am a little surprised that he had not been to see you before you wrote, but I guess

.21 L2 P2

he came that day or the night whitch was last Sunday, I suppose he would want to see brother Hall, & likely preach at hand, Shall the old man Barnes you speak of paying you 100$ was it he whome I sold a mule, & he wanted you to wait one year after peace was made (that is who I understand) You did not tell me who you sold the last mule to nor what you got for him, Cant you spear another or the horse I sent you, if you can at a fair price let them slip, Syphax out to be worked ½ the time & Old Martha ½ that is one, think about it, & then do as you think best, Corn 3$ per bush &C every thing considered, do not neglect to send J.B. Moore note, he has paid me, So you will see if you have gotten the letter & money Ws carried, I can get shoes cheaper from the Govment, but the difficulty is they are to short & large, my old shoes are good yet, but boots Ripped all to pieces, there is heavy firing in the direction of Port Hudson, it is now about sunset & there has been a continual Roar for an hour or more, and occasionally all day, Oh that God may give us a signal victory today & every day & every where until they Shall be compeled to ask for peace on out terms, & then may he have mercy upon us & them & bring both nations to praise & adorn his holy name, good bie Dearest Amie SCK

MARCH 22OND 1863
IN CAMP 30TH ALA REGT 4 MILES OF VICKSBURG MISS

.22 Pl

Ten oclock AM Dear amie I sent a long letter by mail this morning, & I have nothing of interest mutch to write now, but I have a chance to send it to Talladega, by hand of old mr Linsey a Sitizen of that Co, & I think you will get this one first, & as Lt Pike will be coming back soon, I want you to make me a hat as I will have (as I understand by your letter) new clothes & shoes, I want a new hat also, my old one is good enough but looks so old & weather beaten, I think that you can cover my old one with something either jeans or black cloth & make a nice hat of it, a cloth hat entirely will flop down, & that old hat has a good brim, & if it is too high cut it down, I can buy a poor thing worth in common times about 3 dollars, for 25 dollars, If you can cut it down, let it be 3 or 4 inches high & sow the cloth around the top, then round of the top in the same way a cloth hat is made, I want you to understand me, Cut the crown out of the old one, I take it all back you know better how than I can tell you, fix me up a hat if you have time & send with my other things if not time I can buy me one, I intend to save my new clothes for

Sundays, & extra occasions, this coat is not near worn out yet my pants are pretty good also, at home would last me, for every day all winter, I am afraid my D that I Require too mutch of you, but if you cannot get

P2

them without a great deal of trouble, Say so & I assure you I will not think any the less of you, I can buy nearly every thing I kneed but it is not worth while for me to buy until I know whether you are making them, We had preaching this morning by our Chaplin he is a good preacher for his age he is young, were a good turnout, all is quiet today except on occasional shot from our side to keep the Yanks out of the canal they are trying to clean it with what is called dredge boats & we shoot at them every ½ hour some times night & day, There was a call last night for volunteers to go on board of the captured Indianola, to man her , Seven were called for out of the Regt & about 50 to 100 offered, the Coln chose out of the number, I must close, with my best wishes & prayers I remain as ever your own

Sam

PS you will see we have moved by the letter, Refered to we are better situated, all well pleased with the position, we are in front of the Rifle pits & in the same field we occupied the nights after the battle, I had my letter sealed & heard of the capture of 5 Yankee gun boats up the Yazoo, it is official & this is what detail was for that Bowman was on, they were one behind the other, River narrow, the foremost had a saw to cut the shaft, it got down & could not work the next run down to help it off, it also hung & could not turn & so on until the whole five, & our forces came up & down the River & they could not turn on them & capture the whole squadron, I hope it is so, it is believed, God be praised, Oh that he will continue to give us victories until they will see the error of there ways & sue for peace

(23rd written in margins)

23rd 12 oclock it rained all night & the old man did not start till now, all quiet I am well, it has raining, I have heard no more from the gun boats S.

.24

March 24th just before sun set, in same place My Dear we are ready packed up to go on pickett to night & ret in the morning, All well & it is as cold as Dec, a northern the drum has beat & I must go God bless you & yours good bie

SC Kelly

I send this in PS letter as mine is sealed it has been written 2 or 3 days but failed to get off S.

March 27th 1863
Head Qrs 30 Ala Regt Chickasaw Byo

.27 P1

(Talks of attacking gunboat on the river)

My Dear Amie I have been expecting a letter from you 2 or 3 days, I want to know whether you have Rec that money, I have not Rec one since the 14th (LE) dated 14th, I Rec on the 21st, I have sent one by mail a few days ago, but it was dated & redated & at last sent by mail, Oh the night of the 24th our Regt, went on Pickett on the bend of the River just 2 miles this side & above Vicksburg, the ground wet & the wind blew & it quite cold, but we lay down & slept tolerable after putting out Sentinals along the in front of the Rifle pits & in full view of the River, just about the break of day the men along on the line of Sentinals began to fire, bang, bang, I was laying on a hill in plain view of the River, I throw the cover of my face & look & saw 2 gunboats close by not more than 4 hundred yds (apparently) The Coln came running down hollowing fall in, fall in, & in less than 2 minutes all the Regt was in the R pits just in front, Shoemouth deep in mud & water, but it was but verry little in the way, by this time the batterys had opened upon them, the nearest one to us not more than 2 hundred yds, the first one that fired, by this time they had passed the bend & us, & them then the

Roar of cannon, told the distant vollies that Yankee invaders were nigh, they did not Reply, We stood & looked on with a heart praying that we might succeed in Smashing them up, We could hear the balls strike, & the wild shrieks of joy went up from our side, the wheels seased, heard that & saw the speed checked but it floated down out of our sight to the bottom, Some of the crew escaped on a skiff on the La side

P2

the other one was badly damaged & was met by one it is said & towed off, One of those we suppose that passed port Hudson, the whole fleet was fired up & tis said 2 others started down I saw one going back, on up the River, Our Batterys fired at them, across the peninsula, I have no doubt but one of them that passed is sunk, & it was large & iron clad, going down to help out the two that passed Hudson, the papers this morning confirmed me, Tis said that they have but two left, I think if they attempt to pull, We will change them to Rebbles boats or sink them to the bottom of the farther of waters, Oh that God will have mercy upon us as a nation, & give us power to beat back the invaders until they Shall be compelled to sue for peace, this is past day, & I am observing it, the drum has beat for worship, Well my Dear I went to meeting, just before the Colns tents & can say that it was good to be there, to worship towards Gods holy temple, to see the hardy Soldering been in humble supplication at a time of grace, & Revoking his mercies on us as a nation, acknowledging that we had sined as a nation, & asked forgivness & then hear their coarse voices singing the praise of god, n no woman voices to soften the strain, All duties except guard are suspended, Although most of the men do not observe the fast & a good many of the officers I am sorry to say it, but in my co, but 3 observe it, that is Person (who is a Methodist) Palmer, & I, & but few went to the meeting, In fact they are a heartly set, I do not believe that out of the whole co 106 here & elsewhere that there is more than 10 or 12 proposed Christians & several of them furnish but a poor light

P3

I think that all the other companies have more professers, I hope so, if not then that saying is verified, Lord are there few to be saved, I am well pleased with our preacher he is young, but, that will have the better affect, he is able, & a workman that kneedeth not to be ashaimed, he Read the 78th Psalm, & preached from, these words, When he slew them then they sought him, and they Returned and inquire early after God, Oh my Dear I do hope that the Christians of the Confederacy will this day observe, & seek after God, & Return & inquire after him with their whole heart, Oh that God will give the members of Liberty of his Spirit & grace that you may all meet in one mind & one consent to Sacrafise on the alters of our country, humilation fasting & prayrs, I shall close for present, I think that I will get ma letter this evening, & then I will finish, I have neither eat nor drank any thing today, nor do I intend to until after sun set, I will try to spend the time in the way I would wished I had at night, my pen is Rusty or paper greasy or something the matter good bie, May God still protect & keep us my prayr Your own S 5 oclock PM well my Dear Amie I am fearful that I shall not get a letter & I must close this one, or hold it until the next day, Well the mail has come in, Sure enough I got a letter but wait it is from a man in the Hospital, I am disappointed but by no means blame you, I suppose that I am over anxious, I will get it in due time yet, but will be after this is gone, just all that is in it I will write you another in a few days, I have a goodeal to do, we drill often & long

P4

& I have not drilled in so long a time that I am Rusty in it & the Coln has addapped the Rule of not explaining but give the Command & the Capts have to execute, the first evening he did so I was the worst confused I ever was in my life & Rendered more so by my Co being the Right Co, on which there is more Responsibility, I twisted & worked round just like a drowning chicken, the more I did the worse I got, the Coln came up laughing, I said to him Coln I am confused, & he took the Co & streightend us out & I have not been cought in that predicament since, the next evening we performed the same & I did it as well as I expected, he scolds & frets, but I can say that it is not all at me, I am going to do one of two things, (See) I will be a better officer if I can aquire it by studdying or I will Resign, I had serious thoughts of Resigning, I thought that the Coln was inclined to find fault, but I hope I was mistaken, he said once since the evening I alluded to that he was not mad when he spoke short, that we as officers aut to speak Short, that it was more impressive, &C I believe that I am an average Capt, but it seems like that they want young men, what could you get me a substitute for or could you get one at all, if I Resign I shall have to have a sub, but not for this Regt unless he preferred it, I shall also have to have a predicate to found my Resignation on, that I coul do, I can say incompatency, if the Coln prefer, that I would leave to the Sib, Cant you hire N Allread for

2 thousand or less or John Turk, hint it to T & see, for I tell you now I will not stay in any concern if I am not Rested

APRIL 1863

APR 1ST 1863 CAMP 30TH ALA REGT CHICKASAW BYO 4 MILES OF VICKSBURG MISS
3 OCLOCK PM

.01 Pl

My Dear Amie I Rec your letters & things by the hand of Lt Pike, I began to think long of the time but was fully Repayed when they did come, I am well pleased with the things sent, my shoes are made to order, my coat fits to the notch, I have a nice set of buttons & can have them put on, but not today, we had inspection this morning at 9 Oclk, & then an Alarm & we got off to the Rifle pits, just above us & this evening we have to go on pickett down on the River unless another gun boat make out like it is coming up the byo, if so we will go to our own R pits, I think my coat & pants pretty & nice both & I love you Still more (if sutch a thing is possible) for your kindness & self denial for them & those other articles sent me, I have not tried on my pants, but have every competence in them fitting & pleasing me, I have not opened the box of provisions yet but believe that there is something substance in it, the Reason I have not opened it, is this J Palmer & S Penland opened there to divide it & P had a nice ham, & a nice pone of light bread, & a cake, the bread & cake got a little wet & was likely to spoil, & it was late in the night & this morning & all day so busy, I concluded that it could wait & tonight on pickett, In fact it will last longer, one at a time, Lt person & boy board with us, he brought in some things when he come

P2

That was verry acceptable & I am glad that we can Return the favor, Although he is a glutten, & eats just like he was raiseded to shair by the truth, I shall open it tomorrow, if the Yanks don't have us in the pits, I would fight them verry hard for these precious things, I do not anticipate a fight here soon, but it may come soon & it seems to me the quicker the better for them, My Dear I feel from the weight of that box that you have really sent me more than you aut to have speared never the less I am thankful to you for your self sacrafize, we get plenty now & have since we quit beef, the swap of Sugar for pork, I spoke of in a former letter but, about 3 weeks ago I tell you was hard times, Any thing from home is better than what we draw, Still I have no reason to complain, for I am well & hearty, & Dan is one of the best cooks in camp, & he controlls the chitchen & smoke house appointment, we can have a good bread out of corn meal by putting a little soda in it we get it for 15o cts a per lb I believe, Still I do not know, & I is not near to ask in a word he buyes any & every thing he sees & thinks we aut to have, & I depend upon him, & believe he is proud of me, I scarcely ever have to schold him he is always ready, always cheerful, still patient that she kneed not be uneasy about him, for where I go he goes, & when I quit the army, that I will give him a final discharge & if we both live (whitch I hope & pray we may) will come back to our loved home together, God being willing Oh that our Father in heaven will continue to bless,

good bie Dear one SC Kelly

APR 3RD 1863
CAMP 30TH ALA CHICKASAW BYO

.03 P1

My Dearest Amie I wrote to you 2 days ago in pencil & have nothing new to write, but in that I promised to write again soon& now I have a chance to send this by hand to Oxford & think you will be sure to get it, So I conclude to answer all those letters at once, But before I proceed let me again Return you my sincere for the box of nice things you sent me, but still I am affraid that you will kneed them worse than I do, the bread was a little molded but Dan wets it & tosted it & we emajond

It the best in the world, the sausage are just to order, I appreciate the eggs highly & will have some of them several days, the butter I know is nice, we have not eat any of it yet, the pears & every thing else was highly appreciated, My Dear do not

miss understand me, All is Right but I am now getting plenty & I did not expect so mutch, I had the buttons put on my coat today, for whitch I paid one dollar it fits like a bag shirt, it is , if any odds too small, but when I get off one of my shirts & loose some of my flesh by the warm weather it will be large enough, I can button it & wear it buttoned, I am well pleased all round, my shirts are 2 linsey 2 calico, You know where they came from my 5 dollar shirt & a nit shirt all of them I brought from home, & all good but the 5 dollar one, the calico ones are apparently as good as ever, the linsey ones are a little dingy & wearing slick, drawers good, I think I can make out till fall & then may be we will be at home by that time

P2

My Dear I knew we owed J.R.G. a goodeal but if we have not paid him a sight, I think G has acted gentlemenly all the time I have been gone, & If it is any accommodation for him to wait, pay Cary Estice, I think we owe Montgomery a note of 170 or upwards, I hope it is paid but fear it is not, You cannot pay any one after David until you get more, I do not know when I can send you any more (Swan is a joke) I hope we will soon get out of debt, unless you get me a substitute, or buy Linda & her children, You cant do that whitch had you Rather do, give from 12 to 20 hundred dollar for a sub, or from 20 to 25 hundred for her & children, I am sertain that I could pay 25 h D, in cotton easier now than I could have paid 15 hundred at the time, Teague bought her, I am in earnest about sub, I have the subject under consideration, I do not know whether I could I could resign or not, I do not know whether Coln S would sign for me, or not, but I have got a little hurt, Still I do not believe that the Coln ment any harm, he seems as frenly as ever, & is now sick, & talking himself of Resigning, he I am in hopes will be up in a few days, he is the best Coln in the Brigade any how &sf , to the estate money do not take it unless you can use it, You might if James deserves it take it from him & deposit it at Woodwards or else where, if none of the heirs will take it, Or if they will all take a part, You might take your shair whitch will be one 1/5th leaving out Hendrix, I hope you can arrange that business, I am not uneasy about the interest, & I can have a partial settlement when I get enough

P3

to settle, It seems like that Miller children might use some of it, as they are a long way behind, but it is Confederate, & it is plenty, If money was scarce all would be Ready, Did Robt Miller come to see you, I suppose he did not, I wish that I was at home & then you could see me Strut Round in my new Suit, & you may rest assured that you would get as many kisses (at least) as there is buttons on it, I think that I shall work Sam Penland out of that scrape yet, Still I think he did, he has not done wrong, but for the sake of his correction &I am disposed to lend a hand the 20 days labor & unless I am ordered other wise I shall make out the pay Roll, so as to show that he has just drawn 2 month swages ahead,

I appeared in R Cooleys defence before the Coln & cleared him, So I have got all straight & he is the proudest fellow, out of jail, Tell the boys to learn fast & mind what ms B & you say, that is the way to make men of themselves & now Right here my Dear A let me caution you again, If I never get home do not neglect the education of our children, for ma man without is no man at all, Only as a hewer of wood & drawer of water to him that has, and as an illustration of that I have 109 non commissioned officers & privates in the Co, Airheart the best chance & I have my doubts about him passing the examination, Bale Pike was Rejected, & I expect to have to go to another Co for one, I have the election tomorrow, I am verry glad to learn that you have quit crying (nearly) Oh that we could have faith as a grain of mustard seed, be thankful be prayful , trusting in God who has blessed us in so many ways, You say you wish that you could come & see me &C, There is a talk of us going to Vicksburg (our Brigade) as a city guard, & the balance of our Division (Stevensons) going back to

P4

Tennessee & Gen Tracy Com of the post, If we do, Several officers are talking of bringing their wives & boarding them here, but this kind have no children, but I suppose if that be the case, that you might make me a visit, & bring the children, also, don't start until you hear from me again, You kneed not fear wearring me with long letters that is the sent, I am glad you called on Mrs Teague, I expect that D would ask 25 hundred for Lindy & children & at 20 cts per pound would take nearly all the cotton we have, but cotton is worth 40 cts in Montgomery, You can see what can be done, I do not know what I will do, but I Rec that I shall not try to Resign, give yourself mo uneaseness about this matter for I am in hopes that I may make an efficient officer, I am studdying more than I have ever have before,& acknowledge that I have neglected too mutch, I go to prayermeeting nearly every night Mr Underwood has meetings in the Companies, night after tomorrow is the night in my Co, last night there was a good turn out & they seemed to Respect & esteem the preacher, I also go nearly every night up to the Colns to family worship, I hope that the cause may prosper in the Regt, Still it is cold times, Oh that God would Revive us there is lots of Baptist in the Regt more than any other denomination, but in my Co but verry few, All is quiet here, may be fight but don't seem so to me, I believe I have told you nearly all I can now, when I come home I will talk you to sleep, God bless us & Save us from harm good bie your own Sam

APR 16ᵀᴴ 1863
CAMP ON CHICKASAW BYO

.16 P1

My Dearest Amie we returned to camp between sundown & dark tonight after a trip of 10 days all well that went with me but M Henderson, he has Rhumatism so bad that he couldnot walk, we left several in camp together with the crippled all whitch are improved but two Taylor & davis are bad sick, I had with me 47 men we went about 70 miles by water & 25 by land & 9 more before we took water making in all about 100 miles, the Yankees were up Deer Creek but when we got up there they Skedaddled, burning every thing before them, I cannot give you a description of what I saw now, but simply write this to let you know that God in his mercies has still been with me, I am well & found

Dan well on my Ret, I stood the trip finely & saw one of the

P2

best country in the world with some objections, but I got lazy while gone, I got to camp just in time to read one of your letters before it was to dark to read, then eat Supper off of ham & Sausages & egg bread whitch I had preferred, (he saved it), I then had a tub of water & took off as black a shirt as is common for a Capt to wear, took a good wash & put on clean clothes (full suit) then went to meeting, at the Colns, & can really say that it was good to be there, there was 10 or 12 who came forward desiring an interest in the prayrs, I then came back read your other letter one of the 2ond & other 8ᵗʰ, I was thankful to read them, & Read one other on business then I concluded that I would burn more of the candle you sent me & scrabble this & but for that you would have to wait another day, It is now late & I have traveled about 80 miles today &9 on foot since 2 oclock PM, So I will bid you good bie God bless us still, S

Tell Emma & Jame that J.P. & S.P. went & Ret with me & are both well, S

APR 18 1863
CAMP 30TH ALA REGT ON CHICKASAW BYO
.18 .19

.18 PI

My Dearest Amie, I wrote you a letter thursday night & then promised to write you another soon, & I now have the chance to send this by Wash Wells who is here to see his sun in my Co & will start home in the morning, It was about 10 ½ Oclock when I lay down that night & just at half past (11) eleven the Yankees undertook to pass a fleet of ten boats 8 Iron Clads & 2 transports, a Sharp fight ensued, but they still steamed on down the River, they hurt no one on our side while we hurt one gun boat & Sank two others, they killed several mules & done some damage to the City, we must have killed some of them, one of our guns went off prematurely & killed 2 men, I will send you the dispatch if I can get one, They fired occasionally all day yesterday & today but too far to reach the city, well we got up when the alarm was given & lay in lines just in front of our Camp & lay there until about 3 AM, & then got permission to go to bed, but I was already to bed on one blanket & covered with another, We were awaiting orders & I reckon it was well enough that we did not have to go for the men were tired & Sleapy, & I am asshamed to say so of co (E) Some of them took sick, I was some what excited but not scared & would have went as far as any one else, if I could, I have what Bowden calls the Soldiers faith, but my trust is in God for protection & not in cowardice, true I have not in a long time withstood a Shower of Shells, Dan was Right up to go with me & I told him to lock the trunk & be ready & he should go, he was the proudest negrow you ever saw when I came from Deer Creek

P2

after we left that night, cooked up a bucket full of vietuals & the next morning started to Snyders bluff, expecting to find us there but to his great dismay, he met the wagons & they told him that we had taken the boat & was gone to Deer creek, he had stopped of that night & was not there when we started, I asked old Henry where he was & he told me he was gone to Dr Smiths about 1 ½ miles off, I told Henry to tell Dan that I was mad at him for not asking me, & that rendered him more ressles, but D says that he did not go to S. but had stepped over to the 31st quarter off, it was at 8 oclock PM & that is the time our brigade beat the drum in all the Regt & every co calls the Roll, So he paid no attention to the Drum, but if it had been at an unusual hour he would have come darting, Well I will tell you some thing about our trip to D creek we took passage at Snyders, & went up the Yazoo, 35 miles then turned to the left up Big Sunflower 30 or 35 miles then we took down Little Sunflower 4 or 5 miles & stopped at the mouth of Deer creek, as far as the boats could run, on act of the timber cut in to blockade the Yanks, we then got off on flat boats & turned loose without oars up the creek, I had my Co & ½ of Fransics on one, he had the other half of his on a smaller we embarked about 9 oclk PM & worked & tugged & finally tied up & took up two of the loose plank & made them into oars, we got on some better than with the old broken ones, we landed about 3 AM, after Rowing our flat about 4 miles, I will say in a few words that that, that day we did not see 5 acres of land all put together after we left Snyders, all the country was inundated except the old Indian mounds, & on every one a house, it is nearly ^ unbroken forest, the people live in houses on Stilts

P3

& they seem as happy as ducks in a pond, Dogs & chickens both in the house, Cows & hogs either on a flat boat or on an Indian mound, Cribs & stables perfectly easy about 4 feet deep gardens, pilens up the chim & the old gin house standing quietly off to one side with plenty of water to keep the dust from rising, abut the door of the dwelling you will see a Skiff or Canoe & every thing Seems to go easy with the inmates, Some of the boys asked them what they done for water in this country, I think that place any where on either side of those Rivers is one place that Conscript will not effect, But Deer Creek is a good country but wet as the others except along the bank of the River or creek, Whitch varies from ½ to 5 miles wide & is over 100 miles long, not only so this year but every year, I will close for the present it is so dark I cannot follow the lines

19TH 6 AM

.19 P4

We had quite a Storm last, Wells slept with me on my cane bed, but I know that he did not enjoy it I was sorry for him, I slept well, but he was cold I know I was, he leaves this morning, he has promised to call & see you & tell you all about things generally, Well Deer Creek, is the place for good gin houses, all been by Stream, Some have as many as 4 gins of 100 Saws each, the seed drop in a long trough on a ban that carries them off &so constructed as to drop them either in the seed room or carry them out the doors, Seed is of no use only to plant & feed cattle, the balance is in the way, the land Ritch enough & as little as your garden, the negrows look well & there houses shine like a village, the dwelling houses, Some of them very fine, I will say here, that those gin houses have the Iron Screw (that I was anxious to see) grist & saw mills, all under one shelter, covered with Sypruss Shingles & all the lumber of the same, & the most of those gins are

P5

Supplied with water out of the Creek, they have never tried any wheat till last year, & one gentleman said he sowed a verry low piece & gathered it in Skiffs & got 20 bushels per acre, I saw 2 places that looked fine it was on dry land it was just beginning to head, was nearly waist high, just one week ago today, it best for to make 20 to 40 bushels, they make on there up land from 1 to 2 bags of cotton & from 50 to 100 baskets corn & the low lands that are now under water, after the water dries off in June they will plant & make from 40 to 75 bush, the water is full of fish, & the air is of musketoes, I made me a hook out of a kneedle & caught several myself, I caught out of one place 27, they looked like I had caught out of Nancies C but the water is to high to fish now, when it is down they say one can catch as many as he wants my dear I have tried to interest you in this letter, but it seems to me that I have failed

P6

I know if we have no bad luck we will get put of debt, but hold on to the cotton until you can trade it for Linda, & Teague to get her out o the law (at that) I will not buy a law suit, Cotton will be money after the war, I saw where lots of cotton was burnt to keep it out of the Yanks hands, up DC there is lots of cotton & corn both up there yet, after all the burning, the Yanks laid waist about 25 miles of it, I do not want boots until winter I have 2 pair shoes & an old pr boots, I rather have shoes for summer, I am glad to know the stock are doing well, have the Jack put in the stable & if you choose kill the goats, I am so glad that you appreciate home & ort to be more themselves, I have not had the chance to visit my sick only in our Regimental Hosp, the most of them that is sent off go to Canton, we have 4 in Regt Hosp & Joe Hobbs the cook he is well but home, Had you have known that Wells was coming you could have sent my hat, but I have the verry nastest sort of hat, I swapped with a gentleman of colour on DC & gave him 14 dollars to boot, is Dicky going to school, precious children may they learn it is the education that makes the man & I am better satisfied or rather reconciled, & am bound to believe that I am Respected as an officer to the 30th Ala Regt, but I do not consider it a disgrace to get a Sub, I do not intend to be coowred, but the Coln is not well & any man is ill when sick, I appreciate your advice & have never doubted your love, If I know my heart, I love you in Ret, I never fail attending meeting there is a brother Howard from Ala holding a meeting in our Regt nightly, there is good congregations & some good feelings & lots that go up & give there hand for prayer, they will be meeting at 3 PM, would be there at them but for saying to mutch to me, I appreciate your advice, I am pleased with my clothes but abused them that DC trip, take good care of every of every thing, I must close with my prayers & wishes

Amen Your own Sam

.19 found in letter

Apr 23rd 1863
Camp 30th Ala near Warrenton 10 miles below
Vicksburg
.23 .24

P1

My Dearest Amie I Rec yours of the 17th on the 21st I was happy to receive one so late, & Yet do seams that (You all were well) I hope that you have Rec two of me, Since I Rec from DC, I think that Dan wrote some thing about my being gone but suppose from yours that he said nothing about it, in fact he, & So did we think that we were just going to Snyders Bluff, I am glad to hear that Spinning improves your health, I do hope & pray that you may be healthy, I Rather blame myself with your infirmities, Oh that I had been one week later getting home, I am glad you have a good prospect for a garden, I believe that your garden is as forward as any I saw in this country, but Vicksburg has more pretty flower gardens than any where I ever saw, I do pray that the Lord will give us a plentiful harvest, Oh that he will forgive us a nation our sins & keep off Rust & mildews & Send us Rain in Season, & make us a plentiful nation, dependant on the mercies of the living God, I Regret your chickens are not doing well, If you could rise lots you might Swap bacon for Sugar pound for pound or perhaps do better, I believe if I were in your place I would S barter pounds in that way, Judge Walker will swap, I suppose I want you if convenient to see John Weaver, & write to me about him, Elisha W, I guess is done, that is has seen his best days & likely his best health, You had better keep some money on hand for I tell you it takes lots to do me here, my Comissary bill was 22 ½ dollars for march & every thing Turn it

P2 WRITTEN BETWEEN LINES OF P1

in proportion I owe for Apr but am inclined to think that it will not be so mutch as you as you sent me sutch an abundance, it did not last as well as if we had not gone off, about all gone but one piece of sausage, We can draw plenty of Rations now but high I am nearly out of money but we will draw in a few days I suppose, there is nearly two months wages due me will be the last of

Apr & if we do not draw I can borrow, the Cavalry after Fergerson was a good Reply, I guess the Cavalry annoys those inclined to Shirk, How many notes did you take last year on the Jack, I never knew & If Old martha is in fold & she will not have it until sometime in July, I have not been well since I wrote you by well I was affraid that I was going tom have chills, I took some pills one night & a dose of calomel the next & been taking some pills occasionaly & we have moved twice, day before yesterday, down from 4 miles above to 4 below Vicks & was just getting fixed up when orders came to strike tents & be Ready to move, this was at noon & the Regt, in fact the Brigade moved off at 2 PM, we got there about 2 PM the day before & before we had time to put up our tents, Oh how it did rain but I kept dry by leaving home & going to Coln Smiths & who had his up & that night it Rained all night nearly & arrived here a while before night, both moves I did not start with the Regt, but stayed with the baggage & came with it on a waggon, I think that I am about well, I did not want to stay yesterday but Lts thought best from 2 considerations

P3

frst because of my health & 2ondly to look after our bagage, I have not been down but was verry unwell I think I am well now & will Resume my duties we had an alarm last night, I was going the Yanks Run by some more boats last night & also

lost some, I saw the light of one, said to have been burnt to the waters edge, about sutch another affair as last week I guess, nothing official as yet, my Dear one do not be uneasy about me, I will tell you the worst, I think that I took cold after sleeping in those gin houses that is all of it, I spoke of the bad effect at the time, but did prefer a good cotton bed to the wet cold ground, We are in a nice place now on the level of a small branch covered in green grass with an occasional tree, Sun around on all sides with abrupt hills covered with beech, oaks, gums & magnolia trees, with the prettyest grass growing beneath there shades, far preferable to the old hill side corn field we stopped at last, we are at the place we used to come picketting about 1 ½ miles from the River, where , I Reckon, that the Yanks may attempt to land but I guess that they will meet a hot Reception, I believe that I have told you all I know, You see the difference in this line & the above ones, that was written on my knee, I am now writing on my trunk, You will perceive that paper is scarce as well as money, ten miles from market & horses all poor, & the verry sorryest sent there (3) dollars per quire (my trunk to low) J Palmer is now on orderly, I appointed him, he is still unpopular in the co, but the best Sgt I have, I let B pike go back to orderly, but the Coln said that it would not do, So I appointed P. who knows that he is unpopular & consequentally ask no favours & grants none, I have less trouble, John is not so unpopular as he was a while back, he has his faults but is as clever to me as any man in the co, All are opposed to my Resining , Lts & every one that has talked to me, I do not know what to do about it, nor do I know what the Co would do for a Capt to answer questions, I think that I am not the man but do not know where he is that can be heard, my pen is bad or ink or paper greasy or something the matter, I will try my pencil, I have the largest Co in the Regt & more men for duty & have Refused 5 or 6 who want to be transferred to the Co & having said to the Co that I would give any one a transfer that wanted off, but have never had but two applications since I have been Capt & they failed & they seem satisfied perfectly.

24TH 4 ½ PM

My dear the weather is verry hot here now & we are all sun burning as fast as I ever saw men, the water is verry good for Missippi, All quiet yesterday & today no excitement, but do not know how soon, The health of the Army good, Soldiers in good spirrits, all seem longin of success, if we are ever attacked here, I am still on the improve, I drilled the company this evening in Battalion drill, feel no inconvience from it, I doctored myself all the time, I have quit Smoking, I have not smoked in 6 weeks or 2 months, never smoked regularly, & will have to quit chewing or give 2 dollars for the verry poorist sort, per plug, I have not Shaved since you saw me, my baird is (the longest) 6 inches, not mutch gray, not like my head, my mustash is not mutch longer & has been shedding out all the time so has all my baird, I believe that in one year all of mans baird shedds out,

My Dear Amie I do want to see you so bad, do have your teeth fixed if there is any good chance, if I am old & gray I want you to look well & I think you have paid nearly all the debts you can, I will close write tome at least once a week, I will write that often unless on a trip, God bless us Your own Sam

PS I believe that Arheart will s tand the examination, I hope so

APR 26TH 6 ½ AM
CAMP 30TH ALA NEAR WARRENTON MISS

.26 Pl

My Dear Amie I just started you a letter day before yesterday & have nothing of interest to write now, but I have a good chance to send by Lt Warlick of Francis Co who has had Small Pox & is verry near blind, he & Lt Finch of the same co both have furloughs for 30 days, One of Charles Littlejohns, Sons has lost one of his eyes by S.P. he is well in other Respects, I am well, have not been Sick since I wrote you, except a slight headache last night, I went to preaching & there was a large croud, a brother H Swan from Ala preached, but I am not testify for nor against the sermon for I was like the desiples, my head was heavy (& I had to sit on the ground & from sitting to leaning, & from leaning to laying clean down & from there it was not far to sleep, I never wake but once & then strove against sleep, but was perfectly over come & the moving to pray awoke me & I came off as ignorant of the sermon, all but the text, whitch was, & Ye are my witness &C I felt condemned, there is to be preaching today & to night & I think I will do better, , Our brother Howell, is gone to Mobile, & our having to move Rather broke the meeting, but I hope that the Lord will Revive his work among us, Some 3 or 4 convertions during that meting, the preachers of the Brigade met together & do it now at our Regt to hold meetings, all of them are Baptist but one, he a Cumberland presbyterian, Jim or Joe Weatherly one, the Chaplin of one Regt, I Scraped up an acquantance with him, he knew you & all of you, he brought a letter for me

P2

from Martha Gladden, a couple of weeks ago, All is quiet no fighting, Our Regt sends out one co a day on pickett, today is Francis co, wendesday is our day, they go down on the River to watch the Yanks if they should attempt to land, Well Amie I have never been at so great a loss to know what to write to fill my paper, I Reckon you will go to Hopewell to meeting today, Our Little preacher has got his wife in the neighborhood, She has no children, as we move he moves his boarding house, I think he will do well with us, the men Respect him & esteem him, he visits the Sick in tents & Regt Hospital, he distributes tracks a few testaments & occasionally a Baptist on two to the Co, the boys on pickett have some fun fishing, the levee is cut, & they get in the water & dip with a hamper basket & catch from 1 to ten hickory shad about 4 or 5 inchs long, they will spoil in 2 hours unless cooked, there was a fish party in the neighborhood yesterday, I will close I have written all I know that will interest you & the time is out, May God of his infinite mercies still have mercy on us, & keep us in the way we should go, & bring about a piece honorable to us as a nation & then all the wearied Soldiers could Return to stay at home,

good bie my Dear one Your own Sam

MAY 1863

NEAR PORT GIBSON MAY 2 OND 1863

.02 Pl

My Dear A. We are all well that is here & all together, Our Co went off under Lt Pike wednesday morning on pickett to Warrenton, that night we started at Sunset for Grand Gulf, we traveled until 2 Am, arrived at Big Black R where we lay down & slept until after Sunrise while the balance of the Brigade or those before us were crossing in flat boats, we were ready in our turn & crossed on a Steam boat, about 7 when we took up line & marched, until about 5 PM, passed PG & halted within 2 miles of Port Gibson, drew rations but had nothing but boards to cook bread upon boiled bacon & eat mostly without bread, at dark we took up line & marched about

5 miles passing PG & halted in line of battle, Well I had those

of the Co. that were on duty & came in on the day that Lt P left, the lame & mame & Convealessent, making in all 24 besides myself Lt Arheart, 1 Sgt Palmer, Corporals Ford & Tode Wolf, Privates Alexander, Argo, Bowman, W.P. Garrett, N H Graham, Booker Henderson, Jim Peace, B Pike, Smith, Bill Stewart, Jim Tygrett, Reaves, C D White, Rad Wilkinson, all these went in the fight & JimTygrett killed, C D White & Reaves missing all the rest untouched, Bill Estice fell out or rather give out the last day, Nance Gulledge, Joe Dunker, Pinter & Jay Wingo fell out the first night, all of the men acted bravely & we stood our ground until the whole Right wing gave way & in the Retreat was where we lost the missing, they have the field, we fell back in Rather bad order for about one mile bringing off

P2

all our guns & accoutrements (but leaving knapsacks & blankets) where we formed & came off in order, we fell back about 6 miles from the battle ground, the casualties of the Regt, 7 killed, 28 wonded & 45 missing, Capt Tom Pattison was wonded & left on the field not mortally, Gen Tracy fell in 5 steps of me &

Coln Shelly & I helped carry him down the hill, was shot through with a minee ball, in the Roar of my Co early in the fight, the Battery that we had to support was badly damaged & left on the field & Several horses, they were forced to Retire about 10 oclock, & we our Regt held the position until 5 PM, on our wing we had no artillery after the silencing of the Bat, Capt Johnson of the Bat is brave & his men left all & we had to Det men of our Regt to drive the pieces off the field, the officers did there duty & 2 Lt & several of the men killed, Our forces were too Small for the enemies, they I expect were Reinforced all day & ours did not come in time, Lt P. was among them & met us about one mile on the Retreat, we lay in the Sun from

6 AM until 5 PM, the battle opened about 7, our ammunition Run Short & we Received fire all day, it came at last, & we sent for but did not get til after the fall back, We were gaunt & in fine fix for Running, I aet Wednesday dinner & been snacking since, had

breakfast, we are in fine flight for fighting, I sent Dan back 4 miles across the byo, I asked God to have mercy upon us, & if I in the battle should forget him, for him to Remember me I tried to pray & feel more thankful than ever before, I must close my time is out Dick Weaver did not get there, he is a poor hand to walk, we traveled 40 miles in 24 hours, God stil bless Yours Sam

Near Warrenton May 4th 1863 7 oclock PM

.04 .06 P1

My Dearest Amie I wrote to you on the 2 ond at Byo Pier, We stayed there after destroying the spendid wire bridge until one oclock the 3rd, when we took up line of march for big black river, we would have arrived there by 12 or one oclock but the enemy annoyed our rear all day & when we arrived in 4 miles we took accross the direction of the main Road (& the one we were in) & went out 2 ½ or 3 miles Square off we lay there expecting a fight (but no fight) & we were ordered across the R, we went on flats tied together, the whole army passed over unmolested, where we met heavy Renforcements, who had come to our assistance, we got to camps about 1 mile about 5 PM, & about dusk, the bridge was to be cut, they went at it & had cut it pretty well to pieces, & the enemy took advantage of the hill & flew in with there Cavalry & turned them loose & drove them from the boat, they yelled & hoped but no was hurt, but our Sharp Shooters kept them from the Shore, So ended the day after a march of 22 or 3 miles, Rations Scant but all seem in fine Spirits this morning, there was some pickett firing & one of our batterys Silenced all that at a few shots, they haven not pressed us today, We evacuated G Gulf, & blue up the magazine

The 6th 7 oclock AM

P2

We have traveled about 10 miles today, I will quit for is so dark
Same place nothing strange occurred yesterday except we got plenty to eat & nothing to do, we are (I Suppose) in line of battle,

which extends from Warrenton to Big B. Brick Road & bardge, we are in 1 ½ miles of our old camp, Lt Coln Pettus who was taken prisoner & carried as far as the River (15) miles & got away & came into camp last night (he belonged to the 20th Ala, all thought he was killed, he Says that there dead lay thick on the field, that they had 40 thousand, while we only had 3 brigades the largest one did not number 12 hundred, we did not have more than 2 thousand men engaged at any one time, there was General Bowan Baldwen & Tracys brigades & Gen Green came up & covered the Retreat, we were Scarce of ammunition & Reserved our fire all day until about 4 PM when it came & we sent for it & before it came they had flanked us on the Right wing & Reinforcements not up, So it was a critical time on the 20th (who were on the Right) Lt Coln Pettus charged them with his Regt & drove them back to the woods where they were in column & forced him to Retreat, they fell back under a cross fire & passed our Regt & we Rec orders (of Coln Garrett of the 20th who was in command of the Brig) to fall back, we could have held our position if they had held ours, Coln P Said they told him that they began to fight by Single Regt to Regt, but we poared sutch deadly fire into them that they brought up Brigades in Colllams against Regts, I saw two flag bearers with flags in hand running

P3

not spread (5) but rolled up, I saw no stars nor stripes on them, they were not more than 30 yds apart, So that shoes that there was 2 Regts at that one place, & I am satisfied that was too many bullets come over our heads for a Single line of battle of only 2 deep, It seemed like at times that they came as thick as drops of Rain in a common slow Rain & the artillery who whorled their missils of death over us all the day, we lay in line in the hot Sun 10 of the longest hours that I ever seen seemingly, We had only 2 Batterys of Artillery & ours was disabled about 9 or 10 AM & we held the position until 5PM, Capt Patterson of our Regt is wonded & a prisoner, Coln Hanlly of the 31st also, a prisoner that the 31 took, who was carrying of their wonded said that his Coln was killed & that a Brig Gen also that he knew of, that we carried off our dead & wonded verry fast or else that we had more compared to theirs, ever evidence goes to show that we killed lots of them, we did not let them get nearer than 6 or 8 hundred yds, before we opened on them & then we could not see them only when they ran, for they were in a gorge or hollow, it is the brokenest country you ever saw, all or nearly all of the fighting was guess work, I took one crack at the front of woods where I saw some run out of, I saw one fall, I thought one of Francis men killed him, my men all acted bravely in fact all the Regt, they Shot deliberately & the orders were not to Shoot until they saw what to shoot at, the Rifles is the fellows, the muskets fell long way Shot, I told the Coln & he ordered them not to Shoot till they came closer, whitch was not that day

P4

not in front of our line, but worked Round to the end, George & Charles Loyd were both in the fight (31st) C. was wonded in the arm late in the day & is missing, I think that we will fight them again, we are not half whipped if we did fall back 50 miles, it only strengthed us while it weakened them, we are close to our Supplies & Reenforcements while they are mutch farther off, the men are in good health & fine Spirits, I am sorry for the inhabitance that fall into there hands, & especially the poor negrows , they are scared to death nearly running too & froe around some cabbins & the poor things were scared & running & hollowing, from the time we got there (10 PM) until after the battle opened lugging their children & baggage from place to place, & after the batt opened I hollowed to them to clear out & Run clear back out of danger, they took my word & went as fast as possible, I never saw them more, I must close for I have not but little time as I expect to send it by Lt McGee and now my Dear wife I may never see you more but hope I shall yet to live to help gain our independence, & to enjoy the Sweet of piece we gain by it & to shair with you the Sweets of a cottage home, but If I am not so blessed, I am willing to submit to the will of God, who Rules all things, in whome I trust for life & for Salvation through the Richeousness of his own son Jesus Christ, trust in God for he will hear his children when they cry unto him, tell the children & negrows this, So if we met no more on earth that they may prepare to meet me in heaven, where there is no war, God bless us, good bie Your Sam

AUGUST 1863

DEMOPOLIS AUG 12TH 1863

My Dear Amie we arrived here about 12 Noon yesterday, I am well as to health but Sick at heart Co E consists of Lts Pike & Arheart, & S M Penland, Sam was put on duty as all the barens Creek prisoners are those that were payrolled on the field & those that were carried up north that passed Silty Point before the 3rd day of July, The Regt Rendervoosed at the R Road & arrived at Selma with about 70 men officers & all an average of 7 men to the Co, I hope we will not Stay here long under sutch circumstances, Your Sam God bless us all good bie

TALLADEGA ALA AUG 24TH

My Dear amie we arrived at this place this morning & to my great Surprise & dissatisfaction but few of my Co, The Coln Said he intended to Send me back today for them but he has gone off & it is nearly train time & nothing more said, I am better but not well, Old Mrs Denson is Sick, on the mind, I must close it is uncertain how long we stay here look fo__ me 2 or 3 days & if not by then ___ ___ You may give it out Your own Sam

God bless you all good bie

PAYROLLED CAMP 3 MILES BLOW TALLADEGA CLOSE ON RR AUG 29TH 1863

.29 Pl

My Dearest Amie

I was glad to get your letter but was Surprised to hear of

Fannys death, I thought when I left home She was better & would get well but the knowledge of God is above the knowledge of man, & in his ways far more Richeous, I do Regrt our luck & do deaply sympathise with Patient but it is a debt that we all owe, may we all by the mercies of God our Savior be prepared to pay it willingly, Oh that we could Resign ourselves to the will of our heavenly father who givith us all things, I Do hope that you are all well now, I expect to come home as soon as I can get off (IE) when Pike & Arheart comes back, I hope the girles are with you yet, I hope the Colts are over their worst by now, it is nothing uncommon for them to swell

P2

Still it will do no harm to keep the wond washed & grease it & keep it Runing, the orfaice or gash is closed up with matter that should Run out,

My Dear you ask why I did not write more because I had nothing to write, we are in the woods & nothing to do & know but little to write, in fact all seem disappointed, Some getting furloughs for 3 days, I have 4 men out on furlough, I wish I had a word of news to write, I went one night to see my old friend Mr Headen, he is not well, Matilda as usual, it is about 2 ½ miles, I think now that I Shall go back to see them again, I am thinking of going to Talladega to church tomorrow, write me often, excuse Short letters for I will tell you all, I will try & Sign my name to this as

P3 written in margin

as one that loves you dearly & pray God to have mersy on us & bring us together often during the war & once for all when it is over S C Kelly

September 1863

Demopolis Ala Sept 25th 1863

.25 P1

My Dear Amie ___ am well as usual & a great deal better satisfied than I was when we were here in payroll camp last month, we came to Selma Wednesday _____ morning & stayed all night, yesterday morning took open box cars for this place, arrived in good time, I have with me 45 men, about as large a co as is in this Regt, I look for all our boys with Lt Arheart & I hope he will come soon, It they do not they will be <u>h</u>unted & treated as deserters, I have ____ thing to write that will interest you, <u>I</u> think the prospect good got us to stay in the western Division & not go to Tenn, I hope the news is true about our victory, Still I have some doubts may God have mercy upon us, we are expecting to be Reviewed today by Gen Hardee & we are scraping &

P2

Swaping around generally, I Shall send some money to J. R. Graham, Some of li___

Shinplasters, I had Redeemed for him, it____ all my time the evening we got to Selma Running about for that, but I do not mi___ that for him, Shelly is acting Brig <u>adv</u> Gen & Francis in Command of the Regt, they want things done to the notch, I must close & Superintend the closing up, write to me Direct to Denopolis 30th Ala good bie

Your own Sam

PS I have just Rec one of yours the 13th May have not Red it, but will, SK

Camp 30th Ala Near Demopolis Sept 29th 1863

.29 P1

My Dear Amie I have been looking for a letter from you, but suppose that you wates to send by Arheart who I expect today, I have nothing mutch to say, only that I am well, that we are drilling with a <u>min</u> that Rations seem scarce & poor (after leaving home) that I have no one cooking for me & not allowed any one, that I do myself, Dan the most immagenable that I have not heard a word from _____ Coln S paid the men that arrived _____ _____ _____ _____ that I eat the last of my provisions brought from home Sunday, that all kept well, that I was sorry when it gave out, &C I am messing with the Pikes & John Allen, bacon is worth one dollar & every thing else in proportion & have to pay the cash as we go, if I had a negrow I do not nor could not draw Rations enough to feed us, unless it was Dan, I would Risk

P2

but alass poor Dan, is either dead or cooking for those who is our enemies, My Dear I find out that I kneed another blanket if it will not disfurnish you too mutch, you will please him over that old one I carried home & send it to me by Dick Prater who has a ferlough home for seven days, we can draw them they say but when I have no idea, So many waiting, I Shall draw money in a few days I am anxious to hear from you, I fear you are sick, I want to know how the boys are doing, how the sugar corn holding out, how mutch wheat halled to the mill &C&C my boots hurt my feet a little but the weather is dry & they seem to draw, but they are better, I think we will have Rain today, there is quite a Revival going on in the brigade (meetings of night) lots of members, all seem anxious to hear, a good many convertions & 9 saved, the several churches 5 of them the Mis Baptist, Still goes on, I do feel so thankful, but regret to say that but few of our Regt, & none of my Co seem to take an interst, I will close as I have neither time nor matter to fill the other page, Oh that the crewel war was over & we as a nation have gained our independence, & the poor Soldiers could Ret to their former familess, So mode it be, Your own Sam

OCTOBER 1863

CAMP 39TH REGT ALA VOLS NEAR DEMOPOLIS ALA OCTOBER 4TH 1863

.04 P1

My Dearest one I Received yours by Lt A in time & was glad to hear that you were all well, I feel thankful that God has still speared us, as a nation & more especially as a family, Oh that we as the heads of our family could be more greatful, for Shurely the Lord has been verry kind unto us, Shurely he has heard our prayers, Shurely he has taught us on whome to believe & to look to for the life that now is & the one whitch is to come, wherefore we should (the more earnestly) to give ourselves unto God, as a living sacrifice, whitch is but our Reasonable service, There is quite a Revival going on in our Camp , the meetings are of night & Sundays, we had a sermond today, by Brother Weatherly after whitch was a conference to Receive into Babtist Church by experience those who had previously givin their names & Regt

P2

the ordinence of babtism this evening at 3 oclock in the River on whitch banks we are encamped to about ten or eleven converts the Methodist have Received (I believe) 6 the Cumberland Presbyterians 2 or 3 & there was one who come to join the primitive Baptist, but no one to Represent his church, Our preacher told him that he did not want to baptize him, because his church the Primitives did not Recognise it as a valid, So the case stands (did not hear his experience) There was quite ma number of Baptist at the conference, & when the Right hand of fellowship was extended, Showed who was on the Lords side & who were Babtist, burried with Christ in babtism, Oh it does my heart good to see sutch interest taken in the one thing kneedful, the Salvation of the Sole, although we are Sundered by the sins of war, Yet there is a joy in the Religion of our Lord & Savior, this world is full of troubles, Still

P3

now & then there is a bright spot, & although we are separated, Yet we meet, around one common mercies seet, It is hard for me to be a Soldier & face the storm of bullets, believing that if I should fall, that I fall depending on the Richiousniss of Christ, Oh how could I be a Soldier without hope, Still there are thousands who are brave, who go into the battle as the horse, Oh that God would use his professed followers as exstreme stabilities, to bring them all in to his army, then this would be a brave army indeed, brave in defense of their homes & families & brave in the cause of our blessed Redeemer, pushing forward from victory to victory, until the kingdom of this world become the kingdom of the Lord and his Christ, more after the babtism, good bie 4 ½ PM babtism over, & sutch a congregation some say

P4

one thousand, but I think 5 hundred, it is a bluff place & but little chance to get near the Presbyterian preacher sprinkled 4 at the place of meeting, but few there, the methodist preacher is sick, I have nothing else to write as I know of, I have been looking foe a letter today, I Rec one from John Palmer dated 1st October, he informed me of the Deaths of Bowman, & Lt Pikes negrow that there was a great deal of sickness in the neighborhood, that he had & was taken sick, that you were to see them the day before & that you were all well &C I Suppose that Swan is dead & John Mtgomery has a flesh wond in the thigh, My Dear I left my bible, I reckon I havent it, I want you to send it the frst chance, I also lost your letter, I Read it & stuck it, as I thought in my pocket, but it is gone, We are doing as well as we kneed to, no complaint, but for the want of cooking vessels, I have 60 men & only 3 small ovens

P4 (WRITTEN IN MARGINS)

Up to yesterday we got 3 or 4 Kettles we will do well now, we have drawn armes & accouterments knapsacks Haver Sacks & Canteens, nothing sertain as to where we will go or when we are drilling & going through all the Regular Rotueendy of duties common to Soldiers life, except picketing, Oh I forgot to tell you, that Coln Pettus is a brigiadier general before Coln Shelly, he was Lt Coln of the 20th Ala under Garrett, who was Killed in Vicksburg he is a noble fellow & I hope will be our brig, Coln S, is acting now Lt Coln, Patterson is with us in command of our Regt, he is about well, Still he limps a little, he is a thorough babtist, I will close with my best wishes & prayers upon you & yours, praying that the Father may still be with us Yours S C Kelly

Camp 30th Ala Demopolis Ala October 4th 63

.04 P1

My Dear A I am in a mighty hurry to get you a few lines in time to get it off in this mornings mail, I Rec yours by Prather yesterday, & was glad to hear from home that you were all well, but you were in sutch a fit that you had like to had forgot to have told me that you were all well, & my Dear one I am sorry that you are so low down, trust in God for he will yet save you, Still I would have liked to know how mutch Molasses you made, as to the other enquires in your letter, I will try to answer them verbally in a few days, I think that I will me at home next Sunday morning if nothing turns up more than common, I Shall stay but a short time but long enough to tell you howdy & good bie, I Shall start from here friday at 1 PM & Stay in Selma until P AM Saturday, come to your Sisters that night & try to get a horse from them & if I do I Shall be there by 3 AM Sunday morning, God being my helper may be you want to come down to see your kin if so, do so & we could go home Sunday, Suit your own convenience about that, I can get home sooner

P2

than the first way proposed, but, then I would not have your company, I am well & doing well as I expected, we drill all the time allowed & I could start tomorrow but for a review by Gen Hardee, on Thursday, (I am well) & get along as well or in fact better than I thought, The meeting is Still going on last night, Espy preached, & with goof effect his first time, there was 9 Joined the church last night besides seven, one other night this week babtizing to day at 2 PM, the babtist get full half or over, Sam Hall came out & stayed all night with me one night this week, he is buying corn for a Government Cole mine in Shelby or bibb, I will close now & try to tell you the rest next Sunday, God being willing may the Richest of blessings Rest upon us as a family * a nation is my prayers Your own Sam

OCT 5TH 8 AM

.05 P1

My Dearest A I have been verry busy all morning Capt or Coln Ritchie is here & I want to send this letter by him at least as far as Selma, to keep it from going through Montgomery, I have made out Bowmans Dis List & will send it to you to give to Mrs B. then she can send it to Judge Wood, & She will be better satisfied if she sees the Paper, than she will be, if I send it to Wood & she not know only by say so, Recollect that Bowman owes me out of it 44 dollars, You

P2

can have the better chance to get it by giving her the out, or you can stop it in the hands of Wood but he has so many papers & so very apt to forget it, I think she will pay it, I have drawn 2 months pay & Arheart paid me, I could send you some, if you kneed it, I have over 3 hundred dollars, I must close it is drill hours, we had a good meeting again last night Good Bie S C Kelly

CAMP 30TH REGT ALA VOLS OCTOBER 12TH 1863

.12

My Dear Amie I wrote you a letter yesterday, but forgot to stamp or frank it, so I now proceed to write another, I was sorry of it, more especially so because I wanted you or Billy to meet me at the head of the Road on Saturday night, as it is I may get home before this, I expect to start at 1 PM on Friday, if all parties are willing & nothing turns up I am well & nothing that will interest you & must close or miss the chance today Your own Sam

.CAMP 30TH ALA OCTOBER 16TH 1863

.16 P1

My Dear Amie I am so sorry to say to you that I cannot come home, have a pass for 2 days but I cannot Risk it, & besides the Coln will not say that he will not Report me if I fail to get back in time, whitch I cannot do for it will take me 40 hours to get home the best I can do, I tried this morning after I received my paper of his hand to extort a promise from him, promising to start from home on monday night, & Return to Camp on wednesday at 12 oclock, but he said he could do it but for the example, he had let several run over their time & said nothing about it, but I am not from Talladega, he intends to make an example of some body & I do not want it to be me, Could if I were to do so, Costin me, that would do him too mutch good, I know that he

P2

does not like me, or it seems so to me, he seems inclined to blame me on every account, My Dear one these are unpleasant things to write to you, but I feel it my Duty to let you know the worst, I try to do the best I can, & do not think that I have givin Coln Shelly any occasion to been down on me in sutch a manner as he has done for the last 3 months, God Judge between us, & if I am to blame I trust that I may by the mercies of God be enabled to see & make the necessary amends, I Rec yours of the 1st in it yesterday it explained some things that you wrote, Some whitch you wrote like I knew & would have known, had I got the letter in time, As to Selling that horse & mule, Sell them & let the thrashing (another year) take care of its self, I will not do to feed them for that we can make out

P3

without them & had better do it, The meeting is still going on with a goodeal of interest, Still there are lots of men that have never been, although it is Right in there midst, none in the Brigade have to walk more than ¼ of a mile to the place whitch is opposite our Qrtrs & not 50 yds from my Qrtrs, Still several of my Co have never been in fact but a few of us go, I missed last night the first time, & havenot heard who or how many joined, I got me a Sword it cost me 55 dollars, I have got my watch at the Repeares & will go today for it, I Shall have to close, Still I feel like I aut to say something about my clothes, I Shall kneed a pair of pants soon, but if you had Rather, I can buy them Tell Palmer that

P4

I Rec his & was glad to get it, that I wanted him to get that trunk or valuables or either from J R Graham & being it to me, paying him for it, Say to JRG that I may have sent him to mutch money, but do not know it for in making change I got his & mine mixed, Oh that I could interest you we get plenty to eat (Sutch as it is) if we always do as well we will pass through the war well, You need not look for me until you see me coming, I want to come but do not know when ever I will get the chance, John Cooley & Dolf Evans Deserted there Camp night before last, talking off more than belonged to them, May God our God continue his mercies towards us, & bring blessed times of peace of Your own S

CAMP 30TH ALA NEAR DEMOPOLIS OCT 17TH 63

.17 .18 P1

My Dear Amie I wrote to you yesterday by Jack Dale but I was hurried & confused So I thought that I would try it again, not that I can promise to intrest you, but I have no other one on earth that I can tell all to but you, not that I have no friends but that you are to me more than a friend, Yes you are the partner of my life, Oh that we could enjoy that partnership together but sutch is the fate of war, War for what, for you & yours, Oh that I may be enabled to act well my part in this war & that God in his providence may give us those Rights & that Spedely viz the independence of our Confederacy, I feel encouraged at the signs of the times, I do hope & trust that the tide of war has again turned in our favor, the troops all seem to be in good Spirits & condition, we had a Review yesterday by Genrs Johnson & Hardee there was 3 or 4 Brigades out quite an army, Salute guns were fired by the Artillery & at this writing the guns are firing, I suppose as a salute to President Davis, whome we expect to Review us, we have a big Review on Monday any how, Do you see any difference in my hand writing & whitch is the best this or the original, whitch is this, I have been practicing a little the new stile whitch is to hold the pen, between the 2 fore fingers, instead of between the thumb & for finger, the advantage is that I can write without moving the paper

P2

on any part of a muster roll that I can Reach, Still it tires my hand worse, I can write backhanded & straight, I saw an advertisement in the Demopolis written backhanded, it looked nice & was plain, I will quit & see about getting some dinner & good news, the news boys come out every day & we can buy the Selma Reporter or the Daily Missippian either for 25 cts, I nearly always buy the Missippian for it contains the same telegraph & 4 times as mutch reading matter, in a word it is the best Daily in the Confederacy, I am so sorry that I wrote to you that I was coming home I fear you will come to the head of the Road & I not come, for it will put you to so mutch trouble, but I felt confident that I would get to come from what the Coln said, that if I would wait until after thursday that he would fix it up, So I took it for granted, that he would not Report me, nor coshur, nor have me arrested, if I were to go home on a 48 hour leave of absence & Stay a day or two over my time, but alass when I went to have my paper approved (on thursday morning, Ready to get off Friday) he said that officers had got to abusing their privileges & that it had to be stopped & that if I went I must be back at the time, So I told him that that paper pas no use to me & left him, I know one officer who has been gone 8 days today at 1 PM & the train has come in, likely he come but more likely he did not, I will soon hear what is done

P3

in his case, I guess nothing as has been the case with 4 others in the last week, but I am not from Talladega neither am I a favorite & I believe he hates me intensely, not mutch love lost to be Shure. Still I thought that we settled all in Talladega, & so far as I was consearned was, but to my certain knowledge he does not treat me as he used to & I fear he is not Satisfied, although he said he was at the time alluded to, it is now Review & I will close for the pre,

Oct 18th 9 AM the Review I spoke of we had a grand one, all the troops about this place strung out in main st & it must have been ¾ of a mile long & there stood for a ½ hour when the President of the Confederate States passed in Review, The Soldiers Regiment after Regt presented arms & gave 3 cheers to the President whitch went out with enthusiasm, Davis is a plane neat old man, Rather Slender, & Seems to be the man for the times, he is on his way to Miss, we are expecting to move soon, in fact we are Ready & expecting orders to move as soon as we can get transportation on the train, some sooner some later, I suppose we are going to Enterprise, & from there I do not know where, I have nothing new to write, I am officer of the day today, as usual for me to be on Sunday, I am looking for John Palmer soon, I want him to come & bring my pants as soon as they are done, I shall kneed them

P4

soon, I tore a hole in the knee of these yesterday & am going to try to get them patched today, I have also worn out the seat, I tried to draw me a pair the other but there were ten times as many wanting as was pants for, I think that I have certainly fattened since we have been here, my clothes are to small especially my pants & coat, I got my washing done for 25 cts per garment but it is not well done, I Shall have to close because for something to write, we got yesterday a lot of Southwestern babtist, the preacher sent on for 12 copies. So I hope we will get one every week, we will unless we get out of the way of the Regular line, I am inclined to believe that we will go up towards Corinth Miss, Still it is verry uncertain, I must close & have my patching done, & then go to meeting if it does not Rain, looks like it now, I will get a taylor to do my work, The meeting is still going on, but not with sutch Results as brother John Rinfrow writes he has, Still I do hope that there is a great work begun in this part of the army, but we have no sutch preachers as they have in the 10th Ala Regt, May god of his infinite mercy and grace, Still keep us in the way that we should go & bring peace out of confusion & that to our interest & honor as a nation, that the word of God may run & be glorified until all the kingdoms of the earth may become the kingdom of our Lord & of his Christ (Your own) Loved one Sam

CAMP 30TH ALA OCTOBER 19TH 1863

.19 P1

My Dear Amie I wrote to you yesterday by mail but it will not leave until to days train 1 PM, & I have a chance to send this by hand to Talladega & it will go (likely) Sooner than the one by mail for I think that they go up to Montgomery one day & back the next & then Strike for Calhoun, I have no news to write, but what I have written in the other (that is we are expecting to be off in the morning to Meridian & from there we do not know when nor where, The meeting is still going on & I believe with more interest than usual, there was a babtist yesterday & 5 Sprinkled, I am well & doing as well as I kneed expect, the object of this letter is to let you know that I have Sold that (Colonel) to Capt E Johnson (for I suppose 4 hundred dollars) provided that you have not Sold him, now My Dear I never told him anything about his eyes & if they have got well (all Right) let him come (but if they are still running water & he keeps them shut up, or even one of them, when he is standing, tell

Sgt J. M. Smith (of Co B 30th Ala, who I shall give an order to you for the horse) that he has got something the matter with his eyes & that may be he had better not take him or in other words if you have not Sold him & he is all

P2

Right let him come, if he produces from me in my hand writing (dated

19th October 63, Demopolis Ala,) for that Sorrel horse for Capt Jackson Act, 2 M, 2ond Brigade Ala Vols, I hope you will understand it, If the Coln (the horse alluded to) is still bad off with his eyes, Sell him to Wells for 250 dollars or 3 hundred or keep him until he gets better or worse, or do what you think is best & I am content, but dont send him here, as good as blind, like he was when I left home, do not tell Smith how long his eyes have been bad but pass it off in the way I say,

COPPY OF THE ORDER TO SMITH
CAMP 30TH ALA DEMOPOLIS ALA OCT 19TH 63
SGT J M SMITH (SIR) OF CO B 30TH ALA

I have Sold Capt Johnson

A horse (Sorrel) known at my house as Colonel, You will show this to Mrs. A.E. Kelly (My wife) Near Tadiga Calhoun Co Ala as an order from me for the horse, & if he is all Right bring him to Capt Johnson for transportation Yours Resptfull

S C Kelly Capt Co E 30th Ala

I know from that you will under stand, So many Rabeals now a days that I send you a coppy of the letter or order to Smith so you can compare them, Sell old Kit the frst chance 1 hundred bushels corn or its equivalent May God bless us Still in my Prayers

Your own S

CAMP 30TH ALA NEAR DEMOPOLIS OCT 24TH 1863

.24 P1

My Dearest Amie I have concluded to writ to you this cold day not that I expect to interest you with any other news than to say that I am well & have enjoyed myself after my disappointment as well or better than I expected, We have been drilling every day & the officers have to Recite a lesson in tactics every day but yesterday it rained, So as to break up the School, We met in a shade before the Coln Qrtrs, Set down on the ground & answer to the Coln attentively Rather a dull set of scholars because but few have books, Last night was quite cool & we in our hog pin house with 2 blankets for all people & brush & leaves for a bed & 2 blankets turned cross ways for a covering, we done well kept dry if not warm, blankets are in great kneed ever

P2

in my own Co, there are about 15 men in my Co who have none at all & about 30 who have are as good as nothing, Sleep together & make out some how, nearly every 3 men or 4 have one or 2 blankets stretched for a tent & cover with the balance, some one & some none, we have but one fly in the Co & it is a poor thing, I have the largest Co in the Regt & about 3 times as large as some, I have 77 men & officers & Still they come (every day) Some one or a Recruit comes in, I had 5 from Conscript Camps the other day, Bob Foster was among them, Brother J was anxious to come but I told him he could do as well any where,

& stay at Talladega, I got a letter from him day before yesterday, in whitch he said he would have been clerk in an office (in Talladega) but when the detail was maid he was home

P3

on a ten day furlough but there was yet another vacancy, if he missed both these, he thought of joining a Cavalry Co near Gadsdon who are employed taking rt Conscript & deserters, my advise to him is to stay at Talladega as long as they will let him, I would swap chances wit him & give him one hundred dollars to boot, (if I could) Still I am not discouraged with my chances, I hope yet by the protection of God through the mercies of out Lord Jesus Christ to out live this Crewel war, & I do hope & trust that I may be enabled to play well my part, & then Oh then, when we have gained our independence, to Return to my loved ones at home to enjoy that loan, whitch has cost so mutch, & Oh if that shall be my happy lot, may I together with all of similar luck be prepared to give praise to the Father for so Ritch blessings, in whose hands I dedicate all that I have & that I am

P4

I Rec a letter from Palmer yesterday it came in 2 days, My Dear I think you do not write as you might, Still I may be mistaken or I might not get what you write, I have not had but one letter from you by mail since I have been here & it was 12 days old, had several by hand, I do not insist on you giving up your carpet for blankets, do as you like about it, I suggested a plan of sending an officer or two from the Regt for them & the plan was adopted but I was left out, Well may be all thing are working together for good, I submit without a murmur, (only to you) I expect Palmer in on wednesday & I shall get a letter if nothing else, I must close now for the best of reasons, out of matter to write, out of space out of time & Cold

Good bie My Dear Amie Sam

DEMOPOLIS ALA OCT 28TH 63 9 A.M.

.28 P1

My Dear Amie I Received your kind letter by Sgt Palmer yesterday I was glad to hear from you, I had not had a word from you in so long a time that I began to think what was the matter, You will no doubt be surprised when I tell you that instead of going to Miss that the order was counter manded & we took up as we thought winter qrtrs, & were well fixed up, as well or perhaps better that we will get again this winter, bur (as is not uncommon in a Soldiers life) we did not enjoy them but a few days, until we were ordered to Chickamagga & are on our way now having been up since 2 AM, & bidding fairwell to old camps & qrtrs about 6 AM we are now waiting transportation, the longer ½ of our Regt having gone off on the morning train, We will go by Selma & Montgomery & not get

P2

to come by home, I would like the best in the world to do so but it is strictly forbidden for either officer or men to straggle & if so to be Reported & treated as deserter, I could (do so) go by home but if I were all the men in my Co, without one single exception would go & not only go but think that they had a perfect Right to do so, as the Captain do so do we, so they think especially when you turn towads home, , my Dear I have nothing to write but I have time now, I am glad that you did not let Smith have that horse he is a blind horse, I was in hopes his eyes had got well, Sell him as a weak eyed horse, I think that you can do without him & old kit both, Sell them both & de shure to ask enough for them, & let the thrashing another year provide for itself & you will have more corn to give to the other 5 whitch I think can make 4 good hands, more of them for Sale

P3

I hope you may succeed in getting Graham to see to your business, If not I have a notion to try to get John Palmer but I prefer G, but I would take P, rather than Turk, I hope you will have money enough now to answer your purposes, but I do not know when I can send you any more, I kept about 150 & spend of it every day we pay for Rations as we go, I am verry mutch oblige to you for the box of provisions sent although I have not opened it yet in the bustle & stir I thought that I would carry it along so as we already had 3 days Rations drawn when it came, Yet I know that there is something nice & Something that would make a Soldiers mouth water, I am sorry that you are troubled with sutch a poor stick as Turk, but do the best you can & his time will soon be out & then if you do not get ,G, You can do better than to have , T, & have to pay him the 6th &C

P4

I am in hopes that we will not kneed many blankets as we have got here 360 here for our Regt, I think you are Right about yarn carpet, I think it too heavy, Our Regt will not kneed many more than we have got & will get today, these are good English blankets, (as the boys say (Bully) I hope that I shall get along with the Coln well, I heed your advice, I am glad that you have gotten over the blues, look on the bright side, trusting in the Father of us all, Our meeting went on until last night, the interest some what aborted but still moments to the last, I am mutch oblige to you, for your invitation to dinner, but am sorry it was not in my power to attend, I am glad that my letters cheer you up, but I was afraid that they were not at all interesting, because I had nothing to write, I am so well pleased with my pants, I have on my old ones yet but they need mending

P5 WRITTEN BETWEEN LINES OF P4

but it is so dirty traveling on box cars & Steam boats Decks that I thought to save them, I must close for want of time & space & if sutch letters as this will please you I will try to write one every week, May the Lord Still bless & Save us is the prayer of one that loves you dearly good bie Your own Sam

Newnan Ga 2 PM Oct 31st 1863

.31 P1

My Dearest Amie I thought that I would drop you a few lines to let you know that I am well & we have had a verry good trip so far, Still it is like all other trips of the same sort, Crowded & dirty (more a mom) Water tank stopped for a few moments, I will have to write in broken doses, My Dear I hope your Dream may be fully Realized, (about the big piles of Snakes) I think it has already been partly, by the frst battle at Chickamauga , I thought of it, but had verry little idea then that we would go there then, but we are going, laughing, singing hoping all glad to get the chance to go to Tenn, I do hope & trust to God that we may gain a complete victory over them, You wanted to know who was our officers, I forgot to tell you in my last, We are under Brigadier Pettus & Brig. G. Moore is acting, as our Maj General, I do not know who will be our Maj

P2

General, I suppose that we are in Polks Corpse (more a mom) Direct your letters to Capt S. C. Kelly 30th Ala Regt Pettus, Brig Chickamauga Tenn, I had so mutch provisions cooked & when we got to Montgomery we drew 3 more days the last bacon & crackers that I concluded that I would not open the box you sent me, & did not until today, I find it all nice the potatoes a little molded, I wrote you a letter from Selma, I suppose you have, I shall close now we are within 7 miles of Atlanta & car running now, non stopped so we go, go & stop & stop when I think we are going on, the boys running back & to, now we go, go to At I hope this time, if so we will get there about sun set, Atlanta Sun Set we are going off at PM no news as I know of Sal & Joe Dunkin & Rile & Dave Cooley left me at Selma, I hope that they my

P3

meet their Reward, I must close for I have a chance to send it by hand S

7 Oclock PM brings us 24 miles from At I lay down to take a

nap at about 2 oclock when I woke the car was moving, 20 miutes after Seven PM, I suppose we will be in Chattanooga in the morning, this leaves me well, I pray that God may bless us all good bie S C Kelly

NOVEMBER 1863
(Written on scrap letter)

Capt S C Kelly
Co E 30th Ala Chattanooga
Pettus Brig

That is as many words & as many letters in a word that aut to be put on a letter I think they are more apt to come, I expect that we will be under Stevens again, I understood his division came up the Mountain yesterday, We certainly have a vast army in & around this Mountain, but wood & water is plentiful, no fire

WEDNESDAY NOV 4TH 1863
CHICKAMAUGA STATION 8 MILES SOUTH OF CHATTANOOGA TENN

.04 PI

My Dear A I Rec yours of the 1st this morning, I might have got it yesterday morning but F forgot it, I was sorty mad about his carelessness, but that is characteristic of him, in sutch matters, I am so sorry that you are so afflicted, be patient & do the best you can not taking hardships to heart, but trust in God who is the author & finisher of all things, truly these are times of trouble, it is to be hoped that they will end some day but the question is who will live to se it, then the all important thing is to be prepared to meet our lord & be ready when our change comes, I think this is wendsday & sunday was the first, Still you speak of making company of your work & your letter is dated 1st & I know that F started Sunday, I hope you do not do like we do, as mutch on Sunday as any other day, my paper is wrinkled & I am writing on my knee, is my apology for this blotted letter, I hope you have Rec mine of the 31st who I wound up in a hurry in order to send it

P2

by old Marvin Keath, who I found in Atlanta & said that he would go to Rome & likely to Ladiga, it will tell you both Cooleys & both Dunkins deserted us in Selma Ala on the 28th, I was in hopes that they would be taken up in Selma, we came on that night from Atlanta, Started at 9 PM & Stopped at big Shanty at 11 ½ PM & staid there until 9 AM Sunday morning (about 30 miles from Atlanta) come on to this place that night at 7 or 8 PM, Stopped in the muddyest place, Staid there about 1 hour & then took up line of march & went through the mud & brush ½ mile Stacked arms lay down for the night, next morning moved 2 hundred yds & set up at the foot of a Rocky ledge & in the bushes & stones doing verry well, no duties but camp guard & call the Roll every 2 hours, I have but little Idea who long we will stay here, nor where we will go, it is said that we will be thrown into Breckinridges Division, may be so, I thought that he Commanded a Corpse, Tis said that Rations are scarce here, we have had plenty so far, I saw John Clark & J

P3

Foofinder & Several others use to know at home, as to news of the army you know more of that than I do, I knew more at Demopolis than I do here, for there we got papers every day, here it is all Rhumor, except the boom of Cannon occasionaly (none today), It is now 3 ½ PM & I have been writing all day by spells, I have been busy today I am officer of the day & we have got several prisoners & some punishment to inflect sutch as, marking time & one fellow to promenade before the guard line with a board tied to his back, every alternate hour with the inscription on it, The way of the transgressor is hard, We have orders to move immediately, to Report to Gen Walker, we are cooking with a double quick, I do not know where Walker is, we are in tolerable good health as a Co, I am well, May God still bless & Save us all & give us a great victory

P4

good bie, I must close Your own Sam

I have on my new breeches & clean clothes all Round, I expect we will leave our baggage , if so I want the best I have, I cannot carry my carpetsack , I shall try to carry my best blanket & over coat Sword & Rations & wait till the waggons come up with the rest, our Reggimenttal waggons have not come yet, & transportation is scarce & Roads bas as can be, we may be in a fight or we may not, the Lord only knows, Still I trust in him for the life that now is & the one that is to come, pray for me yet the more that I may be enabled to bear my part in this world & be prepaired to meet death when ever it may come, Tell the children that I have not forgotten them, that I try to ask God to be to you all a father, Tell the negrows that I try to pray for them, too, that all must die & appear before the Judgement

good bie my Dear one

Lookout Mt on pickett Nov 6th 2 Oclock PM

.06 P1

My Dear Amie I snatched this moment to write to you I have but a very few So I hope you will not be disappointed, I am well & in plain view of the enemy & Chattanooga, we have traveled the last 2 nights & it Rained all day on us yesterday & a good portion at least, the Cooleys & Dunkins got in, I expect they will be punished, Some little firing with Artillery, I see no more prospect of a fight

P2

now than I did several days ago, all our baggage is at Chickamauga Station, I have but one blanket, we are about 10 miles from Ch S, I will close with my best prayer & wish for you, Your own Dear one Sam

Lookout Mt Tenn Nov 9th 1863

.09 P1

2 oclock PM My Dear Amie I wrote you a note day before yesterday, I was in a hurry & had to wind it to a close in double

quick time, I fear I will not interest you now, but you love long letters & I will try to fill my sheet with something, I will begin by saying that I am well, except a slight sore throat, whitch was caused by the Rain & fateigue in climbing the Mountain 3 evenings ago, & by laying on the wet Rocks in the Rain that night, I hope that I shall be well soon, it hurts me to swallow, but one thing certain we have little to swallow but spittle, beef today but no bread, but I think that when our Regimental waggons get here it will be better, for the Roads are so bad here that the traines have as mutch as they can do, to supply, there own troops but this is the first failure, & we will have plenty (I hope) by morning, as to the beef they drive the to the cook yard, whitch is at the foot of the Mt on the other side about 4 miles off we are

P2

on the west side of the Mt about ½ way to the top, our

Regt just came off of advanced pickett last night, my Co was not Relieved until after dark, as I occupied one of the most important post on the whole line, the Coln told me so, Still they fish, frst one & then the other end of the Regt, to get them off to their motion, & leave me that post, whitch would not been my lot had they confered there detail to either end, I never let on like I noticed it, Still I believe that got as good a position as any one else, all the difference is Relieving, & being Relieved after in dark, I am willing to take it, again next time we are laying here on this Mt in Reserve, Should a fight take place, be Ready to go either way, the whole Brigade laying round here in full view of the Yanks who are on the Raccoon Mt, Right opposite one Regt out of the Brigade or pickett at a time &Stay 24 hours, & could not without exposing the whole Co be Rel Sooner (use for me here, but verry little use when in Payrolled Camp, but even there too mutch to have any favors shown, but I thank God that I can do without or have done so, & another thing is presentable, to the whole Co, that I am not talked to so short, as when there is no danger, I shall say no more on this subject for it is unpleasant but I feel it my duty to tell all to you, the partner of my life & by far the better half, Say nothing about this digression) We were in plain view of the Yankees all the time, Still we had a RR bank for protection had a fight took place, our advance post were on one side of Chattanooga creek & thers on the other, in the night, in the day time they fall back about 4 hundred yards

P3

& we about one, the creek is about as long as Tarrapin, Still to deep to ford any where, I think when all our Regts of our Brig. Stand 24 hours each that we will go back on the other side to our cook camp, Where we will get sop or soop or dip or truck that comes out of our beef whitch with corn bread is at least one third more than we get here, (boiled beef brought to us in bags, Still I have not suffered yet, Sometimes our meals are late & always irregular, & another Brig Releave us, We Releaved Longstreets men, & it is said that they are gone to Dalton, Still more troops have come in from Demopolis, I know but little of what is going on only what I see & hear in our own Brig, We Shell them a little every day from the top of this Mt (the Shells passing over us) but what effect I cannot tell, we can shell them & they cannot shell us, the battery on the Mt, for the height, I want you to send me the dispatches in your letters, I have not seen a paper in a week, I want to know what they are doing at Charleston & the news generally, I will close now & finish tomorrow when I will have a chance to send it, May God still continue his blessings towards us is my prayer, good bie my own Dear Amie Yours Dan
PS I have a chance to send it now S

LOOKOUT MOUNTAIN TENN NOV 11TH 1863

.11 P1

My Dear Amie I have written to you 2 since we have I have been here but I now have a chance TO SEND BY THE HAND OF Lt Thomas, who is a methodist preacher who has resined to be Chaplin in some other Ala Regt, but who is going home first, we still on pickett it is the same place, we just came off last night, of advance post again, I thought that we would have to go every 4th or 5th night but we have to every 3rd night, I cannot tell now any thing about the army, or but verry little except that we have not had a fight yet & no more prospects than there was when we first come, They shell our troops as we come up the mountain & we shell them from the Mt where ever we see them in boddies, & also there waggon traines, they do us but verry little damage & I suppose we do as mutch at least to them, we make them skedaddled & fall & the waggons go as hard as the teams can carry them, Rations are scarce yet, I fear will continue beef is scarce too, we got some sugar & rice yesterday

P2

& our quota of bread, today we sent out 2 men from my Co &others from other Cos & got a fine beef from a house this side of our lines, that they (the family)say is a government beef, they are dividing it now, I fear the Rations, If we had plenty, I think all else, considered is Right the men are in fine health & would be in fine spirits but for Rash, but I fear that if we do not get more & that soon, that they will desert by the whole sale, 4 men out of Co H (that is Capt Burns Co from St Clair County) deserted night before last & went to the Yanks, & Yesterday the Yankees told up on pickett about it, & Said that they had understood that we were short of Rash, Sutch men under sutch circumstances aut to die the death , I could & would live all of my appointed days before I would desert & go to them under these circumstances, I thank God that I can do on as little as I can & be satisfied, Still I know that it takes more to do some men than others, I have not

P3

suffered yet, & we are not allowed to draw but as mutch as the men, but we save ours better, Lt Pike, Airhart &myself are themes, this side of the mountain & Sgt Palmer, Bale Pike & John Allen are on the other side at the cook yard, Sgt P. is acting as company commissary (not able to carry a gun) Pike & Allen as cooks, they cook it & bring it over, W Estes, B Henderson, G. W. Killpatrick & J R Taylor, N W Journey as Co cooks about 10 sick, none bad off most all convalessent, among them is Bob Brown, Wm Dale,

Jasper Wingo & other besides the guard of prisoners (George Raburn is one of them we got out of Jail at Selma & has been under guard ever since waiting a corts martial to try them) guard Phillips, D Patterson, R Prather & Ben Pease, Jim Pease there with the sick, In all there (cook yard) 21 men nearly as many as Co D has, I have with me 58 men with guns & 3 of us with Swords (61) present 82 all besides 2 with the waggons 84 aggregate total. Present & absent 103 aggregate 107, I have about 10 men

P4

more present for duty than any other Co in the Regt, I do not know why it is, but it is a popular Co, Still I feel like that I am not an efficient officer, I try to do my duty, & do justice between my men, I think that I am in full favor with every man I have, more than I could say one year ago, but then I did as I do now, I would be obeyed

May God direct us still, I do feel like that he has been with me & hath heard my prayers that he has shown me great mercy, Oh that he will continue his mercies to us is my prayer, I Rec your of the 5th, I was so thankful for it & especially when I saw you were all well &would likely have bread enough & to spear, If you get ½ meat enough you may be thankful, I must close good bie Your own Sam

PS cant you send me the part of the map of this country

Lookout Mountain Tenn November 15th 63 9 PM

.15 .17 L1 P1

My Dearest Amie we are on pickett yet & we are in advance, we do our share, I wrote to you last Sunday & said that I thought that we would go in every 5 days, then I thought every 3 days but I now tell you that we are on every other day, in consequence of a heavy pickett & a small Regt, one Regt is not able to do the pickitting & then they take off of the rest, all is quiet along the line, except an occasional shell from both, the enemy & our batterys, both shelling each others waggon trains, day before yesterday it Rained Right smart in the morning, as it happened we were not on advanced posts, but then we were on the side of the Mt ready if any difficulty should take place with the picketts below, who were about ½ mile to the nearest front, Right in full view of the Yankee Picketts, one on one side of the creek & the other on the other, they talked & trade with each other, I saw lots of them but did not say any thing to them, the last time, before this that we were on, & my whole Co was deployed 3

L1 P2

men in a place & posts no where less than one hundred yards apart & some places two hundred, my line was about 1 ½ miles long, Lt. A. had charge of the frst post at a Raft, where he stayed all the time & I the balance, (Lt Pike Commanding Co (A) who had no officer) I visited each post 4 times during the 24 hours, the Yanks are keen to talk, but our boys do not talk mutch, for it is forbidden, but still they will pick there chance & talk & trade a little, Rations still short, bread plenty, but only about one meal of meat a day on average, but still I have had all the time, enough, not to suffer, Our waggons have come up & this morning unexpectedly we got beef, I hope we will do better in the Ration line, than we have before, when we full of beef we draw bacon, & if both we draw sugar whitch is better for health occasionally at least once a week, I think, the men kneed a change, They say that I am getting fat, I have had good health except the sore throat, I wrote you about, that I cured by wilting a handkerchief in cold water & tighing it round my neck one cold night & letting it

L1 P3

There all night, We have had a nice spice of weather for about 8 or 10 days except for Raney day spoke of , If you have had sutch will be a great advantage to the farming interest if well employed, I suppose that by this time you are sowing wheat, if the stock has sufficiently eaten out the pasture, if not you have had the gin house gathered whitch will make six loads of 20 bushels each, I understand by your letter that you have 80 loads in all, that includes the 6 loads of the bottom fields 20X80X100 bushels if you have 7 more loads that will be 42 bushels & Turks portion will be 7 loads whitch will give you 35 loads or see (700) bushels, but of that you owe (Tax) 60 bushels, one hundred be exemped whitch will leave you 640 bushels & against you fatten your 11 or 12 Shoats, whitch will eat in fattening one hundred bushels, will leave 540 or say 530 bushels my guess is that you will not have mutch to spear, Still the horses & old kit for you can do with out them & you will

Ll P4

the more corn to give to the old Sows & Shoats whitch is the chance for more meat another year, Make Barney wash that horse again, I expect he is foal, do not feed the horses mutch corn this winter, but make them eat shucks & fodder & a little corn, not so apt to take scratches & then next spring after when you begin to plow them give them plenty, they will fatten, when they are all done pasturing have the cuckleburs all pulled out of their mains, tails & bellies, let Syphax get poor the rest, no so apt to be stolen, & then it will not hurt him in after life, work him some, but not more than a half hand, this winter, See Dugger & let him take the Jacks & keep them one a pen & Return in as good, for (1/2)half he can make with him, I fear if you do not get him off that he will be a greatest of trouble & expense & at little profit, My Dear I am sorry for you, You so often have the headache, I fear you work to hard, take it as you can stand it, hire the weaving

Ll P5

of all your clothe, I am sorry to hear you are out of some thing to eat, You will have to learn to do on what you can get, I am sorry of your misfortune your ovens & chickens, but you will not kneed many vessels we have but 3 ovens & 2 small kettles for 88 men & the trouble with us is, some thing to cook, I do hope & trust that you may always have enough & Some to spear, keep the boys all the time (after they get the wheat sowed) & get the wood too, keep the waggon running, hauling wood & rails, I do not want that lumber cut, up there between the house & Ladiga nor between the house & Mrs Stewarts, all the Rails & wood aut to be got out of the bottom, Sell the old mule for money or corn, You can use the money every thing so high, Speaking of blankets, they (that were sent) got fully ½ in old quilts, sutch as the men will not want, the rest about ½ of Carpet Blan

Ll P6

ket & the rest (one forth of whole number) in bed blankets, My Co will get in all about 24 or hopes 30 at 10 dollars each, I could make out verry well with that many good blankets, but the item of Shoes deploys me, In 4 more weeks on this Mt half of my Co with be as good as bare footed & what we are to do, I know not, but for adventure, there will be a way provided, I trust so, I know that you would be glad to see me, but the Lord only knows, when you will have the pleasure of it, but I hope on, hope ever, trusting in God for the life that now is, & the one whitch is to come, I am looking for a letter from you, Yours of the 3rd come to hand last monday whitch was the 9th that was in due time, I wish that you would write to me every 4ort day & may be that I will get ½ of them & I will do the same, I have been writing that often since we have been here, but you kneed not expect all long ones, I write you this long letter because I have time &

Ll P7

nothing to Read, (except a Novell) My Bible over at the cook yard in my Comfort Sack, John Patmen is over there attending to the drawing & cooking Rations, We have several sick, mostly chills, Lt Pike was Right sick, night before last & yesterday, I have not heard today, he is on the Mt, John Cooley has arrived under guard he & George Raburn, both waiting there trials, My Dear one I believe that I have told you all that I now think of that is worth telling, I got no papers, write to

me often & if you

Sam wrote on back of this page in Ink, it bled through & can't read the rest of the page

.15 .17 Ll P8

over my ink & spilled nearly all, & then I watered it & it is so poor you will not read it all, My Dearest let Billy Read these letters, encourage him to Read, tell him to be a good boy & set a example for the others, tell them that have not forgotten them, They we have orders to go over the Mountain, that is off of pickett, I hope it is so, I shall close for the present, hoping that you are all well & enjoying all the blessing of life in the form &future of our Heavenly Father

.15 .17 L2 P1

2 oclock PM 17th my dear I have not had a chance to send this off before now, we had orders Sunday night to move & wait all night until about 8 in the morning, & then we come over here (JE) on the east side of the Lookout Mt the Yanks shelled us a little but none of our Regt hurt, I heared that one man got killed & another wonded, I thought that they could not throw shells to the top, but they can & do but do not but little damage, there was an alarm this morning & heavy & fast cannonading on our Right, lasting ½ hour, I have not heared where it was nor what was done, I have been verry busy the last 2 days making out muster & payrolls, am not done yet, the men will draw 2 months pay, that night we were waiting orders, I did not go to bed until 12 oclock, but lay down by the fire, blanket & over coat rolled up & went to sleep, my head on a Rock, I lay there to long took cold & had the headache bad last night, feel better today, but think another night when waiting orders that I will unroll my duds

.15 .17 L2 P2

the firing spoke of was Robersons Battery of 15 guns moved down in the night & took position on the bank opposite a Yankee camp & attacked them at daylight, they Skedaddled mightly but Rallied their gunners & replied rapidly, Sent sharpshooters to the bank & opened on our Battery & they (our) battery Retreated loosing one killed & one missing

NOVEMBER 19TH 1863
CAMP 30TH ALA REGT
IN FRONT OF CHATTANOOGA & 3 MILES SOUTH AT WHAT
IS DESIGNATED IN MY FORMER LETTERS AS COOK YARD

.19 .20 P1

My Dearest Amie I had a letter written on Sunday, whitch was the 15th & this is Thursday the 19th & I have not sent it yet, I did not have a chance until yesterday & then I was busy paying off the Co & had 4 men, whose application for furlough had gone up & I thought that I had better hold & Send by them, as I discover in yours of the 13th (whitch came to hand on the night of the 17th) that you do not, or have not had got half of my letters, that one on the 11th I sent by hand, by Lt James, & it appears that you have not got any by mail, Since we got to Chickamauga, not my fault because I have written every 3 or 4 days since we arrived here, I shall send you the one I wrote Sunday for you will see in it some directions, whitch may be some advantage to you, I fear that you are working too hard, take it as you can stand it, I would like to have sutch a pair of pants as you speak of do not line them farther than the legs they will be to clumsey round the body, & the legs are not protected by the over coat, You can send them by Turk, as the 19th is but 2 or 3 miles from here, I see some of them every day, Jack Robinson was over yesterday, he is a Sgt, but says that he has charge of the Co ½ the time, as he has but one Lt present he is sickley, Tom R has been sick, but convalessent, Ran is also there, Tell the children the chinquepins came safe & was duly appreciated by me, I would like to have a lots of little things that you all at home have, that I cannot get , one thing in particular that I kneed & if Turk comes send about a peck of dried fruit, a little butter in a cup or con, a few gobers &C I know that he cannot bring mutch, we are getting better Rations now, we get sugar rice Molasses flour beef corn meal, & occasionally a little bacon, we have camp guard & Send 4 or 5 men from a Co per day, to work on the fortifications & about as many on pickett in front, the balance cook & eat & wash & some times fight a little, the Cooleys are all three under guard & 2 Dunkins, for deserting us, I hope that the penalty will be light as they (4 of them) come in themselves, George Raburn is still under guard, the men I spoke of getting furloughs are Pallerson, Keller, Landers & Sgt Boozer,

on the ground of furnishing a Recruit each, Sgt J B Palmer can get
a discharge, but he has some hesitancy, but he cannot carry a gun
nor baggage, & I guess that we will be pickitting at least one third
of our time this winter, If I were in his place I would take it, I am
glad that you helped that old father (Witt) it is more blessed to
give than to Receive, I know that all at home, must work, the old
& young, male & female, black first & white finnish, while all the
able bodied white men in the Confederacy are engaged in the
army, & while you at home are sorry for us in the army, we do
deeply sympathize with you in your toils & disadvantages, but
we must bear it, the curse in whitch we are engaged demands it,
& if subjugated, we will be worse than slaves, poorer than the
poorest, Oh God forbid that sutch should ever be the case, & give
us power to drive the enemy from our soil & make them Sue for
peace

P2

I wish that Dicky Thackerson would come & preach for us, we
are out of a Chaplin, I think that 150 dollars per month will pay him
verry well, as a Regular Chaplin only gets 50$ per month but
Rations & horse feed furnished, Our Rations cost us from one dollar
to one 50 cts per day, I drew 1 months pay this morning & been
sitting round generally, I have about (200) two hundred dollars, I
have been paid up to the 31st Oct 1862, I hope that Bro Smith will
give us a visit, this winter, ask him if he would accept the
Chaplancy of the 30th Ala Regt, when he comes to see you, Never
give yourself one moments uneasiness about me doing any thing
wrong unless I do it ignorantly & as to deserting, I for one will stay
as long as any one else & that is as long as we can get bread & water,
Will you have salt enough to do you, now at those high prices, I
hope , so, the bacon we have been using is the best I ever eat, it is
the freshest & to eat the fat raw (without a lean streak, eats like
butter, I know that it will take lots of corn to fatten your pigs (or
hogs) but it does not take more than half of the salt to save meat,
that I used to think, Send me the dispatches for your last letter came
in 3 days & I have not bought but one news paper since we have

been here, My Dear you say that you fear that I cannot read it, written by fire light, no danger that, I can read any thing you write, I have never asked help to read one yet, I assure you that no one will ever see one of your letters, unless I should fall into the hands of the enemy & they would not if I had time to tear them up, I keep 2 or 3 of the last on hand & when I get new ones I burn the older ones, I guess that you can get rid of all your tax corn at home, by letting stock drivers have it, but b e sure to get the Right sort a Receipt, I think that you will have corn enough to do you, by being saving, I believe that I have written about all, I kneed not tell you that I want to come home & see you all, but I have no idea when, but be assured that I will embrace the frst opportunity, I see no more prospects of a fight, than was 10 days ago, I will close for the present give my love to all who inquire after me, & Recto yourself my verry best wishes & prayers own Sam

   4 Pm I thought I was done but I forgot to tell you that I wanted a pair of socks as I have got a whole in the toe of one of these & if you can spear me a fiew onions, & send by some one, I heard that old man Brown & Keller Furrow & McBee are talking of coming soon, enquire about it & send by some of them in prference to Turk, for they will come to my Co let it be where it will, I close, furloughs hasnt come yet, but look tomorrow Yours Sam

   20th 7 oclock AM I Dear A I conclude to send by mail as it will be 3 or 4 days before the furloughed men get off, all quiet we are still in camp, nothing unusual, Frank Rountree came in yesterday, he pass your house tuesday, acted the puke, for he did not bring a single letter, nor nothing else, I will close, Oh if you have a chance send me a small wax candle, not so long by ½ as the one last, to Miss, I sometimes kneed one, I am compelled to close or miss another chance, Your own Sam

DECEMBER 1863

DECEMBER 1ST 1863
CAMP 30TH ALA REGIMENT NEAR DALTON GA

.01 .02 P1

My Dearest Amie I now write to you again, my last was from Chickamauga Dated 25th the battle was still raging at the time of my writing & our forces were still holding on, held their position until about 4 PM when the enemy forced our left center, Our Brigade held there position all day & until after dark, when the whole army were ordered to Retreat, Our Brigade did well, we fell back to this place where I suppose we will make a stand, I have been on the sick list ever since monday week whitch was about the 22nd of last month, I hope that I am better, I traveled with the sick & waggons, the excitement keeping me up, I came to the Company yesterday morning after hunting them for 2 days, it is no small job to find a Regt in a large army, They Yanks followed us close & made a big effort with heavy loss in killed & prisoners, Since then they have not been so Savey, Cleaburns Division, whipped, Shermans Corpse, They captured the day, before one battery & I expect one hundred waggons,, So terrible bad was the Road, the most of them captured were already mired down, Our Regiment was not in hottest of the fight on Mishionary Ridge but filled a space in the line, the Regt lost 3 or 4 men & 8 or 10 wonded & a few prisoners, my Co one man wonded (Barney Baxter Slight in the leg with Shell, Our men say that the ground was literally covered with dead & wonded Yankees, they charged our lines 5 times in double collums & were Repulsed 4 times but the 5th they forced several places of the line, the loss on our side must be light, I saw lots of wonded, Our boys think that we killed more of them than they killed wonded & taken prisoners of us, but they had the forces & Longsteet & Bukckners Corpse both gone to East Tenn, they took the advantage, never did troops fight better but we were out numbered at least 5 to 10 to one, I was with the straglers detailed & sick & they were demoralized & a thousand Reports, I was lost off from the command & was determined not to take prisoners if I could help it, I was going to take the woods, had they come up & I expected it, I have a notion to Report for duty, I think I am about well, but am taking quinine, I thought that I had slight chills & did have the worst cold & cough I ever had in life, I was fearful that I would take the pneumonia, I coughed so bad that I would have to get up of nights to Relieve myself, I am sorry that I was not able to be in the battles but sutch was my lot, It is the first time that I have ever been behind the Regt, in the 21 months that I have belonged to it & hope that it may be the last, unless on some other score, I did get so tired of sick men & straglers at least ten thousand, & they as a mass were demoralized, but at ___ ___dge at Resaca, there is a guard to stop all &

P2

Send them under guard to there Commanders, the two Dunkins, Green, Raburn & others of my Co were among them & several others did not acquit them selves with a greateal of honor, George Raburn & John Cooley got away from the guard & are gone I know not where, I hope to the Yanks, You kneed not say any thing about that, Still I do not care mutch for none of those I have mentioned, is what I call good Soldiers, Lt Arheart came up, he was out on pickett & I was fearful he had gone up, I by being with the waggons, got Lt Pike a pair of shoes, The men had to march on the Retreat night & day, & wade creeks, because it took to mutch time to hunt & cross on logs, I & my squad took the R Road & crossed some verry high bridges an narrow strips, In a word the Roads were full of waggons, Artillery men on horses & mules & on foot back & ever conceeivable way to get along, & had Sherman of whipped Cleburne at

Ringgold, it would have been one of the worst Stampeeds of the war, but thanks be to God who gived us the victory there & saved our army & perhaps our Country

My Dear one I have waited long & patiently for a letter but under the circumstances I have not waited long enough, Some letters come in today, the last I Rec was dated 13th, I had rather you get mine than for me to get yours & you not get mine, I know your uneasiness, but hope that you have Rec mine of the 24th eve this, Rations were a little scarce yesterday, but today plenty, I think that we saved about all our Comissarys, lost some corn at Chickamauga but that was all, I did know that we had so many beans, until we Skedaddled, The weather for the last 3 days has been very cold, & before it was verry Rainey, it is moderating now, we lost most of our cooking vessels & tents on the Retreat, the waggons brok down & mires &C, poor mules as well as poor Soldiers, Suffered, I believe that I have told you all that will interest you now, I will finish tomorrow when I have a chance to send it, good bie your own Sam

DEC 2ND 3 PM

My Dear I saw no Mr Graham last night, he is tolerable well, I heard from him that Bryan was with him, they are out about Dalton, I wanted to go out there but could not get a horse, I saw Alford Witt this morning he is hunting Jack, he will find him today, the male has come in maybe I got a letter, I wait No, no letter, I do not know what to think ½ the men in the Co got letters but none for me, I am still improving & am going to Report for duty tomorrow, I shall send this by hand, I must close, God bless you, good bie Your own Sam

CAMP 30TH ALA DEC 2OND 1863 NEAR DALTON

.02 Pl

(Letter burnt on edge)

My Dearest Amie I thought that I would have a chance to send m___ ___ed out this morning but missed the chance _____ concluded that I would write you a secr___ this & one that is for no other eyes _____ see but yours & when you have read it, make a burnt offering of it, My Dear you know that I have always been in for the war, but I tell you now, that in my opinion that we as a nation & a people are whipped, our army is demoralized to, to great an extent, I hate to say so but, I feel it my duty to let you know the worst, So as you may be prepared for ____ as well as you can, our Rations are so scarce ___ men are deserting & going to the enemy, So ___ the Tennesseeans & Georgians who ___ in the Yankee lines are going by ____sale, & in a few word the whole country _____ have fallen back over is Ruined, Stock all ____ & fences & houses burned, I hope to God sutch desolation may never reach our _____

P2

_____ it does, or the army does, the best thing I know ___ you to do is to Sell out every thing on ___ place that the army wants & gather up and ___ South in the waggon, hauling as mutch Rat___ as you could pull, the Reason I say this is because, if our army were camped on those two creeks, you would not have in one week one Single <u>meales</u> <u>victuals,</u> if you would sell they would buy all, they would buy all, & if you would not sell they would take it, So there is no chance to live in an army unless you draw from the Comissary, If our army falls back to Rome then you had better sell out to the government _____ _ants all your wheat & corn, meat cattle, __eep, hogs , fodder, oats &C except what you ____ _____ with you, that looks like destruction ____ ____ but down about Demopolis is plenty of corn ___ ___ is the staff of life, Still at home you ha__ Shelter & So many going South, You may not ___ ___ that, as to the negrows they will be ___e if others are free, & the best way is

(The rest of the letter is missing)

DALTON GA CAMP 30TH ALA NEAR RINGOLD GA DEC 4TH 1863

.04 .05 P1

(Burned around edge)

My Dearest Amie I am astonished because I do not get a letter from you, letters come in every day to the Co, but none for me, I have not had one since about the 15th Nov & that one came in, in answer to mine of the 11th, I thought then that I was doing well, So I was, I do not know what to think, if ___ were sick & could not write, Emma Palmer ___ ____ know it, John got a letter day before yesterday f___ ___ dated the 30th Nov, She said that there was nothing ____ &C My Dear I do not blame you, I cannot blame you

I believe that you can clear your self of any blame, but it is a mistory to me, I have never but twice since I have been in the army been so lo__ without hearing from you, & that was, while we were in Kentucky & last summer in Vicksburg, both times no one got letters, I wrote to you day before yesterday, & sent it by hand by Mr Eeton, of Co (K) who went home on furlough, I hope you have got it before now, Mr A White is here in camp, going to start home in the morning & I will send this by him, he promised to stop & see you & tell you all about me, he can tell more about the army than I can, we counted up & it is just 77 miles home, to his house about 100 miles, John Palmers papers for a discharge have started up today, I think likely he will get but it will be a week first, how will ___ ___ for an over seer, if you do not get Graham ___ ____ him the best chance, I know of, You & Mrs S ____ talk about it, I believe the chance for Graham a ____ one, If you cannot sell that horse, or have not sold him, Bryon says that he will take him & work him for his feed, it may save one of your best mules from being taken for the government, So if you have not disposed of him, & Mary sends for him let her have him, & sell old kit to Mr Whitesides & I think that they will let you keep the rest, they pressed one of Bryans

NOV 5TH AM SAME PLACE

P2

(Sam put down wrong month)

My Dear Amie Mr White will be along this morning early, & I now haste to fill my sheet, I am well, & on duty, I hope all is right with me again, I took quinine & it stopped my cough, Rations are tolerable plenty now but cook vessels scarce, we have but little duty to do, ___ ____ to drill, we have inspection & dress parade, besides _____ details from each company for pickett, some _____ guard & some for fatigue, to go to Dalton to load cars, I am officer of the day today, camp _____ ___ard, I am sorry to say it, the men are deserting every night (nearly), 16 left last night out of our Regt, none out of my Co, I have the largest in the

Brigade, this is saturday morning & we have been here since monday, it was a perfect wilderness when we came, but the night cold & wood is now getting scarce, we clear the woods as we go, I must close soon for a verry good reason, I have nothing else to write, & the drum is now calling the guard, think on that secret letter & then do accordingly to your best judgment, You certainly know better than I, but I wanted to drop you a hint or two,

May God bless you & yours, good bie Your own Sam

Camp 30th Ala Near Dalton Ga Dec 9th 4 PM

.09 Pl

(Middle of letter burnt)

My Dearest Amie I Rec yours of the 3rd just now & was so glad to get it, for it was the first one I have had since 16th Nov, Whitch was Ritten on the 13th, I did not know to account for it, but I know by your letter that you have written, I am sorry to learn that Sam is sick, but I feel thankful that you still have health, I do greatly sympathize with you, because you have the burthen of the whole family, black & white & it is no small job, but My Dear one, take things as you can stand it, & __oose Rather that goodly part, that can not be taken _____y & oh prey for me, for I am mightly tempted, _____ mutch to try my faith , think of me, a c_____ of the toughest companies in _____ all of t__ _____ & it is ____is & Capt th___ & Capt _____

Hope that _____b, I am quite _arlly now & have been d__ _____ 5 days, the health of the Co is verry good, only ab_____ ___n in20 sick, mostly colds, yesterday was a wet cold _____ but during the night cleared of & to day is a nice warm ___m day, We have a good board shelter bilt, keep dry & warm but, badley smoked, we have orders to put up Shanties so as to make ourselves comefortable

P2

not exactly winter Qrters, but a kind of make shift, but the scarcity of troops, the progress is slow, we are 6 or 7 miles South of Tunnell hill, where our advance line is, we do not go there pickitting, but more than half o our Brigade is on Detail, working the Road, Lt Pike & 5 men of my Co are out, they have to stay 5 days, but 2 days gone, then the Rest of will go, I have nothing mutch to write, John Palmers papers were not approved by Brigade Surgeon, He will not come home yet, Graham started home day before yesterday, he was so keen to go, he did not come by, I have got money plenty to answer my purpose, if you kneed any let me know, I suppose that you are done ____wheat, & that Turk has given out coming to the army, _____ Dugger have the Jack, I will close I have a ch____ ____ send by hand

Your _____ _____

Camp 30th Ala Near Dalton Ga Dec 12th 1863

.12 .13 P1

(Letter burnt in the middle)

My Dear Amie I Received yours of the 26th Nov yesterday, but I had Rec one of the 1st Dec a few days before, & have answered it, the mail has come in & I write to see if I get one, _____but I am doing well in the way of letters, _____ is pooring down rain, but we have a _____ten & one to build our fire under, I have nothing interesting to write & besides the paper is so damp that I will quit until annother time, but before I quit I must tell you that I got foundered yesterday on potatoes I drew (whitch were not as sound as they once were) & a quart of gobers (for whitch a paid one dollar) I feel none the worse of it now, Oh & Yes I got a letter from James, dated 7th at Talladega, he says that he is clerking for Coln Lockheart (Chief of Conscripts of Mo) he is well pleased with the Coln, that he thinks that he will be Released from the service by Christmast, that Judge Wood has petitioned the President to that affect & that Coln Lockheart forwarded on the 2ond enst, Respectfully approved, I do not know the plea, nor he did not write me, he was in a hurry, & said that he came from home that morning, I must close the Shanty leaks   Turn the paper from you

P2

I understand now why it was that you sent Billy with the horse & mule to David to sell, I expect that, that lot of horses will sell low but I am anxious for you to get rid of that horse, Sell him & perhaps that may save one of your mules from being pressed, My Dear one (You ask if there was any chance for you to get a furlough) I think not, I do not know how unless I were Sick (or pretend to be verry sick) I would like to come home, but do not want to get sick enough, as to be compelled to leave the service, I prize my health verry highly, Tell the Children that I have not forgotten them, would be so glad to see them & stay with them, but I must serve and defend my Country & Your precious homes, Tell the negrows, to be good servants & in the end they will be as well (if not) better off than they will to be contrary, these are trying times, hard times, & My Dear _____trouble about sending me some _____ had better take care of it for the g_____ can, & let me, get what I can here, if others can live on little, I less, & besides I had as well begin to learn to do on a little, for I am satisfied that I mail have to do it, Our Rations costs not quite one dollar a day apiece, I must close, May God bless us all Sam

DECEMBER 13TH ELEVEN AM

P3

My Dear Amie it Rained a goodeal last night & is still driseling, Yet we slept dry & well last night, Lt Pike & his Detail came in last night, the signs are that we will not stay here long, but I do not know, I think the chances are against John Palmer getting off, I think the same objections will apply to Pink Palmer an Cowden being an overseer as to Turk, all too far off, but of the two, I think if Cowden would undertake would suit you best, Pink is not able to make a hand & Cowden would not try to make it, & he could come once a day & see what the boys were doing, & besides that he is Sober & Steady, Still I do not believe that it will suit Cowden at all, he has so mutch practice to do, I believe that Ferguson could do better than either of them, _____dertake, but he thinks that he _____ he can do besides, You can try _____ & see, I think all of them clever gentlemanly men, & will come nearer filling their contracts than Turk, Tell Sam that I am verry sorry to hear that he has got so big, & more especially before the children

P4

I think that the Rest will try to do what is Right, I hope so at least, they have to live until they die, & it is to there interest to work & make it & if in the event that all the negrows are Set free, they too, will be free & the best way for them is, to do their duty & wait until their change comes, Sam I fear will have to be hung, unless he will take warning, I am sorry to hear of so mutch Stealing, I do hope that there will be a stop put to it, day before yesterday there were 4 deserters in hearing of us, all were Alabamians, they went home to bushwhacking, mostly deserters, there was 17 left our Regt about a week ago & were caught 2ond night, I am oblige to you for the nice suit of jeans, you speak of, I do not kneed a coat, nor do I want pants bad, I have 2 pair, the ones I left home with & those you sent me, both good pants, except the seets, my socks are worn in holes at the toes but I darned them & bought a pair from_____ making out for the present, Camp is a _____ on clothes, Shirts all good, I have thus far kept clear of lice, but do not know how long I can say so, As to fair we get (only tolerable Rations) of the verry poorest kind of beef corn meal &C I can get Sugar at 75 cts per pound & a few potatoes, but Arheart & Pike do not want to buy sutch things, we mess together & have for us 2 men to cook

Dec 13th 4 pm

.13 .14 P1

My Dear Amie Capt McBee has got here but left the box you sent together with 7 or 8 others back some 15 miles, I will try to send for them tomorrow if I can get a waggon, I got the letters, the waggon they hired to bring them would not come any farther &

the Roads are nearly impassable, tell Billy that I will answer his soon, I am so sorry that you are so troubled, I told barney to split Railes around the fields close to the fince & my best Recollection is that I told him that, I wanted Rails split in the bottom to do up all the fince along the Road & this side of the creek, that I did not want that timber cut up about the house, but I expected that they would get some before the bottom got overflowed, I do not want him to split in the water, but I know that there is high places around the farm, where he could get them if I were there to point my finger to the tree, I know that if I were there that he & Sam could cut & split & Toby could drive & unload, & they help him load, but the Reason that they do so little is that they cant do anything without help & that alluded to the time that I expected them to work before the bottom got wet, but to late now, there is places yet in the bottoms that Rails & wood can be got, but it is a long way to haul over bad Roads, well let him get any where, & especially close to the fince

P2

I think the fince between the house & Ladiga can be Repaired without Rails by putting on all the stakes & riders & a few polls cut long & the others getting Rails & wood & Reparing fence, Oh well dear one do the best you can, no telling if we save the place whose hands it will fall in, even if we live to see the war end, & I do not know but what you had as well use every thing as suits best, & I do not know that there is not another Sicklyer Set of negrows in the Confed & but few who are less account than ours are getting to be, I cant think that they have hurt themselves, if they have done more than any body else, what to make & gather 42 loads of corn ,how many hands, 4 to count Dice & Turk made 5 the same number I had the last year, I was at home only I had Dan in place of Dice, when I made more wheat a worse year, all told, fodder more, oats more corn, 50 loads cribbed, Cotton 20 bales more railes coalwood &C Oh no use talking, If I were home next year as good crop year as this, I could with Barney & Billy make more than has been made this year & there would be no grumbling about doing more than any body, Your wish, about the Yank having them, they wish so too & they begin to feel the free, Streaks Running through them now , that is the Reason that they cant do this & that & the other, If I were there I would out a Spear to them, one on the head

14TH 7 AM

P3

this is unpleasant to me, do the best you can but do not flinch, they are servants for God has made them so, it is night, more tomorrow, God bless good bie,

Amie if you can get hens at 150 cts you had better buy, you said nothing about the boys, I want to know, but supposed you forgot it, Yes I do Recollect that you said they were improving & you had not killed & as to the (Secret Letter) I believe your views are Right, it is ruin either way, but if the army takes all you have they will not turn you out of doors, & can but draw Rations from the government as lots of families are now doing, after I have studied it all over, my advise is Stay at home & take the chances, as to the Sale yes send them & let the horses sell at any price, but you had better send G word to buy Kit, in unless she will bring a Reasonable price, well I must now quit & go see if I can get a waggon, no waggon today, well we will have to get McBees waggon to go back after

P4

I hate to tax his kindness, but it is the best we can do now, I will send 2 men with it any how, Wm Palmer come in to see John this morning & brought him a fine chance of provisions, Bale Pikes wife sent him some, So maybe that mine will come in, in good time, I intended to have sent this letter by an old man from Talladega, but while I was gone for the waggon, he left & I now think of sending by John Webb, who stats home in the morning, I am mutch oblige to you, for your long letters & am perfectly satisfied about not getting letters, & hope that you will be

So, Tell me all your troubles for I assure you that I will give you the best advice & consolation I can, Say nothing about that Secret letter, do as seems best to your own judgment without asking ever asking my advice & my word for it, well in all I will be satisfied, I close for the present with my best prayers & wishes Your own Sam

PS I sent you some envelops already backed, if sent by mail try one of them S

Camp 30th Ala Regt Dec 17 1863

.17 P1

(Letter burnt top & bottom)

My Dear <u>Amie</u> it Rained consistently last night & this morning we <u>were</u> to convenient to water, it is (Creek) within 2 feet of my feet & has been for 3 0r 4 hours, while some under water, the while some under the same shelter were compeled to move, after the water run under them, we will move our house this morning if it does not rain to hard, My Dear I had my tooth pulled out, it has not hurt since I had it pulled after about one hour, that tooth has not done me mutch good since I had the other pulled last winter at Vicksburg, Some times I could use it, I send it to you to give to Virgil the two plugs of gold are worth at least one dollar each in gold, the ammunition to Billy, but in your charge, the tin cup to Dicky, the gold pin that will not rust nor wear out to you, you can take care of it & I can get a steel point & use with my stack, I had lost it & John Wilkinson found it, I shall give him (5) dollars for it, this is all the chrismuss gifts that I have to send you, tell the Negroes that I am sp poor that I have nothing to send to them but my good will & wishes, that I try when praying for you and the children, to pray for them also, that the lord may save us all through th__- times of trouble & bring us tour grav__ ___e preparred to meet the Re_____ in heaven ____ ____ will be no more war

P2

My Dear I am on duty th_____ ____ looking daz not mutch to do, I am ___ __rry & am some what confused, but well work out,

I feel like I have not time to write a word & will close. May God bless you & yours, hear & answer your prayers, is my prayer, Good bie Your own Sam

PS Send you my old pants & Socks, I have enough without them & the pants are to small for any one in the Co who kneeds them, & they are too light for winter but do me first rate next summer, S

CAMP 30TH ALA REGT NEAR DALTON GA DEC 21ST 63

.21 P1

My Dearest Amie 7 O AM I Rec yours (by Mr. W.) of the 14th Yesterday noon & they are going to start back this morning, there stay is short, they were long coming that they want to start back so as to get home by Christmas, the roads are bad, I was glad to get it, the last I Rec was by McBee of the 9th, that letter you spoke of going so quick, was sent by Dr. Gorman our surgeon who has gone home on furlough, did he leave it at the office, or throw it out at the gate, I want to know, I am glad to learn that you are all well once, hope that you may so continiew, I am glad to get a letter from Sister A & to hear what has become of James Reid, I have never heard a word of him since I left home, also that you Reminded me of writing to my Mother, I am too negligent, about writing to her but the Rest do not write to me, nor I to them, because I generally have as mutch as I can do writing

P2

I wrote to Mother yesterday evening & will send it by Mr. W. & asked her to write me a long letter, My Dear nothing would give me more pleasure than to spend a short time with you, but the army must be held together & although it would take but 24 hours to get home, yet there is 200 men in the Regt that have as good claims as I have, the hail Storm you spoke of blew down Mothers gin house, so old man Wingo wrote, there was a hard Rain here but no Storm, I hope that Graham may be able to Render you some assistance but I doubt his health, oh for got to tell you that I am well, I think My Dear that you can make a living if the war will stay far enough off, as it those who has, & those who has not, are all alike, all have their troubles these times, for instance Lt Airheart has asked a furlough for 8 days, on account of getting wood &C for his family this winter, papers started up yesterday, I see how he comes out in a few

P3

Amie all the chance that I know of for me to get a furlough is, to go home to see about the Settlement of Fathers estate, If you know that, that business neads my personal attention, write to me & that is the best excuse I can fix up, I am glad that you are out of money, for I have but little< I have loaned out something like 100 dollars & have about that mutch, & will send you some by the first chance after the month is out, then they will owe me 2 months 260$ dollars, but it tales at least one dollar a day to do me, I can buy Sugar at 75 cts per pound &, P. & A. do not want to buy it, So I thought that I would buy it all & send to you, I have only about 4 lbs now, I will get more today & if Arheart gets off I will send it, it will save meat, the best you can do, I Recon is to stay at home, perform & make a crop, have as mutch wheat ground up as will take to do you, & Sell the Rest for sutch of yourself are obliged to have, take care of yourself & family the best you can & trust in the

P4

Lord & Savior for the balance of the things of life & for the one whitch is to come, time is out, the beaugle sounds for Review God bless you good bie

Your own Sam

CAMP 30TH ALA NEAR DALTON GA DEC 23RD 63

.23 P1

My Dear Amie I just wrote you by Mr Wilkinson day before yesterday, but I have a chance to send this by the hand of mr Cannon who will bring you 8 lbs of Sugar, most of whitch is verry nice, but I had a little wet in the bottom I thought that I would mix it all together, I know that you are not out of Sugar, but you can use it & it will save the meat, I have nothing to eat it with but Rice & I do not love sweetened Rice, I eat lots of it dry so & love it as good as a monkey, but I send it to you, who will use it more economically, I can only draw but a pound or two at a time, I have nothing to write in the way of news, You see all that I know in the papers, I get papers nearly every day, My Dear I have built me a house, with the chimney (the boddy) in an old stump, the Roof, a fly cloth stretched, I am snugly fixed, my mess is Sgt Palmer, James Young & Shaw, P & I sleep together & the other two, they cook for us, & I am to pay them, there is no cooks excused from duty now & it is pretty tight on the officers, but I shall pay 2 men to cook for me & if one is

P2

on duty I have another, but my Cabbin is snug we commensed it yesterday morning cut & toted the lumber (nearly quarter of a mile) & half the time we could not get anything to work with, I have as good qrters as any one, the Coln not excepted & a nice mess, the mess we left was to large (10 in it) all good fellows, but getting enough cooked was the Rub, If my box had not come till now, it would have done me more good, but I was obliged to divide, I have all of my fruit & bacon yet a part of my butter goobers &one pie, about a third of my bottle of wine & a few hickry nuts, The pies molded a little for the last few days, I am proud of my fixing beds off of the ground, & plenty of Room, good fireplace, Cracks chinked & daubed, dirt floor as a matter of coarse, but no danger of greasing the floor, high enough to walk about straight up, I will finnish in the morning it is night now & cold enough to Snow, good night May God bless & Save us all is the prayer of

Your own Sam

PS I wrote this on my knee without any thing under it, SCK

CAMP 30TH ALA NEAR DALTON GA DEC 24TH 63

.24 P1

My Dear Amie I have nothing new to write, the weather is cold

& clear, I have on my new pants & think do first rate, all of the men are drawing clothing as mutch as they need except Shoes & Socks, Short coats at 12 dollars, pants 9, good linsey cloth, coats lined, Shirts thick domestic or osingburgs 3dollars drawers same & Some good drilling 3 dollar, hats (poor wool) 450 cts, Shoes good brogans 6 dollars, all cheaper than they can get at home, but the difficulty is, getting them when we need them, I can draw money any day now, two month pay & will send you some the first chance I have, on hand now, about one hundred dollars, I have no use for it, but to buy something to eat, Pay for washing (whitch cost me one dollar per week) & tobacco, Ink paper & invellops, all of whitch are high, my boots are holding out first rate, I grease them once a week, if I cannot get

P2

tallow, I get morrow, whitch I believe is better, the health of the Co is good, I have sent 4 men to the hospital since we have been here & only have 4 now who are excused from duty, Love Alexander has applied for a furlough, I doubt his getting it, hope he may, I have not applied, think my chance a slim one, unless you could fix up some excuse, the mere fact that a man wants to go home, will not do, we have been at home, not long since, while there be in this army, men have not been at home in nearly three years, no one loves home & wife & children better than I do, but for the cause of my Country, I would be then, be assured my Dear one that I will bite at the first chance to get home, if it is only for a few days, I have written more by half than I thought so, I must now close, I hope you a pleasant Christmas week, & a bright new years morning with good health & bright hopes & May God our heavenly father still continuw to bless you is the prayer of You Sam

CAMP 30TH ALA NEAR DALTON DECEMBER 26TH 1863

.26 P1

My Dearest Amie I received by W Hendricks today, I was glad to hear from you, I began to think long of the time but I thought that you were waiting to make a sure case, the letters come by mail now in 3 days but I have notice but one from you only by hand I have been at this place, Wm H took dinner with me, II had confederate beef confederate corn bread & confederate pies & potatoes, this is a cold wet day not raining hard but driseling all day, I have a chance to send this by hand, So I thought that I would write to you, to let you know that I am well, & have enjoyed my self finely during this christmas, before a good fire & having my friends & acquaintances come to see me, Bryon took dinner with me yesterday & Jack Clark was to see me (the workman Jack, that helped Hicks build my gin house) he asked me about you & Billy, My Dear I fear that you will be troubled all the year with Sutch fellows

P2

as those waggoners, Sutch men are the cause a goodeal of damage, I feel that they will burn more bailes than the boys will be able to make, I get paper now, I have not time to write mutch now but will have a chance to send another in a few days, Dick Weaver has applied for a furlough, in fact, one man of every 30 men out of the Regt are allowed furloughs long enough to stay at home 10 days allowing time to go & come, Harris Foster & Bale Pike of my Co are alas going, all of them will be together, the same order allows one officer out of every 3 in one Company present for Duty, to go on the same terms, So Arhearts papers came back disproved in consequence of that order & consequently he will go first, if they get off Sunday night, then time will be out on the 12th Jan & then I shall start up one & allow 3 days for the papers to go up to Headqrtrs it will bring 15th , So I if nothing happens expect to be at home on the 16th or 17th night, I suppose they are going to keep up a listing of furlough, hope so, God bless all Good bie Your Sam

CAMP 30TH ALA REGT NEAR DALTON GA DEC 29TH 63

.29 P1

(Letter burnt in center)

My Dearest Amie I write to you this morning because I have nothing else to do at present, I just wrote you day before yesterday & sent it _____ erday by Capt Patterson of our Regt who will ___ ___ house this evening, the man that I intended _____ by left before I knew it, he _____ _____ let McB____ _____ _____ one of _____ (Odens)

brought _____ provisions _____mers box ____ hand last_____ another box____ P's that Ed Roberdsons wife _____ him, the last one is at the 19th, & he has sent for ___ so I think we will do well for a while, at lea__ _____ these Some fellows helped me eat up what you sent me, & I pitch into theres as though I were one of the family, Amie I have not drew money yet but can any day, I wish, & could send you some, but I think that I will get to come home as soon as Aheart gets back, but that will not be before the 17th or 18th Jan, it takes the papers so long at least 4 days to go to head qrtrs & back, Amie I have been thinking a goodeal of hiring out the negrows & renting out the place & letting you & the children go off some where & rent a place & live where you will not be annoyed every day & night with passerbies , but then there s the stock, provisions to sell, & who will take care of the farm, I do not know what to do, I fear that if you to make a crop the Soldiers will burn up the fense, & kill up the stock, hogs, sheep _____ & steal your mules & every thing else that they _____ hands on, but the question is _____ can you _____ you get _____ Oh that the _____ _____ but _____ to do

P2

4 PM Amie I have been down to the 19th Regt. & Saw several of my acquaintances & have just come back & find that Lt A is about Ready to Start, I have nothing to write more than I have written _____ can consider that matters will be th____ that I come home, whitch I am sure _____ some chance ___ to _____

PS Amie I can draw a _____ts & Short Coats as would do your _____ at less than you can get the work & f____, good lensey cloth, pants 9&, coats 12, good shirts 3, good Drawers 3,

Say nothing about this, but let me know, I draw more than the men want & can charge to some of them, & I pay them the money, & it come out of there Commulation money, & they get the use of there money now, Write to me on this matter, once or twice , So as I may know what to do, by the time I get to come, Yours S

CAMP 30TH ALA REGT DEC 30TH 3 OCLOCK PM

.30

My Dearest Amie I hasten to drop you a few lines to let you know that I am well & am quite busy making out muster & pay rolls, we muster for pay tomorrow, I have a jacket by Mr Brown or Powers, as it was cheaper than you could get or make them & the man are supplied with them, nothing strange or new in camp, look for me home by the 18th 19th or 29t0 if nothing happens, I must close as Harris Foster wants to start, My best wishes to you, Your own Sam

1864 SCK Letters Transcribed

January 1864

Camp 30ᵀᴴ Ala Regt January 3ᴿᴰ 1864

P1

My Dear Amie, I Received yours of the 27th day before yesterday, but it was not mailed until the 29th because there was not Stage on monday the 28th, I was glad to hear that you were all well, but I thought that you had quit that way of crying, oh yes you said it a thing that you had not done in a long time, & I do hope that you will not have any occasion to cry again, I was fearful that it would be a dull christmas, it is the second one you have passed without me, but I do hope & trust that before another comes that peace may overshadow us as a nation & that I may be at home with those I love best on earth & those boys, in their nice jeans Suits, & you my Dear in that Confederate dress, & all in fine health & spirits, I have been fearful that you would work yourself down, yes take my advise in that, I fear that you did not get to go see mother, & meet Ann, I heared from Emma they were all well Emma said that she would send something, but they were too heavy loaded to bring it, W.H. left a few days ago for home, the candy that the children had,

I guess was not nicer than our Molasses we made out of Sugar, & one pound will make one quart, Soldiers are up to getting meat & bread, but be I judge a scamp, Speaking of bad weather, the last 3 days & nights has been (bitter) cold, & the 4 days before them rany & cold, How mutch would you give me for a Substitute if you could buy one, all our Cotton, did Mr Argo & Cannon stay all night, you said you were asleep when they came, I will try & bring you some more Sugar when I come

P2

I am now letting Palmer have some, & we can make molasses out of them, & the beef is so poor, that it will be rather scarce, to Your shear that I could wish Eggs would be verry acceptable in camp, but we have no greace to fry them, but they are good any way, if it was like those I eat under the shade tree, my pants yes, I said the box of things was according to order, I like the pants the best kind, I have been wearing them 2 weeks I believe, the candle I got it, & have used it every time that I wanted a light, it is a good one, I have my piece of bacon & two ears pop corn yet, for hard times, Oh yes my cook is making us a pot of lie hominy, you may think that it will not be nice & clear, it is all of that & as good as ever was made in any kitchen, I tell you that we are living high now, Since those 2 boxes I spoke about in my other letter came in, old man Farmer is here yet, one of his sons was sick & he did not go, but wish start in the morning, & will carry this letter to Rome, Dr G was so surly that I wanted to know about the letter, all Right, he can if he will do Right, Madesons negrow told you a lie, he had not seen me in a week before he started, but I was well, but he knew nothing about me, for it is ½ miles to Johnsons qrtrs & I have not seen that negrow in camp since we have been here, as to buying turkeys they may go like those you Raised & I think the better plan is to quit the business, as to accommodations for you in Stump house, I think the chances, slim, they will do a Soldier but not a Soldiers wife, too many bedfellows, I must close I am well &nothing of interest to write, May God have mercy upon us & Save us as a nation is the prayer of your own Sam

PS Stamp your letters & back as I directed, may be they will com

CAMP 30TH ALA JANUARY 4ᵀᴴ 1864

.04 P1

My Dear Billy I have about 2 minutes to write this morning, to let you know that I am well & nothing new or strange has happened since yesterday it is day light & it raining, showered a little all night, I am writing by candle light is now Roll Call & close good bie your Father SCK

CAMP 30TH ALA REGT STUMP HOUSE, DALTON GA JAN 10TH 63

.10 .11 P1

My Dearest Amie I received yours of morning of the 8ᵗʰ by the hand of Raburn, this morning & was glad to hear from you, but was sorry & Some what surprised to hear that Ella was sick, I have not Received your long letter you spoke of nor have I Received one at all since the 27ᵗʰ by Wm H, No that one came by mail, that is the last one, I expect to get it today, I suppose you sent it by mail, I intended to have sent a letter by Dr Francis, but he promised to come & see me before started, but slipped off to keep from carrying any, & Started 2 days before he told me, he was going, that is not the first time that, that family has done the like, & the letter you sent by John, to me at Demopolis, he kept for 2 days before he gave it to me, Said that he forgot, he had it, after I had ask him, if he did not bring me one, all Right that ends Right, I expect to send this by B. Prichard if he does not do likewise if he does I can send by Charly & if I miss him, I expect that John Palmers papers will

P2

be back in a day or two, & if I miss all, I will send by mail as the last chance & if Airheart gets back according to promise, it will be thursdsay night the 14ᵗʰ & then I will start up my papers friday morning, & look for them monday evening, & if all work well, will be in Rome Tuesday morning & if I can get the Stage I will get home tuesday night, My Dear you see Mr Woolum & tell him that I want one of his best suits, or a suit good or bad that he must play one of his best tricks to get an old Soldier a suit, load or no load, that I Shall expect it, & must not be disappointed, I know that the time seem long to you, it does to me, Still I have nothing hardly to do, but I dream about you & more anxious than if there was no chance of getting home, as to that pen, I have missed it every time that I have had any writing to do, & when I get home I will collect the pay & buy it back, at the same price, & pay in cash at the same Rate

P3

I fear from your letter that Ella will die, but all have to die sooner or later & it looks like that we are in a bad streak of luck, but we must be contented or Submissive to our fate, the Lord giveth & the Lord taketh away & blessed be the name of the Lord, I Really feel thankful, that we have had so mutch mercy shown unto us as heads of a family, Let us hope on hope ever looking unto the Lord, for the life that now is & the one that is to come, I will wait til after the mail comes in & see if I get a letter, good bie your Sam

Stump house 3 ½ PM Well my Dear Amie, I Rec your long letter & was glad to get it, it told me of lots that I had not heared, I love to get long letters from you, where is James, You said but little about him, is he at Talladega yet, has his boy Alfred, the Scarlitt fever, or what, had Mother got my letter before she went to stay with Ann, I saw Bryan christmas, he told me about the land Renting, he is about 2 miles from here

P4

I have not been to see him yet, he has the better chance, to come to see me, he has a horse, & I have not, & besides that I am all the officer in the Co now (Pike being in command of Co A) & I have to be about, expect by a pass approved by the Brigadier General, but I do not want to go after, I have not had one pass since we have been here & that was to go to Dalton to buy me a pair of blankets, but no blankets there, I was notified that the Quarter Master had boots to Sell to the officers at 200 dollars, but I did not want any, I think it is verry well that you let Morgan pass, when I come I will see what can be done &C yes I know that it is the duty of C, & F to assist you & direct you but, the misfortune is, that so few people do there duty, As to breaking up, I was excited when I wrote to you, & thought that sutch trains would be passing likely all year & but I fully agree with you, that there is no place like home, Sweet home, so often do I think of my Dear ones at home, Stay there & Risk the consequences, until you are driven, by dire necessity to leave home

P5

I hope that you may kill your hogs before I get home, & have lots of fatty bread when I come besides chitlings, & souse & all good hog meat doings, that follow a hog killing, & especially some old sausages from the first killing, I have eat beef until it is too poor to write about, but still I am getting fat, there is so little fat that there is no danger of the grees, Rising on ones stomach, I glory in your pluck, about making cloth for the family, /that box I wrote Powers would bring, was put in, Browns & Little Johns waggon & they were to haul it until they parted, & then Powers was to take it, as he was going by, but it is at Browns, I guess, My Dear you complain of the cold weather, & pitty us, we are doing verry well, & no danger of freezing, it is too cold to Snow, we have not had any yet, we sleep in the Stump house & hardly ever have to get up to warm, more than once or twice during the night, I Shall close for the present, know no chance to send by hand until tomorrow, more amen, Good bie

MONDAY JAN 11ᵀᴴ 64 8 OCLOCK A.M. STUMP HOUSE

P6

My Dear I expect that you will get anxious for a letter before you get this, but I had better wait 2 days, & send by hand than put it in the mail, for then instead of sending them by Rome, they send them by Montgomery, & hence the delay at least 4 days longer, As to getting Rails, I know that there is lots of the ground yet not covered in water, the verry best time, for timber to split well, Oh I believe that Barney will do, if he had some one to tell what, & where to work, I hope that the weather may be good, the time I get to stay at home & I will try & look around,, & give them a start that they can go on, at least a while, My Dear I fear that you will run short of money, have you no wheat nor corn held as a reserve, Did you have your wheat ground up, as you spoke of doing, you have never told me, I Shall, if we draw money before I leave have about 350 dollars & Suppose that 50 to get me home & back, so I can spear you 200 dollars, but if I get off, before, the men owe me

P7

about 120 dollars borrowed money, & if I fail in getting that, my bank will be small, Tell those pretty Romping boys, that I had two messes of whit caps, out of the corn they sent me, & when I come home that, if they turn over my ink, that we will have a big Romp & that I intend to tickle them for you, any how, you have not, nor has Billy, told me how his ammunition done & especially the caps, I can buy a box of caps of the small size, if those will not do, Speaking of those Deserters, Barry told me all of them, I, two, expect that 2 men them belong to my Co, Sweet fellows, by hanging time, You said that you were saving eggs for me &C they would be verry good, but I think would cost more than they would come to, I do not expect you to send me anything now, I have some fruit yet & Sometimes draw bacon, sugar, rice &C I guess that old man Bail could be Speared as well as any man, Still it seems strange that a man, would kill himself

P8

It is now eleven Oclock we have had a General inspection, Sutch brushing up old guns &Sweeping yards, you never saw, but all is over now, & I have just seen Mr. McRobberts of our County who (lives over in Rabbet town) going home & promised to leave this at the house, best chance yet, I think him a clever good old man, The weather is yet bitter cold, & has every appearance of

Snowing but, I think it to cold, We make out considering everything Scandalous well, hope we may never fair worse in the war nor out of it, & now my Dear Amie I think that I have given you all the information that will interest you, or at all events, all that I now Recollect of, May the God of all things, direct us in all our ways, & hearts of gratitude for past blessings, & hearts of prayer & Supplication, for sutch mercies and blessings that he seeth we so mutch stand in kneed of, bringing peace out of confusion & Save us as a family & a nation, for Jesus sake is my Prayer Amen good bie Your own Sam

Camp 30th Ala Regt Stump house Jan 14th 9 PM

.14

My Dearest A I Snatch this moment to drop you a few lines to let you know that I am well & that Airheart has not yet got in, but I look for him in the morning, & if so I think the plan laid in my last will be carried out, J Palmers papers Ret today, & he ids ordered to Report to Dr Stout of Atlanta, for hospital duties, he will start tomorrow, he is going to stop at William P. a day before he Reports, & get a furlough from, A, home this evening, I think of sending this by him, the Small pox is in the brigade the 46th Ala Regt, I fear I will be short run for money, the men has not drawn yet, good bie Yours Sam

February 1864

Camp 30th Ala Regt Near Dalton Ga Feb 9th 1864

.09 PI

Letter burnt top & bottom

My Dear Amie I would have written before this time but had no chance to send it by hand & thought that you would get it as soon, to wait 2 or 3 days, as to send by mail, I had quite a pleasant trip from home to Rome, more so than I expected, we got to Rome about dark, where I gave 3 dollars for a poor bed to sleep on, next morning we left at 8 oclock & arrived at Kingston at 10, where we stayed until

1 PM & then for Dalton where we arrived at about 4 PM, but we left the train at the last water station this side of Dalton, whitch is not as far to camp as, tis from Dalton, I got here time enough that evening to look Round & See the most of the men who, all seemed to be glad to see me, there has been some sickness in the Co since I left & Some 7 or 8 sent to the hospital & one of the number died in Hospt Marietta a

Mr W. B. Griffin who came to us at Demopolis, from conscrpt camp, he owed me 20 dollar, Riley Leasley owed me 30 on

P2

J Palmers account, he has not paid me, he says that he lost his money, one or two others, who went to hospital owe me small amounts, the most of them have paid me up, It takes lots to carry an officer through, beef is 74 cts per pound & to poor to eat (at home) when we get it, bacon 250 cts & none to buy, flour 150 and scarce at that, Corn meal plenty at 6 cts per pound (good) sugar 150 & scarce but I think that we can make out, we are better fixed up here, than at the old camps, as a general thing, I am about the same, my mess all well & all on duty the day I got to camp, The duties are heavy, guard & Police duties, drills &picketts, I have not been on duty out side of the Co since I came, The most of the companies are Reenlisting, but mine seem slow, I have been using my influence, towards Reenlisting since I came to camp, I look at it this way, that by Reenlisting it will not protect either our

P3

time, nor the war, & likely it may have an effect on the enemy, & the benefits that we derive is that the men are allowed a furlough of (10) days at home, all Reenlisted men, one out of ten, besides the other sistem of furloughing, that is one for every 25 men present for duty, if my Co were to enlist, I could get 3 men furloughed on the 25 for duty score & 7 ½ on the 1 for 10 score, or Reenlisted men score, whitch is 10 per cent, I think that the influens has been against it in my Co, but I know that it will not be many days before I shall have several men home on the score, I have not Reenlisted yet, but expect to the first chance, Tis hard to part from all I love on earth, for 2 long years, & then to Reenlist for the war, let be longer or shorted, but tis harder to submit to my family to sutch a despotisms as is offered to us, by our enemies, No never will I just (be compelled) lay down

P4

my armes, & calmly submit to sutch fate, My Dear Amie do the best you can for yourself & family (praying for me at the same time) I am a Soldier & may the blessings of god Rest upon us as a family & a nation is the prayer of your own & affectionate husband Sam C. Kelly

PS I traveled with an old methodist preacher from my house to the camp, he has been a chaplain in the original army, Resigned (he says because of the extreme cold there) he is looking out a situation, he preached for us Sunday, & did verry well, I thought he would preach babtist doctoring in spite of all he could do, he may become our Chaplain, I saw Jack Roberson, he says that all that Cavalry (loose Cavalry) sutch as Jim ,G, Bob Alsup, Jes Boozer &C are every one absent without leave, but I do know you kneed not say anything about it, There is lots of my Co who would be glad that John Graham could not get his papers fixed, but let it Run, they say whitch is better to let him, or some poor man with a house full of children, they owe support, just to get every body out as they are, unconditionally willing to let the negrows do nothing and the army may_____

Your Sam

CAMP 30 ALA FEB 14TH 64

.14 .16 .17 P1

My Dearest Amie I Rec yours of the 11 this morning & was delighted to read in it that you were all well, & also that

Grahams papers were signed up by Reece, he was going to send them to me by Sam Pendland but did not get them Signed up in time, I am sorry to hear that Estice is no better, I fear he will die, as to that Casulite, I cannot say that I am mutch surprised at the old Colonel, they never send out any other sort but Sharp ones, I began to think it full time that I was getting a letter, but I suppose you did the same, & I hope that you have got the one I sent, end this, more now

Feb 16th My Dear Amie I thought that I could have had time to send this off or Rather finnish it before now but I have been

P2

busy nearly all the time & the weather is cold, I could have yesterday, but it was not finneshed & it is now after sunset & as cold as December was, but Frank Rountree has a furlough pending & we look for it tomorrow & then I will send it finneshed or not, I have nothing verry interesting to write , but a you love long letter, & I can write any thing that I could tell you(if I were with you) & that is all that I know, Our Regt has changed off our muskets for Rifles & Some of the men are not verry well pleased, the Austrian Rifles, like that one, Bryan left at my house, My men are not inclined to Reenlist, only ten have Reenlisted, although congress has passed the act, Retaining all in the field between the ages of 18 & 45, I must close for the want of light, God bless you Good bie

FEBRUARY 17TH 1864

P3

My Dear Amie I have nothing of interest to write you, the Rations are scarce meat especially, & some Rhumors about our leaving, but all Rhumor no Sertainty about it, the weather is seveir cold, last night about as cold as we have had this winter, I had ice in the blanket, in the Shanty nearly an inch thick this morning, My house is not as fixed as I had it before we moved the door, is in the north end, & the Roof is not good, we have a good chimney & fire place, wood is plentiful but not as handy as I could wish, I had my bed clothes out sunning on the top of the house yesterday & one of the quilts caught fire & burned 2 great holes in it before we found out what was on fire, it will do to lay in, but shall leave it when we move, the time drags heavily away with me & it seems like my trip home has only increased my desire to go home again, Oh that God would have mercy

P4

upon us as a nation, & cause this dreadful war to seas & let us poor

Soldiers go home in peace, who are wasting the best years of their lives in the camps, Oh that he would cause our enemies to think that they are prosecuting an unholy war & cause them to give up the notion of subjugating us, &cause them to Return to their own homes in peace, & leave us to ourselves, to worship God under our own vice, & figtree, according to the dictates our own sincerest, is my daily prayer,

May the god & father of our Lord Jesus Christ keep us in the way we should go, guiding guarding & protect us as a family, is my prayer, good bie

Your own Sam

PS all the other companies are Reenlisting some, nearly all, all more than mine (back wards set) They will not be charged, that it is to there advantage, S

PS This is a poor letter but I have nothing to make it more interesting, S

CAMP 30TH ALA FEB 21ST 1864

.21 P1

My Dearest Amie Yours of the 15th came to hand yesterday evening, I was glad to get it & read that you were all well once again, I was some what surprised to hear of you boarding, but under sutch circumstances & sutch people, it would be different to taking in any & every body, though but for the scarcity of provisions, you could make a lot of money, in that case, What are they to give per day or week, You did not say, I have traveled through Chambers County in 1855 when I was selling flour & frankly it is good land & tolerably healthy, but the larger portion is as poor peney, would say & sandy as Randolph Co, I think that if the war was over & I hat home in health & strength that we would make out where we are or could go some where else, but there is the (if) & Since it is, as it is, you & I will both have to stay where we are & try to fill our several duties, towards each other & our family & country, trusting in God

P2

I am sorry for the loss of that cow, She was best you had & that how she was quite young, I am not surprised at her dying, that is frequently the case, the other Sows & there pigs will be enough to breed them well with the Shoats already on hand, it is not best to have too many hogs for then they are neglected, I am not surprised at you to be thankful for my good health & protection (I try to be) for it is bad enough to be separated, enduring the preservations & hardships of war, & in all & if I was unwell it would be a hard time in deed, pray for me, daly, hourly, & imminently, for I feel the kneed of your prayers, & as it is a source of so mutch consolation to me, to know that I have one (thought far away) who I can trust & believe, is as king God, for the sake of Christ to keep me, in the way that I should go, giving unto me all necessary blessing & at last bring me (when we have gained out independence) home to my own dear wife & family, The Reenlisting is about played out in my Co, they Remind me of the saying of one,

P3

who cut off his nose to spite his face, they say that they were promised a 60 day furlough when they started out, yearly, & they have not got that, & now the thing is certain that one in every 10 that Reenlist can get furloughs & they will not expect the last because, the circumstances of the country was sutch that they could not get the first, I cannot see that it will protest the war, nor, not, to shorten it, I am in for the war, let others do as they will, the Colonel blames Pike & Airheart for not taking the lead in this thing, nearly all the Regt has Reenlisted but my Co, & the Coln said to me last night that mine was one of the best Companies he ever saw & never behind only in this thing, I have sais as mutch as I intend to say, without some sign on part of the Co first, I have done my duty, I have laid the example. & I now leave it to them & to their own consciousness, I have no assurance that I will I will get a furlough on the Reenlisting Schore, it applyes only to noncommissioned officers & men not to commissioned, I am sorry you did not understand it,

P4

You need not look for me home soon, Mrs. Reese is she lucky or unlucky, any woman who has a husband, to be left at sutch times, I am mutch oblige to you for your invitation to dinner, I will accept the first opportunity, I had a dinner at home today, & for fear you cannot guess, I will tell you I had corn bread, Stewed fruit & a little butter, all said & ate& was satisfied, not a morsel of any thing else, though we are not entirely out, Yet we know how to economize & have to do it, to keep fasts from coming to often, You can certainly make out on the meat you have killed, I hope so, If Golden will give you 1000 dollars for Syphax let him go, but I do not care to sell him at that, I had Rather keep him, what are you about to sell the cotton, I expect that you had as well sell those worst torn up bags, & perhaps all of it, I cannot advise, You & Graham for that, I leave it with you, What are you going to do with your wheat, Sell it, or had you not better sell the flour, Where had Josh been, I know that he had some business above or he never could have found time to come to see you, more tomorrow good bie

Camp 30th Ala Near Dalton Ga Feb 22ond 12 oclock

.22 P1

My Dearest Amie I promised on my last sheet to write you more today, I have nothing strange nor news to write, I am well & do sincerely hope that when these lines reach you that you all may be well & in the best kind of Spirits, there is certainly a big move on hand in the lower post of Ala & east Miss troops are hasly moving from here, A Rhumor says we will go, but it is uncertain, I do hope that our Army may gain a decisive victory over them in that Campaign, the battle is Gods, Oh where is that Sermon you were going to send me, there is one in the Regt but I have not read it, the weather is pleasant now, the health of the Co is tolerable good, H. Slaton is not well, I expect he will be sent to the hospital, I Rather that you would not say any thing to Pike about Reenlisting as he will think that I am the cause, let him alone & let him be Conscripted

P2

with the ballance of the Co (as they will) & he be there Captain, if they want him still & do not want you to understand that, I think myself unpopular in the Co, no by no means, I know that my men think well of me, & as a proof the men or Recruits I am getting, but here is the point, I had Rather command a Co of volunteers than a Company of Conscripts & the choice is with me whether or not I will command after we have served out our three years, or Resign & go into some other command, My Dear one my (home) Rations are mutch out & the chance is scarce & high here, but you have not got it to spare, & if you had had a lot on hand & we were to move I could not get it transported, So I would loose it, as there is but 2 waggons to the Regt, to haul all filed & staff & cooking utensils, axes &C, So do the best you can & I will try & make out, God bless & Save us & bring peace out of confusion, is my prayer Sam

GEN STEVENSONS DIVISION NEAR DALTON GA FEB 24 64

.24 P1

(*Letter very faded. This is all that can be seen*)
My Dearest Amie I Rec yours of the 19th late yesterday & was glad to hear that you were doing well

P2

P3

---

going, the waggons are all gone South, it was thought that the Yanks were coming to tunnel hill, about 6 miles north of here, but my opinion is that the army going to fall back to Resaca, & we are waiting for all the stores & waggons &C to get off & then we will follow as a Rear guard, we were up all night before last cooking up & fixing up, Ready to fall in at day light, We were Ready but we did not leave till about 10 oclock PM, & moved & stopped & then moved again & took up here about an hour by Sun, & are here yet, 12 oclock Noon, More anon, Good bie god bless us & our cause your own Sam

P4

4 oclock PM 24th My Dear we are still at the same place, & in hearing of the cannons towards Ringold, They have been firing there about 2 hours, we were ordered into line (as we thought it move but it was) to be Reviewed by Gen Johnson who was cheered by the men as he passed, I must close as, I have a chance to send it to the officer immediately with my best wishes & prayers good bie Sam

MARCH 1864

CAMP 30TH ALA REGT MARCH 1ST 64

.01 .02 P1

(Corner of letter missing)

My Dear Amie I Rec yours of the 25th by Pike yesterday & was glad to hear you were in fine Spirits, I do Rejoice with you about your own escape from what you so mutch dreaded, all Right on that Schore now, I was some what uneasy for you, but am now Satisfied, we are in our old winter quarters, as snug as if no fight had had taken place, I shall not give the particulars about the fight for you know as mutch or more than we do, except what came under our own observation, the account of the affair in the papers is about correct, it is about all that I know, we were held in Reserve to support Cummings Brigade or Renolds as the case might be, but thank God they were able to Repulse enemy charge that was made against them, & we lay down on the ground & let the missiles pass over us, inspection now more anon, Well Dear it is now about 4 P.M., & has been Raining & is now very cold, I was (after inspection) making out my muster & pay Roll, ____ it rained so hard & the Shanty leak so hard

P2

that I had to quit, & then went to bed to keep myself employed, I slep until just a while ago when I was aroused by drum & fife passing through the Qrtrs, escorting a fellow carrying an inscription (on aboard in large letters) Cowardice. For Shirking out of the fight, I have written you2 letters within the last week & had them put in the citizens box & if you did not get them it is not my fault, & besides that, the one of the 27th I said that I would give (if sutch a thing was possible) ten dollars for its safe delivery in due time, But Estice has not come in as he aut to have done & I have not got my onions, but that is nothing compaired to the damage he is doing the Company & himself, he will be Reported absent without leave & the furloughing will be stopped so long as he stays out, Oh that every man would do his whole duty, I got my candle it does first Rate & my old tooth brush I had forgotten that I had left it, I can make out a while longer without clothes, but my boots are ripped but I think that I can get them fixed, they will give out as soon as my clothes, cant you have me a pair of shoes made out of some of the best leather

P3

I want mines in lengt but verry low the instep, Old man Tigrett is a good hand, but is so slow that I Recon you had better get Kathy to make them, I hate to give

160 dollars for a pair of boots, but if you have bought them all Right, I think that I shall know both by the 1st May & probably I can get a short furlough to go to the rear for to get me clothing &C, I shall try it for 4 days at that time, but if the estate settlement

needs my attention, May be that I can get off on that before, I write to you about it in my last, I want to come home again, as bad as I did before I went, I dreamed of being at home last night, of seeing you &C, may the time soon come for a Realization of that dream, fund your money as fast as you get it & let the law take its coars, write to Gladden & see if he will take Confederate money or my estate notes now, & if he will, you can get a good trade out of Graham for cotton enough to pay them off, all that I hate about the taument is that the Shackeling Cavalry get it, & the infantry who do all the fighting have to eat poor beef & corn bread, or do without, but dog has his day

P4

I am glad you demanded his papers, I wish all the women could read as well as you can, but my Dear I think you aut to pay more attention to figures, I Really do not know how mutch money you sent to Dr Cowden, here is your figure (200,20) that if it is dollars, is two thousand & 20 & if it is dollars & cts is two hundred dollars & twenty cts, but I think you for two hundred & twenty dollars, whitch aut to have been in only three figures, thus (220) or (220.00) two aughts to show cts, but even dollars without cts, Say 220$ the dollar mark either before or behind the amount, but when dollars & cts both are in the amount the dollar mark before $00.00 cts after, I think that you can spear old Kit, you say you wish you could sell her, that young mule will make the 4th hand, what time you Run four ploughs, & that leaves old Martha to do the jobbing, I hope that you may get them all good hats, & mine I want made low crouned about like this one & size (7 & 1/8) Seven and an eighth, I hope that money matters will settle soon, & the people be satisfied, but some will

grumble, any how, it seems like that the doctors are favored, but they must take care of the women & children, H\John Frances went to Jims wedding & then went on home, he has Returned, I have only saw him on inspection, I will see him again

P5

Will Weaver I thought was wonded, but that did not keep him

305

from wanting to marry, I suppose that they mutually agreed to put it off, Soldiers will marry for all of the men in the world, they do appreciate the worth of the woman, I think that Bryan aut to have sent his negrow, at first, as to Rations, I think that I can make out, as any one else, but Rash (as the boys call them) from home is verry acceptable at any time, my Dear one I am Really sorry that you do not get my letters, I do write, & will continue to write, & may be out of a good many you will get some, I am so glad that the Cavalry in the neighbor hood has done so little damage, it is discouraging to men in the field to have them tear up their homes, I do not think that there is as mutch stealing going on, as was 2 months ago, I don't think that I will approve Dick Praters papers, (& if I do not the thing is dead) because he has always been on the Shirk &no man in the company who has been well has been home as mutch as he has, he has never been in a fight & besides all that & worse than all that he is not, a practical Smith, as that paper sets forth, his interest might as well suffer as mine, & he is not a Smith & has not done his, the duty that I have & has been at home twice to my once

P6

2nd March I have nothing new to write this morning, I am well & the weather has cleared off tis cold & windy, I will close, God bless us all good bie

Your own Sam

CAMP 30TH ALA REGT MARCH 8TH 64 NEAR DALTON

.08 P1

My Dearest Amie I Rec yours of the 4th yesterday evening, & the first thing that struck my attention was that you have not Rec my letters, not my fault, my dear one, for if possible I were more anxious, than you were, under sutch exciting times, I assure you that I had written 5 letters (two of whitch I put in the citizens box) that you aut to have gotten before the 4th of March, I cannot account for it, but I do not want you to think that it is any inconsistency on my part, I Received the one from James also &

was surprised to think that Gladden should hesitate to bond the money, indeed I thought that he was my ageant, & besides that when I was at home, I could not for see what congress would do, if I had known that G was so verry timmid, I should have appointed an ageant, I have written to Gladden & expect to send it this evening by hand with this, I also Rec a letter from Mother in whitch I learned that James was County Surveyer (a thing that I did not know before) about the selling of the cotton you, You certainly know more about the money, I had not heared any thing about them

P2

You must depend upon Dr. Cowden, Fergerson & others for advice, I am not capable and now, My Dear one do not ever think (mutch less write to me) about your long interesting letters, they have never been to long, & nore are without interest to me, if it were possible I would like to know all about every one on the place, & every thing on the place, just as mutch if I were there, but I do not ask that mutch of you but fill your sheet any how of sutch as is not interest to you, may be to me, I am sorry to hear of your bad spells of headaches, I deaply Sympathize with you, I have oupon the affaires of the estate, applyed for a furlough of 12 days, Setting forth the facts & the danger of delay of funding the Money, The Coln had it & said it was a strong petition & Really did more than I expected him, not only, approved & fowareded but certifyed that it was fact, I thought that it would go through but was told by Francis that Gen. P. could not approve, but Respt forwarded upon the grounds that I could have an attorney, It may go through Right but I begin to doubt it now, if it comes back approved by Gen Johnson, I shall start home fryday night or Saturday morning & it will take me 2 days to come home, for I will have to stay all night in Rome, & will get home as good to start Sat Morning as Fryday night, I am on guard & have no more paper, but hope soon to see you, then I can tell you all, God bless Sam

CAMP 30TH ALA NEAR DALTON MARCH 9TH 64

.09 P1

My Dear Amie I wrote you a letter yesterday but had no chance to send it, only by mail & I consider that no chance at all, as you do not get the letters I had sent that way, I have nothing new to write, but I am still well, & I thought as I had a chance to send it by one of my own Co (Sgt. Adkins) that you would be Shure to get it, I wrote to Gladden day before yesterday but preferred to wait until, Adkins Started, as the Shurest & Shortes time to its delivery, My Dear I think it quite doubtful about my getting off, I have been thinking about you Selling cotton, if you were to sell it for Interest paying Confederate notes, they will pay the interest of 2 cts on the one hundred dollars per day, whitch is 7 dollars & 30 cts per year payable, every January, the notes are Recivable in all government dues except export & imports & payable on day, two years after a piece is made with the M. S., where as money bonded only draws 4 per cent, & payable 20 years after date, I had Rather have them than the bonds, but the question is, had we Rather have

P2

the money (sutch as it is, on the) cotton, The cotton is wasting & is loosing in weight every year exposed to fire & Yankee Raiders, heavy taxation while the money is subject to legislation & an indeffinate payment, & to a taxation &C but it is easier carried off or to take care of in time of a Raid, but more dangerous at other times, (Ps)is more subject to theaves & plundererers, but the interest arising from 20 bales of cotton averaging 500 lbs each, Sold at 50 cts per pound would be ($365) three hundred & sixty five dollars per year, Due on payable the 1st January, every year until 2 years after a Ratification of Peace, when the whole amount would be due, now If I knew that the government would not Repudiate its currency after we have gained our independence, I would say Sell the cotton, put the money in a jug & hide it in the ground, & there let it wait until it was due, the tax on the cotton last year was 9 hundred dollars, it surlely cannot be that mutch on the money, last year it was one dollar on the hundred, whitch, if we had had the value of the cotton it would have only been 50 instead of 200&, find out about the tax on those notes & or cotton & advise with your friends & then act accordingly and I am content, May the God of all the earth have mercy upon us & direct us & save us is my prayer,

Your own Sam

MARCH 12TH 1864

.12 .13 .14 .15

P1

My Dearest Amie I expected a letter from you today but did not get it & disappointed about my furlough & having a chance to send this today or tomorrow by hand, have concluded to write to you, to let you know that I am well & the health of the Co & Regt as good as ever, I saw it, the strength of the Army good, all have unbounded confidence in Gen Johnston, General Hood is our Corpse Gen. Inplace of Hardee, who is gone to virginia (I believe) the men of the Company are Reenlisting now in a hurry, 40 have Reenlisted within the last 2 days, that makes 50 in all, in my Co, I believe that in the coarse of 8 or 10 days that all the whole Co will, except for 4 or 5, We have started at 4 new furloughs today, & 3 pending on the order for 1 man for every 25, present for duty, but the 3 pending were before the others Reenlisted, I cannot run both orders at the same time, that is if 70 were to Reenlist, then there would not be 25 left & then I could not use that order, but the other whitch is better, 7 instead of 3

P2

13th 11 oclock AM My Dear one, Yours by Ector come by hand just now, I see that you now know by the no of letters that I had not forgotten to write, I cannot account for it, I get your letters as soon by mail as by hand, & you do not get mine under 8 or 10 days, I shall send you my disapproved furlough, I want it kept, it may be a good witness after the war is over, if they (the <u>bums</u>) should alow me, whitch they may do, I am so sorry that it did not come approved, on your account especially, you will be so badly disappointed but hope on, the war will close some day, I write to Gladden to fund the money or do other wise if in his judgement, he thought best, If you send him 2 hundred dollars, what will you do for money, & that is hardly a drop in the bucket, compaired to what I owe the estate, I think you have yet on hand about 25 bushels of wheat, whitch is worth from 35 to 40 dollars per bushel, 25 bushels at 35$ will bring 875$ that with the price of old Kit, whitch aut now in the old currency bring Bout (wont <u>quite</u> give you that) all that & about 2 bags of cotton would pay the notes & leave you some besides, I think the face for the note was 1225 dollars & the interest for 5 or 6 years will make it, at least, two hundred dollars

P3

I believe that we aut to sell something enough to take up those notes in the old currency, as all the rest of the hiers have paid thers in the same, if it can be done in this month & the money bonded, So as to set me up on equal footing with the Rest, I fear it will give you a goodeal of trouble, but it aut to be attended to, I was in hopes that I could have come home & not put you in so mutch trouble, you have better sell the cotton or enough of I, &go to Gladden as soon as possible, You have written to G & sent him the 200$ before now, & if he takes it we will take the balance if in time, but if in interest paying bonds, it is already bonded & you will only have to pay it in, I to wish that I could be there to see to it, but you will have to do the best you know, But I believe that you see what can be done, I cannot spear you but little of my wages, as it takes at least one dollar per day to buy my meal & beef & salt and other to keep me in tobacco, paper, cakes & gobers &C

P4

I have on hand about 150$ & am loaning it to the men & wating until they draw in the new issue whitch will be about the last of Apr 64, I broke my watch & fear it will not do any more good soon, I let it fall & broke the cristal too, I shall see if I can get it Repaired & if not I shall send it home for you to keep until I come,

I still look for another letter, that one I got did not come up to my expectations. Still I was glad to get it, good so far as it went but you was hurried, I have not seen the Dr yet but will soon, I think that I have written all that I know that will interest you, I wait for the mail good bie Sam

14th one oclock P.M. Well my dear I wated yesterday for the male & today both, but no letter, only the hurried ½ sheet that you sent by the doctor is all that I shall get until about fryday, you genneraly write wednesday & I get them fryday, I have nothing new to write, I am well as I could ask to be & hope and trust that I may Remain so for above all (but bullets hums &C) I dread sickness most, if I can have my health I hope to get through this war Safe & Sound, hoping you all the same good health, through the mercies of God, I hope we may meet before long in peace & plenty, good bie Your own dear husband Sam

PS 15th one oclock P.M. drill hours nothing new I was disappointed sending last night good bie

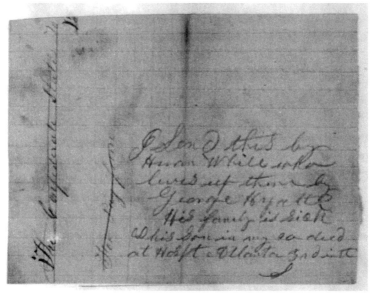

(.17 was in envelope with this letter dated 17th this is front)

(back of above note of death)

after dress parade My Dear I have been so busy making out a historical Roll of the Co for the 2 last days that I have not had time to answer your letter, I am scarce of paper too, I send you ½ sheet that you can croud lots on if you will write it fine & not be in quite so big a hurry, the weather cold spitting snow, I fear the fruit is killed, I fear that you will not get this until tuesday night if then, I hope you all the good luck &C good bie S

CAMP 30TH ALA REGT NEAR DALTON GA 2 P.M. MARCH 17TH 64TH

.17 P1

My Dearest Amie I Rec your letter of March 14th today, I was glad to get it & more so to hear that you were all well & doing well, I did not know that that Patent had any teeth to have the toothache in, I knew she had some old snags, whitch, she would do well to have pulled out, I do not doubt, but that her health would be better after words than now, I am so glad that you all getting along well, tell the boys that it does give me so mutch pleasure to hear that they are trying to make a living & to do their duty, that they are not like me exposed to all the dangers & frusrations of camp life, & occasionally exposed to rifle fire of the enemyes bullets, where they come thick & fast triming limes & striking stumps & trees & often the man by my side, Sleeping on the ground with one blanket, living at least ½ the days on not mutch (flour beef)meat as they eat

P2

at one meal, corn meal & but short allowance flour, a stranger in camp, but I do not complain but simply make the comparison to show to them that there is by far preferables to bring a Soldier & the Capt of a Company, who has to stand between them & the opresors, but I thank God whome I have trusted thus far & who has sustained me, I still trust in him & hope that he will bring me safely through these war times in peace to my Dear family, My health is fine, Tell the boys that I know if they will try that, they can beat the last years crop, I considered Turk a disadvantage, My Dear I do not know what to advise you about the cotton, more than I have, You have Rec the letters on this, Still it seems like the interest paying notes, money would do as well to take up those notes as other money bonds, they are the same as bonds & better because they are due 2 years after peace is made, & the bonds are not due until 20 years from date, If the war was to go on 20 years from date would be best, but I hope better things, I must close the bugle sounds for drill, No drill passed down the line, booly for that, Replied 20 voices, & I fully concur, I hope when Mr G get back that he will come & see you & you can advise with him & all accordingly, I will close, I think I will have a chance to send by hand,

good bie S

Camp 30th Ala March 24th 2 pm

.24 Pl

(Letter extremely faded)

My Dear Amie Yours of the 19th & 2 others came hand today, I was glad to get it & agreeable to the time you sent it, to the office (Sunday morning before Stage hours) I aut to have gotten it tuesday instead of thursday, I see on the envelope it was mailed on the 22nd, when it aut to have been the 20th, there was no Stage monday , could not come on the 21st, either the one you sent it by (to the office) or vess did not do there duty, I wish you would investigate this matter, for sutch negligence should not be passed over, you hurrying to get it ready, & then it lay in the office 2 days later, the boys have got letters 2 days later than mine, tell vess you will pull his nose if he does not do better, I have been on pickett with 35 of my Co, Started yesterday morning early & went to the top of the Mt about 3 miles, Started in the snow about 4 inches deep, but the Sun shined & melted off nearly all on the south side, & we had a better time then, than

P2

Really could have expected, monday night & tuesday it

snowed nearly all day & then me & boys & nearly the whole army were _____ Shall fight, _____ with this, officers, Regiments with there Coln, Brigades with there Generals, one Right against the other

CAMP 30TH ALA REGT NEAR DALTON MARCH 26TH 1864

.26 Ll Pl

My Dear Amie I thought I would have started my letter yesterday, but the furloughs did not come in, I write you more, thinking, that I can send this evening, John Wilson Thackerson is _____ to my knowledge or consent got started up a Sick furlough for 30 days, how is that you may inquire, Airheart while I was on pickett wrote it out & Signed my name, whitch I had no idea of sutch a thing, if I had been in camp it would not have been signed, he may be Sick, but he looks just as well as ever I saw him, he left us last March & Rejoined us about 2 weeks ago, has not been excused by the Dr from duty, but will_____ a furlough of 30 days,

CAMP 30TH ALA REGT MARCH 31ST 1864

.31 Pl

My Dearest Amie I have been expecting a letter for 2 days & Still look for one today but we will have to drill before the mail comes in & I have not time to write after drill before Sgt Ford will start, I have nothing interesting to write except that I am well & have been all the time, but busy, & Seems like business crowds on me, I have to drill the Regt this evening, in turn the Captains out drilling, I have never attempted sutch a thing & fear that I shall make a bad out, but will do the best I can, Rhumor says that our picketts were Scirmishing with the enemy yesterday, & I Reckon if they were, they are today, we can hear artillery in that direction, my opinion is that they are practising the artillery as we have been practising with small arms, the weather is plesant today & the time will soon come for us to leave these Smokey huts & go

P2

forth to meet a Strong foe Oh that the God of battles may go with us to victory & bring about that peace that we so mutch desire, To God be all the praise for his wonderful protection towards us, & bring us together as a nation & as family is my Daily prayrs, Good bie my dear one, Your own Sam

PS Sgt Ford promised to stop & see you a few moments, Sgt Atkins stopped but you were not at home, nor Lt Pikes wife either, he Reported to us that both of you were trying to marry again, in a joke SCK

April 1864

Camp 30th Ala Near Dalton Ga Apr 4th 1864

.04 P1

My Dear Amie I Received your of the 24th March, Witch was monday morning but your date was 27th but written monday morning, I think you were mistaken in the date, I was getting anxious for to hear from you, I looked Tuesday Wednesday & got it Thursday, I am so sorry for you, but alass, I was fearful that you were Sick, but I am thankful that it is no worse, it is my prayres that you may enjoy good health, and am in hopes that you may be better here after, I guess that you will have plenty of money, now those bags will weigh or aut to weigh at least 500 pounds a piece. they will bring about (3 cts lb) (1100,00) eleven hundred dollars, that will pay some towards those notes, My Dear I suppose that you sold that cotton from what I wrote after you had decided to do otherwise, Still it may be best, Yet you certainly know better than I do & you are at perfect liberty to do the best you know & I am content, I am sorry that you have no one to help you, but I am puzzled to deside whitch is the safest property, cotton or negrows, as to Confederacy money, just as

P2

mutch as will take to answer my purpose is enough, I had

Rather have cotton than the 20 years bonds, I think that you can pay those estate notes this year & then or by then, we will see how the matter goes & the currency will either Settle or to nothing, those bonds cannot be used only in taxes & I fear that I have done a bad business in having the money of the estate bonded, but it is too late now & if we can gain our independence & the Government Repudiate the whole of it I am content, for it was Ruinous as it was & was injuring the Cause, True it will fall hard on some & especially on us in this estate for we bought nothing while others did, but I thank God that we (if the war was over today with what we have) could live with out it, I believe it is the first step towards Repudiation, I do not know but what it would have been better to hold on to it until new issue came out & then Swapped 3 for 2, then done the best we could with it, I am glad that the Children seem to learn, Cant you keep Tom about you, to call for you & do little jobs, is he

P3

yet bloted & lifeless as he was when I was at home, My Dear when you are so bad sick why do you not keep Dice or Billy one at the house, The Grahams are lucky (to what I am) to get to be & Stay at home, better lucky than Ritch, looks like the women are in for the war from the number of boy children, J Palmer wrote to me to fix up & Send forward his papers to go before the board to be examined to be a Retired Soldier, I did so with the form he sent me, but I have but little hopes of sutch a thing, his was 29th, he said that was the first day, that he had left the house since 29th Feb, he said nothing about his wife, I am not surprised at Julia L, it looks like that some of the women will go crasey yet while the war lasts, but I have not heared of a single Soldiers wife in our neighborhood disgracing herself, I am sorry for any Sutch (good Soldier favr fellows) it is so dejecting, Is Ruth a widow, it seems to me that I heared something about her but have forgotten, I should keep Sims & Bam another year if it all agreeable, I think that Hyatt is a good hand with Stock, You will find out enough without inquiring of him (from others)

P4

I hope that the fruit is not all killed, was not a few days ago, I hope that you may yet raise plenty of chickens, they will help out your meat, I want you to have plenty if I occasionally tight run, Our Rations are more plentiful than they were a while back, we get some bacon, & Rush(as the boys call it) are always more plentiful when bacon comes, instead of (poor) beef, 5 of my men passed your house Friday with a waggon coming to the Co, they brought Letters &C for lot of the men, & I was a little fretted when they told me they did not stop, Patterson was one of them, Young & Shaw (of my mess) got some bacon & flour, & they are good to divide, all goes in until all is gone, & then if I can buy, well, & if not well any how & we eat our poor Rash & are as well off likely as if we had eat more, Only those 2 in with me now, the company is in fine health & good spirits & as large and as good a Co as is in the army, that has never been consolidated (ie) 2 camps put together, I have 79 men present for duty & none sick, I am proud of sutch a Co, & I think Head Qrters is to, The Colonel is having the Captains to drill the Regiment in his presence, alternately, I am the 4th in Rank & it come

P5

to my time Friday morning (would have been Thursday evening but for a Brigade drill) I did as well as I expected, I know that I some of those that Rank me, I was Shocked at the Idea when the Coln first told us tat we would have to drill, on the Saturday night before, I went to Studdying & the weather was too unsettled to have but one Brigade drill & the one spoken of above, & I learned a or Rather Reviewed more than I had for months before, the Coln told us the evening before, that I would have a drill & if an hour was to long that I could turn it over to the next Capt at the end of ½ hour, but I drilled my hour out before I was aware of it, I wish now that he (the Coln) had but us at it a year ago, I think that I will in a short time take a pleasure in sutch a drill, in stead of it being a task, The Colonels have to drill the Brigades then Brigades the Divisions & I saw Gen Hood who is our Corpse

Commander, he is a fine looking man, & a good General, he has a wooden or cork leg boot & spur on it as the others, The evening spoken of in my last letter was the

P6

Yanks, (following our example) Sham fighting Hardees Corpse, was to have a (Sham) fight Thursday evening, & we were to be Spectators but it was a Raney day after the morning & they put it off until (monday) to day & it is a bad wet day, Rained all night & Showering this morning, Saturdays is a wash day, Sundays inspection, Yesterday was a nice Spring day not cold this morning, Reminds me of old times when we would be planting cotton, The honorable Jube L. M. Curry visited us Fryday night, One of our Captains formed a procession, not with standing the inclemency of the weather (the wind whitch blue almost a gale) & Serinaded the Colonels quarters where Curry was Stopping, halted, fronted & called out, Sutch from the honorable Curry, Repeated by hundreds of anxious Soldiers, where upon the Statesman walked out in the croud (in the dark, thick dark) & adress them as friends & fellow Soldiers, he said the inclemency of the weather for bid him making a Speech, but that he could not let this opportunity pass with out acknowledging his thanks for the

P7

high honors paid him, The Rough Soldiers formed a complete wall around him, So thick that the wind could not penetrate, but passed over our heads, he Spoke (in the dark) about 40 minutes, while all seemed to be Spell bound, Standing so thick that one could scarcely Spit without Spitting on himself or some one else, he wound up promising to Speak at length to the Brigade some nice day, by consent of the officers in charge, the Called out 3 cheers for Curry when the enthusiastic Soldiers Sent up the almost deafining Shouts & then dispersed in Silance to there quarters, He is judge advocate General for the army of Tennessee (this is so called)

My Dear Amie you ask me whither I will get a furlough for

Reenlisting & a bond, I will not get a furlough & do not suppose that I will get a bond, No I have no idea when I Shall get to go home again, nor when we will draw any money, the men are nearly all out of money & wanting to borrow, I have loaned out about 60$ & have 62.50 cts on hand, I shall suspend (loaning) my clothes are all gradually wearing out, my hat fast, my boots also

P8

If you have me a pair of shoes made, you had better get old man Rennolds or Lem Phillips to make them, on the same last that Phillips made Lt Pikes on, Pikes shoes fit me only to high in instep, caution the maker about that, I Require a nine in length & not more than a seven in size verry low in the instep, thin fine leather lined in qrter thick without, board bottom, & low heels, with a nice thin iron plate on heels, but I can have the heel irons put on, if I can get the shoes, What about my hat, Tell Billy to write to me, I want to know what he is doing in his words, & besides that it will give him practice in both writing & composition, tell Virgil that I want him to learn to Read well by the time I come home. Tell Dick that by that time he must learn to spell on the book, than he spelled off when I was at home, for all of them to learn all they can, for it is learning that makes the man, My Dear Amie do not work too hard yourself but try and make the Rest do their part, Do you ever get tired of my long uninteresting letters, I feel like, that I weary you, & like an apology is necessary, this is a wet day & no duties, hoping that it is satisfactory, I now close, by my best wishes & prayrs, I remain your Husband good bie SCK

CAMP 30TH ALA APR 5TH 64

.05 P1

(Written on small scarps of paper)

My Dear A yours of the 3rd came to hand just now, I now haste to write you a few lines to let you know that I am well, & nothing more, Mr. Briant is here to see me for the first time, I have not talked but little with him to, is now 4 PM & the train leaves at 5 ½, So you see that Wingo & Hollingsworth cannot wait, both on

P2

furloughs of 40 days from Recruts, both of my Co, I am sorry that Cavalry are not dismantled & sent to the front, May the God that we serve still guide, direct & protect us, good bie Your own Sam

P3

PS the mail has come in & in it your long letter but they are in sutch a hurry that I have not Read it all, but think that you had better hold on to the balance of the cotton, I read a letter from South Carolina the other day & Cotton was selling at one dollar & every thing else in proportion, we are drawing plenty of good bacon now & I have never used a single bit of the bacon or flour Sent

P4

me yet, I did not know a word about the lard, we are healthy enough but have not kneeded it, I have about ½ my butter & Some of my cake & today the 2 mess of peas & the 1st of the fruit, I am so sorry that you are so unwell, I hope that you may be Stoubt, I close SCK

P5

PS 12 Oclock they did not get off on the 12 Oclock train but will go on the 5 ½ oclock train, well I heared the preacher & he is a good preacher (babtist) Sent as missionary to the Soldiers & has done good & will yet do good, I trus, he is an old man white headed, but able & a good Christian, we hneed sutch a man, he preaches

P6

in all of the brigades, & Says that every where is attended with good Success, we have no chaplain, I must close as Price is anxious to get off,

Good bie SCK

CAMP 30TH ALA DALTON APR 9TH 1864 9 AM

.09 P1

My Dearest Amie I Received yours of the 6th & 7th by Mr. G. also the Ritch box of provisions, all in due time (yesterday) Mr. G. staid with me last night but it was so wet & disagreeable that we did not open our box until this morning, I am more than oblige to you for your kindness, Still at this time we are getting better Rash & more plentiful than have before, all I fear is that you will Stint yourself, I can live on as little as any one, & if I know my heart I want you and the children to have plenty, but I fear for you, having a continual draw on you, by Soldiers passing & an occasional box to me, would in the course of one whole year exaust a full supply whitch you have not got this year, Do not understand me, as being dissatisfied, no, by no means, but I think that I can do better on a scarsity than you can, you have always been used to having a plenty, & I want you to keep plenty, The box (the contense) was just as nice as could be, all in the verry best

P2

Still & Order nothing Ruble nor injured in the blast, Oh my Dear one, who would not be a Soldier to defend the Rights of sutch a wife and my prayrs daily are that I may live through this struggle & humbly do the part Required of me in it, & See us independent as a nation, & Return home to those whome I love best on earth, to enjoy the blessings of that liberty whitch has cost so mutch, Sacrafise, Death, limbs, & blood, I only have 2 in my mess with me now, but our other who is a waggononer, I divide with, he since he has been driving, divided with us, If we can stay here this box together with what we draw will do us a long time, more of us of us big eaters, Some men (looks like) are dissatisfied unless that they eat all up, little or mutch we are not so enough is as good for a man as a feast, Yester day was fast day, Read out on parade, the evening before, & all duties suspended even Roll Call, drills, but I say it, to our Shame as a Company & I suppose as a Regt, Brigade, Division & army that it was not generally observed, in fact to my knowledge, I do not know of a single

P3

individual that did except myself, I suppose some others did,, I tried to the best I could, we had no preaching, no public prayr, but it was a wet day, after 12 Oclock & windy & cloudy in the morning, the men seemed to be inclined to make Sport, more than other wise, but I felt that I had fasted & (tried to) pray, in days that were passed, & felt nothing worsted for it, in fact that I had been protected & kept from some cause, while others whome I considered better by practice had fallen on the Right hand & the left, Really I considered it a poor Sacrifize, for the innumerable blessings that God in his mercy has seen fit to bestow upon me, I do not say so to boast, but it is my understanding of the word fast, that one should neither eat nor drink, nor use tobacco in any way, from Supper time one evening to the same time the next day, or from bed time one night till Supper time the next night, the last is the usual time, then I drank water & chewed tobacco until bed time, then slept until the usual time got up, but put nothing in my mouth to chew nor swallow until about Sun Set, about the time we

P4

usually eat, but my mess cooked & eat & Rather insisted on me eating, but I told them no it was my duty to Sacrafize, & I felt like it was a poor Sacrifize compaired, with the blessings Received, & that I would eat with them tomorrow, Yes one says if it does not make you sick, no danger that says & Rather be an advantage to health than other wise, So I fasted & feel I venture to say better than any who did not, for I did my duty & did not eat any thing more than a hearty Supper, & am well prepared to appreciate the worth of that Ritch box, So liberally bestowed by you, Oh that I may prove worthy of you, I kneed not write what I want, you seem to anticipate my necessities & had fixed a bill I would not have been better pleased, The Sham fight came off Thursday, I was on a high hill surrounded by the thousands, & among others some women & children, it would have been a grand sight to you & those bright eyed boys of ours, but I hope that you all may never see sutch a sight in Reality, The Yankees are fighting Sham fights too, we hear there artillery on sutch occasions, I think it a good thing, we see the necessity of drilling by it

P5

(written in margins of other pages)

Mr Curry is to adress the brigade this evening at 4 PM on the

State of the Country & I must hear him, Still the wind blows hard, this is Saturday wash day for the army, but there will be a crowd, I expect that Graham will get his dictoral & if so I hope that you will not have so mutch to do, but I feel in hopes that if the cavalry & Yankees will not disturb you that you will make a living, & Some besides with the start you have & liberal blessings from God the sorce of all good, If you think best let Sam go, G. said that Appleton wanted him to take an interest with him, if (G) does it will be all safe, I suppose & I think it would suit Sam better than the field, & that will be a good trade even after the war, I will write to mother, Good bie My Dear wife Sam K

CAMP 30TH ALA APRIL 16TH 64 NEAR DALTON

.16 P1

My Dear Amie I have been expecting a letter since tuesday but no letter yet this week, I shall have a chance to send this day (likely) on to morrow, John Price, Tode Wolf & Kirby will come in the neighborhood on furlough, leave camp today or tomorrow, E. Johnson is broke of his Commission as Quartermaster & is going home he said to make a bond & to investigate the matter, he tells it that they notified him from Richmond that he had not made a bond, but he went home in the Summer of 62 for that purpose & on his Return paid off the troops, I do not know what is the matter, but I would naturally suppose that there was something yet behind that has not been told, I have heared him brag how mutch money that he had made, & I know that his wages are only 140 dollars & mine 130 dollars, & I have bearly paid a few debts & if I bought as many clothes & at high prices, I could not have sent you more than 500 dollars, but he has bought land, negrows &C &C, he said that he cannot walk but that he will go to Forrest in preference

P2

My Dearest you must not make this thing public, let others tell it first, these are the facts so as I can learn & write to you so as you may know the truth, not with standing what Rhumors says, he is as good a Qrt M as we will get, tome, but may be not for the interest of the government & that is what concerns us all, The Masonic fraternity has taken a powerful stand in our Brigade, & Johnsons Qrtrs are the place where the lodge meets, Nearly all the officers in the Regt have joined, I have not joined, I do not know what object they have by joining, if it is for protection I shall put myself in the hands of the living God, who has kept me safe thus far & I shall still lean on his almighty arm & not depend on an arm of the flesh, or as David said, let me fall in the hands of God & not in the hands of men, now 8 AM & the furloughs have come in, all Right & they will start in 2 hours, Ready to take the cars at twelve & will be at Ladiga Sunday night if nothing happens, I have no news to write mutch, there was 5 men condemned to be Shot to death in the

P3

18th Ala Regt,& yesterday was the day but it was postponed 10 days in consequence of a petition sent up for there aquital, there was 3 of then babtist on a profession of

faith in Christ by Espy, I under stand that the Repreave has passes Gen Johnson approved & sent them on to Secretary of war at Richmond & to the President, I hope that they may be pardoned, Amie John Price has promised to bring my Shoes if you can get them done, I shall kneed them by that time, my clothes are all wearing out but will last a while yet, I am wearing my coarse pants & saving my jeans one, I have no idea that I can get to come home under 4 months if then unless I should get sick or wonded or Run away, & I abhor the verry idea of either of them & do hope & humbly trus that it may never be, my old hat is failing fast & I have not yet money enough to buy a new one, it will do a while yet, I suppose that we will draw money the last of this month, then they will owe me 390 dollars, I suppose that the new issue is out, I have not seen any of it, it is nicest, Said we are

P4

to have preaching today at 10 AM by D. D. Teasdale, I want to hear him but am afraid that I will have to go out to Shoot at a targett, it seems like that it always falls to out lot to Shoot on

Saturday while other Companies are idle, all are busy writing this morning, those furloughs came in unexpectedly, the order for one in ten (Reenlisted men) is suspended & we are sending one from every 25 present for duty, I have 80 men besides the officers, the whole Co (Regt I believe) is proud of Kellys Battalion as it is Called, one of Gen Hoods inspector Generals, inspected us the other day, he said it looked like old times to see sutch a Company, & said other things to encourage & ulogize the Co, Oh that I may prove worthy of the confidence Reposed in me by the people of Calhoun County, in Recruting my Co, as mutch or more than any Co that has ever left the County, I must close duty calls & I must bid you good bie, may the God that we serve be with us & provides good, for us as a family & a nation is my prayr, good bie Your own Husband S C Kelly

CAMP 30TH ALA REGT NEAR DALTON GA APR 17TH 1864

.17 .18 Pl

My Dearest Amie I now take the Lone Some Sabbath evening to write to you in answer to your long letter of yesterday 9th inst, it was a long time coming, but the train Ran off tuesday, suppose was the cause of the delay, I generally get them the Friday after they leave Ladiga, I do love to get long letters from you, but if you do write the longest letters, I certainly write oftener than you, & will not give it up with out an investigation that you write the worst long letters, I always write one & verry frequently two a week, I had never touched my flour or bacon & did not know that you had but any lard in at all until Read your letter yesterday, having plenty without it, we let it stay as we said for hard times, but this morning we hauled it out & had some bread with fat and soda both in it & it was quite the idea, it seemed like home bread, I have never undone my bacon, & had I known that our fair, would have changed so soon, I should not have said any thing about it to you, I did not say so, with a view or indication of getting any thing from home, but a simple comparison between the fair of the negrows at home & the Soldier in the field,

My Dear I expect that I was mistaken about the amount of taxes, I have under stood that the Confederate tax is besides the tenth) 5 per cent on all Real & personal according to the

P2

value of sutch property in the year 1861 one thousand dollars exempted for a Soldier, five hundred for his wife and one hundred for each child, at that we will have exemped 1800 hundred dollars, Six Negroes at least 5 thousand dollars, 57 hundred dollars of land, 7 hundred for Jack (besides the cotton & other things liable) making (9400) nine thousand four hundred dollar, take the exemptions off and it will leave (7600) seven thousand six hundred dollars, and five per cent on that (or five dollars on a hundred) will be 380 dollars, (So mote it be if it is the law of the land) So you will have some use for flour cotton money, but I think that now had better hold out on the balance of the cotton until the money matters settle, I have 2 interest paying fives but will have to spend them for tobacco, that money you said that Capt Duglass lost, you can do as you wish, but I think that you kneed not Reflect upon yourself in the least, not your falt, Send it to me I can spend it, I am sorry that you could not go to the meeting & keep the fast, did any one in the neighborhood keep it, I wrote boys about it here, but sent the letter by mail last monday or tuesday, You may get this first as I expect to send it by E Johnson, I heared him say that his wife would never back his letters to Capt J. but to E J she considered the title of Capt Significant & would not

P3

title him until he got to be a Gen, verry well I Reckon, She can still back in the same way (to E Johnson) in Reality, the most men that I have heared speak of it are glad, but I cannot Rejoice over his misfortuns, Still some times he acted as if hr though that he was the head of the whole conceson, my lines are Rather close to inter lines & I think that I shall make up the dificiancy by writing the out lines now, My Dear Amie you will certainly admit that I do write oftener than you, wont you, Say yes, I am in fine spirits about our wheat and oats from what you say, & I know that it is not a worse looking chance than it was in 1857 at the 15th Apr, & there was never a better crop in the County than that year, I do not want a coarse pair of shoes, I can get them sent here, I must go to preaching more anon, I went and heared a young man, I suppose a methodist, he done well for his sort and age, this morning after inspection we had preaching in our Regt, I thought him a babtist, but that old brother Teasdale, that preacher yesterday did me more good than both of these today, that is my sort, the Simplisity of

P4

the gospel, tell Billy that I will answer his soon, that he must try and improve, Dear Amie do not know what to fill the balance of this with, it seems like I write the same thing over & over again to you, I know that I do, now yesterday I wrote a little & then lay it down & do some thing & then take it up & write a little more & so on, I am nearly always busy doing some thing, we get & Recite a lesson nearly every day in tactics & Regulations, The army Regulations would be a good book for Billy to Read & in the scarcity of school books for boys, I think would do verry well, Sam P. has not mentioned what you alluded to, but I though at the time we got the boxes that something was Rong but did not let on, if I have my enemies in the Company they are favoring my end, it seems to me because they are my neighbors that they think I aut to show them the more favors, but not so, I treat all alike, asking no favors, show none to the prejudice of any one, now dress parade more anon,

John Wilson Thackerson did not get his furlough, but I never saw it, he is doing duty Right straight along, I never until this moment knew you sent Sausage, I will have some for Supper, I will go to the bottom of the box & find out what you did send, I mearly expected (after you wrote that you would send a box) some bacon & flour with some little pees & a cake, but I am more & more obliged to you than ever, found a piece of soap more, now you may

PS

(written in margins)
know that I am not suffering Really, I did not expect so mutch
& only 3 of us, so we can live well as long as we stay here, if it is
long enough to get a mess of Polk Sallad to boil with some of the
bacon, we draw splendid bacon the third of a pound a day to my
mess one pound, & it is enough for a soldier,

My Dear I know that tis is a trashy letter, but I know that you
will Read every word in it & I could not write sutch things to any
one else, but you know if I were with you that I could & would
tell you all, So that is all the apology, but more kneeded, it is
almost dark & raining at that, So I will close, may our heavenly
Father still be over them, good bie Your own Sam

PS 18th 6 AM nothing new, this morning, Cloudy & threatening
rain, we are to have a Grand Review this morning at 10 Oclock, I
under stand by the word grand review that all the Generals & big
folks, Sam

CAMP 30TH ALA (CO E) NEAR DALTON GA APRIL 21ST 1864

.21 P1

My Dear Amie I wrote you a long letter the 17th & expected to
send it by E. Johnson, but he left earlyer than I expected & I
thought then that I would not send it, but I can send this by
Airheart & I will send the other along for what it is worth, it is not
worth any thing to me, but may be some satisfaction to you, A's
papers has come back & he is all Right, out of the war, now I do
not blame him under all the circumstances, I Received yours of
the 17th by Rountree, all in good time, I was glad to get it, & my
Shoes fit me verry well, but they are, I fear most to narrow for
traveling, I could have done without them a while longer, but
Rather have them to soon than to late, I shall wear my old boots a
while longer, if I do not send them home by Arheart, I think that
I shall send my old pants too & Some other things, my old calico
shirts are wore nearly out, but the weather is so cold that I still
wear them, they are not worth sending home, I think if you have

some new calico to make me some new ones that you had better send them by Price, my socks are holding out better than other clothing in consequence of some cotton socks that I am wearing, these old boots would do to frount & be as good as ever, but I am a little afraid that the shoes would hurt my feet as we are going to leave our winter qrtrs tomorrow & going to the front, I suppose about tunnel hill where we had the fight, I have never touched my bacon yet & Stand

P2

a good chance to loose it, but will do the best I can, we lack only one week of staying here 5 months, the longest time we have ever stayed any one place, but the time seems short to me, we will now take the woods, & good bie to winter Qrtrs, we will bivouac as the military men call it, I was in hopes that the cavalry would get done passing there some time, but I Reckon not while the war last, & I think have got so in the habit of Stealing that they would Steal from there own families (especially fodder), I hope that some of those thieves may get Reward, warren Slaton wrote to me all about Charley & I have no doubt but what that was Charleys & Evalins business up here, to per suade off warren & Green, I asked Joe what about it & I said that he (C) told him that the boys were all safe speaking of George & Babe, I hope that he to may get his Dues, I shall send my watch home as it is broke & I cannot get it mended here & it is no use in that fix, I wear it in my drawers pocket & for got to write about it, You can keep it until you have a chance to have it mended, the lever is broke & the tinkers in the army are not prepared to do that sort of work,, All furloughing is suspended except on a Recruit & I am not certain it is not, Your chances for letters will not be so good as have before, but I will write & send by mail at least once a week if I can, they will be from 3 to 10 days going, Frank Rountree is

P3

assigned to post duties, (but I do not know when) only the application & surgeon surtification is made & he is home, I think it verry uncertain about John Palmers papers, but I will try it again, he nor F are any use in the field, I am in hopes that the Confederate prisoners will be exchanged, I think that J. H. will come in home one of these days, & me & Lt Pearson we will hold an election soon for one to fill Airhearts place, & Sam Pendland is Running, Mr Gladden is too busy (I Reckon) to come, is the fruit all killed, is the wheat as high as a Rabbit, if so & is green & greatly it will make wheat unless it does freeze & kill it here after, I would like to take dinner with you when you kill the gobler, (in that the hen is Stolen) but do not wait dinner for me, if I am not there at dinner time, for some of it cold will suit me verry well, I am sorry for Mrs Whitesides, but the old man is at Rest, out of the war, out of the world, out of sin, in the presence of God, Safely on the other side of this vail of tears where the weary are at Rest & the wicked sease from troubling, J. L.s Soldier husband is not mutch purkins, from all I can gather, but every Sweet has its bitter & So has the bitter its Sweet, I saw a letter from old man Brown concerning his son Jim, I do not look for him soon, If Graham was to come home soon,

P4

I do not suppose that he would charge you the full price of a years wages for the (3/4) three forthes of a year, in fact only 2/3 two thirds if he gets home by the 1st May, I am in hopes that you were mistaken about Rs folks being pouting or mad, they are so busy getting Ritch, Give my Respects & tell them that I would have been glad if I could have been home that night they were there, to come again, that not to wait because I am not there &C I am sorry for you my dear for I know that the time drags barely by because you are not well, I suppose in fact, the time flue swiftly on to me, & I frequently Sing Fly Swiftly Round, Ye wheels of time and bring the long Saught day, as to Jr__, I believe that he is a Christian & am almost led to believe that he is impressed to preach, Oh that it may be so , So true, is it that there is not but little true gospel preaching, but my dear we must trust in the Lord & prayer, hoping to the end, Tis bad to be so annoyed by the worthless Cavalry, but do the best you can, You had better save from your money enough to do you until I can send you some, buy your negrow if you wish, I shall close this as it is getting dark & we Rec orders to quit cooking that we will not move tomorrow, it is Raining now, God bless you & yours is the prayr of your affectionate Husband S C Kelly

Camp 30th Ala Regt Near Tunnel Hill Ga April 26th 64

.26 P1

Mt Dearest Amie I Received yours of Saturday this evening, I was glad to get it & See that you were all well & doing well, we moved this morning, the move anticipated in my last, (the one by Airheart) we may fight soon but we only moved here because if a fight was to take place we would not have to travel 7 or 8 miles & besides that the wood & water both were getting scarce, I am pleased with the move, I think that there would have been Sickly there, there was so mutch filth all about there, not with standing the <u>police</u> every day, I am afraid that you will lay yourself up weaving Shirts for me, that I do not kneed at all unless I throw away or send home or dispose of them some way, they are not near worn out yet, the chances to do any thing with them but throw them away, is bad, My Dear Amie I do not consider I need any clothing except those under Shirts & I could do with out them as to my over Shirts, Coat & pants, keep them until next fall & as I want any thing I can draw (as most of the officers do) pants & a short coat whitch is better for Summer & more

P2

in uniform with the Rest, (of officers) I had a notion of Sending my overcoat home & if a good chance would send my other (or military) coat & get Cannon to Ref it to pises & make it over the other side out, it can be done & it would look like a new coat, it is a good coat but dirty & the button holes torn a little but I do not know of any chance to send either now, Frank Rountree could not get his furlough on his Recruit not with standing the Surgeons Sertificate that he was not able for field service, & he is assigned to Hospital duties & ordered to Report to Atlanta, he left fryday, Sam Pendland was not elected, he got 28 votes & Landers 38, L is the old Lieutenant that first started out with the Company, he is as brave as any one need be, & that is a good Recommendation for an officer, my Shoes does first Rate, they draw my feet a little but all new Shoes do me that way, I wore them today, & Rolled up my old boots & bacon in my bed clothes & they all came through safe, we left all our boxes , benches &C, but the waggons are gone back after the boards, we will build Shelters but not Cabins, I think we can make out as well as usual, we are sharing provisions

P3

I do expect that they will Row Mrs. W up Sold River as the saying is, I am glad that they have caught or about to catch that old fox of Ladiga, he has run a long time first, I am in hopes that you will have fruit, I hope that you will make wheat & every body else, I have not seen Dick Weaver, I suppose that he is at camp, Whealers Cavalry had a Skirmish with the Yanks the other day, I suppose you saw it in the papers, the news is encouraging today, It is Reported that Tom Hyatt & Scott Raborns & some one else of that croud is to be Shot for desertion, they are at oxford or on there way to Cave Springs, I am in hopes that you have got the letter I sent by A, & the watch &C I Rec a letter from J Palmer yesterday, he is still at Greensboro yet, I sent forward his papers again yesterday, he is getting particularly anxious,

W Estiees letter of Saturday says that J Graham is on 15 days furlough, I believe that I have written you all that I now think of that would interest you & it is about dress parade time, So I will close for the present, Will write a poscript in the morning if I have time before it has to be mailed, God bless yours S C Kelly

Salvation & & us as a family is my Daily prayrs, Good bie Sam

P4

PS Wednesday morning, this is a nice morning all seems quiet, You say that you are having lie hominy, we have out our cold corn bread (that accumulates on our hands) Cush or fried bread or poor do, or some thing we fix it up & we eat it with a good Relish, I fear that I cannot have your broch, pin & Rings made out of the piece you sent, all seem afraid to under take them, they say that it is not a good piece tis to hard, We tried one Ring off of it, & it broke & would nor Stretch, You never said who sent it, I know that I can satisfy you about it, but the owner I do not know & more over we are in moving position & the chances are bad to get any thing atall done in the way of work, All the trinkers say that the old Ring will not do for Sets, it is white metal Smoked over & the Smoke is wearing off, I wish that I had sent it home by Ar, I have a piece of Silver on my knife, if I can get the work done will use it for Sets, I now close, the news in papers encouraging, there is a Right Smart feeling of a Revival in one of our Regt 25 Ala, I do hope that the Lord will direct all of our affairs & the great Capt of our national Salvation & us as a family is my Daily prayrs, Good bie Sam

MAY 1864

CAMP 30TH ALA 4 MILES NORTH DALTON MAY 1ST 1864

.01 .02 PI

My Dearest Amie I Rec yours of wednsday 27th April yesterday evening & was glad to get it & Read its contents, I am so glad that you all may are getting along so well, I do hope that you all may do your part as a family in making a support, the truth is this, If other negrows are bad, ours will be too & they will get it just as soon to stay & do their part towards making a living as to do otherwise, for let them be free & they will have to work for a living, to get it honorably, & then if it is Gods will that they Shall be free they will be so & besides all that, if they behave & work on until their change comes, they will be more Respectful than any other coarse, I think that it is soon to alter lambs, my Father always let his wait until the fall Shearing, but may be test Sooner I think the wheat (from your description) will make a good crop, not time for oats to show what they will do, I think that Bryans negrows is a bad lot, (between us) it is a goodeal oweing to there raising, all just to say or think that we were spoiled

P2

that we were Spoiling our negrows, but it seems to me like, that our negrows have always done us as mutch good as any one,s & now they seem to be doing better, just so in army, Some seem to think that I am too easy on my men, but one thing I know is, that I always am at the place in time & that all seem to think that they will do to stay close by in time of a Squall,

May 2ond before Sunrise, Well My Dear A I understand that J.R.G. has got his papers at last, S Pendland has Rec a letter to that affect, do not know the content of it, I think that you have done well to hide some corn, while you have it, you aut not to hint it to any one, I shall not, feed your hogs pretty well one a day & they will do finely, feed them the Refused corn first & if that is not enough splice out with good corn, the boys aut to Shuck the corn for the horses, of wet days & throw the Refused in a pile to itsself for the hogs & pack up the shucks & give to the horses about as many shucks as would come off of the corn they eat, in that way you can get Refused corn for the hogs & not give the horses bad corn

P3

I am still wearing my old boots, when I think there is any danger of looking or getting in a tight I put on my Shoes, I am well pleased with them, I know my shirts will be nice & I can wear the new pants if you send them, my drawers are as good as ever, As to money I have about the same amount, I was making out muster rolls yesterday, is the Reason that this is not finished, I have no idea when we will get it, I wish that I could see you in that now days, I know it is nice if for no other Reason because you made it, I am verry sorry that you are not entirely well, I never enjoyed better health in life, for whitch I try to feel thankful, I think that we have bettered ourselves in the move, we all have shelters & have to do no drilling, we pickett & work on the fortifications, we had taken a day at each, we get the daily papers nearly every day, the news on the whole Spring campaign is encouraging, There is a great Revival in nearly all the Brigades in the army, only Slightly in our yet, but I do hope that it may Spread like fire in stubble, Sam Henderson preached for us Thursday night & is to preach again to night, he is Soft but a good one

P4

Oh that the Lord would Revive us & make us as a nation bow before him, compels our Souls & invoke his forgiveness, thanking him for his great mercy towards & ask a continiewance, Submitting unto his will & then ask him (in faith) to give us peace, Oh that the people at home may be Revived as well as those in the army, Our Rations are good & a plenty of it, Sutch as it is corn meal & bacon with a little of the &C occasionally, I have some of my butter & fruit yet, the butter is good fir, one of my mess does not eat only fresh butter & the other is a verry moderate eater any way, but I do not have butter every meal, I tote it in my haver Sack when we pickett or work or go out to hear noise &C there was quite an alarm the day we come off of pickett, but we were behind the excitement& came in & gathered our Rash & followed on, but did not get over ½ way when we met them coming back, We thought that the thing was going to happen but it is now 2 days since & no fight yet except a cavalry in the extreme frount, My Dear I have written this hurriedly, May the God of our fathers still be our God & guide & save us from the hands of wicked men & bring us peace & Save us all in heaven is my daily prayrs good bie Your own husband SCK

Camp 30th Ala May 2ond 1864 (5) PM

.02 .03 P1

Well My Dear boy Billy I was disappointed in Sending off my letter this morning to your Ma & thought that I would write you one this evening, This day has not passed without some excitement, this morning we could hear distinctly the Roar of muskets & the Still more dreaded Cannon, We were expecting to be called on every moment but are yet in camp although firing has been heard all day, at intervals troops have been passing to the event today, I think that a fight is now certain in a few days, this evening I went to the babtizing, Brother Espy administered the ordinance to 5 willing Subject, all young men but one, Youth is the time to Seek the Lord & now My Dear Son these may be the last lines you ever get from me (the Lord only knows) and my advice is to you to Seek the Lord while he may be found & call upon him while

P2

he is near, Let the wicked boy forsake his ways & the unrichous his thoughts & let him turn unto the Lord who will have mercy & to our God who will abundantly parden, My Son I do not consider you a bad boy, but you are a Sinner & must be Reconsiled to God, or he banished from his presence, are you afraid of God, Yes because you are a Sinner & not Reconsiled, are you afraid to die, Yes because you are a Sinner, think of these things & pray to God our heavenly father & ask him to have mercy upon you & be your friend confess to him that you are a poor little weak boy & ask him to become your friend and father, plead to him the Richousness of his Son Jesus Christ, who died for Sinnes & you are one, & he has promised to hear & answer prayrs, that is the only way you can be Saved, no other name, but Jesus that will do to depend upon for Richousness, Ask your Ma about it She is a Christian & will be pleased to tell you any question, May God be help us all is the prayr of your affectionate father S C Kelly

MAY 3ᴿᴰ 64

P3

P.S. Same place in camp the Sun is last Rising all quiet So far no firing heared this morning, but I may not write another line before we hear the boom of Cannon all seem to think that a fight is inevitable, the weather is fine this morning Right Smart frost, I hope we may be prepaired to Receive our enemies in a

P4

Hostile manner & gain a complete questor, the troops are in good plight & spirits, The Revival still in increases, not with standing the cold, I must close or be to late, I have not Rec one of your last, God bless you & yours & our Country is my prayr, good bie Your Husband affectunatly S

Camp 30th Ala May 6th 64

.06 P1

My Dear A it is quiet early not Sun up & we are all packed up & ready to move, but I do not know where to, all seems to be quiett so far as I know, no firing, Rumor says that we are going to two or three places, but I do not believe that Coln S. knows where we are going, I Received your letter & the Short you sent by Price, I was glad to get them, we are not in line of battle yet, nor have not been, but do not know how soon, we have been on pickett & working on the fortifications, a goodeale & have kept two days Rations on hand Ready for any emergency, has been no fighting yet only Skirmishing with the Cavalry picketts, I saw 15 men shot day before yesterday for Desertion, bushwhacking Rutine & Robery &C, I Close God bless good bie

The back of letter May 6th

P2

Dear Wife I Sute my self this morning to Drop you A few Lines to Let you now that I am Well and Doo hope When these few Lines Comes I endorse the above must close with my best wishes & prars, I remain as ever your own Dear Husband until death good bie S C Kelly

Line of battle Near Dalton May 8th 1864 twelve oclock noon

.08 P1

My dear Amie we have been in line Since yesterday evening, have not done any fighting yet, the Skirmishing began about 7

AM, one wounded man from our Regt passed just now, Some fiew bullets passed over our head, we all expected it to open good fashion this morning, it may come yet before night, we are all hopeful, I try to be Ready, let the worst come, The Lord only knows who will be speared this great battle, I know in whome I believe, Oh Lord help though my unbelief, I try to be Resigned to my fate, the Lords will be done, I have your prayrs, all quiet now good bie more anon, God bless us all, & Save us as a family & a nation, Your own Dear Husband S C Kelly

P2

PS about 5 PM the battle not yet opened, Some Skirmish firing occasionally, think will wax hot tomorrow, We have moved on the top of the mountain in plain view of the enemy below on our Right hand facing the South & our forces on the left, we are waiting them to attack, I close for fear that the mail will go out, I have been looking for a letter from you God bless good bie my Dear Amie SCK

my hands is dirty & water a long way off S

LINE OF BATTLE 30TH ALA REGT MAY 10TH 64

.10 .11 P1

My Dear amie we are still fighting away, we have been fighting since Sunday (I wrote to you then) the enemy has not gained a single point as I have heard, thank God our loss light, my Co one wonded Morton Keller Slightly, we have been bushwhacking away all day, in front of the line of battle, ____ ____ wating for a chance, or until we were _____ whitch has not been done, we are as Skirmishers in front of a bad line, to chance I don't think they will try it (mountain side) I am well & fine heart, trusting in the Lord in whome hands all things given, Capt Elliot Reily wonded John Francis also

Sun Set

P2

it is now most dark, I am detached all day, do not know any

news, my guess is all is Right, God bless you & yours & give us a speedy peace is the prayr of your own Husband (affectionately) good bie S C Kelly

11th 2 or 3 PM we have been standing around the forces all day in rear of our line wating for action, got a moment, we were Relieved last night after dark & those that ____ yesterday are bushwhacking away, but I think that they will not change those works, Some of our Brigade now is _____ move, we all expect to follow, Yanks are certainly scarce now, our place is on Rocky face Ridge in full view of the tunnel, good bie S C Kelly

MAY 14TH 7 AM
LINE OF BATTLE HOODS CAMP 2 ½ MILES NORTH OF RESACCA

.14 .22 P1

My Dearest A I Rec yours of the 6th by W. night before last, was glad to get it, got the Shirt & paper, we evacuated the Mt that night at 12 oclock, the enemy could not take it, & flanked off towards this place, Some Skirmishing yesterday & this morning, I had charge of the pickett line of our Brig on the Mt & was the last that left it, they did not pursue that night but pressued the Rear yesterday, Maj Francis was wonded, I wrote you as dead

THIS IS WHAT WAS WRITTEN ON BACK OF PAGE P1 FOR MAY 14TH

S. C. Kellys Book
Capt Co (E) 30th Ala
I hope that Gen J

.22 P1

The piece of comb you sent was to hard that it could not be worked to an advantage, the old Ring was white metal Smoked one & I ____ to & showed it to 3 ring makers & all said that it would not do, at all, for Sets, plain Rings of that Sort Selling foR 5 dollars a piece, I will send what I can get made out of it as soon as possible

P2

PS 22ond day light nothing new , this morning A is Ready to Start this moment I think that I can have your Jewelry made, man the hustle & hurry about moving over, I sent my watch old pants & an old pr a socks, Good bie God bless You & Yours is my daily prayrs, Your own SCK

Army of Tennessee May 22nd 1864 Near Altooney Ga

.22

My Dear Sister I Rec your kind letter have not time to answer, but say that so far I am safe & well as to health for fear that my Dear Amie is driven from home, I write to you, You may know something of her, I have written to her every chance & I have not Rec a letter since the 12th written the 6th, May God bless us all as a family & a nation, I bid you good bie Your brother S C Kelly

Army of Tennessee Altooney Mt Ga May 24th 1864

.24

My Dear Amie I am well cant tell any thing about the army only we have been here 5 days & no fighting since the 12th, I must close as I have not time to write, God bless you & yours Affec husband S C Kelly

(written on back)

Private J W
is hereby relea
and will sep

Line of Battle Ackworth Sunday evening May 29th 1864

.29 P1

(Names dead and wounded)

My Dearest Amie I thank God the father of us all that I am yet Spared, We have been under fire 3 days Since last Sunday, My last note to you was tuesday or wensday, Since then until yesterday morning we engaged the enemy, we are know in Reserve, our loss in the Regt is 40 or 50 killed & wounded, mine was in one/2 day in front on Skirmish, one killed & 6 wonded, Love Alexander killed mortally, wonded S R Wilkinson in thigh & hip, W M Nance through Right breast, Severely Harris Foster in thigh, M Sproggins in ankle, Slightly Corp

P2

Franklin Ford in Shin, W A Raind in face & knee, I do feel thankful that it is no worse, for my Co & an other Small Co, both under my command were ordered to take & hold a position that a whole Regt were run from, we held on from 11 AM until after night (when we were Relieved by 4 Comps of our Regt) against a double line of the enemy, at least 4 times our No, hot work, but I was Sustained protected & kept by him on whome we trust, My Dear one do send Billy to G V & gt my letter and Send me one, I am so uneasy to know & hear from home, I have heard that up to thursday was yet clear, I think that   .

P3

320 have there hands full here, we have not had a general engagement all day, the line only in places & from accounts their loss is heavy, tis said that in front of Cleaborns Div alone that our people but killed yesterday 3300, there is no doubt of it, that there was a tremendous Slaughter there, one of our Regt lost 100 killed & wonded, we have taken lots of Small armes 280, waggons & teams, brought out from 50 to 80 waggons & all of the mules & 110 prisoners hungry, One of them begged me for bread & Said he had not had a bite since last night (& it then night 10 or 11 oclock) & only one cracker at that, he said that they were nearly marched to death

P4

On Rec a piece of cold corn bread was the most thankful creachure I ever saw, & bid me good bie & told me to take care of myself, we got plenty Rash, the troops all in fine spirits & think that Joe Johnson knows how to manage them, I try to be prepared for the worst, Oh prey for me, I try for you, I trust in Johnson &

the army as instruments in the hands of living God who givith the victory, heavy Skirmishing along the line all day, I had my Shirt & drawers washed today, while I wore my pants & over Shirt & now changed to have the other washed this time, I have changed since 4th or 5th past, Some little Sickness, I must close, My Dear, I could write you a letter but time to short, male go out 5, Lord Jesus be our Richteonsness. God by while living affectly SCK

JUNE 1864

.06 L1 HERS P1
(Hers that he has written back using her old letter.)
This was dated 24th I write back on Same paper because of the Scarcity of it with me, Sam

this summer Barva says the bottoms smells so badly since so many soldiers camped there, I believe I have told you all and will send this paper for you to write back, one of Crous sons was killed at Calhound, Geo, Torrey is also dead, May God continue his blessings, to us and keep us in the right way and save us at last, God by

Your own Amie

Graham has been here says the yanks may be here before night the Lord only knows what will become of us I will try to send the boys with our provisions off if I can get them to go with graham and I will try it awhile longer May God direct us how to do and what to do, In haste A

NEAR LOST MT GA JUNE 6TH 1864

.06 HIS P1
My Dear Amie I do not know (hardly) where we are, but it is about 10 or 11 miles to Marretta Ga, we moved night before last from the place I last wrote you (whitch was on the 2 or 3rd) my Co & one other Co were on Skirmish a wet day & a wetter night & we were firing all night at irregular intervals, & they at us, & we were not Relieved until about day light & then we followed on in I

believe the worst Road for mud I ever traveled & came up with them about Six miles where they had halted & in the evening (yesterday) we were sent back here about 2 miles as picketts, but our two Companies are held as Reserves, but will have to go out on advanced posts to night, the enemy did not press us the last time we were out & the firing was at long range & on our part was to feel there where abouts, they are now calling for the letters & I have just began, I must close by saying that I Rec yours of the 15th 24th & 29th May yesterday & the day before, I was glad to get them but was afraid to hear from home too but I was truly thankful that the Yanks have not been on you as wrote to you my opinion of affair, I must close or miss the chance, I as well in good Spirits, the enemy are Still flanking going east, May God bless us is the pray of your own dear Husband good bie S C Kelly

Lost Mt 6th June 5 pm

P2

My Dear A I was too late to get my first off, it was not the regular mail man, but one that was going over to the line & Said that he would take all the letters over to the Regular mail carrier, You say that I write to so little, So I did, but the best I could do under the circumstances, for the currier would come to the lines irregulary & was in sutch a hurry that he would not wait a moment & I would Scribble down a little rather than not send at all as a great many did, as to news there is nothing but Rumors, mostly favorable to our side, one of whitch is that Lee has gained another victory & Run the enemy 15 miles capturing 1000 prisoners & another is that Gen (Sornsebody) some says Forest & some say Chalmer has Retaken Rome &C another yet is that Capt Reece (now Mayor) has telegraphed to Gen Wheeler that there is a Yankee Supply train coming across from Huntsville Ala to this army with a guard of about 10000 men & if he (Wheeler) will send Reenforcement that they can all be captured, &C the Cavalry are all keen to get off on a Raid of Some Sort, for Joe makes them leave there horses & go in the trenches & act as picketts &C & they do not as a general thing like to be so confined, I have seen lot of my acquaintance in the Cavalry in the last few days, but have not seen Sims Milton yet, hop I will soon, My Dear Amie I do try to be thankful for the abundant mercies that God has seen fit to bestow upon me, for I have been in some danger for the last 30 days & 20 of the 30 under the fire of the enemy & I believe in hearing of firing every day, we left our Qrtrs on the 4th May & they threw there missils over us on the next whitch was Sunday 8th, Since then we have seen hard times, but I do feel thankful that it is no worse with us than it is, my own Amie I am in hopes that they will not come down there, but the Lord only knows, & if it is his will that we Shall be conquered we will be, but I cant believe that he will Suffer sutch a heartless

P3

enemy to triumph over his people, are there not 50 Rictheous in the South or not even 5, Yes I do hope & trust that every day that there are tens of thousands of petitions, going up to the giver of all things, to give us our independence & are not those of the elect, who has promised to hear when they cry unto him, oh Yes & he will hear, but we have Since & come Short of the glory of God, & when we weary thoroughly Scourged them we will Repent & turn unto the Lord with a full purpose of heart, Oh our heavenly Father are we not Scourged, Oh help us to Repent & to Call upon the in this our time of trouble, & not depend upon Genrs Johnson & Lee, only as instrument in the hands of the living God, Oh God hear the prayr of the wife, of the mothers, the daughter, the Fathers & the Sons, brother & Sister, & in an special manner those of the widows & orphans of our distressed South, & now my dear A it may be that we have not properly viewed this matter, we have been happy together, not envying any one, have got along in the things of the world well, had in a word a happy home, had plenty & not enough to be burdensome, had we bought the best negrows (in our opinion0 of any body &C&C but this crewel war has separated us & 28 month & no telling how mutch longer, & what other Sacrifices we may yet have to make, may be that we may be like many others, loose all & still after all that God will find us our independence , & now my dear, prepare yourself for the worst, my home is in the Confederate army as long as I am any use to the army, if we fall back to Florida & the whole country behind, be as Tennessee, but my advice to you is to Stay at home & trust in God who has kept you thus far, Send off the negrows when necessary, God bless us all Your own Husband S C Kelly

LINE OF BATTLE LOST MT JUNE 7ᵀᴴ 64

.07 FRONT

I am well nothing new today
S C Kelly

back

SUN SET 7ᵀᴴ

LINE OF BATTLE IN R ROAD 5 MILES NORTH OF MARIETTA & 3 MILES SOUTH OR BELOW BIG SHANTY GA JUNE 9TH (12 OCLOCK NOON) 1864, NEAR KENESAW MOUNTAIN

.09 PI

My Dearest Amie I wrote to you day or two ago from Lost Mt, where we were on picket & I hope you have

Rec it, I had Rec yours of the 1ˢᵗ before, whitch is the last, but hope to Rec one today when the mail comes in, Sam Pendland & J Price have Rec yesterday letters dated 5ᵗʰ inst they say that there is no general news, & I take it for granted that you are all knocking along & have pretty well gotten over your Scare, Oh I do hope that the enemy will yet be Routed, whitch is Scattered, & driven from our dear homes whitch is a greateal of it destroyed, by the blessing of God I hope to see it, we have not been under fire Since 5 oclock AM 5ᵗʰ inst when we were Relieved by Cavalry from Skirmish line & our Regt & Brigade & Division & Corpse moved to Lost Mt, where our Regt went on pickett & Remained until the night of the 7ᵗʰ when we Ret to line & lay there one night & yesterday morning moved here, North east about 6 miles we have built breastworks out of Railes, Rocks & dirt & may fight here or we may not no skirmishing in hearing neither yesterday nor today, all Seem confident of Success if the Yanks should attack, Some lament the desolation we are making, but all say, better that them for us to run on there works & be cut to pieces & be whipped, then all behind would be gone, the truth is they flank & we follow on the inner track, form line & offer them

P2

battle & they Refuse & in a day or two they are moving (or flanking) to our Right, & we have to follow or let them go Round the end of our line & get in our Rear or wherever they choose, So it does not make any difference how good our works are, with no foe in front, they are of no more use to us, & we leave, but Some seems like they cannot under stand it & some at home seem to blame Johnson, like in the days of Washington so tis now, We have the advantage by having the inside track & greatly in the choice of the ground, I Hate this for your Satisfaction & So you may have a Reply for the Croakers that may chance to meet you, I Say that Johnson has the confidence of nine tents of this army, & if our battle line was formed in my yard, I would Say to you, gear up & take what you canto the Rear, & expect that my wheat would be fed down, my finses piled up for breast works, garden torn down tredded down & eaten up, Roads & paths running in every direction through the fields of corn if it were not as high as an inch or any height to fully Ripe, In a word a line of battle has no more Respect for property than a hurricane in the night, why not, you ask, because mens lives are at steak, there wives & children & all of the interest of the Confederacy is also at steak, My Dear I must close, I drew me a pair of pants yesterday (Linsey) & not before I kneeded them, I had darned & patched the old ones, both on the Seat & knees, my old coat & hat is nearly out of the Scrape, but I will take the chance, my shoes are good for dry weather but it worsts them through sutch bad mud as we have traveled through, I hear the Roar of distant companies to the Rite of our front, May God bless & Save us as is my prayr aff

S C Kelly

PS I drew one month pay today but cannot Spend it, it in large bills, Ie, 1 of 100$ 2 tens & 2 fives, I have yet of old issue 15$ Yours Sam

JUNE 11TH 12 OCLOCK NOON

.11 P1

My Dearest Amie I Rec yours of the 4th day before yesterday but had just written & Sent it out & on his Return from carrying off the mail he brings what letters comes, So you see that I cannot answer a letter Rec the same day, I was glad to get it even of that (date) but J Price Rec one the same day dated the 6th, I know that you loose time by sending them to J V, (even by Woolem) for he drops them in the box likely after they take those out that have been deposited there during the day, & then stays there until the next night, where as if it were mailed at Ladiga it would be already in the Sack & would go Right on, I do not know as I have any thing to write, more than I wrote the other day except there is more firing to day than here before, the battle may yet come off here, we are all hopeful God give us the victory is constantly my prayr, I am sorry for you, I know that you are troubled, let Dice Stay & let the boys go if they will, If the Yankees get them they will put them

P2

Right in the army & my word for it the time will come when they will wish that they had gone South, but if they will not go I know that you cannot force them off, & if you do they can Run away & be a total loss anyhow, If you could get some one to carry them off that would do to depend upon, but all are as deep in the trouble as you are & all have there own things to take care of, It may be that the enemy will not force them off against there wills, if they choos to Stay, & the best you can do under the circumstances is to Say to our boys that they have to live until they die, either bond or free & that if they will not go off with the Yanks, but will Remain & make a living, That if the balance of the negrows are Set free that they shall be too, & it is far preferable working on the farm than being a Soldier, I know by experience, I Close may God he continiew his blessings to us is my daily prayr good bie your own affectionate Husband SCK

P3

PS I will send this envellop Backed you can turn it & it is the olde Ready Just altered S

P4

Take a pencil or pin staff & Roll it along between the folds of the envelope & you can open it without tearing the paper & especially if you first wet it, I have no chance to get any & none to carry

LINE OF BATTLE OR RR BETWEEN BIG SHANTY & MARIETTA JUNE 14TH 1864 9 AM

.14 P1

My Dearest Amie I Rec yours of the 11th by Graham last night was looking for one & had been for 2 days, I wrote you on Saturday the 11th & put a hundred dollar bill of new issue in it, You say that you have written 6 letters since the 6th May, on the 12th May I Rec (by R Wilkinson) yours of the 6th, on the 4th June I Rec yours of the 15th & 27th on the 5th, yours of the 24th & Since then in due time of the 1st, 4th & 7th that accounts for all. But I thought it a long time from the 12th May to the 4th of June, but could not blame you, but could not tell whether it was derangement of the mail or whether you were Sick or gone from home, I do try to feel thankful that it is as well (every way) with us as what it is, You did not say in this what was the date of your last letter from me, I wish you would in every one, So I may know, I think that yours of the 4th Said that you had Rec mine of the 29th, I then wrote on the 31st or

1st & put two Rings in it, I wrote every 3 or 4 days if there is any chance to Send them out, is not when there is, Some times but little I know, but I try to tell the Reason & ½ tellen is better than none, I have not Seen Graham yet, or do I know where he is, a army man gave_____ terday it had_____ found its way here Some how, You _____do not get all my letter, or you would have known the casualties of my Company, I have given it in two, together with the Sick Sent to Rear & what I write is so (or if it does not come under my own observation & give it as I believe it) not withstanding the Rumors, to the Contrary, I hope that all have heared same now, we have not had any one hurt since the 26th May & I think that, in my former letters that I

have given all that been sent to the Rear Sick except old man Hiram White who went up a few days ago, with Something like the ericipulas, I have to write about the Co, or els my letters would be shorter than they are & I give the names of the men that I know you are not aquainted with, Yet I do not know, who may ask about them & those in the Co that I do not mention you may take it for granted that they are all Right, the Wilkinson boys Tom was taken Sick the 8th May & sent to Rear, I Suppose to Atlanta or some other hospital, Rad & John Remained with us until the 26th May when Rad was wonded & Sent to Rear or hospital, we have what is call a field hospital both of Brigade & Division & Corpse, if a man gets Sick he is examined by the

regimental Surgeon & treated by him, if he gets worse he is Sent in a day or 2 to the brigade Surgeon who sends him to the Division hospital & if he continues worse

P2

is still sent back still farther to the Rear to the Corpse hosp & there if the Chief Surgeon of the Corpse thinks propper he sends him to Atlanta or Some where else, Just so with the wounded, lots of men get well, with a few days Rest & a little medicine & never get farther than the brigade or Division field hospital & are Returned to duty in a Short time while others, we may not hear of for months, My dear this Sounds to me like I had verry little to write about, but I Suppose that you did not know how these things were managed, John Wilkinson is with us now & has been all the time except 3 days in the Rear Sick, if I Say a man is Sick & Sent to Rear he has gone as the Brigade field hospital & I cant tell whether he will be Sent Still farther back, or Ret in a day or So, time only Reveals that, You Speak of your oats I do think that you had better let them get Ripe & cut them, if they have full cheat, & ret tall oats enough for Seed, I guess you have had plenty of Rain by this time, It seems to me, that I never Saw So wet a time, it has not Rained any today, but the Sun has not been seen little since Saturday, & Sunday & night & all day monday it Rained nearly all the time, Yesterday it turned cool & is yet cool. We my Co & 4 other Companies of the Regt went on pickett in front of our Brigade Sunday morning at day light & were Relieved monday ____same time, Slight _____

____ all day _____ an attack, but they did no____ no one hurt' I had to act as officer of the day (Ie) in command of the 5 Companies, I am the Senior Captain the Regt now, for duty & have had to act as Staff officer Since May <u>64</u>, I did also as officer of the line (or Capt of my Co) when n sutch duty, I do Reg the loss of F, also Capt Elliott (wounded) who is my Senior, So is Capt Deshago who is Sick, it seems to me like it is pretty tight on me but I am thankful that I been enabled to perform in Some Sort of way, the duties, though not with entire Satisfaction to myself, My Dear I do not want permission, but seek humbly to perform the duties imposed upon me, trusting in the Lord for Strength in every time of kneed, we have moved about 2 ½ miles to the Right & have thrown out picketts, (the whole Corps) & one now Resting in the woods, but very little firing today, Cant tell when nor where the big fight will come off, I thought we were in Reserve now, but am not able to tell, I close & now my Dear A. pray for me& the cause that now Separates us & all of the whole army & may God hear your prayrs & answer is the prayr of your affectionate husband good bie) Sam

This below is written in margins of P2

I will send this for you to write back on. A.

This paper seem greasy or my haver sack has greased it so cannot hardly write

LINE OF BATTLE NEAR MARIETTA JUNE 19TH 4 P.M. 1864

.19 .20 P1

My Dearest Amie I wrote to you 3 or 4 days ago while we were in Reserve, we have not been engaged Since neither in Skirmish nor battle but been moving about to Support (if necessary) those who were, true 3 evening ago we were moved up on the line & during the night built breast works & Stayed there all day 17th & night until 3 AM yesterday morning when we our corpse were to our left in Rear of Hardees who were fighting the enemy & had been for a day or two previous but I thank God that he did not need our assistance but Repulsed them (tis said in every assault, yesterday 18th) the most insissant Rainy day I ever saw until about 12 then Showry all evening, we left about 3 AM & traveled in the Rain & mud until about 8 AM then built fires & Stayed until about 4 PM & traveled back within 1 mile of the place we left, though by different Rout & Camped about 9 PM, Stayed there until about 2 PM today, when we moved to this place, making a muddy tromp of about 10 miles, one of the most tiring tromps that ever I took, Rendered more so to me, from the fact that I was Sick with the disntery & had to Stop frequently,& have runs & am now poorly for 2 days, but am now reported not for duty, we have sent off to hospital since I wrote you Wiley Garrett & Nim Argo. & have Returned from hosp John Rhoads & Ben Piece, I have not Rec a letter from you Since Graham come, I saw him about 4 minutes today, don't give yourself uneasiness about my Sickness, I hope that I will all be Right in a day or So, if whorse I shall go to the Rear, the Coln is also complaining, 2 or 3 men in the Co complaining, none of your acquaintances, the wetest June I think that I ever saw, I am anxious to hear from you, I think Gen Johnson is doing the thing about Right, You will see in the paper about the 31st Regt, being captured on pickett that is 185 men & 11 officers out of about 300, the Coln (Henley) & the acting major (Capt Thompson of our County) included John Hyatt & Browning that you know, May God Still continue his blessings towards is my daily prayr Good bie Your affecty husband SCK

P2

PS 20th June Second line of Battle Same place as yesterday, except we moved (after we got our works done) about ¼ mile to Right, where we had to work all night by detail all night to build protection for our Selves from Shells, we (our Brigade) are the Reserves for Cummings Brig of our Corpse, who are Georgians & what are left are good fiters, lots of them have Stopped at home, whose homes are in the Yanky lines, but little firing today in hearing, they throw a few Shells over us about 10 AM, it is now 12 & the Sun is Shining, no telling what a day may bring for __ the heavy Raines, likely have Retained the operations ___both armies, I was off in an old crib writing in time of heavy rain, & the mail carrier went out & I missed the opertunity, but he brought me one letter from you of the 12th whitch Speaks of that Rainy Sunday that you will Read about if you get my letter of the 13th whitch I enclosed to you a hundred dollar bill of new issue, I am so thankful that I have a trusting believing praying wife, I feel like I need your prayrs, I try to pray but I have so many things to try my patience that I feel like that I am So verry unworthy & negligently, ungreateful but unto whome els I can go, or who look to for Strength to bear me through the perolous times, but unto God, the maker & burden of my prair , & I try to go to him not in my own name but in the name of Jesus Christ his only begotten Son, who died for Sinners, Rather that, than for me to get your & you not get mine, I have no way of carring paper & write on Slipps & notches &C I hope that you can Read them if not let me know & I will try & write on clean paper, I can buy paper nearly any day but cant get less than a quire & have no way to keep it dry, you Say that want to See me so bad, Do, but alass this crewell war has Seperated us, but Oh God forbid that that Seperation may be but just a little longer, until he has enabled the Confederate army to have gained her independence, & peace Spread over the nation as a govment, then the way warn Soldier Return Sound in body & mind, to his long absent ones, with a heart full of gratitude to God for his abundant mercies & blessings, Tell the boys that nothing of the kind in life would give me So mutch pleasure as to over the crop, that I know that they feel better in the full discharge of their duties, that at my coming I may say well done, good & faithful servants, I am better today, hope I get well Right away, Good bie Sam

FN to this letter. This letter is written on a scrap order with this written upon it with the most beautiful handwriting.

MAY 21ST 1864
QUARTER MASTERS DEPARTMENT
CAMP NEAR MARIETTA GEORGIA

Captin
I have this day relieved Private J H
Duncan from duty in the department and ordered
Him to report without delay to his command

——— ———

2 OCLOCK PM MARIETTA GA JUNE 22OND 1864

.22 P1

My Dearest Amie the weather continued so unsettled & we had so mutch hard marching to do, & my health not improving nor could not under those circumstances that I turned in to the hospital yesterday morning while our Brigade was passing & thought that I would rest until I got better or the weather broke, I am glad to Say that I have greatly improved in the 2 days I have been here, I am with the Brigade Surgeon who politely asked me to Stay with him & I accepted in Stead of going to the Regular Hospital, I have taken but little medicin, I do not need it, more Rest & a vegettable diet whitch I get more than at the hospital, our Corpse has moved again on the left in Rear of Hardee, again, it has not Rained today but I think it will this evening, I visited Several of the hospitals today, I find them a bad place for a Sick man, the wounded Rec mutch more attention than the Sick, 4 others of my Co Stoped & Sent back Since yesterday morning, Sgt

J W Ford, Privates G W Jenkins, B Henderson & J Green, Coln Shelly also Stoped, but would go to the front this morning, So would I have gone, had I had a horse to ride, they are out about 2 ½ miles west of this place on the powder Springs Road, Still Skirmishing all the time no general engagement, I had a good dinner of vegettables today for whitch I paid in new issue five dollar, Cheap enough for he gave 150 cts per pound for flour, my bowels are checked & I feel 100 percent better than I did when I came here

P2

do not give yourself uneasiness about my Sickness, I am determined to take care of myself if I can, I don't care if Some one is Ready to Say that I am bunking , I do not intend to do duty when I am not able, I can Say one thing in truth that I have come as nigh, aways being on hand as one tenth of the Regt, 9 tenths have failed before me, & if I were to go til I dropped dead, from fatigue, what honor,

My Dear this is about all that I know to write, that will interest you, May God our heavenly father Still have mercy upon us & Save us is the prayer of one who is Your affictunate Husband Good bie S C Kelly

PS I have not Rec any letter from you since the 19th dated the 12th, I answered it, our lines are Slightly changed in the last week, I just heared that our Corpse has or is going to move Still farther to the left, If I Still improve I expect to go to the front tomorrow or next day, I would not have done any good the 2 days I have been here, our command are Bivouac in Rear of Hardee who is Skirmishing with the Yanks, Yours SCK

LINE OF BATTLE ABOUT 4 MILES WEST OF MARIETTA GA JUNE 23RD 4 PM

.23 Pl HIS

(This letter has been wet, ink runs & is faded out in places. Amie had written him back using this letter)

My Dear Amie I Rec yours of the 17th came by hand today & I

was glad to get it but, Cannot tell why my letters are 2 days longer Coming than Some others in the Co, Sam Pendland Rec two today one from Ladiga & one from <u>Cross Pls</u> 2 days later, I am Sorry that you are so troubled about the negrows, if the Yanks come & they want to go with them you will have to let them go, for if you send them off by themselves then they are sure to go, if they want to, & <u>Do</u> know all about that, no Say they are more trouble than they are worth & if they can do better than take my advise just go it boots, no don't be to Rash with them that if they will not go off out of the way, to Stay at home & not go off with them, but Stay & finish the crop & gather it & help use it, & that will be better than go off with them Y where they are shure not to make any thing & I am Shure but what you had better divide the meat & give them there Share & when they come let the negrows tell them that this is our meat & that is hers & if they take it & then, beg them not to take yours, God only knows what will be the end yet, I still feel hopeful that God will in his mercy, in his own appointed time give us our Independence & if in his providence we should loose our negrows, I hope that he may Spear our lives & health & bring us together after peace is maid & that Soon verry Soon & I trust that we in his mercies may make a living & be happy, & live in his fear & favour, until our time on earth is ended & after all be prepared to meet around the throne of God in heaven, Our Division charged the enemy yesterday evening &drove in there outer line with considerable loss to us, (our Div) our Regt lost in killed & wonded about 25, only 1 or 2 Killed most Slightly wonded, other Regt more or less, my Co W Thomas little finger on left hand, Lt J W Pike Cmd Co, he was Struck with a grape shot in hip, Only Slightly brushed & J Price on arm Same way, I have Ret to line, I feel well but not fully Regained my Strength must close or <u>miss</u>

God bless you & yours good bie SCK

P2 HERS

I got the rings you sent all safe and the larger one pleased me better that if I had made it my self. When you come home I will settle with you for it, I did not think you could do that well, I am rather lonesome this evening all are out in the wheat field but me and Dicky he is grubing about as you used to say. I do wish you could come home and Do to thing here for if the Yankees do come they will ruin us. In point of property and I can not help my self they take and destroy all as they go. May God save us from such a fate but we are no better than others, sometimes I think our negrows all want to go to them and then again I do not know. I am in a peck of trouble about it, if Bro j would come and see me it would help some but I do not know where he is whether in the army or no. May God direct us and save us is my daily prayer. Your own Amie

4 MILES WEST OF MARIETTA LINE OF BATTLE JUNE 29TH 64

.29 (LETTER FADED)

My Dear _____we are yet in line _____you will see we kept a sharp fight day before yesterday Lt Pike got wonded in the charge on _____ slightly, I wrote that to you, Cheatham & Claborn were attacked the same day in the main line & Slaughtered them powerfully, You will see all about it in the papers, I am quite well & stood the night well, the other day , I am truly thankful for the kind protection that God has seen fit to bestow upon me, I Rec your & billys letter day before yesterday, I was glad to get it, I will answer when I have more time, keep this Record this is an exact coppy of what I put in my muster Roll, all in good spirits, think Joe knows how to meet Sherman on any point, May God Still continue his blessings to us is my daily prayr, Good bie your own affectinate Husband S C Kelly
(The Report mentioned above is the movements from winter quarters to the end of June)

MAY 1ST RECORD OF EVENTS SINCE WE LEFT WINTER QRTERS
NEAR DALTON GA

P1

We Remained in winter quarters up to about 1st May, 64 Near Dalton, when we moved out to line, & were engaged by turn erecting fortifications &n until the night of the 6th May took our place in line on east side of Rocky face Ridge, Remained there until the morning of the 8th, then sent out 12 men from Co as Skirmishers, who engaged the enemy at about 10 AM & kept up a Slow fire until next evening, & were finally driven in by a Strong force, who attempted to Storm our works in front of the 20th Ala Regt, our Regt being ready to support them, that night (the 9th) our Co were deployed as Skirmishers (on the west side) who annoyed them all next day by Rolling Rocks & Shooting at them as they dodged, we were Relieved at night, & Remained on line until the night the 12th, when with our Regt brought up the Rear, except the picketts, 13th moved to our place at Resacca, we were in Reserve both 14th & 15th, Jeremiah Kiney killed, by Minee ball 12th, J Plocpe left arm broke by Shell 15th , fell back that night 16th at Calhoun, 17th Adairesville, 18th Cass ville

P2

19th built works, 4 PM passed through town, forward line, 20th crossed River (Hytour) bivowacked near Coopers old Iron works until the 25th, our Co on pickett at River, Regt & Brig, Division & Corpse moved to New hope church 7 or 8 miles S. W. Co evacuate & caught up in evening, built works that night, 26th 11 AM Sent out in front of Brigade as Skirmishers, we engaged the enemy immediately & held them in Check until Relieved at night, lost one killed 3 mortally 3 Severely & one Slightly wonded, 27th behind works , night moved to Regt & back evening in Rear o position last night before, 29th moved to Right & Rear of (whole Corpse) and Bivowacked the until the night of the 31st, June 1st took position in line 6 miles west of Acworth built works, 4th Sent out on Skirmish, Slow firing but Regular as the Rain, Relieved at day light 7th by Cavalry, Command fell back to Lost Mt, the Co came up about 10 AM a distance of about 4 or 5 miles, our Regt Sent on pickett (we in Reserve) relieved on evening of the 7th Returned to line, 8th moved 6 miles N. E. to

Kenesaw Mt built works, 9th 1 oclock PM moved to Right ½ mile on Right of R.R. with in

P3

Reserve, in Rear of Cummings 11th moved to line Relieved Bakers Brig 12th 60 on pickett Slight Skirmishing day & night, (Rained incossantly) Relieved at daylight on the 13th moved to Right 2 miles 14th bevowacked 15th 1 PM moved to frount & built works, Remained until 3 AM, the 15th moved to left 5 miles, in Rear of Hardee, 4PM moved in Rear of place left in the morning, 19th 1 PM moved to line built works in Rear of Cummings, 20th 6 PM moved ½ mile to Right, 21st 4 AM moved 4 miles to left Bevowacked until 2 PM, 22nd when the whole Division moved forward and attacked the enemie Skirmishers & drove them to their main line, loss of Co one Lt, 2 men Slightly wounded, fell back at night about 1 mile, built works, 23&4th our co on Skirmish ½ , 253 others, 24th evening of the 26th the whole Brigade on the Skirmish, 27th 8 AM the enemy with 2 lines of Skirmishers & a line of battle attempted to drive us in, but we Repulsed them in 5 minutes but a heavy fire was kept up all day by Sharp Shooters, we were Relieved at night by Reynolds Brigade, Ret to main line & are there yet 29 11AM we lost none out of Co, 2 out of Brig killed, 7 wounded

JULY 1864

SAME PLACE ON LINE JULY 2OND 3 PM

.02 FRONT

(On small scrap of paper has been used on back)

My Dear I have not time to write only to let you that I am well & nothing unusual has occurred God bless you good bie S C Kelly

Dear Captains___ have attempted ____sutch that I co___ I have heard ____ Let me know. ___ Percent & also ____ & died. Any

asa____ I hope to be ex_____ you to write as____ I got acquar____
of Silver Run ____ =its Lts Gow ____

.04 P1

FM on small scrap of paper has been used on back My Dearest
Amie I have not Rec a letter from you Since the 20th dated 22nd
Yours & Billys, I am anxiously wating to hear from you, look
Shine this evening, I have not mutch to write but knowing your
anxiety at sutch times I try to write often, though the news would
be unimportant to any one but you, I know that you thank God
on the Reseption of every letter, that announces that I am well &
yet Spiritual though Sutch times, Thank God that sutch is our case,
Oh that I could be more humble & thankful, trusting & Christ like,
Lt Pike has not Ret from hospital _____Soon _____

Sick sent to ____ on the evening of the 2ond my Co & others of
Regt were sent on pickett Same place where we fought them the
monday before (27th) spoken of in my Records of events, we kept
up a Sharp Skirmish until dark when we gradually let the firing
die out until about twelve oclock when the whole army fell back
& at one AM we evacuated the posts (Stealthily) & followed the
main army (all the picketts or our Brigade under Coln Shelly) &
came up about 2 AM about 4 miles from old position, we built pits
& are Ready for them, (So far as I know) they pursewed after day
light & Some Skirmishing last night & a goodeal this morning,
Some anticipate an attack this evening , we in Reserve of
Cummings Brig (Georgians) J Keller Ret to Co from home
yesterday

P2

John Prier has been Sent off to Atlanta or Some where else, I
did not think him hurt bad enough too that, Wyley Garrett was
furloughed for 60 days from hospital 25th, Well my Dear A the
mail come in & no letter, but not your fault I know close & will try
to write Billy a few lines May God Still continue his blessings
towards us is my daily prayrs, Good bie your own S

W Pace Kelly Dear Son I am thankful that I am Speared, to drop
you a few lines of advise apply yourself to Reading writing & the

pursuit of knowledge, for a man with out it is the Slave or tool, or the heaver of wood & drawer of water for him that has, and above all Remember thy Creator in the days of t_ ____ of the evil ____ comes not that thoughtless Say I have no pleasure in them, Seek the Lord be converted & live said to the honor of God, you are not to young to become a Christian, & the hope tha_ __ld I die, I Shall be saved from hell & Saved in house to dwell with God, & the Spirit of just men made perfect , through Jesus Christ, is worth all els on earth, Son I am pleased with your letter, Some your words Spelled wrong, but you must try to improve, I know your chances are bad but imply what you have & be truthful and obedient to your Mother, be kind & obliging to your little brothers, teach them how to do by your example, May God direct you in the way you Should go is the prayrs of your affectionate father S C Kelly to W Pace Kelly

LINE OF BATTLE NEAR TURNERS FERY IN CHATTAHOOCHEE RIVER JULY 8TH 4 PM

.08

(This letter was written on blank page torn from old Sermon Book)

My Dearest Amie I Rec yours of the 21st by mail yesterday but we were on pickett & had not the chance to answer it I have not Rec the one by Arheart nor the last, nor did not know he had Started until I Rec yours, I have not heared of all, all are well with us, Since I wrote we Sent off Sick John Wilkins & Henry Shaw & have Received from Hospital Lt Pike, Nim Argo & Bob Brown, all look well & Say they faired well at the hospital, John Palmer wrote that he was coming to Co & look for him, we have been under fire of Artilery & Scatering minies every day lately, but have not been engaged, I feel under Reniuwed of obligations to our heavenly father for his kind protection every day, on the evening of the 3rd or 4th I narrowly escaped having both legs cut off by a Shell, it Struck my pants just below my knee & Struck the ground in less than 3 feet & Rickashed to a considerable distance, came near hitting 2 other men in Company after it bounced, (we are on pickett whole Division) guarding the River to prevent them crossing, true we have fallen back but we are not whipped nor bad Scared, they keep flanking Rather than fight, they are Shigh & want to compromise on pickett & not Sharp Shoot, I hope that it will work out, will yet God being our helper, we will conquer a peace, if not it will against us (Ie) the Lords will, will be done

P2

My Dearest I am writing on a blank back of a Sermon book taken from Mr Lesters house, that we tore out of the way, It seems like my letter all go, but scattering, I am quite well & have improved ever since I Ret from hospt, we get vegettables now & forage a little, I expect that Robinson is getting Ritch in Confederate money, but my place is not for Sale unless you know of another to buy that you had Rather live at, I live for You & Children & my Country & try to Serve God the maker of us all, You will not loose mutch by discount on your old issue, I have only about 12 dollars, the boys drew 22 dollars apiece today (or 2 months wages more or less & Some of them owe me Some, the Government owes me 4 months wages yet & I hope you will not need before you get Some), as to paper use that old book or any thing, make your own envellops & write to me certain every 5 days, I cant think that it will be long before I am at home, not six months more & I do hope Safe & Sound & in a free & independent Government in peace with the nations of the earth, I upon hope ever, I am sorry that you are so hard Run for bread, but I think that you had better Sfen out your corn & eat your wheat, I would like to exchange I have not eat a biscuit but the 2 days at the hospital in over a month, only once or twice crackers, but we get plenty, in the wet weather when your hogs were diging, it was the musherooms they eat, I guess, I am proud of the crop from what you say, Wilse aut to have been in 3 years ago, may God Still bless us is the dayly prayr of your Afctly Husband SCK

Turners Ferry

This is a picture of the Mayson -Turner Ferry which operated from 1844 to 1897 at the location of the Veterans's Memorial Hwy (former Bankhead Hwy.) at the Chattahoochee River. Calhoun Turner and John Hooper are in the picture.

LINE OF BATTLE NEAR GREENS FERRY ON LEFT LINE JULY 12TH 12 NOON

.12 Pl

My Dearest Amie I Received yours of the 7th last night after night when we had come in off of pickett, where we had seen 14 hours fighting the Yanks a cross the River we had one wonded Severe in hand Sgt J W Ford one other in Co H who was in my charge (welfour Brig) have been down here on pickett 4 or 5 days, we expect to be Relieved today & we will Rejoin our Div, whitch is between here & Atlanta, the news from Va is encouraging, the papers Say a fight is pending here but it has been one Continual fight, Some times, hot on us & them hot on Some other part, but more or less fighting all the time, our moving codition & uncertainty of our where abouts is the cause of my letters not Reaching you Sooner, they go to the Div Hd Qrts one day & then to Corpse another, & about 3 day take the cars for Ala, but Sutch is the Chance, I was a little Surprised at Arhearts coming, but am not disappointed at not getting my pants, (I drew a pair about the 20th June, I thought you knew that my pants are better than the balance of my clothes & I can do on what I have a while longer & then there will be a way provided, I am Sorry for you but I Rejoyce that you put trust in God, & if you fall in the hands of the enemy Still trust on though they Stay, your God forbid that they should be allowed to disolate that fair Country, but the Lords will, will be done & we will have to Submit, tis hand, & but hundreds & thousands of So miles have fallen in there hands, & a great many badly treated, I dear Say but trust on trust ever, Submitting your cares in the hands of him that is able to Save both Sole & body, I think that it is a bad time to buy a waggon, too, to make out with the large one, Oh yes James is too busy & always has been, to see, or know, or

P2do anything for you, if the Yanks comes & takes all, he will not be any better off, than if he had Speared a little time, & trouble in seeing to you & giving you a word of advice occasionally, it has always Seemed to me, like he has not acted the part of a brother in this matter, not So with Ann, Wm. H. takes some interest, I think that if I had been at home & he in the army fighting for my Rights as well as his, that I Should have done a better part by his wife than he has mine (You) I wrote to him about it, that is the Reason you got that letter, more Anon, Ordered to move 3 miles of Atlanta 6 PM I am Sorry that Sam is Sutch a fool, & if I happened on him about the time he was in his tantrums I think that I could have quited him, he is a fool, & if the Rest are set free he may go too, & he will be more Respected, by doing Right than wrong, the next news I hear from them I expect to hear of him going to the Yanks, ungreatful wretch, for the Sickness that he has had & the attention he has Received, but Sutch is the depravity of the human heart, You tell Barney privately (for me) that when he gets in them big ways, to raise a dispute & fuss with him, & whip him good, for I know he kneed beating to death, I do hope that I will get home some day & wo unto the negrow that dear Sause me, God being my helper, we will yet gain our Independence, in the fear of God & under his protection & all negrows will (if they been away) be in duty & it will be better with them than Sam, either bond or free, I have hopes of the Rest, & I just want them to wait & See, & let God deside this matter, they have to live until they die, even if they were free, & why not Stay there & work & live of the fruits of there labor, I close God bless us Specialy in our deliverance from our enemy is my prayr Yours own husband S

JULY 13TH 64 NOON

.13

Still at the Same place all quiet with us today, J Thackerson Ret to Co today, Some little Skirmishing on the Right, I must close I have a chance to Send by Ab Littlejohn, write oftener than usual these time good bie Your own S

CAMP NEAR ATLANTA GA JULY 16TH 1864

.16 P1

My Dearest Amie we are Resting (apparently the whole of both armies) about 4 miles of Atlanta we have been here 3 days & 4 nights & there is but little firing in hearing, Rumors are Current about Price & Forest passing in the Rear towards Nashville, or Some other point, & the Yanks here making to the Rear & tearing up the RR Iron & carrying it with them &C&C good if was only true & also Cheering news from Va, Grant falling back, Martinsburg in our possession also Hagerstown, Harpers ferry, EC, & that our forces under Buckner (or Breckenridge) Carty & Yewell are within 4 miles of Washington City Shelling, the Shells Reaching with in 2 miles of the verry heart of the City & Baltimore & Philladelpia in a perfect blaze of excitement good if tis ½ of it true, Sutch is our hope, while we feel confident under the direction & protection of God to Repell any assault that they may make upon our lines, they may (& will I fear) flank us out of Atlanta, but the cause is not gone up then, all seems to be in good Spirits & think Johnson a

P2

Christian & General, looking to God the Author of all things to direct us him in the management of this great national affair, but oh when I think of our fair Country & of you (my love) & those bright eyed boys, falling into the hands of Sutch enemies, my heart Sinks, my tears flow, & my prayrs are lifted to that God who tears down on our nation & Ruses up another, Who is the maker of us all & who only we can look to for healp in this the hour of kneed, Oh that he would have mercy on us Speedely, Oh God are we not Scourged enough, we have Sined but is it not enough, have we not Repented, & turned from our idols & Seek after the only God, Oh our God if we have not Repented as a nation & a family, help us to begin this day, & come humbly to the footstead & ask for Jesus Sake to forgive our Sins & give us our Independence & hearts of grattitude to praise the as we aut, The mail has come in no letter for me, & none from our end Since the 12th dated 8th from Prathers wife, letters from the lower end dated 9th, Say there is no more talk of the Yanks than usual, but I saw a Soldier from near Oxford who left there the 13th & in my Co this morning who Said that the talk was that they were at Gadsden & had crossed the River about 300

P3

of them & a good many on the other side, Sutch are the Rhumors, I hope it is no worse than we have heared, My Amie in Sutch times of excitement I wish that you would write me a few lines every other day or I would not object to every day, I am so uneasy about you but hope for the best, but try to prepare my mind for the worst, God grant us mercy, We are having a good time to what we have had, we have been washing up our clothes & the officers baggage were sent to us today, all my things were present except for my piece of bacon & a polk of salt, they went up & I got my other linsey Shirt & drawers & sent back those I had worn all the time except Shirt too bad to send, I kept the Same cotton Shirt I have worn Since Wilkinson brought them & have one in my Satchel, I have never worn also one of my old calico shirts & 2 pars cotton socks & Co books & papers is all in that line, as to bed clothing with waggoner one Blanket & over coat & an old tan cloth that they are Rolled in, So you see that if I were to loose all it would not Set me back mutch, as to what I have, My hat old & patched coat dirty & Raged, Shirts passable for an active campaign, drawers (one par with me) good, pants faded (of the Confederate linsey)

P4

& knocked out about the ankles, Shoes at least ½ worn & never knew what blacking was maid for & totally unused to tallow, Socks 2 par one good, others worse off wear, that mutch with a blanket, sword, &C haver sack & canteen makes me a good load for these hot days & is about as little as a man can do well with, we all started from Dalton fat & full, but now look like horse that have been worked all the time until the crop is laid by on Short Rations of a night, but I believe that we are tougher than when we left Dalton & in as good Spirits, Some times up & Some times down, but time flies Swiftly by, Oh that it may not tarry until we have gained our Independence & peace is made & we meet to thank our God for his abundant mercies, There is a meeting going on 5 joined the churches last night, babtized today, Capt who is in command of the 46th Ala Regt of our Brig preached last night, good preacher but the circumstances surrounding him deprives us of his labor in the gospel, all seems interested & the army to a great intent has Reformed, Oh that the gospel may Run & be glorified until it may become the church of the living God, Oh that God will give us deliverance Soon is my prayr, Your own Sam

ATLANTA GA JULY 27TH 31/2 PM

.27 P1

(This letter has significant burning around the edges and center. Sam wrote his letter on back of a letter sent to him from Hiram White. In turn Amie tore part of the letter off and wrote back to Sam between the lines of Hiram Whites letter)

My Dearest Amie I thank God that he has yet Speared me, we have been under fire for several days, no general engagement on our part have been Skirmishing all the time, I had one man killed & one Slight wonded since I wrote to you, John Keller shot in fore head never Spoke, Josh Pinter in leg but he still with us, that occurred on the 20th, I had just moved from the spot where Keller was killed __ not exc_ding a minute, just in the edge of the ditch, a good seat but dangerous, The enemy are Shelling the City Some & have Shelled near us but doing little damage, we are Shelling them more than usual, Our artillery has been ____ ____ waited for them to charge ___, they annoyed us all the time we were in Brush. Gen Hood told them to shoot when & where ever they _____ that they could do any harm to the enemy, & they Shoot _____ appeared at J Removal, Still no objection to Hood hopeful _____ will work out well yet, Our Gen S D Lee of Miss is our Corpse Commander now troops still in fine spirits, I Rec yours by Tyler _____th, I was so thankful to hear that you were all spared yet, I think that you had better sell the cotton, Do the best you can, I hate to loose all & do not know how to advise, If you sell it & get the money & let the negrows know it & the Yankees come they will tell them, they may take it from you, Send it off & Sell it and let on as though you had sent it to Selma to store it, You must work it some how that ___ in Secret as to

---

P2

(This letter is from Hiram White to S C Kelly)

yours nor the Co Since I left, I would like to be with you very mutch but cant tell when I will be able to get there, I wish you to write back to me on the Receipt of this letter and let me hear from you and all the boys how you all come out whether there has any news of _____ been killed or wonded Since I left our far__ is Pritty bad here but I will not grumble ___ I saw Martin Keller and Smith they bou__ came here after Transportation, They had ____ boath a Sixty day furlow and was a going ____ try to go home, I have heard they are Paying off the Soldiers now, I wish you if you can Draw for me, to do so is as I am Kneeding Some mon__ very bad here & if you cant draw my money by assigning my name, I wish you if you Please to Send money use ____ ___ to me and _____ a few Dollars for I tell you I am in kneed of a little and if there has come or should come any letters to the company

forward please forward them to me Direct to me at Covington Ga
_____ _____ Hospital ward no 3 write on the pice__ ____ of
this I Remain your most Honorable Servant Hiram White to S C
Kelly

P3

*(Amie wrote back to Sam between lines of Hiram Whites letter whitch
Sam had used. Sam wrote back to Amie answering her question. As
best I can tell the letter was used 4 times)*

Sam I can do without him but may be I had better get Arheart
to bring him but he could run away as easy as from here   (this is
from Amie)

no do not send him unless he is willing to come, Sell him to
Gladden good bie I must close write again good bie yours S C
Kelly

LINE OF BATTLE ATLANTA JULY 29TH 2 PM 64

.29

My Dearest Amie I do feel thankful that I am yet Speared there
is more or less fighting every day, we are about one mile north of
the City on the left of the R Road, in the Support of a battle,
yesterday on our left there was a hard fight, but I have not heared
the particulars, but from what I hear we cannot make more of it
than a draw fight, Gen Loring was engaged & is mortally wonded,
also Gen Stewart (commanding Popes old corpse) Slightly. there
is a constant Sharp shooting & artillery firing all the time day &
night, I got Hobbs to wash my clothes today & an alarm broke out
& I had to put them on before they got dry, we have to be Ready
to go to the trenches at a moments warning, about one hundred &
50 yds, Our Regt lost a man yesterday, by a Shell, I heared that
Davis Weaver got his heel Shot off & it had to be cut off last
fryday, It is Raining I must close May our father in heaven, have
mercy on us, good bie Your own husband S C Kelly

AUGUST 1864

ATLANTA AUG 1ST 64

.01 P1

FN PS written upside down in margin & on small scrap of paper.

My Dear Amie I am yet thankful that I am yet Speared while others are falling around me, as good & perhaps better than I am, but it has pleased the Lord to protect me thus far, & I know of no other help but to trust in the mercies of the living God through the merits of his dear Son Jesus Christ, I try to Submit my Self & all (You) my dearest at home & my Country into his hands, & try always to Say not my will but there to be done, we are Skirmishing with the enemy every day, with a goodeal of artillery firing on both Sides, it Remindes me of vicksburg, Some loss on our Side daily but I have not lost any of my Co Since I wrote you, Our Regt were in Support of a battery Saturday & lost in Killed Lt Colonel Patterson & Capt Wm McGee, Wonded Ed Clark & Several others, Ed is Son of Coln C of Jacksonville, that night the Regt went on pickett & while Relieving Capt Derrett (of Randolph Co) was mortally wonded, & died before he Reached the hospital, on Fryday while in

P2

Rear of the battery a man of Co A was Shot through the breast with a 12 pound Shell, Sutch is the horrows of war & at this time the Roar of artillery & musketry is Sounding & the Shells & pieces are occasionally passing over me, we are not at the front ditches, but at the Reserve line, looks like they want to tear all the houses down, they annoy us, but looks like they mare not going to attack our lines in a Regular battle, the army is in good Spirits & feel confident (through the mercy of God) to hold the position against any assault that they can make, if they can be kept from flanking, we had a big Rain yesterday & were Cold last night on pickett, My Dear one, I do want to hear from you, but am waiting patiently until the communications are opened, the last I Rec, was by Tylor, the 15th, I have written several & sent by many chance, I

Shall Send this by Capt Kicks, father who is go to Ala, Start in the morning, Still pray for me & thank God that it is as well with us, as it is, Oh God hear our prayrs & continue, for Jesus Sake,

Your own husband Good bie S C Kelly

PS I have not Seen nor heared of Lt Pike in 8 or 10 days, he was able to come to Co then, but only on a visit, may be sent off to Macon or elsewhere SCK

PS

Since the above , Baird has Ret from Division hospital & Says that Pike is there & talks of coming to Co, it is on the far edge of the City (Sun Set) SCK   all the boys are well tell the people that those who are hurt & if no names all is well S

ATLANTA AUG 2OND 64

.02 P1

My Dear Amie I have about one moment to write long enough to thank God that I am yet Speared & well, Lt Pike Returned to Co this evening, it is now Sun Set & we are going on Pickett to night But little firing today, the boys all well except Some Slight Colds, I close may God bless us & the Cause that Seperates us, good bie your own husband S C Kelly

PS I have heard of no Casualities today SCK PS If you can Spear J. Hobbs, wife as mutch as five dollars let her have it & he will pay me as I am Scarce of money I have about 60 dollars but owe 42 dollars of it to men gone to hospital & may Return any day, & may not John Wilkinson is one of them 22 dollars Shaw the other, I Started it in a letter to them but it Ret in consequence of the Raid they are at Covington Ga, where is it that your kinfolks lives, So I might find Some of them if I be so unfortunate as to get Sick or wonded & had to be Sent off & Could not get to Ala, If I die I hope to be prepared for the change, I try to do my duty (unassuming) both towards my Country & my God, though verry unsatisfactory to my Self especially to God, but I am what I am by & through mercies of God through the Richusness of Christ good bie yours SCK

LINE OF BATTLE ATLANTA AUG 5TH 64 3 OCLOCK PM

.05 P1

My Dear Amie I Rec yours of the 22ond yesterday & of the 26ᵗʰ today I was glad to hear from you, but had not heared that S was gone, I Suppose that there is one bearing date Some where between the 15ᵗʰ (the one Tylor brought) & the 22ond whitch I Suppose would tell when he went &C, but he is gone & no more than I expected, I would be glad to Save them, but the Lords will be done & I try to be thankful that it is no worse &if it will please the lord to Spear our lives & give us our Independence & health, I think that we can make a living & be as happy as we need be on this trouble Some earth, My Dear I am So Sorry for you to be in Sutch a dread, but if they come, trust in the Lord, & be true to our cause & do not provoke them but humbly contend for womans Rights, could do without my pants a while, but send them, I need a coat hat & Shoes, worse than pants, my things I had with the waggons were burned by the Raid So Say Rumors, You Say that you need help from a true power, Remember that main extremity is Gods opportunity, Oh that God may

P2

make bare his arm in our deliverence from this crewel & warerful enemy & give us piece out of this confusion, The army was dissatisfied with the Removal of Johnson, but are better Reasembled & again taking courage, If you can Sell off your Surpluss Stuff & Stock do so, but who would buy the carrage or the Jack, I hate for you to sell Syphas but if you get his worth let him go & the 2 good mules & cotton, So if the Yanks come they will not take them & the money you can take care of it better than the property, If you cannot Sell the Jack let him stay at Hs & Risk the chance you have enough to trouble you, besides, My Dear your Pa ust to Say, so not cross the bridge until you get to it & Remember the bright side, Oh that the whole nation could prey & Call to God for his help in this time of need, There has not been any General engagement but at this time heavy Skirmishing & nearly every day so we go on pickett again to night, Mr Bryan is not verry well, H Graham & Hyatt are all safe so far, I heared that Dave Weaver lost his foot on the 22 last month Lt Coln Patterson & Capt McGee were both Killed & Capt Derrett that night 30th, our Lt Coln will now be Capt Elliott, who was wonded Rockey face (absent) Capt Deshazo is Senior who will _____ making me Senior Capt, God bless _____ husband

    S C Kelly

P3

PS I Rec a letter from S. Miller Kelly (one of Bro As boys) of Miss he is home wonded at Gettysburg, Mays not well yet, he Says all well at home, Sims is with Forrest, the Yanks have been in 12 miles of his Place, that he has 4 grown sisters single & one married, one at home & 2 little ones & a little brother, that 2 of his brothers in law with the army & Nathan is a prisoner Since Gettysburg fight, they have not heared of him in 6 months, been to wet in Miss this Season, Dated 15th July 64 Philladelphia SCK

LINE OF BATTLE ATLANTA AUG 7TH 64 2 OCLOCK PM

.07 P1

(Written on scrape paper dated Thursday morning June 29 from Amie)

My Dearest Amie I Rec yours of the 20th today whitch explained all about Sam, I wrote day before yesterday but did not get it off So I concluded to write another & Send them both together, This is Sunday & Comparatively

Speaking quiet, Some artillery a long way off towards the left, whitch is between here & home, I am Some what afraid that this will not Reach you, but not mutch trouble & perhaps you may get it the Lord only knows, Some Rhumor about a Raid in our County, but nothing Said in papers about it, Some talk about them at or about Mobile, No news from Graham yet, but I know that he will not come as long as he has a half of an excuse, Tylor is Staying around here he can make lots of money on papers, envelops &C I must close or miss again God bless us good bie yrs Sam

P2

FM Amies letter & Sims PS

yours of the 14th came today, I was so tired scouring but when I found the letter I was rested lots, I am nearly out of paper and do know where the next is to come from, but it will come, I will have to buy, 10 or 15 bu of corn or feed away to mutch of my wheat we are feeding on wheat now, I do not think we will make more than 100 or 125 bu, May God bless you and keep you in all in all the way and bring you home safe at last is my daily prayer, Your affectionate wife Amie,

PS this is a part of the letter written to Send by Airheart & as paper is scarce I use this Sam

.1 LINE OF BATTLE ATLANTA GA AUGUST 14TH 1864 12 OCLOCK

.04 P1

(Letter has a hole in center top & P3 is written between lines of P2)

My Dearest Amie I have been expecting a letter from you 3 or __ days but alass no letter Since the 20th July whitch came just came 2 weeks ago today (I believe) at an___ Rate it came in due time, I have answered them all ___t have not written in 4 or 5 days, Still expec___ to get one, but My Dear I will try, & do better I ____ know if life & health & opportunity, & material & ___ chance to Send them last that I will write at lea___ twice a week, I have been expecting that Graham o__ __rice or Palmer one or all of them would come back & _ring me letters &C but no come, All of them are absent with out leave, now Palmer was Sent from hospital & ordered to Report to Co on the 28th or 30th July & Prices time out about the same time. I Suppose that they are both at home & will Stay there as long as they can, I cant blame them mutch, that they aut to come back for there is no telling when we may need them bad, & the duties are already verry heavy, we are on pickett every 3rd day besides detailes for fatigue & guard duties, Rations only tolerable & especially every 3rd day when we draw beef, vegetables are about played out, we are Skirmishing with them more or less every day, Some Shelling of us nearly all the time, doing Some little damage, but less than one would immagine, Last night they kept up a Regular Cannonade all night across our lines & some fell in the City, One man killed & 4 or 5 wonded in our Brigade, Jasper Wingo Slight in thigh, So Slight that he is not sent to hospital & Lt Pike is Sick again & Sent to Division Hospital also John Patterson not Sick but a Sprained knee, Kim Argo Sent off Sick, N Baker Sgt N D Atkins Joe Kirby all Sick Sent to Regt, Old man Cornelius Hiram White Returned to camp and Frank Rountree was on post duty in the City of Atlanta & got Struck with Shell night before last on the leg (Severe) I fear will loose it, he is sent off to Rear, no General engagement yet, nor are the Signs any better than 10 days ago, I heard of Bryan a few days ago, he was going to come to see me, but has not yet, I cannot account for my not getting your letters, I hope you get mine, I had Rather do without my self, It the Yankees does not come through our country it will be a wonder to me, I am So fearful that they will come & take my Suit of jeans & the nice linsey Shirts & my Young Horse, Syphax & every thing else & tear up & destroy every thing and above all to insult you my Dear one, the partner of my youth may a just Lord forbid, Oh forbid it oh my God

P2

I do know but what I Shall need my clothes & haver sack, if I get justice I will be the _____ jor of the Regiment, but they may skip me on an exam__ion, If they do I Shall be perfectly indignant, & _____ tempted to quit the Regt (if I can) because Since _____ day of the death of Maj Francis (11 or 12th May 64) ___ this date I have done the duties of the office, in this Campaign (as hard a campaign as this Regt ever passed) with the exception of 2 days (being 21st & 22ond June) & have never heard any on complain about it except myself & when not on the duties of the Maj were in Command of my own Co, All is well that ends well & I trust that God is yet with me, I feel like he has thus far Sustained me & I yet trust him, tomorrow I am to be examined & if it goes well with me, then I will petition for a furlough to go home to Supply myself with a horse & Suitable clothing, but do not be disappointed for at this time I would have no use for a horse & at this crisis they may not let me go, but after the push is over then I think it will take, I am a Sight for Rags my old hat by, I got Tylors old one & am wearing it, my coat is out of credit, Shoes gone up, pants & Shirts best of all but if I had good clothes I would

Sport them mightly but I do hate to look worse than any one else Ie) & be Major of the 30th Ala

Turn it bottom upward & you can Read what letter else

P3

I have never Sought promotion, but if I were to let another pass me & any one of the 3 be absent or die I being the Senior would have the duties to do just as in the Campaign from Dalton, I had 2 Senior Captains one off wonded & the other Sick & I have the duties to do getting none of the proffets or advantages of the office, going on foot, packing & cooking up my own Rations &C So I conclude that if I could & had to do being Capt that I could do as well & be a full Major, My Dear I know that I have Said to mutch about this mater already, but I have nothing else to do but to write & nothing of more importance to write & besides that I feel like I aut to tell you all, I think that there is annother Captain that is preferred before me at head Qrtrs who may be a better officer than I am, but who has never done as mutch duty in the Regt as I have & a favorite when there is favors, for Since 26th Sept 63 he has seen home 4 times to my one & all but once or twice my claims were as good as his, enough of this, I will write you Soon & if you have ___ Sold Syfux hold him until I write again, I went to pr___ng to day, Brother & Capt Brewer preaching again, I wri__ you of him had a dozen or more morners, this sunday all is ____ quiet than usual, I wrote that I had lost my clothing not so, I Suppose, Tell Li___ W. that I have met with & got acquainted wit a Dr Thomson of Lovings Div, who took dinner whit him as they passed up here, he loves to talk about it & Sends his Respts &C may God have mercy upon us as a family & us as a nation & help us Soon to extricate our land from the en____ & give us peace is the daily praer of your own husband S C Kelly

LINE OF BATTLE ATLANTA GA AUG 18TH 64

.18 P1

My Dearest Amie I have not Rec a word from you since the 26th July, I cannot account for it, Joe Duncan Rec one from his wife today dated 14th Aug & mailed at old man Garretts, (Ragan post office) I

suppose by it there is no Yankees in that County but did not find out whether there was any mail line by Tadaga or not, I hope the best, but I am fearful that Something has happened, I have no war news to write, maters are, after the Same old Sort of Sharp Shooting & artillery firing, all the time more or less, Rhumors of both good & bad news every day, So many that a man to tell any thing has to Substanciate it by the best of authority, we are doing well under the circumstances, get plenty to eat Bacon & Corn bread & one day we drew one ear of new corn to the man, Some peas & about every 3 days beef whitch decreases the Rash, my Co Remaines about the Same Size, Sent to hospital Since I wrote you Wingo & Wm Dale both Slightly wonded Shell old man Cornelius Sick, Returned from hospital H Shaw, N Argo & John Wilkinson, heard from

P2

Lt Pike (no better) Rec notice that M Spraggins Died of Gang green (of wond Received 26th May) at Griffin Ga on 26th July, Rec a letter from Palmer dated Aug 5th at Macon Ga he was well, I have given out Grahams coming, I went before the board to be examined for Maj (as I wrote to you) but was Rejected, I am displeased at it, (I might say at my self) for I have acted for the last 3 month, but kissing goes by favores & I have never been a favorite but as the Coln acknowledged to me & others that I am always on hand & no objections to my official acts, but let it pass, if I have been Speared & protected & given health & Strength thus far I pray God to continue his blessings towards me & bring me through these days of trouble & then I will try to give him all the praise, I Simply want to do my duty in the fear of God, looking to him & expecting from him all the mercies & blessings that I So mutch Stand in kneed of, May God bless you & yours is my daily prayr, good bie Your own husband S. C. Kelly

LINE OF BATTLE ATLANTA AUG 20TH 64

.20 P1

My Dearest Amie I Rec yours (by G) today & was truly thankful to get them & find out how you all were, I thank God that it is as well with us this day as what it is, Oh that God will give us hearts of grattitude & thankfulness for his mercies towards us & that he will Still bless us & answer our prayrs, we ask for Christ Sake, I am well Duties about as usual, Sharp Shooting & Shelling more or less every day, Rhumors about as common Some favorable others unfavorable, Rations plenty except every 3rd day we draw beef, I was examined for Maj & Rejected, I thought hard of it, but may be it is all for the best, I thought that they prefered another to me (may be Rong) There will be annother chance Soon (I believe Shelly will be a Brigadier) & then I think that I can come in because I am Senior & also the next best chance & then all of the favorites have plaid out, I could tell you all if I were with you but enough of it for now, You Spoke of paying out all of your money, my advice is

P2

keep enough to do you whether those notes are paid now or not, I would Sell the wheat or flour & Save the money, Still those notes are a good excuse & do not let on but what you pay it on them to the negrows & children, So I conclude tis not best to let them know how mutch money you have, as to Selling Syphax I may need him, Could you not Send him down to James, on Ams & let him keep him & tell them that he was a Soldiers horse, or D Weaver, he is at home or will be soon, (he did loose his leg, Jim Montgomery was killed) as to the Cotton you cannot hide it, with out the negrows knowledge & there is no confidence in negrows now, I cant advise, do with it & every thing else on the place, according to your own notion for the best & if we loose it I will never once blame you (my dear) I feel like I cannot advise, because circumstances alter case & now I tell you, in this war I expect to sacrafise, but God being am helper, if I get with my life & sound & my family, I will try to be thankful Still they cant move the land but may get it from us some way, May God have mercy on us & Save & answer our prayrs is my prayrs

Your own Sam

LINE OF BATTLE ATLANTA AUG 23RD 1864

.23 P1

My Dear Amie I was in hopes that I would get a letter from you today but alass no letter, the Road is in order again & one man in the Co got a letter mailed at GA the 18th Aug, If I could get one that late I would feel like I had heared from home, but I am truly thankful that it is as well with us as it is, the enemy were not there (I feel assured) the 18th, Does the mail male come to Ladiga, if not do try to Send the letters where it does come even to GA, You can Send Bill on old Martha at least once a week, I Reckon that She is so poor that no one would take her away from him & yet She could make the trip, but I cant think that you are driven to that necessity yet, You asked whether to take the oath (If they come or leave your house, take the oath & if you Remain in their lines you can give us no assistance & if you are lucky enough to get back or they are driven back & you have any Scruples about it, You can then take the oath to our Government (or take it back) If you take it at all, You will be scared or forsed to take it & that Sertain not considered binding

P2

You said that you had a nice Calf Skin to make me a pair of boots, I wish I had them now, I was in hopes that G would bring my pants & Socks, I am to cut a long matter short, nearer out of money & nearer naked than I ever have been Since I have been in the army, I washed & patched yesterday, I can keep my self Sorty Respectable yet & do my best, but am no where to those whose good or bad fortune it has been to go home, I Shall draw every thing I can, as Soon as I can, the weather is warm & I feel thankful that I have been able & Speared to beat the heat & burden of this day, as I do hope that the hardest is past, I must close or miss the chance, I would like to write more but have but have learned to Sacrifise, S Pendland Says he will write day after tomorrow, Have to go on pickett to night, May God bless us as a family & nation & bring us together Soon in peace under our own Roof & none dare molest is my daily prayr, Good bie Your own Sam

SEPTEMBER 1864

LINE OF BATTLE NEAR LOVEJOY STATION MACON RR SEPTEMBER 4TH 1864

.04 Pl

My Dear Amie I hope I have a chance to Send you a few lines by Capt Burrs boy who is going to Start home, I am we;; & yet Speared from the missils of death, we left Atlanta a week ago & fought the enemy at Jonesboro on the 31st Aug, we lost out of the Co W P Kirby left arm broke & prisoner, Nim Argo Slight in leg, Sam Pendland Slight on Rump, R W Prater Spent ball on thigh, David Phillips Missing, it was hot times but it pleased God to Spear me for whitch I try to feel thankful, our loss was heavy in the Regt, we are about 25 or 30 miles from Atlanta & 8 or 10 below Jonesboro on the 1st of Sept our Corps left Jonesboro & went in the Direction of Atlanta next day turned east Y have been on the march ever Since until this morning formed here, we are in Reach of there balls & once & a while one comes over, I cannot go into a detailed account, but Say that we have marched hard but had plenty

P2

Our forces evacuated Atlanta on the night of the 1st Sept, Crops are good considering the land all through here, Some of the people are moving back but the most of them Stay at home, my advice is Stay at home, bad either way My Dear, I cannot write mutch, I have not heared from home Since yours of the 20th Aug,

If I Should be so unfortunate as to be taken prisoner & you Should be fortunate enough to get a letter from me, hold it to the fire until you nearly Scortch it, I close May God bless you & yours & hear & answer your prayrs is my prayr asked for Christ Sake Good bie Your own dear Sam

PS I drew coat pants & Shoes & Swapped hats & borrowed 50 dollars of Graham, So as the boys Say, I am all Setting, we have heared no news in a week don't know what is going on, Scarcely any Rhumors, OH that God would have mercy upon us Spedely SCK

CAMP NEAR LOVEJOY STATION GA SEPT 8TH 1864

.08 P1

(Ending of letter written upside down in margin)

My Dearest Amie I have another chance to Send by Capt McCaines boy & have but few moments to write before he Starts. I have just come in off of pickett & you must be Satisfied with Short letter in Sutch times, there is no Yanks in hearing of where I have been, I went on yesterday evening & Stayed 24 hours as brigade officer of the day, I have nothing to write except that I am truely thankful to God the author & fiver of every good & perfect gift, we have been in Camp 3 or 4 days & no Shells nor minee balls to molest or make us afraid, tis Said that the enemy have fallen back to Atlanta or else they are flanking again, though more generally believed that they are falling back, as they left our wonded at Jonesboro & tis Said that they are tearing up the RR, we have got out our wonded W P Kirbey of my Co died, his arm was broken & they too out the bone for about 3 inches & he died after he fell into our hands, Several of our wonded died, our loss on the 31st was considerable when we charged their works, but we paid

P2

them back in double Rates on the next day when they charged ours, our loss comparatively Small, we were Some what dishearten at the defeat the 31st & at the evacuation of Atlanta, but hopes is now Revived & the army think that he has fallen back because Wheeler has cut his Rash, I believe it, & think that it has been cut Since the 19th Aug, but they had about 30 or 40 days Rations on hand & the whole County to forage in, but that cant last, Scouts Report that they have Stripped the County of ever thing, that the women & children are Seen Roving in their Camp picking up every Scrap to be found, their Camp is full of gritters made out of canteens & every indication is that they are Scarce, Oh that God would Stretch forth his arms in our Salvation, as a nation & family, My A I guess that if nothing happens that in a Short time that I will be promoted to Major, I am Still acting, & Coln S will be Brig, then Maj Elliot will be Coln, Capt Burr Lt Coln & then I am the next, I want you to get josh or James or Some one else to keep Syphax for me, I have no Idea how I can get him, but it will be a month or so, before it is confirmed if I had passed the board, I must close May God bless you & yours & hear our prayrs is my prayr good bie Your own Sam

CAMP NEAR LOVEJOY STATION GA SEPT 13TH 6 PM 64

.13 Pl

My Dearest Amie I Rec yours of the 31st aug yesterday & today of the 28th aug & also of the 6th Sept all of whitch I was so glad to get, the last I had Rec before was of the 20 aug, I have written several, if you get you will be posted, I Rec a letter from Sisters Mary & Emma both day before yesterday that told me the Sad tale of the death of my Dear old Mother, You have no Idea how it affected me, & more especially when I Saw it was on the Same evening that I was in charge at Jonesboro the hottest place that I ever was in, if Sutch a thing is possible for God be praised for his wonderful protection towards me, I felt like that God would take care of me, & So he did for whitch I try to be thankful, Oh my Dear I know that I Shall miss Mother at home if it is my lot to ever be there, She was almost as a Statue, but for 28 years have I Seen her busy in the corner or about the house but alass, the Strongest tie in earth to a family & especially to ours is gone, a mothers house was the place to meet each other, but alass She is no more, may we all be prepared to

P2

meet her in Our Fathers house, an house not made with hands eternal in the heavens, where our fathers & Sisters & mothers & o0ne dear brother is gone, Oh these are times of trouble & one by one of our family are falling & we two must Soon follow according to the coarse of nature, we have already passed the

spring & Summer & are now in the autumn of life with leads blooming for the grave, but Oh if this crewel war would close & let us meet again to Spend the fall & winter of our age, in peace & quietude , I feel like that I would be the most thankful on earth, I live for you & the children & oh that God will hear our prayrs & answer with answers of peace, I must close I am officer of the pickett & must Ret to my post, all is quiet a truce of 10 days this is 2ond no guns no boom of Cannon no enemy in 3 or 4 miles, Oh that as this is the first armistice of the war that it may Soon be followed by one in a larger Scale & for the adjustment of this national difficulty, I yet trust in God to give us peace & the cause that Separates us Your own Husband S C Kelly

CAMP 30TH ALA NEAR LOVEJOY STATION SEPT 16TH 1864

.16 .17 P1

(This letter is burned in the middle, written between line & in margins)

My Dearest Amie I have written to you Since I Rec yours of the 6th Sept, but was hurried & did not answer it to my Satisfaction, I will try to answer all the points now, but I will first Say that I am well & as hearty as I could ask to be, all the Co is with me (There is 46 of us all now I believe) so except Joe Duncan & Thomas Connary who are just a little grunty, we have been drawing beef & corn bread only for the last 8 or 10 days, until yesterday we drew bacon (a pound to the man) but beef today, peas, Molasses (Sure Sign the boys Say of a move), It would amuse you to see the men draw Rash, it is cooked & brought in Sacks each to Company then laid out in ___ for 5 men (as equal as they can guess) 5 Stand round and count one 2, 3, 4, 5, 6, 7, 8, 9 10 and then the Sgt will cause Some disinterested person to turn his back, & then he (the Sgt) will ask (& putting his hand on one pile) who tis this & ha answers 7 or any other No & then Says pick up the pile &So on until the whole is gone, then each Set of 5 goes off & divides it into 5 piles & one turnes & it is touched off in the same way, It is just like we divide fish when we go Saining, I introduced it in my Co 2 months ago, when we had nothing to weigh & but little time to go on, & now the whole army So far as I know practice it, it gives general Satisfaction & in all divides there is good & bad peaces & the Sgt is not accused of partiality, I draw in common with the men & take whatever is falls to my lot, Sometimes very light but I frequently Set down & eat every bite of meat before I quit, if bacon I generally have plenty but beef is & will be Scarce, I miss

P2

Bill Estier, he is as free hearted as his mother & is neat & clean as any in the Co, he is Chief Cook, & we make hash & Soup & Cush, & poor do & live generally fat & full, My Dear I feel like I have wasted this mutch paper, but what of that, it only costs 33 1/3 cts per sheet bt $1 worth this morning, I am glad to hear of the Revivals at home there is a considerable Revival going on in our Brigade, but we too are behind, we have the poorest preacher I ever heared other is an old private of a Ga Regt that has preached for us 3 night, & while he preaches or prays all is Right, but if Joe W tries it, it is like throwing water on a fire, I am Sorry for him & try to pray for him, ____ne of my young men are taking an interest in the meeting, I am ____kful, Oh that they _____ Cant you get Mrs ___wart to join the ba_____ I am a little surprised at Mrs Wears girls, joining the babtist, Oh that God would Revive us both at home & in the army, My Amie I am Sorry for you, You are apt to hear So many Reports, but be careful that you do not make me an Idol, I to am in the hands of the living God & if you worship me more than God, I am your Idol I know that you love

383

me, & hope I will appreciate it, but you must love God more & pray to him for me & yourself & the children & the cause of our Country, & for peace &C &C and may he hear & answer our prayrs with answer of peace, You Spoke of weaning the Colt (Taflua) is it fine, & the best way to wean is never let it Suck after it is once taken off, You Say that Syphax is Stancly, I under stand that he is getting fat, is he fine looking, or would he do for a Major to Ride, I have no doubt now, but that Coln Shelly will be Brigader

P3

(he is now acting in place of Cumming who was wonded 31ˢᵗ Aug 64)

& then Maj Elliott will be Coln of our Regt & Capt Burrh Lt Coln & then I inline to contend for Maj again, if I fear the like consequences but I know that Elliott as Coln, &that I as Senior Capt & as good a chance as there is in the Regt, that my chances are good, I was indignant at the idea of acting all through the campaign (& Still acting) to be Rejected before a board of examiners, Some of who are no more competent than myself because, What, because the men that passed me was a favorite of the Coln & was not a better military man, but a more business man, & Set round & tell big tales to officers &C a thing I never done, I am better reconciled & hope that I ____or given, but I never will forget, Sorry Dear _____ you this _____ how the was managed, I am thankful that God has enabled me to Sustain my Reputation as a Soldier as well as I have, & to Serve my Country in the capacity that God may place me is the highth of my ambition, good officers are getting Scarce, Cant you get James or Josh or Gladden to take care of Syphax for you, I fear that he will be procured, or Stolen, & they could Say that he was a Soldiers horse, I am Sorry for Mrs Whitesides, Does Billy seem concerned about Religion, impress it upon him & nex an education, make him Read when he has leisure & do not confine him to close, but keep him in practice, Mt A you aut to See H Forney & ask him if it is not best to Rent the old home Stead again & if So let Mr G go a head & Rent it, Why did you not get mutch wool, was it because I was not there to Shear as I did last Sept, You Spoke of Pee,B. he is (as the mexicans would say) nonao,

Your Shoats are Scarce & I guess Small, put them up or else feed them on high or green corn, You Speak of the abundance of vegetables, verry few come to

P4

my Shear this year, but we have eat every Sugar cane Stalk in 3 miles of here, forage plaid out, as to fruit I get a bite or two of blackberry, about one dozen peaches (all said) about 4 dozen apples at from one to two dollars per dozen, about 4 dozen Roasting ears, as to water melons it has been my misfortune to See perhaps ½ dozen, but not for Sail, I passed Gen P's Staff one day eating one, when they did change hands it was from 6 to 15$ oweing to size, Are you making your own Molasses or getting Tom to make them, where are you grinding it, if you make yourself, I have drawn pants, coat & Shoes, I write you before my own Shirt is giving way, thread bare on the elbows, the other I threw away at Chattahoochee River July, one of my new Shirts (domestic) you Sent b__ W. I have never had on _____

_____ book & papers, I Shall kneed my clothes by _____ month if there was any way to get them, have them Ready by the time we go into winter Qrtrs, if we ever do, I would like to have a good pair of boots, made on the las__ that my Shoes were (you sent me at Dalton) but I want them at least ½ inch wider on the bottom, you Spoke of Selling wheat & flour, have you any more to Sell, & at what price did you Sell it , You never said, as to a Safe place, no where is Safe now, but I think you had better Sell every thing that you can Spare, that the Yanks could take off or destroy, & hire out the ___ grows to the government, think about that & write to Mr Gladden & Josh & get there advice & James too, & take the money & you & the children be Ready to pick with Patience & Dice & Tom to get out of there way, Still it dont seem like that would do either, but if the negrows are not first out of the way they will all go Certain & may go if you move them, So in that case you would loose all & all you left behind, Oh that God would Spear you of that trouble,

(turn letter upwards)

P5

and direct you is my Daily Prayrs, as to the mistake in the taxes if the estate, I know noting about it, let them work it out, I know that I owe on notice besides inline of 1225$ besides Some things bought at the Sale & Some Rent, all of what I want you to pay as you can Commencing on the Smallest first & not pay any on a note unless you have enough to cover interest too, Be Sure to keep enough to answer your own purposes if you Sell the cotton, You will have lots of money, but I do not Say Sell, I Say do as you think best after getting Sutch advice as you can Rely upon, You Said that if the Yankees had come that it would have Killed you __ can not mean but put your trust in God, he has been with us & is ___ trust yet, Still with us & has promised to be with us to the end, trust in, hope or pray on & wh____ in life or in death, all will be well, I have been looki___ ___tter from you 2 days ____ but no letter yet, I did not expect _____ write when _____ communications are cut

but write every 4 or 5 days ___ whenever there is a chance to get them, I try to get chances to Send by hand at least part of the way, they are more certain, I do love to get letters from you, & when I have time, I love to write to you, You better to any one else, but always did love to talk to you & now I am deprived of that privilege & I am assured that you will not become weary in Reading a long letter, & I have nothing else to do, So I conclude that it will by nothing a miss to write anything that I would tell you even I with you, Yes I would kiss you a dozen times in a minute & if money would buy a furlough (if but for one hour) I would be dimeless in 5 minutes but no use talking Sutch things are not possible in the nature of things, but depend upon it that I am coming as Soon as I can get there honorably, Suppose J. B. Palmer is at ease now, I say that

(turn to left)

P6

because he annoyed me while on this campaign with his

petitions to be Retired &C be permitted to join this that & the other, when I had no time even to get & cook my Rations, & nothing to write with nor on & his papers first & last had I complied. Would have taken more writing than the declaration of independence, I wonder if he knows that I Received a notice from the Dr at Greensboro that Sgt J B Palmer was Returned to duty & ordered to Report to his Command without delay, I want you to tell him that, I was looking for him & the next news I heard was he was at home on a sixty days furlough, ask him for me who gave him that furlough, I am in the dark & think that there is Some mistake, I have not Reported him absent without leave yet, but will Report him as on Detached Service if his furlough is g__uine he had better Send me a correct Coppy, My Dear Amie ____ the lines to try _____ home, You are mistak__ I left on the 3rd & arrived at Dalton 5th February 64 ___ _as Mr G ever got Fathers tomb stone if not when he gets, get one for Mother also, I have not Rec yet the letter you Spoke of, the last letter Mother ever wrote, Sent by Joe Gladden, I did not know that Joe was coming to this army, & do not yet know to what Command he was coming to, If Semion Weaver does die there will be a helpless gang, I do hope he may live until Some of those children get grown, Taylor & Steve are good big boys I Recon, how many children has he by his last wife, Is Wm & Henry or both get well of wonds & Returned to there Commands, You Said that David was still bad of & Cole and Liz were gone to See him, where is he at, I was in hopes that he was at home, did he loose his foot as I heared, where is Dick, I never learned whether he went with Wheeler or not

(turn to left)

P7

I am in hopes that Toby has got well, but I had Rather hear of his death than for him to do as Sam has done, then he could do us no harm, Sam is an ungreatful Reach, has been Sick more than any other negrow on the place & had more attention & then without provocation to leave Sutch a home & join the Yanks is base in him,

I Say it to you & I believe it, that he never will do any better than he has done while with us neither free nor bond, May the Lord have mercy upon him, How many Babies has Mrs Ferguson, I have forgotten, You Spoke of seeing Mrs Pike I told him of it, he said that was the latest account of home he had, he is Still verry unwell at the Division hospital, the other day he came b___ ___ up I was Surprised to see him, for I thought that h____ ___ he has never a___ for a furlough but he is in my _____with _____ for this year he is affected in his _____ back, If I were in his fix I would go home, if they would let me & if not I would write to you & let you try for me, I dont want to alarm Mrs P but I believe that if he Stays here that he will not live 2 months, though he is verry tough, but Seems to be going just like Bale, gradually worse, & low Spirited, You Say in your last that you had Rec mine of the 27th aug that you are Sorry for me & thankful that is as well with me as what it is, What do you mean by Saying Send it to me if you Still have it, What it, I have forgotten, I do not know where I was at when I wrote it, L have written more than I expected & I now being this epistle to a close by Saying that I hope we may meet again soon when the war is over & when we can talk to our hearts content, May God our father continue his blessings & mercies towards us is my prayr, Good bie your affectionate husband S C Kelly

P8

17th 7 AM I had no chance to Send yesterday We are at the Same place,

Some Rhumor about our leaving, this is the 6th day of the truce, I have but little idea what we will do, I have not Seen any one who has come out of Atlanta Some Say one thing & Some Say another all Rhumors, you can learn more from the papers than I can tell as to my letters being unsealed, I do not think that they are opened, they do not Stick well at first all this lot of envellops are So, Some of them I Stick with gluton others I Risk So & the handling they come open, I Saw Elisha Orean day before yesterday he is well & I guess a good officer, he is Capt in 29th Regt, he was wonded in the neck at Resacca 15thMay & has been home nearly all the time Since, he is Married about a year ago, he married ___ lady that was with ____ at our _____

Miss _____ Galisville, _____ drill time more _____ that I can Send this as far as Selma by hand & I no_____ ____ise by, Surprised that the meeting is Still going on, last night after a Short Sermon a call was made for morr___ with out any Singing or excitement & the brave Soldiers walked forward & knealt down to at least 100, I think that one 3rd of the congregation was moved or ½ the men professes there 3 joined 1 methodist & 2 babtist M Phillips of my Co one of them, May the lord Still Revive us & Save us all in heaven, Your own S

16th there were 13 babtised today

LINE OF BATTLE NEAR PALMETTO SEPT 24TH NOON

.24

My Dear Amie I have not wrote in a week nor have I Rec one from you in that time, we moved last Sunday monday & tuesday & came to this place & Round about way of about 30 miles, we are now on the west point & Atlanta RR we have built Strong works & laying behind them, we moved to this part of the line wednesday & it was said that the enemy were in 2 ½ miles, but Scouts Report none in less than 7 miles & only Scouts at that, I have never believed we would fight here, but the Lord only knows where we will fight, or where we will go or when, It is not in man that walketh to direct his Steps, My Dear Amie I have not been well Since last sunday night, (this is Sunday) I have had the disentery have it yet, or to use a common expression I am what I used to Call at home foundered but I think that I Shall get well now as the forage is pretty well gone ____h I must Close as I only have a few moments to w__te God bless us Still good bie ___r own husband SCK

LINE OF BATTLE NEAR PALMETTO GA SEPT 28TH 64

.28 P1

My Dearest Amie I Rec yours of 17th Sept last night at 8 oclock & the mail goes out so early of the morning that I have not had time to write, So I will try & have it Ready to Send in the morning, in my last to you I wrote that I was unwell I think I am well now, I have been unwell for 8 or 10 days until yesterday & today, the health of the Co is good 48 men present for duty & nearly every day Some one comes in old Mr Reid from Rabbit town came in today, he left us Sick at Marietta, I am glad that Frank Rountree had got home, I never learned how bad he was wonded, I began to think long of the time, between letters, I believe that I get them, Henry Weaver was out to See my a few days ago, he left home fryday was a week (this wednesday) he told me about David & Elisha & William he did not know anything about John, his (Henrys) leg is not well yet, he has been home on furlough Since you were there Said that his Pa was on the mend but 2 of Backers children were Sick he is about 2 miles from here I fear that my boots will be to narrow & high in the instep Oh that I could get to come home & get my new Suit I Suppose that you are having me a hat made also, J Palmer wrote me that he was going to carry wool to make 7 hats, that includes me, I will Soon be out again, out of everything & money too if I keep on Spending for Something to eat, I buy pork at two dollars, mutton at one & a half & every thing else that is to buy in that proportion, we draw poor beef & we are close to an old mans house where he is Selling out every thing, & Soldiers will eat if money will

P2

buy it, I drew one Months pay just before we left Lovejoy Station, I have about 100$ I have Sent up an aplication to go to Macon for the officers baggage, for a 6 days if I go it will clean me out of cash, my things are not worth the expense, but I cant do well without them & cant buy others & then it will be a Rest from duty that long, I do not know that it will be approved don't care mutch & then there is a talk of us leaving here Some say one place

& Some another none know, but if we travel far we cannot carry them (it is Raining & it Spatters my paper), Some Say we are going to Blue Mt to flank the Yanks out of Atlanta but the Lord only knows when or where, there has not been a yank in 7 or 8 miles of here these are pasable times to what we have been used to, I lost my pen & penset Stock (Silver one that I had when at home) I am now writing with a goose quill pen Tell J Palmer that I Rec his of the 18th inst & that I will answer it Soon, that this is the last Scrap of paper that I have, he talks like he is doing lots for you & Mrs G, for whitch I am glad, make him help you, he hates the hospital So bad, & when his furlough is out, get him to come & bring my clothes & if I can get him in as a courier I will do my best &C if we come to Blur Mt you may look for me, but I hope that this army may never pass through there, it is it is destructive to any country, I think that you have done well by trading old Kit I have written to Mr Gladden today about Mothers estate, (Ie) for him to appraisr & proceed to Sell or divide estate, & be Rented as the balance &C I asked him to act as grant, I am Sorry to hear that you are all So afflicted but thankful that it is no worse, I fear that the cavalry will break you up

P3

(Written between lines & upside down of P2)

but trust in God & he will yet Serve you they have been passing there for the last 15 months & you are yet Speared, I am glad to hear of the Revivals, there is a good feeling in this Regt & in my Co Oh that they would turn to the Lord. Dick Prater nor Sam Prater neither bad off in my opinion when they left, I have been looking for them back, May God Still continue his blessings toward us is my prayr for Jesus Christ Sake, good bie your own Sam PS I will back you on envelope & Send you S

OCTOBER 1864

NEWNAN GA OCT 3RD 64 2 PM

.03 P1

My Dearest Amie I am here on My way to Macon Ga after the officers baggage of our Regt, I have leave of Absence for 6 days, I am now detained waiting for the train, have been here Since 9 AM I left the Regt at 12 oclock no 1st Oct footed it here 49 miles, detained at the River by the bridge washing away about one hour before I got there, an I Should have taken train last night at 7 PM, I got within 5 miles of here last night & learned that car went out at 7 every evening, I left the army at a Cross Roads called, Scined Chestnut on the Powder Springs Road with in a few miles of New hope Church, I expect that it will take me 3 days after this to go to Macon & do my business, I am ordered to Ship the Baggage to Talladega, I expect to be at Blue Mt on next monday Night & if you can or want to Come to See your Sister, I would like to have your Co home, I may not Reach there in that time I will have to Stay one day in Talladega, I will have more than I can carry on a horse, I thank God that it is as well

P2

with us as what it is May he continue his blessings is my prayr good bie your own Sam

PS Do not be disappointed if I am behind the time trains So uncertain & do not put yourself to too mutch trouble I can come on the Stage &C. S

NOVEMBER 1864

CAMP 30TH ALA NEAR FENCE ALA NOV 11TH 1864

.11 P1

My Dear Amie after Seven hard days Ride I arrived at this place & found that Lees Corps had moved across the River, I had no difficulty in getting here except the Rain & mud & one deep creek whitch I went 10 miles out of the way to get to a bridge, I had company the first day but did not get to Gadsden the 2ond 3rd & 4th by my Self except 6 or 8 miles in the evening of the 4th & that evening got off the Mountain, whitch I was alone I was in the lonesomest poorest county I ever Saw, the most of the way among the tories & bushwhackers, but God was my protector & carried me Safely through the balance of the way I had company, I was cordially Rec both by officers & men & was not blamed, I came from Gadsden to Blountsville from there to Moulton by way of Days Gap

P2

then to Florence, making in all 160 miles through bad Roads my pony Stood the trip finely but pulled off in the Mud both pare Shoes, I had him Shod yesterday, I have no news except Forest has made a halt, I guess you Saw the account R S Miller was at the Regt on the 18th Oct I believe he is at Gen Hoods Qrters I will go & See, he left the letter & a note for me Showing his Regt &C I am uneasy about you all but try to Resign you to the mercies of God, I am anxious to hear, this is the first chance I have had to Send & this is by mail, I wont to have my clothes washed today, I Swapped off my boots to Coln Elliott, mine were getting too Small, I think both are bettered, I must close I will write again May God Still continue his mercies towards us is my prayr good bie, Your own husband S C Kelly

NOV 13TH 12 PM ON RIVER BANK AT FLORENCE

.13 P1

My Dear A I am well & have just Started over the R to See RSM he is on the other Side I now waiting on Stewarts Corps to cross, I think that the whole army will cross today & then go into tenn I could not Send this but Capt F is waiting to cross & is going home, I think that Sim will cross today

P2

I wrote you day before yesterday & Sent by mail I was 6 ½ days getting here had no difficulty but came the most of the way by my Self

May God bless us all is the prayr of your own Sam good bie S C Kelly

ARMY OF TENN NEAR FLORENCE ALA NOV 15TH 1864

.15 .16 P1

My Dearest Amie I have written you two (pencil) letters both verry Short, but I now have a chance to Send one by Frank Turner to Talladega Co who is going for clothes for the men of the Regt, he will be here in the morning before I can write, & I now take this evening although it is getting dark, you will See his advancement & if any one wants to Send clothing he is a good hand, I feel like I was well Supported, I got myne from Sim today & am as well pleased as I could be, all Say that it is so nice, & I got a good taylor to put the buttons & lace on it & now I am called by every one that calls me at all Capt, I did not get over the first day (Sim was on the South Side & I on the north) but I got over last night & Stayed all night with him, he has a good position & I advised him to keep it as long as he could, he has plenty to eat, that is more than we can Say, but we make out, & the pontoon bridge is So crowded that Some times we Run Short, but beef cattle & every thing else passing over & occasionally it breaks So we

P2

have to wait until it comes, I have not Suffered, I have Some of my bread yet perfectly good & the larger portion of my bacon, I gave Sims Some of it & he fried a Rabbet for breakfast in the grease, I mess with Lt Landers & Griffith of my Co but Sleep at Head Qrtrs & keep my horse there, I am not Major but Still acting in that capacity, there has not been any promotions yet, but each one is acting in the capacity Senior to his Rank, I have had lots of offers for Syphax, but I tell them that he is not for Sail nor Swap, My Dear I do not know any news (Certain) all uncertainties to Soldiers, tis Said that we are going into Tenn, but when I do not know already 2 Corps are on this (the north) Side of the River &

Gen Forest is here to go with us, I think that Stewarts Corps will cross tomorrow all the Generals are here & the men are all eager for the trip, May God direct the expedition & make it Successful, I am uneasy & anxious to hear from you now to dark to write May God bless & Save us as a family & a nation is my daily prayr, good bie Your own Sam

NOV 16TH BEFORE BREAKFAST SAME CAMP AS YESTERDAY,

P3

My Dearest Amie I have no news to write more than I have already written, but I have Some letter time this morning & for fear that you have not got those that I wrote Soon after my Return, I thought to give you Some of the detail of my trip here the first day, I had company from Lt Pike to near Gadsden where I Stayed all night at the widow Words, next day I crossed the River & went 15 miles on the top of the Mountain & Stayed at a Courier Station at the house of an old tories who had a Son in the Lincoln army, there I Slept in the crib with the with the couriers & got Stocked with lice & got no corn for my horse, next day I passed through Blountsville & 7 miles this Side making about 33 miles & Stayed at an old mans by the name of Putnam, he is a brother to old Mrs Garrett, there I got corn but had to feed myself, next day I traveled off the Mountain about 35 miles & over took in the evening 3 Texans & Stayed all night at an old Widower by the name I believe of Dodrage 4 mile of Days Gap, then I was in the Tennessee

P4

valley, I came on with my Texas friends next day about 2 miles, to a Smith Shop where they came on 3 others of their brigade, who were waiting for others to come up, when they (the party of 10 or 15) intended to make a Raid on Some bushwhackers who had been committing depradation in the valley, & it was Said had lots of horses & other plunders Stored in certain caves, I Stopped about 1 hour & wished them mutch Success, & left by my Self but Soon Struck in with a Tennesseean by the name of Lansten, accompanied me to the River 3 days Ride, that night we Stayed 4 miles this Side of Molton in Laurence Co at an old man by the name of Moore, that night we fell in with a Squad of Armstrongs cavalry under

Lt Barbee, creeks Swimming or deep fording we went 10 miles out of the way to get to the bridge but came near Swimming 2 or 3 Sloughs traveled 27 miles & Stayed at a Mr Hamptons who was in the Service, his wife & Sister keeping house with 80 negrows & only 3 men on the place, next day 4 miles to Ride to Florence but it was 2 or 3 oclock before I got over the River on the pontoon 715 yards wide to Island & 170 yds the other making nearly 900 yds,

God bless you & all S C Kelly

PS I am Sorry that I cannot interest you in a letter but Sutch is the case I know nothing to write it is Rhumored that Lincon is Reelected, I Suppose we will hear in a few days, it is also Rhumored that the Malitia of Georgia Alabama & Missippi are coming here to garrison this place, the Yanks were here when our army came & they got farther they are in 6 or 7 miles of here, Armstrong is fighting them,

My Dear A if you have a chance Send those Co book by Lt P or Some one else, they will be needed this winter, they can bring them on the R Road will soon Run to the River now Runs to 1 or 2 Stations this Side of Cherokee 22 miles from the River, I close may the Lord bless us all , good bie your own S

NOV 26TH 4 PM 1864 NEAR COLUMBIA TENN

.26 Pl

My Dear Amie I have a chance to Send a letter out & this is all the paper I can Start I am well we came here today & our forces are

Skirmishing with the enemy, Forest has been driving them for 2 or 3 days, they Seem to be well fixed here I do not know whether we will fight or flank them out of the place there is a RR Running from here to Nashville 45 miles, it also Runs from here to Decater Ala We have traveled 5 days besides today 5 or 6 days, this is in Murrey Co a Ritch Co & lots of corn & hogs, we had pork issued to us last night I wish that I could wright

P2

Something interesting I am getting along finely, I mess with the Coln & Major & So far we get along finely, My horse is doing well I tend to him my Self, I had him appraised yesterday, they Said he was worth 1233 dollars, we have had Some cold weather Sleet & Snow today Rain, I Swapped off my Roundabout for a vest Sal Duncan had made out of my old coat, does well, May God bless us all & Save us is my daily prayr I have been uneasy about you & our County, we get but little news, I have not had a word from you Since I left, God bless you Good bie your own Sam

DECEMBER 1864

HD QUARTERS 30TH ALA REGT IN LINE OF BATTLE NEAR NASHVILLE TENN DEC 6TH 1864

.06 P1

My Dear Amie I hope that I will have a chance to Send you this letter, I have written before but no chance to Send out, I have not Rec a word from home Since I left but hope that God has been merciful to you, By the mercie & blessing of God I am well & yet Speared unhurt, we are under fire of the enemy & have been for 3 days (

Since here Sharpshooters & artillery) we are in line of battle I Suppose within 1 ½ miles of the city, while they are in there Strong hold in the City, We arrived here 4 or 5 days ago & have been gradually moving up, we are in our 3rd line of works, I do not think that we will assault there works but flank Round or do Some thing else, Forest is doing good Service & I hope that we will Soon have the road cleared from here to Atlanta as we already have Road to Pulaski, we will have a train from the latter in a few days, we had a big fight at Franklin on the 30th Nov. our Corpse was not engaged, we were left at Columbia while Cheatam & Stewarts Corpse flanked them & gave them battle at Franklin, we charged them at Columbia

P2

& drove them loosing in our Brigade 11 killed & 46 wonded, my Co loosing none one man Slightly wonded but with us now (E Duckett) we marched from Columbia to Franklin 22 miles & bivowacked at dark the battle Still Raging & had been from 2 PM & Continued until 7 PM, We were Ready & fully expected to go in the next morning but day light discovered that they had Retired leaving there dead & wonded on the field, It was a dreadful Carnage our men fought them hand to hand across the breastworks, after they had charged through an open field for ½ mile through grape & canister of 48 pieces & at least the minie balls of twenty thousand men but on they went to there 3rd & last line of works, they Strewed the field with our dead while we filled there ditches with there dead, I saw them burring & I Suppose on the field that we had the most dead, but this Side of the town they had the most dead, but this Side of town they had 100 dead & mortally wonded besides the Sitizens Say that they carried off two trains of dead, if that be so there loss is grater than ours, our loss was I Suppose 500 killed & 1500 wounded, among the killed was Capt Elisha <u>Orean</u> Coln Shelly was Slightly wonded but not disabled, Maj Gen Cleaburn was killed 5 Brigadier Genls killed lots of Colns & Capt & Lts & men but thank God we gained the victory

P3

yesterday morning busy about cooking & fixing a Sharpshooter busied himself from there pickett line & Shot at a bunch of our men & wonded Wm Duncan through the Right foot, going in at the instep & coming out behind the little toe, I think under the bones, about one hour after at the Colns quarters another man was Shot through the head & died last night, So you See that we are in the mids of death but thanks be to God he has yet Speared me, Oh that he will continue his blessing towards us, I must close God bless us all, I am Messing with the Coln, good bie Your own husband S C Kelly

1865 SCK Letters Transcribed

January 1865

Near Burnsville Miss January 1st 1865

.01 P1

My Dearest Amie I understand that we will have a chance to send out letters this evening & I now hast to drop you a few lines to let you know where I am & how I am & have been doing, I Rec yours of the 6 Dec & 27 Nov about 10 days ago, while we were camped near Columbia Tenn but we have had no chance to Send out Since, I was so thankful to learn that you were doing as well as what you were, We are in Tishamingo County Miss about 15 or 20 miles above or Northeast from Corinth on the R. R. we have come down the Road from Cherokee Station, we crossed the River about Florence 5 or 6 miles, had but little difficulty in crossing, We were attacked at Nashville on Thursday the 15th on our left wing & were flanked out of our works or, about half the line we did no fighting on our part of the line but at night fell back & entrenched about a mile & a half, there we were attacked by Sunrise with a furious bombarding, even before our works were half finished but over Shells & Shots we persisted & in about 1 hour we were Ready for a bloody Reception, in about

P2

an hour they made there appearence, with a line of Skirmishers & 2 or 3 lines of battle, they soon engaged our Skirmishers who were soon driven in & our boys from the trenches gave them Sutch a warm Reception that they took Shelter in our old pickett (posts) holes & the adjacent hollows & we were not assalted any more during our Stay from that quarter but the Commanding was terrible on the left, they fired incessantly all day with frequent charges, while we were holding our position easily & had but little apprehensions of any one else giving, but to our great Surprise & dismay we Saw men ½ mile to our left Running to the Rear & an incessant Shout (but I thought it our boys) we looked again & Saw the Brigade on our left Run out & in an instant Saw the Stars & Stripes & heard the loud appeals from the Yanks, Surrender you d d Rebbles, I Saw we were flanked out, Shooting at us in frount & a line coming Square down the ditch, it was a Rout, we were not whipped, but it Stood ever man to take care of no one, I was among the last to leave, but Run out under a Shower of bullets & Shells, God Speared me thus far, among the prisoners they Capture or is missing is S Pendland, Sal & Joe Duncan, M Evans, Journey Baker, Dale Green, Rhodes, S S Taylor, I Wilkinson, Wiley Turner wounded & left,

(The rest of letter written in the margin)

we have a hard Retreat our Division covered the Retreat a day & half, we have lost ½ our artillery & half of our army in killed wounded captured & missing I will write the first chance we have orders to move at 12, May God bless you & yours & answer your prayrs is my prayr good bie your own Sam

TUPELO MISS JANUARY 7TH 1865

.07 P1

My Dear Amie I hope that I will have a chance to Send you this letter whitch leaves me well as to health but I have a Rising or Carbunkle on my Rump, whitch has been hurting me for the last 8 or 10 days, I got So bad off that I had to Ride in the ambulance 4 days, I am better now & Rode my pony (Syphax) today, Yes let me tell you about Syphax, he has Stood the Campaign better than any other horse in the Brigade except one other pony like horse belonging to Blunn, (the Dutchman) We had to do without forage Several nights & when we drew only 20 years to the horse, but that is enough for him if it were to come Regular, he had improved up to the time we left Nashville & Since then we have traveled every day more or less, (this is 23rd day I believe) he is in better order than you ever Saw him, but he has been Somewhat neglected Since my bile has been So bad, he is not afraid of any thing but an engine, cares nothing for bulletts or cannon firing, I Sat on him, in less than 10 feet where they fired a 12 pounder & he never moved, I was also that Same night on the Skirmish line on his back Riding up & down the line encouraging the men (Skirmishers) who were under my charge

P2

to Stand there posts while the mimie balls whistled thick & two pieces of artillery (in Short Range) were playing there missils of death above us, he was perfectly Calm, that Same night when we fell back from that place a Yankee horse came dashing up to me & I let him follow on until we came to a high fence & I got one of the men to take my halter & Ride him out, we Stopped about 2 miles from there for the night & I Still on pickett, that night I did not Sleep more than ½ hour, I lay down as cold as I could be, (without frostbiting) & dropped off to Sleep with my bridle in my hand & horse was as hungry as a hound was feeding on Shrubs &C and Set his forefoot Right on my face, but he was careful not to lean on it mutch & I took my hand & lifted it off, So that Spoiled my nap that night, to cold to Sleep any more, I also dropped my gloves & in finding them found a haversack of Salt, So I amused my Self in giving Syphax Salt out of my hand, I also found a tin cup in the Search, that I gave away & bought a nice Silver cup for one dollar, it was on a Captured horse & the Captor was selling out cheap he Sold horse bridle & Saddle for 250 dollars& other things in proportion, I have my cup yet & intend to keep it as long as I can, the horse I captured when day light I found him to a big young, poor, one eyed artillery horse, I let the boys that were barefoot Ride him until day before yesterday & they blessed him, So he paid me for my trouble

P3

all this happened beyond Franklin while our Div was covering the Retreat, we had Some hard fighting & hard marching, for we took the mud & fields & woods & creeks as we come to them, Retreating in line of battle, fighting from hill to hill, we kept them back (that is we would form on pickett ground & wait until they would come in Sight & then let them have it until they would Retreat or Scatter & then we would about face & move off Sometimes 2 miles before they would press us again & 2 or 3 times not more than 4 hundres yds, we lost Several killed & wonded, among the latter was our own gallant (Corps Commander) Gen S. D. Lee Sev in foot, Gen Stevenson is now Comd the Corps & Gen Pettus the Division & Coln <u>Deadman</u> the Brigade, I wrote to you who were captured (on last Sunday) while we were at Burnesville on the Memphis & Charleston R. R. above Corinth, we have traveled every day Since from 8 to 20 miles, Billy Duncan Shot in the foot with out breaking a bone at Nashville 5 or 6 days before, before the Retreat & was Sent off to Pulaski & as we come by he had the lockjaw & had to be left, he was all the men in the Company that was disabled except Some of the prisoners were wonded, it is believed that Wily Turner was S Pendland Sal & Joe Duncan, Baker, Dale, Evans, Green, Jim Brown, Journey, B Peace, J Rhoads, Smith, Taylor, J Wilkinson, Andy Brown & John Taylor are missing Since, I must close may God bless us good bie your own Sam

PS the last letter Rec was on the 20th dated 6th last month S

CAMP NEAR TUPILO MISS JAN 13TH 1864 (IS 1865)

.13 .14 .15 P1

(Sam dated this letter wrong is actually 1865 also it was so brittle it had to be pieced back together & repaired)

My Dearest Amie I have not Rec a letter from you Since 20th Dec 64 at Columbia Tenn, Dated the 6th Dec 1864, I was glad to hear from you at that time, but am particulary anxious to hear again I think that I will get one today as there is a large mail come in, as Soon as it can be distributed we will get it, We have been here Several days,& the probability is that we will Stay here Several more, they are Shipping all of the army Stores South, as fast as the trains can carry them off, I do not know where we will winter Qrters, the health of the Regt is good, I am messing with the Coln & Adjutant have been fairing verry well, but we are in a little Run just at this time, the beef is So poor, but we draw pork today, We

Received a circulation from army _____ Soon as the Road could be used for that purpose, that he would addopt a liberal Sistem of furloughing, So good So far, & if that liberal Sistem is addopted I Shall try my best to come home again, We got no war news, at all, except grapevine, I have not Seen a paper in a month, no papers come to us now I have been

P2

today to See the negrow prisoners, I Saw Sam, he is well, but Raged & dirty, he is tired of his job, & wants me to take him out & let him Stay with me, I have a notion to try him, I can get him by making the propper application, he promises fair, he could help me lots, but if I do get him out & get the least Suspicious of him in any way I Shall have him Shot or hung, I told him So, I Saw Pritchards Dan, they Say that Grahams Jack is dead, Died in the hospital, that about 50 of them that were at Oxford have died about 100 now in the hospital, Several Run away a good many Stolen by Soldiers or anybody that wants on can Steal him, I Saw at Oxford two froze to death the other night, Sam is in a bad fix but a week ago we had lots of Soldiers in as bad, We have drawn Shoes & pants & a few blankets, & _____ give him, for I have been doing with my old blanket until within the last week,

14th I Rec yours of the 27th Dec yesterday evening & was truly thankful to get it & learn that you were doing as well as what you were, I fear that your account of Sherman is not correct, we have heared that he was at Savana, gloomy times these, yet God in his providence may yet have mercy on

P3

us & give us our independence, We are yet out of Winter Qrters, I do not know where we will winter, as to Big bone turn him in Some field or lot & feed him & let him do nothing, I Should not pretend to Stand him but try & take care of him enough to keep him alive through the winter & if he was turned in Some of those Swamps in the Spring he could live without feed, I guess you have made a good trade to get Rid of that girl & I think that you will make a bad bargin (to pay the price that negrows are hiring for) when you get Maria, negrows are not now worth more than there feed & clothing My Dear that is my notion, but you certainly know best (Ie) you know what She can do & what you need, as to J.R.G. he is as good as out of the Service, I learned from a letter from Tyler L. to Sam P. that J.R. & Dave H. were both at home & had temporary Substitutes, also from the Same letter that Miss Nancy N. had a fine daughter &C, I Suppose that you will have meat enough to do you, by you waiting to hire, _____ is easily Seared I Suppose about her Rations, Still I am Sorry of her loss, I am Really Sorry to hear that Dr. C. is So affected with Sickness, go to See him & give him my best Respects, as to Receipt of letters, Rec two at Columbia one dated 6th Dec came by mail & the one Sent by Lt. P. 27th Nov. P. Sent the letter by Griffith but kept the vest, I have a vest made out of my old coat that I got of Sal D., Wm Duncan was wounded in the foot & left at Pulaske Tenn with the lock jaw

P4

Suppose that he is dead, I have writen this before, but I write again because of the uncertainty of mailes, I am messing with the Coln & Lt Keith who is acting adjutant, Capt Burrh was wounded on the Retreat from Nashville but came out,

Since then our mess is Smaller We have also a cook & a hostes we have all got along verry well but I feel Sometimes like that I was Rejected of men, but then I try to look to that friend who Sticketh closer than a brother, I could have finnished this yesterday but I Spent the evening in getting Sam with me, I got him out of prison & put him in the mess to do any thing for any one of us, just for nothing but feed, but he not mutch account, he is poor, & Seems dejected & has the worst cough, I do not think him able to do mutch, I Shall treat him well, if he does well, I am Sorry for him, My Dearest A I have just washed & put on clean clothes the 2nd time in a month had my clothes washed with out Soap (but lye) they are clean but not white, my Rising has got well, it did hurt me nearly as bad as the Chills & fever, I believe I have written you all the news that is worth writing, So I now bring this long _____ to a close, May God Still protect & Sustain us & answer our own prayrs is the prayr of your own husband Sam good bie

ALA REGT NEAR TUPELO MISS JANUARY 16TH 1865 HEAD QRTRS 30TH

.16 .17 P1

(Letter to Sister)

My Dear Sister I have concluded to write you a Short letter this evening time is Short I am well &by the mercies of God I am yet Speared from balls & imprisonment, you have doubtless heard our defeat at Nashville, we lost in captured & the fiew that was killed & wonded about half of our Regt & Some Say ½ the entire army & fully ½ the artillery but fiew waggons, Our Division Stevensons) covered the Retreat for 9 days that was the hardest time we ever Saw, we would form line of battle & when the enemy came up we would fight them back & then about face & about face & march in line to the next hill (Sometimes not more than 4 hundred yds) through the fields, woods, Swamps, creeks

P2

whatever else was in the way & form & fight again, Some of the men entirely barefooted & Some with out blankets, all hungry & tired the whole Retreat was one of the worst I ever Saw, My

Sister I feel like that God has been merciful to me in Spearing me I try to feel thankful for his blessings, I am Second in Command now Capt Burr was wonded at Nashville & has gone home, Lt Coln Elliot first, the health of the men is good, We are expecting to move Soon, we have been here 10 days it is nearly dark, I am messing with the Coln, I have my horse with me yet, I got Sam out of Prison the other day he is not well, he promised fair, I close May God bless us Good bie your brother S C Kelly

17th morning we Rec an order to furlough every 15th man I hope to get home this winter I Rec a letter from Amie dated 29th Dec all well & doing as well as could

Sam

CAMP 30TH ALA REGT NEAR TUPELO MISS JANUARY 16 1865

.16 .17 P1

My Dear Amie I have a chance to Send this by the hand of parson Weatherly who has Resigned his Commission as Chaplin & is going home, to Serve under Some board as army missionary I have nothing of intrest to write, except what I wrote day before yesterday, but oweing to the uncertainty of letters I now write again, in it I told you of my get Sam out of prison that he was not entirely well, that he is not mutch account &C I think that he has improved Some but he has the R Road <u>lick</u> yet, I think that he will get to have Some life, & be Some Service when I get him fed up & clothed, my health is good & the health of the army generally

P2

Never better but we look like worked down Stock, all need Rest & feeding from home, or at home, for a month, Right in hog killing time, but I fear no Sutch good luck will happen to but few, for the winter is ½ gone & no furlough yet, but tis Said that Rearguard has come & that furloughing will be Resumed Soon, we commensed to drill & will every day unless prevented by bad weather or otherwise Our hospital men are coming in dayley & the Regt is filling up, we did not carry ½ our men into Tennessee with us, absent Sick wonded detailed & deserted, Some talk of consolidation, but tis Said when a Regiment can Start 500 that it will not be done, then the 30th is Safe from Consolidation, My Dear I guess that the Spirits of the people are greatly changed Since our disaster & Rout at Nashville, but that was not Gen Hoods

P3

falt, for the battle in my judgment was well planned & the enemy were Repulsed with heavy loss on all parts of the line that they had attacked us, & when it come to Baits turn to be attacked they broke indiscriminately & left the works before the Yanks were within 100 yds, or enough of them to Render the Remainder powerless, So the great victory at Nashville was lost to our army by the cowardice of one Brigade (Finleys Floridans) the Same that Refused to fight at Murfoeysboro, So Say Rhumor, She also Says that Gen Hood Said not more than five minutes before the line was broken, that tomorrow morning I will be in Nashville, that the enemy are whipped on every part of the line they have attacked, & that he now Says that if the line had Stood 5 minutes longer that he would have Swung Round his whole Right wing & would have completely Routed them

P4

but alass the golden opportunity past & we were Routed though not whipped for we (on our part of the line) felt like that we could whip 10 lines, to come in our front, Oh that God had been on our Side, but it Seems like that he was not, but I feel truly thankful that it was no worse gloomey times there, Oh that God the God of our Fathers & I trust our God would have mercy upon us as a family & as a nation & bring this crewel war to a Speedy close, according to his own will is the prayr of your own Soldier husband & let the poor Soldiers Return to there long left ones to be an help meet for them, to plough to Sew to Reap & to mow in quietude & no enemy to molest or make us afraid, Oh my God, So mote it be, May God bless you & yours & hear our prayrs is my daily prayr, good bie your own Sam

P5

PS Jan17th 65 well My Dear Amie the order for furloughing has come, it allows one for every 15 men & one officer to be Retained here for every 15 men, So that lets me out & nearly all the Rest as we have 91 men in Co & Lt Landers & myself God bless you & yours good bie S Sam is Sick today S

ON MOBILE & OHIO RR JAN 21ST 1865

.21 P1

My Dearest Amie the 30th Ala is on there way Some where in fact our whole Corps is on the Road before & behind, we left Tupelo yesterday morning & are now on the Road at a little place called Gaynesville Junction where the citizens had a lot of provisions for the Soldiers but, we were on the hinder part of the train & got but little, they Say that the 20th charged it, We are crowded & it Rained all night & the most of the day both yesterday today & the tops are as full as the insides & the men changed & those on top get in dripping wet & the car is as muddy as your hogpen, Lauderdale Springs about 1 oclock PM We had a bad night but Stopped & Camped from 9 PM until 4 AM, I write to you 2 Letters within a week & if you get them they contain all the news up to there date Since then we have Sent off our horses (we Suppose to Ga) Sent mine by N Sewell & told him if he come near you to call, this I expect to Send by J Sewell who has a furlough & if we go to Mobile he will

P2

leave us at Meridian & go by Denopolis & Selma it is not known whitch rout we will go, Sam is yet with me, he is creeping about but not near well, I got him Some old clothes & made him wash good & put them on & gave him my old blanket, Since I Sent off Syphax & the Rugs, he has improved Some, he is not mutch account to Slow I have not Rec a letter Since 27th, I must close May God Still continue his blessing towards us is my pray Good bie your own

Sam

SELMA ALA JAN 23RD 65

.23 P1

(*Letter burnt in middle*)

My Dear A we arrived here this morning at about 10 AM too late for our furloughed men to get off (Ie) the last two Hollingsworth & Keller,

Sewell & Reaves got off on the morning train they left us at Demopolis & got here last night, we came by Demopolis & not by Mobile as I expected, I have nothing of interest to write only that P _____ Keller got a furlough _____ Frank Rountrees Re cruit & is to pay Frank back what he gave the boy, Say to Frank that I Sold it for him & Keller is to go & See him we have had a wet

P2

bad time but better than to walk, we leave at 5 PM for Montgomery thence to

S Carolina May God Still keep us & bring us together Soon in peace is my prayr of your own Sam

no letter yet but we are moving & I need not look fore one until we Settle God bless you Good bie S

CAMP 30TH ALA REGT NEAR MILLEDGEVILLE GA JANUARY 28 1865

.28 P1

(*Letter burnt in middle*)

My Sear Amie we arrived here last night & gone into camps waiting transportation the R Road is torn up for 40 miles & we will have to walk but have to have waggons to carry our cooking utinsals &C I Suppose that we will Stay here a day or two, we have had a cold bad trip & the men were obliged to have fires whitch they built on ovens & ligts & the Smokeyest Set of men that I ever Saw, at Columbus & at Fort Valley the ladies gave us a meal, out of their own hands, the men bring formed in two Ranks faced inwards & they the (ladies) passed through giving to each one with there clean hands as mutch as they could eat, Wh__

_____ we gave three hearty cheers to the ladies of Ga, I have had the worst cold that I have had in a long time I got So hoarse that I could Scarcely talk at all, but I am better now, Sam is Still with me, I was fearful he would freeze but he is Still kicking, & I think is improving, (not Sick but worn down & as poking, as an old mule), I gave him my old blanket & this

P2

morning gave him an overcoat, that I Swapped my old overcoat for, now I think he will do better, I bought me an Over Coat in Montgomery Ala, one of those State Coats for Ala Soldiers only for 180$ I had to borrow the money & am out of money now, I have borrowed about 200$ Since I left home, whitch I have not got, we have not drawn any from the Government yet, & I am necessarily compelled to Spend more than when I was with my Company, be assured My Dear that I have not Spent money wantonly, I borrowed 125 dollars from Loyfoyett Mattison who lives up Nancies Creek that I promised that you could pay to his wife, So if you See her or have any chance pay her, Mattison went through the County with the _____

he will be home, he may come to See you, but you need not put yourself to the trouble to go to See him, Our brigade lost on the trip from Tupelo Miss lots of men, deserted & gone by home as they Say, our Regiment lost 51, but none from (E) Company all the other Counties are well Represented

P3

My Dearest, I would close, but for your love of long letters & I will not promise you any news, but give you Some of the Rhumors afloat in camp, first that England & France have Recognized our independence or will by the 4th March, That they have given Lincoln until then to make peace or Subjugate us &C That the Reason assigned is that he has Served out the time that he was elected for & has not conquered us, & that we have maintained our Selves as belligerents & that in his Reelection we of the South had no voice in it, 2ond that there will be an armistice in 10 days, 3rd that Some one offered to bet any amount under one hundred thousand dollars, that peace would be made in 30 days &C&C, One of our Divisions of our Corps has gone on, I Suppose to Augusta, I have news f___ _____ but that he is in Savana, It is hard wo___ ____ wright a letter, I have but little hope of getting a furlough, but promise you that I am coming home just as Soon as I can get there honorably, the order excludes all who have been home on furlough within 12 months next preceding the date of the order, whitch was issued on the 15ᵗʰ Jan 65 and My furlough was granted on the 17ᵗʰ or 18ᵗʰ Jan 64 So you See that I am excluded just by 2 days, the object

P4

of the order is to let those go who have not been in a year, under the order only 5 officers in our Regt are entitled , out of the 5 , 3 are already gone, When they get back I think that I will try my luck, My Dear I am So anxious to hear from you, have not heared in a month, but it is not your fault I know that there is letters on the way, we never get letters while we are on the move, I wait trusting that God has parsed you & yours, If you have any good chance Send me 150 dollars, I have no idea when we will draw, I have not written Since we left Selma, the weather was So cold, among the Rhumors is one, that we are going back to Montgomery Ala. I heared no Reason assigned, My Dear I dreamed of Seeing you at home last night, of Seeing the children also Oh that it may come to pass, I do want to come home So bad, I am So tired of this continual _____ thank, will this crewel war ever end in my _____ & I be permitted to Return to my long left & loved ones at home I think that the God who gave me this life & has kept it this far, will accomplish the purpose for whitch he made it & if it is his will I Shall yet Return to enjoy the Sits of home with you, in the autumn of our lives, orders to move at once, God bless us Still Good bie Your own Sam

FEBRUARY 1865

CAMP 30TH ALA 25 MILES BELOW AUGUSTA GA FEBRUARY 2ND 1865

.02 P1

My Dear Amie we arrived at Augusta on the evening of the 31st Jan Stopped there but about 2 hours when we took train on the Savana RR & Stopped about 10 P.M. 25 miles below Augusta & between there & Savana, at a Depo on Road name unknown, we thought that we would go to a Bridge on Briar Creek, whitch is about 4 miles below here, Johnsons Division is al the force that is here, Wheelers cavalry are below here or Rather between us and the enemy We have but little idea what we will do, or where we will go, we are just laying Round loose, no duties to do, plenty of forage Sutch as potatoes peas &C in the country& the people are generally Ritch, Some give us, while others charge high, We draw plenty of bacon & crackers, have not drawn money yet, are nearly out of money, the whole Command, the men begin to kneed clothing again, I do not like my over Coat & if I have a chance I will Send it home & let you have me a dress Coat made out of it, It has no lining at all in it, & is Ripping all to pieces

P2

I will write to you more about it if I Send it, I am in hopes that I will get a chance to come home this Spring yet, though the chances are Slim now, our horses has not come yet, nor do I look for them before the 15th of the month, I wish that I had Some good news to write but alass all I know amounts to nothing but Rhumors, Still I Shall live in hopes, that in a Short time that Something will be done, to Stop the war, God only knows, & he Rules the destinies of men and nations, Oh that he would have mercy on us & bring about the means, & ends, to accomplish an honorable peace & that Speedily, but let us be contented & obedient to his will, & whether in time of war or peace, let us be prepared to Say they will be done, Oh God, Sam is yet with me, black, Ragged, & dirty, he has improved, in health & Spirits & as Soon as I can get him Some clothes & Shoes, I think he will be worth his feed not worth it now, What do you think about my Sending him home, I think that if I get a furlough that I will bring him home with me, he needs Rest & feed, like a young mule worked down, If we were Stationed, he could make money enough by washing to pay his way home, an order for fatigue, I Suppose we are going to fortifying, May God bless you & yours is the prayr of your own Dear one Sam

LINE OF BATTLE NEAR MIDWAY ORANGEBURG DC S CAROLINA FEB 6TH 1865

.06

My Dear Amie my last was written in Ga 25 miles below Augusta dated (I believe) the 2ond, we Staid there but a day or two & then marched 15 miles back & took the R.R. to this place Midway, we are above Branchville 15 miles, I know but little of what the movements of the enemy, it is Reported that they are from 8 to 20 miles of here, we are in line of battle across the Road at a bridge on the South Edisto River, the face of the country is level & the larger portion Swampy & the balance old field pines, but fiew houses & the people generally Scarce, lots of them Reffuged, My health is good except cold & cough, the weather warm, but Some Rain on us 2 or 3 days ago, I cant write you a full letter because I have neither the time nor the news to fill one, the mail will Start out in a fiew moments, I must close Receive My best wishes & remember me in your prayrs May God bless us & Save us & bring us all home in peace Soon is the prayr of your husband (Sam)

MARCH 1865

CAMP 30TH ALA CATAUBA RIVER S C MARCH 3RD 1865

.03 P1

My Dear Amie I wrote to you Some 10 mor 12 days Since but have had no chance to Send one Since I have not written, I think the chance now a Slim one to Send by Some one passing on furlough or exchange from Va, We are our Brigade on the River as a guard to protect the R.R. Bridge on Cahauba River the Charlotte Road, about 20 miles from Charlotte N.C. We went from Columbia to Charlotte on foot & averaged 21 miles per day then we came down after Staying 3 or 4 days to this place last Sunday night, & this I believe is fryday our pickett dutys are verry heavy, plenty of forage good health &C, The weather is wet & Roads muddy for the last 10 days, but fortunately for us we Stopped the Same day it began to Rain, I have not got my horse yet, but look for him Soon, he would have been worth tome 50 dollars a day on this Campaign, The Cahauba River Runs about from North west to South east coarse & the Report is that the enemy crossed at Rock Castle about 35 miles below here going in a northerly direction, all of our Cavalry crossed the River here, the last today, I Saw Dick W Eawen Brian Joe Gladden Pete Pelham Dr Miller Francis Joe Francis Dr Tom White & Several others that I knew, The Catauba is about 3 hundred yards wide at the bridge, but where we Waded it at the Shoules 14 miles below here at Lands ford it was about 5 or 6 hundred yards wide & from one to 3 feet deep & So Swift that one man could not get along by himself without great danger of falling , Sam got within 3 feet of the bank & fell completely wetting himself & our Rations, the weather cold & we traveled until dark after wading before we camped at least 4 miles making in all 25 miles that day, About 3 miles this Side of the ford is a nice church house & a large grave yard, with a great many tombstones of ancient date, & there is the graves of Andrew Jacksons father & mother, This is York District S. C. the district where my father was born, this is a better county than the lower Districts I do wish I that I could know that you would get this letter, I could try harded to make it interesting I have not heared from home in So long a time that I have almost come to the conclusion that there is no way for letters to pass, Still I had Rather that you could get mine than for me to get

P2

Yours & you not get mine, I think that you are more uneasy about me than I am about you, I try to commit all that I have into the hands of the living God, asking him to take care of us, for the Sake of his Son Jesus Christ, in whome I trust, we believe, My Dear I have no war news only that Old mas Joe (Johnston) as he is called has taken command of this army, & that he lives in the hearts of the Tennesse Army, worth more than a Reinforcement of ten thousand men all armed with twelve pounders under any other man in the Confederacy, I cannot hardly expect R E Lee, One cold Rainy evening after we had got off of the train at Columbia & were moving down the Street to the bridge, the frount Regiment in our Brigade turned loose to cheering & the word passed down the Command that it was the old herow Gen Johnson, who had off his hat (& the Rain peppering his bald head) Riding past Receiving the loud cheers of the Rough, dirty, lousy Rebbells, with the Smile of a Soldier, patrott, & gentleman, Oh truly he is a patrott or he would never taken the Command of this army again, the Second time Round Scattered & demoralized, but that is a proof of his greatness after organizing & handling it half through a campaign, if the authorities think that he is not the man, he quietly Submits & after it gets Rundown & they want him to organize it again he goes at it with his whole heart, So mutch for him Oh that God would give unto him all the wisdom knowledge and understanding to do the will of our father in heaven & at the Same time adorn him with power to handle our army Successively. & if it is in accordance with his holy will to gain our independence & that Spedely.

My Dear A. I cannot make an calculation when I am coming home, nor when we will move, nor where we will go, nor what we will do when we get there, I Shall write when I think there is a half chance for you to get it, I Shall not look for a letter until a better chance opens, pray for me, & trust in the Lord & thow Shalt be Saved, I do want to See you & those 3 flaxen haired, blue eyed boys of ours, who are the pride of my life, Oh how I try to feel thankful to God for the gift of Sutch a wife, I dreamed that I Saw you all at home well & hearty God grant that it may be So Son when there will be no war to molest or make us afraid, Oh I do desire to live through the war to Spend with you & yours, in the fear and Service of God our autumn and old

P3 written in margins

Age of our lives for the Sake of our children, So mote it be, oh our father and now may God Still continue to bless us & Save us is my daily prayr, Your affect mate husband Sam

CHARLOTTE N C MARCH 5TH 65

.05

Dear Amie I am well on the train for Some where I Send this by Jack Clark

Good bie God bless you

Your own

Sam

GOLDSBORO N CAROLINA MARCH 13TH 65

.13 .14 P1

My Dear Amie I feel thankful that I am yet alive & in good health & do hope & pray that you & yours have & are Still enjoying the like blessings, for I do consider it a blessing when I think of the hardships and danger that God has Seen fit to bring me through, & I try to feel thankful but when I would adore Some evil is present with me, So I do acknowledge that had I been left to myself that I Should have perished, & I now Stand as a monument of his amazing mercy, but I try to trust in God for the life that now is & the one that is to come, ever looking to Jesus who is the hope of my Redemption in whome I trust, we believe, pray for me that God may Spear my life through the War & bring us together Soon in peace, where we can unite in Song & praise to him who has been So merciful unto us, & where we can be an advantage to each other, in the Raising & preparing our dear children to live to the glory of God, Oh My Dear I do try to ask God to be with you & to direct, guide & protect you, to hear our prayrs & answer us with answers of peace, to go with us through this life & be with us in death & Save us at last in that house not made with hands, where there is no war, to molest or make us afraid, So mote it be our Father. We arrived here yesterday about 9 AM it is now most night, We came from Kinston about 38 mile east of here, where we fought the enemy on the 8th & 10th & Skirmished with them on the 9th on the night of the 10th we withdrew after getting the best of the fight all the time, in fact we whipped them good, but I do not know why we withdrew, without to guard Some other place, we Suppose Raughley or Smithfield, or else to concentrate our forces, Gen Bragg Commanded in person in the fight, the first day of the fight I was in Command of the Skirmisher line in front of our Brigade & after I had gone through the whole fight & the last gun was fired & Stepped off of a log & Strained my ankle So bad that I had to be helped off of the field, I was worse hurt than I have been Since I have been in the Service, I went to the Creek & bathed it as long as I could Stand it & then poured my Sock leg nearly

P2

full of Salt & kept it wet 2 nights & one day & it got nearly well enough So that I was in the fight on the 10th & marched 9 miles that night & 19 the next day & 8 or 9 yesterday, it is a little Stiff, I got me a good Shirt & could have got lots of things but for 2 Reasons, first I oppose prowling in time of battle & Secondly I have not got my horse yet & we have about as mutch as we can carry, Sam washed me a Suit today & I have them on, he is improving in that particular but he will tell Stories, I have a good notion to Sell him or Send him home, Still he Seems to think a goodeal of me & objects to being Sent off in time of a fight, Says that he wants to Stay close to me So if I Should get hurt (he Said) he would Stay with me, but it So happened that he has never been in a fight yet but I will let him go in if he prefers it to the Rear, Ie, to the waggon cook he is fearful that he will get lost (he Says) My boots & clothes are all worn, (not out) but worse of wear, I See no chance of getting any from home Soon, but trust that there will be a way provided, It is now Sunset & we are expecting orders to move every moment, So no more at present but Remain your affectionate husband, may God bless us good bie SCK

Smithfield NC March 14th 6 ½ PM well Amie we left Golesboro about night & marched 8 miles camped & took up line of march at daylight this morning & arrived here about one PM making about 17 miles, I have no news of the enemy nearer than Kinston & tis Reported that they evacuated the Same night that we did, Still we left Hokes Division there & I am not able to Say whether he has left there or not, I did not tell you about the casualties because you do not know any of them in our Regt none killed our loss was Small, they were the easyest Yankees whipped that we ever met with, they were well dressed, & had (Some of them) ladies dresses of all Sizes & description from home Spun to Silk in there knapsacks, they are a heartless Set of men, through S. C. they burned about ½ the dwellings all of the ginhouses corncribs & mills &C all the cotton & corn & wheat that they could not use & tore up generally, Oh God forbid that Sutch a people Should ever Conquer, but I try to Say not my will but thine be done, though God of all the earth, I expect to Send this by Capt D C Mclain who is going to Ala after deserters, hospital Rats & absentees of the Regt generally I want to hear from you, but I wait, Committing all that I have into the hands of him that is able, good bie yours SCK

PS Thursday morning nothing of interest happened Since I wrote only we changed camps & I think are on the way to Roughley, God bless you & yours good bie Your S

HD QRTERS ALA REGT NEAR SMITHFIELD N.C. MARCH 26TH 1865

.26 Pl

My Dearest Amie I wrote you twice Since the 19th Inst but have a chance to Send a letter by hand by an old man of the Regt (discharged) who lives in Talladega Co, we come here from Bentonville day before yesterday after a 2 days march, we have not had any fighting Since the 21st at the latter place We appear to be Resting, draw clothing & today (Sunday) had inspection, was inspected by Gen D. H. Hill in person, he is the Hill that fought the enemy at Bethell Church, the first Small armies that was used in this war, before the fight however he called the Regt to attention & he kneeled down & prayed for them & the cause & got up & charged & whipped them, he looks more like a preacher than like a General, he is commanding our Corps in the absence of Gen S. D. Lee, who we look for in a few days, who (tis Said) is now a Lieutenant Gen, My Dear Amie I do wish that I knew whether you get my letters or not, I hate to write the Same thing over & over, but I think that tis better for you to have to Read it 2 or 3 times if you get them, than not to get it at all, You may get one out of 3 if you get all 3 that is Somewhat a <u>Rutenation</u> but that is my Reason, I thank God for his mercies & blessings towards us, & especially to me, I was Spared all through the Campaign not a Scratch, our Casualties in the Brigade was heavy, Gen Pettus was Slightly wonded in leg, Lt Pettus his nephew was killed, Coln J. K. Elliott of 30th was Slightly wonded, Capt Heacock 30th Killed those were among the casualties

P2

of my old Company wonded Sgt H H Boozer Sev in both hands W G Stewart Sev in Same hand he was wonded in at Bakers Creek Wm Turner Sev in thigh D L Kerbey Severe in heel, Several others Slightly, but Ret to duty, I think that we whipped them badly, every time that we charged them we drove them from their works & every time that they charged ours or attempted to flank us they were hansomely Repulsed, leaving there dead &wounded on the field besides guns & Accouterments knapsacks haversacks blankets oilcloths &C&C we could have got waggon loads but were not allowed to stop & that night fell back to our own works & on the night of the 21st we moved off & came here as before Stated, but they evacuated the Same time & marched on

Goldsboro while we on Smithfield, tis Said that they are at Goldsboro, we feel like old mas Joe knows all about Mr Sherman, now dress parade I must close for the present, but before I close I will tell you that Gen. P. & Coln Elliot is gone to Rear & I am Command the 30th

27th 11 oclock AM, my Dearest Amie Capt McCaines & Heacocks papers have Returned for to go home after deserters & absentes of Regt but Capt H is no more & I have Recommended the name of Lt Ed Clark to fill his place (he is the Son of Coln Cs of Jacksonville) & if he goes he can carry this to Jv. If it were not that I am in Command of the Regt & the only Capt left in it I would try and go myself, but it would look like because I had the power to appoint that I took advantage of it, So I conclude that I will Stick to my duty trusting in God for everything, I have trusted him thus far & he has Sustained me & kept me, & I am what I am by the mercy of God, I feel like that I am dependant oh that I may trust him more

P3

We have just heared that no one can go besides those that were Recommended first, So Clark cant go, I am Sorry for Mrs Heacock but Sutch is the fate of war, Sam is nearly Crazy to go home but (even if I were willing) I have not money enough to bear his expenses, I drew wages up to 31st Aug, I have about 200$ I loaned Col Elliot 130 dollars & also I think that Sam can Stay as long as I can, If I were to come home I would bring him, If Capt Heacocks papers had come back before he got killed I guess I should Sold Sam to him, he offered 3000 dollars for him if I would bear his expenses to Talladega & I offered to take that & he bear the expenses, he is doing me but verry little good, I cannot draw Rations for him & only once & a while buy Rations & it is cost lots, So it keeps me Scarce ____ I divide (whitch I am always going to do as long as I keep him) I let Capt Wise or Gen Stevensons Staff have him for a few days until I determine what to do, I can cloth him better than feed him, Sometimes I am good notion to Sell him but the money is So depreciated & if we gain our independence he will make a good negrow yet, if not the money I could get for him will be no account, So I have concluded to keep him with me yet a while, This is the Smokyest & dirtiest camp I ever Saw the woods were burned off before we came here & but little else to burn but pine my clothes are So Smoked that I cant keep my hands clean, I am nearly out of clothes all getting worn out my old boots have Shrunk from the day I first put them on, So that I cannot hardly get them off without help my coat is Smoked

P4

but it will do me this Summer my Shirts will do a while 2 pretty good ones my drawers one pair good the other worst of wear pants both pair nearly worn out, but I think that they will do until I can have me a pair made out of my over coat & keep the cape to wear on the jeans coat in bad weather, I Shall get me a pair of boots the first opportunity, during the days fighting at Bentonville, my feet were wet So mutch that I have the toeitch like I used to have when I was a boy, but for all that my health was never better, I have the Colns horse during his absence, am looking for mine every day they were Shipped from Charlotte Several days ago, Oh I forgot to tell you about my hat, it is Smoked & greasy & looks like Some old hat that has been worn by Some careful old man for years, I do not want you to be uneasy about Clothing this body but trust in God & pray him who is able to take care of both Sole & body, Oh my dear one I would like to See you all, I Sometimes dream of you whitch is generally a Sorce of Satisfaction but trust in God for mercy & if it is his holy will that I Should be Speared to meet you on earth, & live out the Remainder of our lives to the good of our children & to the glory of his holy name So mote it be, I try to pray for that & try to Say not my will but thine be done, May God Still continue to bless us & Save us al last in that better world is the prayr of your own affectionate Sam good bie

APRIL 1865

CAMP 30TH ALA REGT APRIL 3RD 1865

.03 P1

My Dearest amie I Rec yours of the 20th Fed by Pike day before yesterday and one of the 10th Feb by mail that has Billys letter in it, they were the first letters that I had, had from you Since we were at Tupelo Miss & that one was dated 27th Dec 64, yesterday I Rec one dated 17th Nov one 12th Jan, one 26th Jan & one 4th Feb but the one Pike brought was dated later than all, it was the 20 Feb 65 I was truly thankful to Receive them, for you informed me of lots of things that I did not know a word about, to tedious to mention at this late date, I am Satisfied (my dear one) for you to do as you think best with every thing that concerns us & our children, Still if it were convent I would give you my best advice, Oh I do wish that I could Receive your letters in time to give you my opinion on matters that you ask it but Sutch is the fate of war, & this world is full of Sorrows & disappoints, vanity of vanity, & vexation of Spirit, Still I do hope that there is a better day coming, but for you & our dear children I could live in any Sort of government the Remainder of my days, but you are the pride of my life & I am willing to Serve in the war for to establish a government for you & especially our dear boys, Oh that God would enable us to gain our independence & that Speedely & then the poor worn & tired Soldiers could Return to there loved one, at home, My dear one, I try to live a Christian in the army but I fear that I bear a poor light, but I am what I am by the mercy of God, through the Richtioness of our Lord & Savior Jesus Christ, & as to death I do not know, but what, I am as well prepared as I ever will be, but I desire to live through the war, for the Reason that I trust that I may be an advantage to you, in helping you to Raise our dear boys to be useful men, if the war was over now & we had nothing worth counting I would be perfectly willing to work all the time of them while the other two go to School, I feel & know the necessity of an education & if God will Spear my life I will try to give them that if I have nothing else to give them, It is a long war that will never end, & as I have been thus far Spared I Still look to & trust to the Same almighty power & Someone will live through & have a hope, Still I try to Say Oh my God not my will but thine be done

P2

I feel thankful that you faired no worse by the cavalry than what you did I believe that you will have corn & meat enough to do you if you can keep it, I am Sorry about the colt and also on you account the old mare, but She was So old that Really She was no loss, You have 3 good mules & that is enough for the hands & I hope that you can drive one of them to the buddy, as to the Jack I think that you had better turn him loose in one of the fields, I do not want to Sell him, in fact I do not know what he is worth in Confederate money but Sell him, that will be the least trouble, I think Robinson would buy him as he is So plush & nothing less than two thousand would be fair he aut to be worth as mutch as two men, when I bought him he was equal to 4, do as best you know & I am content, I fear that you will get out of money every thing to buy & noting to Sell, I could have done without the money you Sent me, I drew up to the last of Aug, had 200$ & loaned Coln Elliott 130$, my horse came up the other day he is poor, he had the distemper & had like to have died, but is mending now Coln E came back 3 days ago, I bought me a Saddle for 150$, my old one hurt when on the trip & they used the one I bought & it did not hurt, So I have two the old one I can use on an extra mule we have, I got my vest P had worn it 2 or 3 days, if I had been him I would have worn it all the time, also the Socks & gloves, I have hired Sam out to a Capt on Gen Stevenson's Staff for one dollar per day he has washed & bought him Some clothes, great talk of consolidation, I must close or miss the chance, God bless you & all that is near & dear good bie Your own husband

S C Kelly
direct
Capt S C Kelly
Co E 30th Ala

Pettus Brigade
Stevensons Div
Lees Corps
Army Tenn

APR 17TH

.17 L1 P1

My Dear A I have a few moments time to write you a few lines to let you now that I am yet alive & well, I try to be thankful I can Send this by Nef Priuett who is payrolled & going home the Va army has Surrendered, in the Consolidation my Co & Co G of 30 Ala were put together & made Capt over them & now in the 20th Ala Regt Co B Lts Pike & Landers were both dropped they are coming home as Soon as their papers can be fixed up we (Our Brigade) are a head of the main army they are at Greensboro 40 miles above we were Sent here to protect the place & RR but it were taken before we got here & our coming Run the Yanks off they destroyed all government property we are Repairing RR, Joe Hobbs was in the fight here & is wonded in the leg & knee, Sev but not dangerous I must close, Sam is behind with main army, May God have mercy upon us & Save us from danger & bring us together Soon in peace Your Sam

P2

PS I have got me a good pair of Shoes & Shirt I gave my cup for Shoes & a knife the balance of my clothes besides what I have are with Sam, I think of having me a pa of pants made out of my over coat, Oh that God would Still Spear us, & help us, we are weak but he is mighty & I try to trust him for the life that now is & the one that is to come Save us Lord as a family we trust, that we have been in thy protection thus far Oh leave us not now but bring these times of trouble to a Speedy close according to thy will & pleasure & let us met again as a family in peace health & Sound both in body & mind, where we can unite around the Same alter & give the all the praise that we are capable of god bless you & yours especially good bie Your own affectionate husband

S C Kelly Capt of Co

B 20th Ala

I am acting as Senior Capt of the Regt but Syphax is behind hope will be up Soon We came in cars most of the way S

SALESBURRY N C APRIL 17TH 1865

.17 L2 P1

My Dear Amie I have just written you a letter today by Lt Priuett but Lt Pike & Landers are going to Start home today & I consider it the best chance that I have had lately, I wish that I had Something good to write but Sutch is the case, I have not only that I am well & in the land of the living that I fear I do not appreciate properly but I try to be thankful to God for all his blessings bestowed upon me, & I Still live in hopes that he will bring me Safely through these times of trouble & at last permit me to Return home to my Dear ones Sound in every Since of the word, the balance of the army is at Greensboro about 40 miles above here coming on, we were Sent here (our Brigade) to defend the RR Bridge across the Yadkin River & this place whitch is 6 miles from here, we got there time enough & did Save the bridge but they destroyed the government property & the RR all they could, We were consolidated with the 20th Ala Regiment & go by the name of the 20th Ala My Co & Co (G) 30th Ala, the Va army has Surrendered to the Yanks, & the men & officers payrolled & going home they are passing in Squads from one to fifty every man for himself, these are dark days but the Lords will be done, & if tis his will that we be conquered I try to Say not my will, but thine be done Oh Lord of heaven & earth have mercy upon us, we are Repairing the R.R. it was torn up by Stonemans Raiders about 6 thousand that came accross from Knoxville, we had no garrison here only convalessent from the hospitals & detached men working in the government Shops & a battalion of artillery besides Some 4 or 5 hundred men who had been home and Returning, making in all from 450 men to 1600 all Said firing a gun & then turned our own artillery upon us, from all I can learn there was not more (besides the artillery) than 4 or 5 hundred organized men against 6 thousand Cavalry who completely Surrounded them before they Surrendered Joe Hobbs was here & is wonded Severely in the leg & knee, his battery was captured

P2

Sam is with Capt Wise of Gen Stevensons Staff now at or near Greensboro & Sewell is back there with my horse, I think the army is coming on & it will take them 2 or 3 more days to come here, Our army is in hand & under the Command of Gen Johnston, I Suppose that we will Retreat before the combined armies of Gen Grant & Sherman, only Supposition I do not pretend to know, we heared of Selma going up (as we termed it) & it is now Reported that Mobile & Montgomery both are gone up, My heart is heavy I might tell you lots but cant this far, My Dear I wrote to you Sometime ago about the conditions of my clothes & boots &C give yourself no uneasiness about that for I think that I can get all I kneed I have a good pair of Shoes & a good knife for whitch I gave my cup, I wanted you to have it, but if I had been captured they would have taken it, & likely would not take the Shoes off my feet, my boots were nearly gone up, I wore out one pair of my pants & threw them away the others will last perhaps until I can get more, I had me a new Shirt maid & threw away my last, your Shirt Sam has what clothes I have except what I have on, I have one hundred thirty dollars, & Coln Elliott owes me 150, & I am talking of Selling my over coat for 150 dollars whitch will make me besides what the Coln owes me Two hundred and eighty dollars, My Dear A I have written nearly the Same things in both letters, perhaps you will get one & if both Read them & know again their will (& I am one of them) & others dropped who wanted to be Retained, Some take it as a complement but I do not like Sutch compliments but I am in for the war or So long as I am able, Now my Dear wife I hope that the time will not be long before Something will be done to bring about an honorable peace although these are dark times now, Yet I live in hopes & tis Said that the darkest times is just before dawn, it has been a long night already, Oh that God would take the charge of our affairs & bring about that peace that we So mutch desire, nevertheless not our wills but thine be done Oh though God of all the earth, I will close by Saying that you have my best wishes and prayres Good bie your own husband

   S C Kelly